Four Farces
by
Georges Feydeau

✳

Feydeau at the age of five

FOUR
FARCES

by
Georges Feydeau

Translated and with
an Introduction by
Norman R. Shapiro

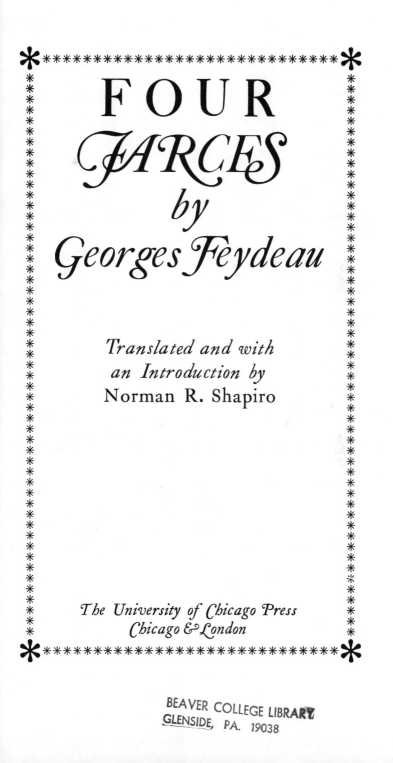

The University of Chicago Press
Chicago & London

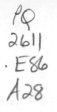
The University of Chicago Press, Chicago 60637
The University of Chicago Press, Ltd., London

86 85 84 83 82 81   3 4 5 6 7
Published 1970

Printed in the United States of America
International Standard Book Number: 0–226–24476–8 (clothbound)
Library of Congress Catalog Card Number: 78–125164

For my parents,
with thanks
for their endless encouragement

Contents

Preface

A translator's task always reminds me of a game played on a pinball machine. When each little steel ball comes hurtling out of its groove, its zigzag route among bumpers, buzzers, flippers, and the like is virtually limitless in its possibilities. However closely one ball seems to duplicate another, no two will ever trace precisely the same path. And yet, despite its practically infinite potential, despite the numberless courses it can follow, each ball is strictly limited within the framework of the machine itself. It can never go bounding off anywhere else. In other words, total freedom within total limitation.

The translator finds himself in an analogous position. Every work to be put into another language presents almost an infinity of possible end results. Certainly no two translators ever come up with identical versions, word for word. But however great his freedom of choice, and however wide his range of possibilities, the translator is no less circumscribed within the limitations imposed by the work itself. Unlike the writer starting from scratch, whose liberty is absolute as he faces the blank page, the translator begins with a very real restriction. He must work with someone else's thoughts and style, not his own. Perhaps this is why translation—like the pinball machine for its own devotees—is so satisfying a pursuit for those of us who indulge in it. It represents a compromise, a kind of equilibrium between the two powerful and mutually antagonistic human desires for freedom and for restraint. In a sense, it is a microcosm of man's struggle within himself between total independence and total submission, between liberty and the willing renunciation of it. The translator enjoys the best of both worlds: like the little balls in the pinball machine, he is very free and very limited at one and the same time.

Still, as rewarding as the translator's job can be, it can

also present no end of frustration. Practical problems, large and small, come up at every turn. How to treat the pun? How to handle a reference that makes perfect sense in the cultural context of language A, but none at all in that of language B? Even something as ostensibly simple as a proper name can raise difficulties when crossing the linguistic divide. And so the translator finds himself obliged to take liberties, though always with the idea uppermost in his mind that he must somehow remain faithful to that nebulous something that is "the spirit of the original."

In the present translations I have, of course, been faced with such problems; and I have consequently taken my share of liberties. Without enumerating them in detail, let me pronounce a *caveat lector* or two for anyone who would believe that everything in these pages is "pure Feydeau." When possible, puns and other linguistic banter, in which the originals abound, have been treated by finding proper (or properly improper) substitutes. Thus, the "Iles Hébrides" in *On purge Bébé* have been cross-culturally transformed into the Aleutian Islands, preserving a lengthy play on sounds that would otherwise have been lost in English. Likewise, in the same comedy, an extended pun on the everyday French noun *cocu* has been recast— with the help of the words "laughingstock" and "two-timer"—to avoid having to use the stilted English equivalent, "cuckold." Such liberties are frequent. Let no over-zealous scholar jump to conclusions about the stuff of Feydeau's wordplay without consulting the originals.

Proper names have been only a minor problem, and only a few characters have had to be rebaptized. For example, in *On purge Bébé*, Adhéaume Chouilloux, whose first name is wholly alien to Anglo-American ears (and eyes), has become "Abélard," while Follavoine has dropped "Bastien" in favor of the more common "Maximilien." And in *Le Mariage de Barillon*, the maid Ursule has given up a name that, to us, has a rather Germanic ring, for the distinctly Gallic "Joséphine." I have also avoided translating any of the names that suggest English equivalents. If Follavoine had become "Mr. Wildoats," he would no longer be very French.

The only sizable liberty I have taken was likewise dictated by cultural considerations. Miss Betting, the governess in *Un Fil à la patte*, is an English lady who, in the original, understands no French and speaks only her native tongue throughout. No one understands her except her pupil Viviane, who interprets her comments for the rest. In an English translation this presents an obvious problem. The character must speak a foreign language, and must not understand what any of the other characters say. Clearly, the foreign language can no longer be English. It would, of course, have been easy enough to change Miss Betting's nationality. But this is where the cultural problem comes in. What pretentious French mother of the 1890s, in search of a governess for her daughter, would be satisfied with a German *Fräulein* or an Italian *signorina*—or with anyone, in fact, but a fashionable English miss, even one who knows no French? Result: a translator's impasse. The liberty I have taken is rather extreme, but I think it is a good way out. And, if any further justification is needed, I think I am safe in assuming that my solution would have pleased Feydeau's own lively sense of the absurd.

I believe the author would also smile on some of the liberties I have taken with his titles. My choices are, needless to say, not very literal. But they are, all the same, in the Feydeau spirit; and that, I submit, is a good enough excuse.

Many thanks are due in many quarters for material and moral help in the preparation of this volume. Foremost, my appreciation to Professor René Jasinski, who shepherded me through my first studies in Feydeau, and who made an intrinsically enjoyable task even more so. To Wesleyan University, my gratitude for its generosity, both financial and temporal. I am no less indebted to Professors Reuben Brower and William Liller, respectively the former and present Masters of Adams House, Harvard University, where, through their kindness, much of the present manuscript was written. To Ninon Tallon Karlweis, my appreciation for her indispensable assistance and her efforts in my behalf. For valued suggestions, encouragement, and constant interest, I am happy to express my thanks to Professor Caldwell Titcomb, whose broad knowledge and sound judgment have been most helpful; to Professor Daniel Seltzer, Lillian Bulwa, Walter Glanze, Evelyn Simha, Dallas Hext, and to another devoted Feydeauphile, Laurence Senelick.

My list of acknowledgments would be incomplete without special thanks to my best readers, my parents, to whom this volume is gratefully dedicated.

NORMAN R. SHAPIRO

Cambridge, Massachusetts
September 1968

Introduction

"I'm getting out of here!" cries the dentist Follbraguet in Georges Feydeau's last play, a one-acter with the extravagant title *Hortense a dit: "Je m'en fous!"* ("Hortense said: 'I don't give a damn!' "). And he stalks out of his house, threatening never to return, half mad with rage, away from his wife and her mad, illogical antics, which have trapped him in a web of madder and madder circumstances until he can take no more.

Obviously, the key word here is "mad." And for good reason: if any one word can be used to describe Feydeau's theater, from beginning to end, it is this one. It is a theater of madness *par excellence*. And the spectators who viewed Follbraguet's turbulent exit, never realizing that it was to be Feydeau's own symbolic farewell to the theater, laughed heartily at all this madness in 1916, as they had been doing at so many of his comedies since his first youthful success in 1886. They laughed the lusty, unreflective, undemanding laughter of the Boulevard, anxious only to be amused, to steer clear of the serious theatrical fare of *fin de siècle* Paris, be it the depressing "slices of life" of the 1890s or the experimental, avant-garde reactions to them. The Boulevard was as little interested in symbolist drama and Wagnerian-type idealism, for example, as it was in the Naturalism of Antoine and the Théâtre Libre.

And so it was the Boulevard, the popular theater, that originally conferred success upon Georges Feydeau. Immense success. Audiences flocked to his ingenious comedies and set attendance records. Colleagues and critics alike outdid one another in their acclaim. Tristan Bernard, himself a comic playwright of no mean stature, recognized him as *le maître* of his genre. Even the poet-playwright Catulle Mendès, a determined foe of the vaudeville,[1]

---

1. The term "vaudeville" is used in the modern French sense: a light, skillfully constructed comedy, farcical in its effects. It has

agreed—though grudgingly—that Feydeau was a most talented practitioner of what Mendès considered an unworthy dramatic form:

> How can anyone win out against someone who makes you laugh your head off? You can't be angry when you're doubled up with laughter; and it's hard to hold a serious point of view when you're holding your sides. It goes without saying that I have not come to terms with situation vaudeville; I continue to deplore the fact that M. Georges Feydeau uses the truly remarkable talents that he was given on plays that will be performed four or five hundred times running and revived four or five times as well, but that will never be *read*. Well, I suppose this young man has the right to throw his talent out the box-office window; still, whatever he does with it, you have to admit, and even admire, his hilarious imagination, his artfully constructed plots, and his irrepressible verve.[2]

(Feydeau has had his revenge. Today, who reads *or* watches Mendès?)

Reservations notwithstanding, the poet's admiration of Feydeau's talents was typical, and it was shared by the public. At the height of Feydeau's career, it was not uncommon for two or three of his comedies to be playing in Paris at once. Some of them toured the provinces almost uninterruptedly for a decade or more. It is said

---

nothing to do with the American variety programs of the same name. Similarly the term "vaudevillist," a writer of such comedy.

2. From a critique of *La Dame de chez Maxim* ("The lady from Maxim's") in *Le Journal*, 18 January 1899. The review is quoted by Gaston Sorbets at the end of the play's first edition, interrupted by World War I (*La Petite Illustration*, 1 August 1914–17 May 1919). This and subsequent translations from the original French are my own, unless otherwise noted.

that, over a period of some fifteen or twenty years, *La Dame de chez Maxim* alone was always being presented somewhere. Nor was that "somewhere" necessarily in France itself. Though he may not have vied with the British Empire for rights to the never setting sun, Feydeau did see his plays translated into many languages and staged abroad almost as soon as they had appeared at home—not infrequently in pirated versions, it should be added. In the United States, the well-known impresario Charles Frohman was responsible for bringing several of Feydeau's most successful comedies to the New York stage around the turn of the century and beyond. (One of his productions—*The Girl from Montmartre*, 1912—should be of particular interest to historians of the American theater. Based on a German translation of *La Dame de chez Maxim* published in 1911, it contained music by one Henry Bereny, as well as by a young composer just beginning his climb to theatrical fame: Jerome Kern.)

In short, for his own contemporaries Feydeau was usually surefire. And he is so again today. After a generation of relative neglect—a far shorter period of oblivion than most geniuses suffer before rediscovery—Feydeau's theater enjoyed an unexpected rebirth of popularity during the early forties. Ever since the entrance in 1941 of *Feu la mère de Madame* ("Madame's late mother") into the repertory of a rather tradition-bound Comédie-Française—despite many a raised eyebrow and gasp of disbelief—this newfound popularity has grown unabated. Feydeau has kept audiences "rolling in the aisles" with one revival after another. Today, in his native France, he has (in the words of playwright André Roussin, to name but one) become "a classic of the French comic theater." [3] The Comédie-Française now welcomes him with open arms and has added several more of his comedies to its reper-

3. Roussin, "Le Cas Feydeau," *World Premières Mondiales*, New Series, February 1963, p. 1.

tory. One, *Un Fil à la patte* (*Not by Bed Alone* in this collection), has itself broken all the attendance records of that venerable institution.

Across the Channel, Feydeau has begun to attract a most distinguished following as well. Indeed, some of the most prominent names in the British and French theater today—Olivier, Barrault, Hirsch, Guinness, Vitaly, and others—have associated their acting and directing talents with his revival. At present writing, this favor shows no signs of waning. On the contrary, any French director, from Barrault on down, has come to realize that, when his books dip into the red, he can usually count on Feydeau to pull him up into the black. British directors are learning the same lesson. Six of his comedies have even found their way into a recent British television series.

Conservative critics may take issue with Jean-Louis Barrault and Marcel Achard, who rank Feydeau second only to Molière as a French comic genius.[4] But few, I suspect, will be willing to deny that he is, as Catulle Mendès had observed, a playwright of talent and comic power to be reckoned with. Yet Feydeau is still rather little known to the American public of playgoers and playreaders. Published translations of his works are very few and very far between. As for actual productions, they too are much less frequent than they deserve to be (though his name has begun to crop up from time to time in college productions). Some American cinema audiences may, indeed, have been exposed to Feydeau without realizing it, in the recent showings of *Hotel Paradiso*, Peter Glenville's film version of his own translation of *L'Hôtel du Libre-Echange*

4. See Barrault, *Une Troupe et ses auteurs* (Paris: Vautrain, 1950), p. 51. Also Achard's introduction to the nine volumes of Feydeau's *Théâtre complet* (Paris: Le Bélier, 1948–56), vol. 1, p. 7. (This collection contains all thirty-seven of Feydeau's extant comedies, including two left unfinished. There is reason to believe, however, that other manuscripts have not survived.)

("Free-Exchange Hotel"). If so, I hope they will not judge him on the basis of that production alone. Not only did Mr. Glenville feel obliged to insert himself slyly into the film as Georges Feydeau, observer. A more basic objection is that Feydeau's comedy does not, I fear, translate too well into the film medium. It thrives on the restrictions of a proscenium stage, where the very limitations of space impart a focus and an intensity that the camera destroys with its limitless virtuosity of movement, its pannings, long shots, and the like. A thousand things happen in a Feydeau play. Much of their comic strength lies precisely in the fact that, on stage, they all have to happen in the same place.

I think the reason for the neglect of Feydeau in America will be obvious to anyone who reads him with an eye to stage presentation: his plays make tremendous demands on the skill of actor and director alike, requiring a polish of performance and a sense of timing in word and gesture that all too few of our homegrown actors and actresses, nurtured on the Broadway ideal of the quick success, have taken the time to master. Perhaps, as critic Elliot Norton suggests, one "does not need a team of Oliviers" to bring off Feydeau successfully; but all the same, as he is quick to admit, "good comedians and comediennes under a wise director" are indisputable requisites.[5] Feydeau's is not a slapdash theater; two weeks of rehearsal will not succeed in infusing his masterpieces with the vitality that they demand.

In a typical Feydeau play every move has its importance; hardly a word can be omitted without somehow altering the whole. As the longtime dean of *fin de siècle* French theater critics, Francisque Sarcey, once said: "In a play by Feydeau, no character comes into a room and puts his hat on a chair without my telling myself: Aha!

5. *Boston Record American*, 31 May 1968.

You can bet that hat wasn't put there for nothing!" [6] It is for this reason that Feydeau's plays abound in detailed scenic instructions and directions to the actors, often of a most minute nature. Though Feydeau professed to have nothing but scorn for the *vérisme* of Antoine—an ideal which, according to his protégé René Peter, he thought incompatible with the true nature of the theater [7]—he was not, all the same, unaffected by it. In many of his comedies he takes the greatest of pains to instruct the actors in exactly the proper way to deliver a line or perform such and such a gesture. When mechanical devices are used in the action, as they frequently are, he is careful to include a note on their precise workings, and what to do in the event they fail to function. Examples are many. One of the most striking and frequently cited is a passage in *Occupe-toi d'Amélie* ("Keep an eye on Amélie"), in which Feydeau, wanting his characters to pronounce a certain interjection in a very special manner, goes to the trouble of writing it out on a musical staff, unto the exact time values and pitch. An actor could ask for no more explicit directions!

This exactitude is such that Jean-Louis Barrault has been quoted as saying: "When I am directing a play by Feydeau my work consists mainly of making sure that the actors follow the author's instructions." [8] Barrault is exaggerating, of course, for modesty's sake. Still, there is more than a grain of truth in his observation. Nor is he alone in his respect for Feydeau's theatrical precision. Jacques Charon, director of the fabulously successful production of

6. Quoted in Léon Treich, *L'Esprit de Georges Feydeau* (Paris: Gallimard, 1927), p. 12.

7. See Peter, *Le Théâtre et la vie sous la Troisième République, première époque* (Paris: Editions Littéraires de France, 1945), pp. 251–52.

8. Quoted (in English) by Wolfe Kaufman, in "French Farce: Timing Is of the Essence," *New York Herald Tribune Magazine,* 6 February 1966, p. 23.

Un Fil à la patte at the Comédie-Française, has summed
up the demands of a Feydeau comedy from his first-hand
experience:

> In staging Feydeau my principal worry is pace. I
> like to keep things moving rapidly, but I don't dare
> make any changes in Feydeau's directions. This is
> difficult because he is, so far as I know, the only
> author who has ever been so exacting. Usually au-
> thors say so-and-so comes on, goes off, or whatever,
> and let the director of the play choose the move-
> ments. Not here. And this is important because,
> alas, the directions, the movement, the details in a
> Feydeau play are part of the play. Once I left out a
> couple of instructions which, I thought, were un-
> important. A few scenes later the whole play top-
> pled, the plot came askew. Not only every word of
> dialogue by Feydeau, but every gesture, is care-
> fully thought out by the author.[9]

A theater that makes such demands on director and
actor alike may be given anything but slipshod preparation, by anything but a poorly trained company. Perhaps
the current proliferation of new repertory theaters will
create a dramatic atmosphere worthy of Feydeau in this
country. I should like to think it will. It should, at least,
provide on this side of the Atlantic a corps of well-trained
actors with the technique necessary to translate into living action the complexities of a theater that, for all its
madness, requires acting and directing of cool, self-con-
scious precision.

But just what is this madness, which, I keep saying,
runs so blatantly through Feydeau's theater from beginning to end? In fact, it is many things. On the simplest

9. Ibid.

level it is the madness of the isolated remark, the dozens of passing *mots* impregnated with that special brand of Feydeau folly that can make the most outrageous of observations appear quite reasonable indeed. Such are the numerous bizarre explanations that our author puts into the mouths of those characters who must try to explain their way out of the mesh of seemingly inexplicable situations. Witness, for example, the reply of Bois-d'Enghien in *Un Fil à la patte,* when his mistress finds him cowering in a closet (for reasons which you will understand when you read the translation): "Well, you know, there are times when a man just likes to be alone." True enough, but delightfully mad under the circumstances. Mad too are the numerous pseudoscientific explanations that so many of Feydeau's characters dream up ingeniously on the spur of a trying moment. Such is the imposing disease "gueula lignea," would-be latinization of the common *gueule de bois,* an ailment we might better recognize under a name like "hangovitis." The disease is spontaneously baptized by Doctor Mongicourt in *La Dame de chez Maxim* to explain his colleague Petypon's morning-after hangover to the latter's suspicious but gullible wife. A few moments later, another mad, pseudoscientific explanation comes to Petypon's rescue. While trying frantically to rid himself of "Môme Crevette"—the cabaret singer he has just found in his bed, dimly remembered result of his escapade the night before—Petypon is surprised by his wife's sudden approach. There is only time to secrete "La Môme" on all fours, under a rug, covering her as if she were a pouf. To complete the illusion, the faithful Mongicourt sits down on the improvised hassock, just as Madame Petypon enters the room. To distract his wife's attention, Petypon affects another attack of the same malady, much to Madame's dismay:

MADAME PETYPON, *in a panic.* My God! What's the matter with him? . . . Doctor, come quick! It's the hangovitis . . . He's having another attack!

MONGICOURT, *without getting up.* Hold on to him! Don't let him go!

MADAME PETYPON. I won't!

PETYPON, *groaning, trying to turn her away from Mongicourt and "La Môme."* Aaaaah! . . . Turn me toward the north! . . . Turn me toward the north!

MADAME PETYPON, *frantic, turning him toward Mongicourt.* Which way is north?

PETYPON. No, no! Not that way, that's the south . . . In attacks like this you always turn the patient toward the north! . . . Aaaah! . . . Turn me toward the north! . . .

[Act I, scene 3]

Madame Petypon complies, awed by the prestige of the scientific explanation, only one of the many such bits of delicious dementia that Feydeau obliges his characters to invent.

A few notches up the madness scale from the isolated remark and the bizarre explanation, is the madness implicit in the mere existence of certain of the characters who people Feydeau's comedies. There is nothing necessarily mad about a man who stammers—unless, that is, he happens to stammer only when it rains, as is the case of Mathieu in *L'Hôtel du Libre-Echange.* Nor need there be any tinge of madness in a person so emotional that he cannot express himself clearly—unless, of course, like poor Lapige in *La Main passe* ("Pass the deal"), he finds himself barking like a dog every time he opens his mouth to speak! And, while an animal may not properly count as a character, who will deny the delightful folly inherent in the trained seal of *Le Mariage de Barillon* (here translated as *On the Marry-go-wrong*), barking out its minimal vocabulary at the most inopportune moments?

More involved still is the frequent madness of those

passing situations into which Feydeau throws his characters, situations often grotesque in their seeming capri-
ciousness. A prime example is the unenviable fate of
Champignol in the comedy that bears his name, *Champignol malgré lui* ("Champignol in spite of himself"). Saint-
Florimond, in love with the former's wife, finds himself
obliged (through a concatenation of typical Feydeau circumstances) to impersonate the unsuspecting husband,
even unto doing his two-week military service in his stead.
But the real Champignol, without warning, arrives at the
army camp as well. Seeing Saint-Florimond's longish locks,
the captain blares out his orders: "Get Champignol's hair
cut!" The command, passed down from one underling to
the next, is executed; but it is the real Champignol who
has his tresses shorn. Seeing Saint-Florimond again, the
captain bellows the same order; and once more the real
Champignol falls victim to the ravages of the razor. And
yet again. When the quid pro quo occurs for the last time,
it is a slick-skulled Champignol—head shaved clean with
sandpaper—who is left reeling beneath the blows of Feydeau's mad, mad fancy. And who will read *Le Mariage de
Barillon* in these pages without seeing that same mad
fancy at work in the very plot itself? What other description so aptly fits the intricacies and complexities that lead
its hero into a marriage that is unrivaled in its grotesqueness?

Intricacies and complexities indeed. And most ingeniously contrived. For, with all its multimadness, the typical
Feydeau comedy is a rigorously, logically constructed machine in the best tradition of Scribe and the "well-made
play." Imbroglio was Feydeau's stock-in-trade. We have
already cited Catulle Mendès' praise of his "artfully constructed plots." In this respect, Mendès was repeating the
accolades of dozens of contemporary critics who, from the
success of his very first full-length play in 1886, *Tailleur
pour dames* ("Dressmaker-to-ladies"), had already ac-

knowledged Feydeau as a clever geometrician of the comical complication. Mendès was, no less, forerunning the many present-day observers who have admired the same mechanistic perfection. Madame Dussane has voiced this admiration most strikingly of all, in comparing Feydeau's technique to that of a strict contrapuntist: "There are moments when—all things, let me say, being unequal—the progression of an act of Feydeau offers the same secure feeling of satisfaction in surprise as the workings of a Bach fugue." [10] No small praise, this, and quite to the point (and counterpoint). For Feydeau is, uncontestably, the Bach of his genre; and his compositions—the word is not out of place—have a kind of awesome grandeur about them despite their levity and seeming triviality. They are like great Bergsonian machines, in which characters seem reducible to the status of inanimate things, mere parts of the mechanism; and situations, growing in size, or gathering momentum, or reversing their elements into monstrous quid pro quos, become almost tangible in their terrible concreteness.

Still, it will be clear from my preceding remarks that I agree completely with André Roussin when he observes that this impeccable craftsmanship is only part of the story, and that the genius of Feydeau is his "extraordinary mixture of madness with the most rigorous logic," [11] not logic alone. It is this mixture, the very rigorousness and cold inevitability of mad plots and situations, that makes Feydeau's comedies verge so often on the desperate; that keeps his typical hero always teetering over the edge of sanity, always wondering if he is going through a real experience or a bad, mad dream. In his late plays, especially, these unfortunates find their tenuous grip on sanity perilously close to giving way. Our poor friend the dentist

10. Béatrix Dussane, *Notes de théâtre, 1940–1950* (Lyon: Lardanchet, 1951), p. 221.
11. "Le Cas Feydeau," p. 4.

Follbraguet is perhaps the most extreme example. Another, not much less so, is his predecessor Follavoine, hero of *On purge Bébé* (*Going to Pot*), the final comedy in this collection.

The group of plays offered in this volume span Georges Feydeau's career and represent its four principal stages. Born in 1862, Feydeau developed an early interest in the theater, dabbling in it even as a child. At least, so he would have his public believe. A charming article written for the Paris newspaper *Le Matin* (15 March 1908), at the height of his popularity, recounts his beginnings, though not without tongue in cheek:

> How did I become a vaudeville writer? Very simple. Through laziness, nothing else. . . .
>
> I was a child of six, maybe seven. I can't be sure. One night I was taken to the theater. What was the play? I don't even remember. But I came back home full of enthusiasm. I had the bug. The disease had taken hold.
>
> The next day, without having slept a wink, I got down to work as soon as it was light. My father came in on me unexpectedly. With my tongue stuck out and my hands feverishly plastering down my hair, tousled by a sleepless night, I was, quite simply, writing a play.
>
> "What are you doing there?" my father asked.
>
> "Writing a play," I resolutely replied.
>
> A few hours later, the governess (whose job it was to instill in me the basic notions of all the learning then in fashion) came to fetch me. She was a nice girl, but an awful bore.
>
> "Come now, Monsieur Georges, it's time."
>
> My father interrupted:
>
> "Leave Georges alone," he said quietly. "He's

been working this morning. *He's written a play.*
Leave him alone."

All at once I saw my salvation, the trick that
would always save me. From that blessed day on,
whenever I had forgotten to do my homework, to
learn my lesson—and, you can believe me, that
happened more than once!—I would make a dash
for my notebook of plays. And my governess, trans-
fixed, would let me be. . . .

We owe the elder Feydeau an incalculable debt of thanks.
Himself a novelist and respected intellectual of the period,
friend and protégé of Flaubert, he would make his most
lasting contribution to posterity, not in his own works, but
in this fatherly encouragement of his son's childhood enthusiasm.

Feydeau's passion for the theater grew throughout his
school years and beyond, and kept him wavering between
two ambitions: to become an actor or a playwright. His
earliest published efforts date from these years at the
lycée. They are slender works, humorous monologues in
prose and verse, of the type so common as the salon entertainment of those pre–radio-and-television days. For this
genre was all the rage of *fin de siècle* Paris: "Nobody
escapes it. You can't go anywhere to spend a social evening any more without bumping into some monologuist
who, on the pretext of amusing the guests or keeping them
busy, will recite *The Fly* or *The Crawfish*." [12] Feydeau's
first monologue, of the many that he was to write (especially during his early years), was published in 1880, when
he was eighteen. Its successors spread his name throughout
many of the salons of Parisian society, where they were
recited by such celebrated artists of the day as Coquelin
Cadet and Saint-Germain. One of them, *Un Monsieur qui*

12. Abraham Dreyfus, *Jouons la comédie* (Paris: Calmann-Lévy,
1887), pp. iii–iv.

n'aime pas les monologues, published in 1882, is a witty acknowledgment of the popularity of the genre:

> No! I'm going! I can't take any more of it! That tall blond fellow is in the next room. You know, the one who's always reciting monologues. Well, he's doing one right now! . . . Monologues! Who ever heard of such a thing! If I were the police department I'd make them illegal. They're phony! Superphony! A man in his right mind doesn't talk to himself. He thinks, and so he doesn't talk. Why, to allow the monologue is to cheapen the human race! There ought to be a law against it! . . .

It goes without saying that, by the time the speaker has aired his griefs and suggestions, he has delivered a lengthy example of the genre he so detests. A pleasant bit of logical madness that bodes well for the Feydeau-to-come.

In addition to his monologues, Feydeau was quick to try his hand at another favorite salon genre, the *saynète.* Parisian society of the period was especially fond of play acting. No soirée was complete without a drawing room theatrical, presented by professionals, if the hosts could afford them, or, more intimately, by well-intentioned amateurs. Collections of such playlets flooded the market, and, along with them, an endless stream of manuals of diction, dramatics, stagecraft, and the like. Feydeau himself, though he soon gave up the idea of acting professionally, did indulge his dramatic flair in frequent amateur performances of this type throughout his early and later years. And he did so with not a little talent, if we can believe contemporary accounts.[13] Feydeau's contribution to this vogue of salon comedy consisted of about half a dozen one-act

13. See René Peter, p. 196, note. Also Jeanne Pouquet, *Le Salon de Madame Arman de Caillavet* (Paris: Hachette, 1926), pp. 174–75.

plays. *Par la fenêtre* (*Wooed and Viewed*, the first translation of the present collection), was his earliest. It was
produced during the summer season at the resort town of
Rosendaël, near Dunkerque, and printed six years later
by the prominent theatrical publisher Ollendorff at a time
when Feydeau had begun to make a name for himself.

Par la fenêtre is a modest little work, certainly a far
cry from the Chinese puzzles that were to make Feydeau
the master of his genre. It is clearly of salon dimensions,
abounding in monologue—the first scene is nothing else—
and sly asides to the spectator. Still, it does give an indi-
cation of some of the elements that were later to fill his
dramatic bag of tricks. Hector's jealous wife, though we
never see her, is a worthy precursor of the many headstrong heroines that will people Feydeau's later plays,
especially those at the end of his career. Nor is Emma, the
next-door neighbor, any less headstrong than his petulant
spouse. She is only the first in a long string of Feydeau
females intent on avenging their husbands' wayward ways;
emancipated ladies bent on exploiting their newly won
social advances. And what of her husband Alcibiades? He
too, like Hector's wife, remains hidden in the wings. But
we know enough about him and his fiery Latin tempera-
ment to recognize him more than once as he swaggers his
way through later comedies. In this volume we shall see
him as the General in *Un Fil à la patte*, where, once again,
his jealous rage will threaten to erupt in one of those
pseudoheroic duels (or near-duels) so common in Feydeau's theater—witness the plays of this collection—by
which he often mocks a contemporary vogue and its over-
sensitive or prestige-hungry adepts. Alcibiades, further-
more, is the prototype not only of the irascible Latin
rastaquouère, but also of the legion of other foreign visi-
tors who had been inundating Paris—even then—many of
whom would eventually find themselves caricatured in

Feydeau's comedies.[14] Most of all, however, *Par la fenêtre*
points to the later Feydeau by the very absurdity of
Emma's request, perfectly logical in its own way but
thoroughly mad nonetheless. Emma will have a long future
in Feydeau's theater, heading the line of demanding ladies
whose special brand of frustrating logic drives many a
man to comic desperation.

After *Par la fenêtre* Feydeau's production continued in
the same vein of monologues and *saynètes;* modest beginnings, which, all the same, were attracting attention in
popular theatrical quarters. It was not, however, until his
first full-length play that the ripple he was making on the
comic waters started to become a wave. *Tailleur pour
dames* was produced on 17 December 1886,[15] though written several years before. Feydeau had experienced considerable difficulty in having the script accepted by a
theater, despite the many theatrical connections he already
enjoyed:

> It took M. Georges Feydeau three years to have
> *Tailleur pour dames* performed. . . . And yet, the
> young author held a hand full of trumps in his
> quest for recognition. . . .
> Son of the late lamented Ernest Feydeau, stepson
> of M. Henry Fouquier, one of our most brilliant
> journalists, protégé of M. Francisque Sarcey (who,
> abandoning his usual reserve, had warmly but un-

14. A letter from Feydeau, written in August of 1897 to journalist Jules Huret, gives humorous proof of his feelings about this
foreign influx: "Where am I?—For the last week, abroad, in Paris!
But not for long; I'm afraid I might forget my French." Published
in Jules Huret, *Loges et coulisses* (Paris: Editions de la Revue
Blanche, 1901), pp. 289–90.
15. Many sources, including the catalogue of the Bibliothèque
Nationale and the Le Bélier edition of the *Théâtre complet*, mis-
takenly give this date as 1887. See my article "Georges Feydeau:
une date essentielle corrigée," *Revue d'histoire de théâtre*, October–
December 1962, pp. 362–64.

successfully recommended the play), Feydeau
needed no less than the friendship of Fernand
Samuel, daring director of the Renaissance, to en-
able him to unpigeon-hole the three acts that had
been drowsing untouched for some time.[16]

Once the comedy was performed, however, it was a tri-
umph; a riotous escapade of would-be adultery and mistaken identity already rich in the inventiveness and folly
that Feydeau would bring to perfection.

The half-dozen or so comedies that followed in rapid
succession could only be a little anticlimactic for Feydeau,
after the tremendous public and critical reception that had
welcomed *Tailleur pour dames.* For him they were merely
demi-succès, half-successes. For the critics too they were
less than total triumphs. The observations of one of them,
Auguste Vitu, are of particular interest. Vitu, drama critic
for the prestigious *Figaro,* had this suggestion for the
young author, on the occasion of the three-act operetta
La Lycéenne ("The schoolmiss"—23 December 1887):

I think that he would work to better advantage if
he took the trouble to develop his ludicrous entanglements and link them together by some kind of
logic, at least a seeming logic.[17]

We may reasonably suspect that Feydeau read this criticism, and that he took seriously the suggestion of such a
well-known critic. It would certainly appear that he did
so; for, as we know, the "kind of logic" that Vitu recommended was, precisely, to become one of the dominant
features of his technique.

The second play offered in the present volume, *Le Mariage de Barillon* (10 March 1890), dates from these years.

16. Guy de Saint-Môr, *Paris sur scène, 1886–1887* (Paris:
Piaget, 1888), pp. 227–28.
17. *Figaro,* 24 December 1887.

It is one of a group of comedies that Feydeau wrote in collaboration with his friend Maurice Desvallières, concerned no doubt with his failure to duplicate the success of *Tailleur pour dames* and hoping to profit from the collaboration. We will never know how much of the play is "pure" Feydeau and how much the work of Desvallières, though it is more than likely that the former, signing as principal author, wrote the lion's share. Today it is hard to read this play, rich in systematic madness and buffoonery, and understand why it was not received with more enthusiasm. Antoine, in his year-by-year memoirs of Parisian theatricals, passes off the audience's reaction to its opening with the terse assurance: "They laughed." [18] But the critics were less amused—still evoking comparisons with the triumphal success of Feydeau's firstborn—and the author himself, quite naturally, was unhappy too.

He spent the next two years in a kind of self-imposed exile from the boards, closeted with the work of three comic playwrights in an attempt to get back the winning combination. For character study he chose the celebrated Labiche as a master. For dialogue he turned to Meilhac, of the successful comedy and operetta team of Meilhac and Halévy. The comedies of Alfred Hennequin served as models for the technical side of his craft. Hennequin, father of one of Feydeau's subsequent collaborators, was the author of many popular comedies of the day, all of which were tightly knit, well-made Scribean constructions. Feydeau, already with a penchant for imbroglio, was to profit from his study of Hennequin's method and was soon to outstrip his master. "Two years spent in this company," one contemporary tells us, "and Feydeau returned, ventured one work, then another, and never again interrupted his success." [19]

18. André Antoine, *Le Théâtre*, vol. 1 (Paris: Editions de France, 1932), p. 244.
19. René Peter, p. 49.

Indeed, the years that immediately followed this brief hiatus were the period of Feydeau's most concentrated productivity, and showed that his "exile" had been well spent. From 1892, year of his reemergence, to 1896, he brought out no less than seven new three-act plays, either alone or in collaboration. *Monsieur chasse!* ("Monsieur goes hunting!"—23 April 1892) was the first of this long series of successes,[20] and was followed within several months by both *Champignol malgré lui* (5 November 1892) and *Le Système Ribadier* (30 November 1892). According to Marcel Achard, the first two had been written in 1891. Feydeau submitted both scripts to the director of the Théâtre du Palais-Royal, and was so overjoyed at the acceptance of *Monsieur chasse!* that he was quite ready to accede to the latter's summary judgment that *Champignol* was "an absurd play" and that it had not even "the slightest chance of success." [21] It was only with the greatest persuasion that another director, the impoverished Micheau of the Nouveautés, convinced Feydeau to let him read it. By the time he had finished the second act, Micheau's enthusiasm was unbounded. He was certain that *Champignol* was just the play he needed to revive his theater's ailing finances, and he offered to produce it. "He had guessed right," Achard tells us. *"Champignol malgré lui* played over a thousand performances." [22] Feydeau was on the crest of the wave.

And the wave was a long, rolling one. Success followed success, as Feydeau regaled his ever growing public with such masterpieces as *Un Fil à la patte* (9 January 1894), *L'Hôtel du Libre-Echange* (5 December 1894) and *Le Dindon* ("The sucker"—8 February 1896). *Un Fil à la*

20. Some eight months before, a dramatic monologue, *Madame Sganarelle*, was performed in the resort town of Spa, Belgium, and subsequently at Poitiers. The manuscript remains unpublished.
21. Achard (see n. 4 above), p. 9.
22. Ibid., p. 10.

patte, our third play, is typical of this maturing Feydeau. Typical in its snowballing of a modest cause into a monstrous effect; in its sight gags, its repartees, its mad situations piled one on top of another at an almost merciless pace—merciless, that is, for characters and spectators alike. Typical in its indelicacies, which, however outrageous, for some reason never do degenerate into bad taste. Typical, too, in its discreet balance of characters both ordinary and extraordinary; for Feydeau wisely avoids excessive caricature. To be sure, the tempestuous General is painted in broad, blatant strokes; and Bouzin, the man who can do no right, the born butt, overweening but harmless, is prototypic of the innocent fool. But, by and large, the characters are ordinary enough. For most of them it is not so much what they are that makes them comical as what they do or have done to them—the part they are made to play in the mechanism. And those who are, indeed, caricatures are less important for their foibles per se than for the levers and gears and springs those foibles put in motion.

This same period saw Feydeau—again with Desvallières—temporarily leave the Boulevard for one of the national theaters, the Odéon, second most prestigious stage in the land. And not without controversy. Antoine records that there was, indeed, "some opposition to allowing two authors considered mainly as vaudevillists a place in the second French theater." But he goes on to add that "the public, however, is having a good time, and that's what counts." [23] The comedy in question, *Le Ruban* ("The ribbon"—24 February 1894) does, in fact, represent an attempt by Feydeau to depart somewhat from the mechanistic brand of bedroom farce and to move closer to the character comedy of one of his models, Labiche. The play depicts

23. André Antoine, p. 302.

the ambitions and tribulations of Dr. Paginet, a staunch "antimicrobian," whose researches have covered him with less glory than he imagines. Still, it is for these misguided scientific efforts that he covets the prestigious ribbon of the Légion d'honneur. Amid the many plot complexities and farcical elements, Feydeau succeeds in drawing a character sketch not unworthy of so-called "higher" comedy, following Paginet in his obsession, until, like Molière's miser Harpagon, he is willing to sacrifice the happiness of a member of his own family to satisfy it.

But the change of style represented by *Le Ruban* was, at most, short-lived. *L'Hôtel du Libre-Echange* and *Le Dindon* are once again comedies of unabashed imbroglio, variations on the theme of marital mix-up; and by 1897 Feydeau is comfortably back in his accustomed groove, constructing *La Dame de chez Maxim*, that "infernal machine" manufactured from an inexhaustible kit of comic parts by a hand that was now that of an unrivaled master.

And yet, for all his talents, Feydeau did not always work with ease and pleasure. Prolific though he had been a few years earlier, it seems to have taken him close to two years to complete *La Dame*, which had already been promised to Micheau of the Nouveautés, anxious for another hit.[24] During this time, Feydeau kept his name on the boards (and money in his purse) with frequent revivals of previous successes, as well as with a group of one-act comedies, possibly written earlier and refurbished for the occasion. Among the latter was *Dormez, je le veux!* ("Sleep, I command you!"—30 April 1897), a spoof on the then current rage of hypnotism, as was *Le Système Ribadier* of five years before. Feydeau gave his own ex-

24. This play, not produced until 17 January 1899, is mentioned as having already been accepted for presentation in 1897. See Jules Martin, *Nos auteurs et compositeurs dramatiques* (Paris: Flammarion, 1897), pp. 214–15.

planation for the lengthy delay in a self-portrait published in 1901. The theater, he tells us, was his livelihood, and work had become a necessity, not a pleasure:

> I may as well confess it: I hate to work. When I was a schoolboy, I used to take great delight in writing comedies, because it was through them that I avoided doing my assignments. . . . Well, today the situation is reversed. The theater has become the rule, my duty. It is my trade. . . . No, I am not one of those who enjoy giving birth! When I am arranging all that madness that unleashes the spectators' glee, I am not amused by it. I keep the cool, calm poise of the chemist measuring out his medicine. I put into my pill a gram of imbroglio, a gram of licentiousness, a gram of observation. As well as I can, I grind them all into a powder. And I can tell, almost without fail, the effect that they will produce. . . . When the work is done, what a relief! I regain my freedom.[25]

How much of this confession is a valid self-portrait? It is hard to say. Feydeau did have a humorous reputation among his contemporaries for being a little on the lazy side. And we know that, on occasion, he was not above participating in theatricals of dubious artistic merit for monetary gain. For example, the libretto that he supplied for a lush ballet-extravaganza entitled *La Bulle d'amour* ("The bubble of love"—11 May 1898) could have served none but such a practical purpose.[26] We know too that, after considerable financial success, he suffered severe

25. Quoted in Adolphe Brisson, *Portraits intimes*, vol. 5 (Paris: Armand Colin, 1901), pp. 15–16.
26. This spectacle, with music by the popular composer François Thomé, is discussed in detail in the review *Le Théâtre*, June 1898, pp. 18–20.

reverses in the stock exchange and was almost constantly in debt. Still, Feydeau, among his other qualities, is basically antiromantic; that is, he delights in mocking and tearing down high-sounding ideas that offend his common-sense vision of life. Perhaps this confession is little more than an attempt to poke fun at the romantic ideals of sudden inspiration and fervent devotion to literature and art in general. We might remember, in this regard, that *fin de siècle* France was rife with various forms of idealism and latterday romanticism, all rebelling against the materialistic philosophies and aesthetics that had long dominated. Feydeau's portrait of himself may well have been only an exaggerated counterreaction, a bending over backward to avoid seeming the impractical, head-in-the-clouds "artist." On the other hand, even if his admissions are true, he would not be the first genius to be so motivated, nor would the quality of his art—and craft— suffer thereby. Even the great Molière was not above writing to feed his troupe.

At any rate, lazy materialist or no, Feydeau scored a fantastic success with *La Dame de chez Maxim*. Critics outdid one another in their search for superlatives to heap on the misadventures of Dr. Petypon and the notorious "Môme Crevette." For the critic of the *Mercure de France* the play qualified Feydeau as "the best of our vaudevillists." [27] For Sarcey, overwhelmed by "the fertility of comical devices," it was the finest that Feydeau had ever produced. [28] No less enthusiastic was Robert de Flers, himself a well-known dramatist, who found it "quite simply the masterpiece of the genre," building his crescendo of praise to an impressive pitch:

27. A. Ferdinand Hérold, in *Mercure de France*, March 1899, p. 797.
28. Francisque Sarcey, critique written 18 January 1899, reprinted in *Quarante ans de théâtre*, vol. 8 (Paris: Bibliothèque des Annales, 1902), p. 189.

Thanks to a geometric precision, we accept the most extravagant situations as well as the most stupefying solutions; and the most demanding philosopher as well as the most intransigent algebraist will bow before the prodigious gifts of M. Georges Feydeau.[29]

Nor was the success of *La Dame* only an artistic one. Micheau found it well worth the waiting. For, through its first hundred performances alone, it earned the Nouveautés the then incredible sum of more than 620,000 francs, selling out every performance for the first time in that theater's history.

I have already alluded to the play's continuing popularity in France and abroad. Yet, despite all the profit that Feydeau must have been garnering from its many authorized productions, it would seem he was having troubles making ends meet. For, in February of 1901, he was moved to put up for public sale a substantial part of his art collection, more than a hundred works, most of them by noted contemporaries.[30] Feydeau, son-in-law of the portraitist Carolus Duran, was himself an avid art enthusiast and amateur painter. Such a sale could have been prompted only by pressing financial needs.[31] At about the same time, though he had been promising Micheau a sequel to *La Dame* for a couple of years, Feydeau was to make another artistic sacrifice to monetary gain by collaborating on—or, rather, doctoring up—the libretto of an ill-fated comic opera, *Le Billet de Joséphine* ("The

29. *Revue d'art dramatique*, 5 February 1889, pp. 206–8.
30. The catalogue of this auction is available in the New York Public Library. There is a catalogue of a second sale, two years later, in the Library of Congress.
31. Feydeau was once asked what his hobby was. "The theater," was his whimsical reply. "My trade is painting. The public has turned all that around." See Léon Treich, p. 69.

message from Josephine"—23 February 1902).[32] It was
not until nine months after the quick demise of this venture that Feydeau finally produced the new comedy that
Micheau was so eagerly awaiting.

La Duchesse des Folies-Bergère (3 December 1902)
can be viewed as something of a turning point for Feydeau, since it may well have been the critical reaction to
it that resulted in the next major development in his
career. Although its broad humor was appreciated by the
public, the critics were less enthusiastic. One of them in
particular voiced a telling objection. Emile Faguet, acad-
emician and scholar of repute, agreed that the comedy
was amusing in its madness, but found serious fault with,
of all things, its construction:

> It does not have that logical cohesion in its ab-
> surdity, or rather in its eccentricity, that is the
> prime virtue of the vaudeville. It is made up of
> several vaudevilles, in which the spectator becomes
> involved, from which he parts company, and to
> which he returns, without drawing out of each one
> all that it contains; a weakness of M. Feydeau the
> beginner, one from which he emerged, and into
> which he is falling once again.[33]

Faguet, traditionalist though he was, enjoyed a prestige
that would not let such an appraisal go unheeded. His
criticism recalls Vitu's judgment of *La Lycéenne* some
fifteen years before, one that Feydeau eventually seemed
to take to heart. Now, after a long series of successes, the
playwright finds himself suddenly confronted with a
criticism implying that he has not only stopped developing

32. The music for this work was composed by Alfred Kaiser. A
full description can be found in the review *Le Théâtre*, April (no.
1), 1902, pp. 14–18.
33. *Journal des débats*, 12 December 1902, p. 1128.

but that he is even regressing to the technical imperfections of his youth. A change is in order.

And, indeed, the plays that came after gave evidence that just such a change was taking place. Not an abrupt change, to be sure, for Feydeau would never wholly abandon his vaudevillistic talents. But rather a gradually developing emphasis on the subtleties of interaction as opposed to the blatancies of action per se, a direction already lightly hinted at a decade before in *Le Ruban*. With the production of *La Main passe* (1 March 1904), some fourteen months after Faguet's discouraging review, critics were once again unanimous in their praise. It seems that Feydeau, who had always made them split their sides, had never quite given them a "respectable" excuse for doing so. Now, lo and behold, they could find in his new play a touch of "higher" and more literary comic devices with which to salve their consciences: "delicacy of observation, a touch of subtle analysis in the characters," and even "a dash of philosophy." [34] What impressed the critics most was that Feydeau did not have to rely entirely on his repertory of mechanistic devices but could still treat the traditional subject of marital and extramarital imbroglio with a much more delicate touch.

The rest of Feydeau's theater shows an oscillation between these two poles: restrained comedy of interaction and unbridled comedy of action. On the one hand, he would produce *L'Age d'Or* ("The Golden Age"—1 May 1905), a fantasy in a Labiche-family framework (and his last collaboration with Desvallières). He would even write a bona fide character study like *Le Bourgeon* ("The sprout"—1 March 1906), treading on risky ground to depict the dilemma of a young abbé at grips with his budding carnal appetites. Both plays are not without occasional touches of robust humor. On the other hand, he

34. From a critique by Charles Formentin in *La Grande Revue*, 15 March 1904, p. 685.

would revert squarely to the jack-in-the-box constructions of his earlier triumphs with such unabashed romps as *La Puce à l'oreille* ("A flea in the ear"—2 March 1907) and *Occupe-toi d'Amélie* (15 March 1908). After change, uncertainty. It was not until the notable success of his next play that Feydeau seemed to determine what his future course would be.

Several months after *Amélie* had scored an impressive hit, Feydeau's name surprised the critics by appearing on the boards of one of the smaller Parisian theaters, the Comédie-Royale. His new comedy, *Feu la mère de Madame* (15 November 1908) was inconspicuously tucked in among a group of three other one-act plays. For a number of years many of the less prominent theaters had been presenting composite programs of this type—*spectacles coupés* —in an attempt to rival the growing popularity of the *café-concerts*, cabarets that had begun to offer a more and more varied artistic fare, with profitable result. However, these small Parisian "off-Broadway" theaters seldom produced the works of well-known playwrights, and there was considerable wonder at finding the celebrated author of *La Dame de chez Maxim* not only presenting a modest one-act play but also sharing the bill with three virtual unknowns.

But for all their surprise at his sudden change of pace, the public and critics were no less delighted with Feydeau's new offering. Henri de Régnier, who had replaced Faguet as drama critic for the *Journal des débats*, was warm in his praise, calling special attention to its unaccustomed simplicity. For in this work, Feydeau "has used none of the skillful and inextricable plot entanglements that have, in part, made for the success of his great plays. In this comedy he goes no further than an anecdote, but that alone gives him enough to provide unlimited entertainment." [35]

35. *Journal des débats*, 27 November 1908, p. 1035.

The "anecdote" is, in fact, a lengthy quid pro quo, but not of the usual Feydeau variety. Mistaken identity, indeed; but in a very different key. For the humor of *Feu la mère de Madame* derives almost entirely from the clash of personalities, not the grinding of gears. Feydeau introduces two characters, the man and wife at odds in a frustrating war of nerves, a couple that will, in different guise, reappear throughout his remaining one-act plays; tragi-comic illustrations of the dictum that "so many husbands and wives are separated by nothing but marriage." And, in fact, it was to this series of plays that Feydeau devoted the rest of his productive life, aside from two unfinished comedies and two others by youthful protégés to whom he lent his collaboration and the luster of his name.[36]

It would appear that the success of our fourth play, *On purge Bébé* (12 April 1910), a year and a half after *Feu la mère de Madame,* confirmed Feydeau in his new, more restrained style. This play, as readers of the present collection will appreciate, is once again an "anecdote," another hectic day in the life of Madame and Monsieur. Imbroglio there is, to be sure. Who will deny that Follavoine is caught up in a network of circumstances? But, as in all these late conjugal comedies, it is an imbroglio that grows from the conflict of characters, no less perfectly constructed that Feydeau's monstrous mechanisms, but far more intense within its more compact psychological dimensions. "I hope that M. Feydeau will continue along this path," wrote critic Adolphe Brisson in his review of

36. The plays in question are *Cent millions qui tombent* ("A hundred million from heaven") and *On va faire la cocotte* ("We're off to walk the streets"), both unfinished; *Le Circuit* ("The road race"—29 October 1909), three acts, with Francis de Croisset; and *Je ne trompe pas mon mari* ("I don't cheat on my husband"—18 February 1914), three acts, with René Peter. Another three-act play mentioned by several contemporary sources, *Ni vu ni connu* ("No one's the wiser"), produced 29 April 1909, was in reality a revival, slightly altered, of *Le Système Ribadier,* originally staged some seventeen years earlier.

On purge Bébé, "and that, without ceasing to be clever and ingenious, he will draw his inspiration directly from life. The great comic author within him holds many surprises in store for us." [37]

For Brisson, Feydeau's change of style gave promise of still greater things to come. And Feydeau was to validate his prophecy, though illness, cutting him off in his prime, would let us follow the conjugal chaos of our man and wife through only three more plays: *Mais n' te promène donc pas toute nue!* ("Please don't walk around in the nude!"—25 November 1911), *Léonie est en avance* ("Léonie is ahead of schedule"—9 December 1911), and finally, some four years later, the already cited *Hortense a dit: "Je m'en fous!"* (14 January 1916). (Let no one think that today's vogue of long Broadway titles is a new phenomenon!) The situations differ in their particular madness, but the theme is always the same, as the harassed husband suffers a crescendo of frustration at his wife's baffling brand of ill—very ill—logic. All the comedies met with the same enthusiastic response. "The things which . . . are presently attracting the public are the one-act plays of M. Georges Feydeau." So one contemporary journalist reported after the first four had been produced. "There is not a little theater to be found," he continued, "that does not want . . . a one-act vaudeville by the author of *La Dame de chez Maxim.*" [38] Other critics corroborated this enthusiasm, though few made the mistake of considering the plays as "vaudevilles."

It is, in fact, worth speculating on just what it was that made Feydeau abandon his broad style to concentrate on these more subdued comedies. There are several possible answers. On the one hand, he may have been affected by a long-standing critical pessimism toward the vaudeville.

37. *Le Temps,* 18 April 1910.
38. Eugène Héros, *Le Théâtre anecdotique* (Paris: Jorel, 1912), pp. 157–58.

Throughout the final decade of the nineteenth century, critics had been intoning constant dirges to this dramatic form. As early as 1891, Henry Fouquier, in a doleful article on the condition of the French theatre, had called attention to the rapid decline of "Hennequin's theater of a hundred doors." [39] Many other critics echoed his words. One may well wonder how critic Fouquier viewed the budding career of his stepson Georges Feydeau, already author of many vaudevilles himself. It seems more than coincidental that after Fouquier's article, when Feydeau reemerged from his "exile," he never again used the designation "vaudeville" for his productions, though he had done so frequently before. From that point on he was to use only the terms "comedy" and "play." Some have suggested that this post-1892 nomenclature is proof of Feydeau's awareness of having advanced the vaudeville to the point of making it almost a new genre for which the traditional name was no longer appropriate. More likely he was merely avoiding a designation that could not benefit his plays, and could only hinder them at a time when critics, his own stepfather foremost among them, saw the genre in decline. Not that Feydeau himself believed that "Hennequin's theater of a hundred doors" really was dead beyond recall. Far from it. If he had, there never would have been *Un Fil à la patte*, *La Dame de chez Maxim*, *Occupe-toi d'Amélie*, and so many more. Now, however, the enthusiastic reception of his one-act plays may have persuaded him finally to abandon the intricacies of the vaudeville for a genre that had won him public and critical acclaim.

Then too, he could succeed with far less effort. If Feydeau had become as lazy as he would have us believe, it is easy to understand why he might choose to exploit this new vein in preference to the old. One act, even

39. "Le Krach du théâtre," *Figaro*, 18 November 1891.

perfectly constructed, takes less time to write than three. It is possible, too, that these plays were all the easier for him to compose since he may well have been drawing on his own marital experiences, albeit stylized, for these intense comedies that tread the razor's edge between the humorous and the serious. For Jean-Louis Barrault there seems to be little doubt in this regard: "Madame Feydeau was in a sense his muse . . . [for] these one-act masterpieces." [40] At this distance one can only theorize. There would, however, seem to be some evidence, at least circumstantial, that Feydeau was, indeed, having troubles at home. It was at just about the time he began to stage these domestic comedies that, for some mysterious reason, he took up residence in a Paris hotel, without his wife and family, continuing to live there until illness forced him to a sanitarium in 1919.[41]

It was this same lingering illness that prevented Georges Feydeau from ever writing again. We are clearly the poorer for it.

We would be poorer still if he had not, artistically speaking, been reborn a generation later. But, in our own day, as we know, this meticulous craftsman of relentless laughter is duplicating, if not surpassing, the great success he knew during his lifetime; success that brought him the admiration of peers and public alike. Yet, although Feydeau the Boulevardier has found a steady place today in the "official" theaters of Paris—a place that he, in his own lifetime, would never have dreamed possible—I imagine that the average spectator, now as then, sees him only as a clever clown in the lusty tradition of French bedroom farce; a clown with a madly fertile and inventive fancy, but a clown all the same. I suspect that, like Feydeau's

40. Jean-Louis Barrault, p. 52.
41. See René Peter, *Le Théâtre et la vie sous la Troisième République, deuxième époque* (Paris: Marchot, 1947), p. 77.

contemporaries, the rank-and-file spectator of today sees in him an ingenious fabricator of what the French used to call "digestive comedy," a nonintellectual after-dinner theater whose characters might, likely as not, cavort about in their underpants to bring down the house; a theater admittedly superficial, unconcerned with the many deep, problematic, philosophical plays of the avant-garde that are obviously saying something about the meaning of life, though who can always say what?

And, no doubt, Feydeau is very much a part of this popular tradition. Still, while the greater public accepts the comic madness of his plays as farcical clowning and slapstick—or perhaps even as a comic relief from the intellectual demands of the modern theater of the offbeat and obscure—many, on the other hand, see in this madness the possibility of a more serious twentieth-century interpretation, and one not unrelated to that selfsame offbeat and obscure theater of today's avant-garde. For many, Feydeau represents a foretaste of that contemporary theatrical current which, for good or ill, has been dubbed "Theater of the Absurd." If by "absurd" one meant merely mad, there would be no argument. Quite clearly Feydeau would qualify. But surely it means more. Theatrically, the term "absurd" can be said to cover a multitude of scenes. It is, in fact, something of a catch-all for many different brands of nonrealistic theater, all of which share a common denominator of implausibility in some form or other, be it in any or all of the basic dramatic variables: décors, characters, dialogue, and plot situations. The "absurd" theater of a Pinter, reasonably plausible in most of these respects, is not that of a Beckett, quite implausible in most. Nor is either just the same as the "absurd" of an Ionesco, which vacillates between the two extremes.

In this sense, Feydeau's brush with the "absurd" is rather light. His décors are all perfectly realistic: a bourgeois drawing room, a hotel, an army camp, etc.

Never any bizarre or impressionistic or symbolic settings like the many we find in Beckett or Arrabal, for example. His characters, except for the happy sprinkling of broad caricatures and unusual types mentioned above, are plausible enough. They are ordinary people: doctors, lovers, mistresses, soldiers, chorus girls, wayward husbands, vengeful wives, and all the rest. Even a dentist thrown in. His dialogue is perfectly acceptable as real dialogue, despite its frequent flashes of madness. And his plots, while always unusual and often grotesque, are nonetheless quite plausible to anyone who has watched them develop piece by piece. We can believe that they are actually taking place, though we would hate to have them happen to us. In other words, there are no expanding bodies, no multifaced heroines, no characters conversing in garbage cans, no people turning into rhinoceroses, no empty chairs purporting to be full, or other such external hallmarks of today's "absurd."

Still, it is in the very grotesqueness of the typical Feydeau situations that he seems to emerge as a forerunner of the "absurd." Because there is another characteristic that pervades a good part of this avant-garde theater: that is, the projection, in theatrical terms, of the aimlessness and unpredictability of man's fate in a haphazard (or, at least, inexplicable) universe, in which things—mainly bad— will happen to him for no obvious or compelling reason. In this sense there is a good dose of "absurdity" in Feydeau. I have already had occasion to discuss this aspect of his work in an article of several years back. Let me quote a passage here:

> Alfred Capus, Feydeau's contemporary, once defined the essence of life as "the struggle of the human will against chance." This "struggle," transposed into the framework of a comedy, is the very essence of Feydeau's theater, in which seeming

chance is really a well-regulated creation of the author. The playwright, like a master puppeteer, assumes a godlike role, creating around his helpless characters a universe of apparent absurdity in which their efforts to resist their destiny are frantic but fruitless. Some, consequently, are tempted to see in such a universe an embodiment of the absurd, finding in Feydeau's merciless and often gratuitous imbroglios a foretaste of the existentialist view of the human condition. . . . Feydeau's characters are often victims of a relentless whimsy, which delights in recreating in a comical dramatic fiction the absurdity and inexplicability of real life.[42]

Examples are legion. On the one hand, there are those unfortunates who, thanks to an innocent peccadillo, are made to suffer the torments of Feydeau's comic hell. Saint-Florimond may, indeed, be pursuing Madame Champignol with less than honorable intent; and Dr. Petypon did bring home the notorious "Môme Crevette." But neither man has yet been guilty of any real breach of propriety. Nevertheless, they are enmeshed in the maze of circumstances, whose cause—their creator's wanton caprice—they cannot even begin to perceive. Then too there is Bouzin, whose misfortunes you will see firsthand. True, he is an overreacher, convinced of a talent that he does not possess. True, too, his every misadventure throughout the play can be traced back to this basic "comic flaw." But a small enough flaw it is, after all, and certainly not worthy of the punishment that Feydeau metes out to him. "I'm innocent!" he cries, as the final curtain falls. And, except for the modest sin of trying to advance his artistic cause with a spur-of-the-moment fib—I am trying not to

42. "Suffering and Punishment in the Theatre of Georges Feydeau," *Tulane Drama Review*, Autumn 1960, p. 117.

give the plot away—he really *is* innocent. But his creator, for the time being, turns a deaf ear; and Bouzin, though we know he will be saved by Bois-d'Enghien in the long run, is left to wonder what kind of blind, absurd fate has singled him out for suffering.

On the other hand, there are those Feydeau victims who are not really guilty of any "comic flaw" at all, however slight. A Champignol, through absolutely no fault of his own, has his hair shaved down to the roots. "It's inhuman!" he groans, a sort of Job reduced to comic size, unable to grasp the meaning of his fate. But no god reveals himself to explain or defend it. If he did, Feydeau, the author-god, would explain to his victim that, deserve it or not, each character has his part to play, albeit a part dictated by nothing but his creator's whim. Lacking this consolation, poor Champignol can only resign himself to the apparent absurdity of his lot. So too with Barillon. What has he done to deserve his bizarre destiny? Not a thing. But certainly that is no reason to spare him the chagrin to which he falls unhappy heir.

At least, in the examples mentioned above, Feydeau takes pity on his puppets and, sooner or later, pulls the proper strings to set them free. Even Bouzin's fate will eventually be put to rights. But such is not always the case. Feydeau is just as willing and able to illustrate man's "absurd" condition, whether intentionally or not, by refusing to untangle his victims or even give them cause to hope in their eventual salvation. Consider the hero of one of his last monologues, *Un Monsieur qui est condamné à mort* ("A gentleman condemned to death"—1899). He has come to Paris from the provinces to visit his aunt, who lives across from the courthouse:

> My first day in Paris! As soon as I get out of the station I ask this guy: "Which way to Court-house Boulevard?" "Easy," he tells me. "There's

a bus that goes there direct." Sure enough, on the
next corner, what do I see but a bus, all painted
black, standing in front of this shop that's got like
a lantern hanging outside with "Police" written on
it. . . . So I ask someone: "Does this bus go to
the courthouse?" "Damn right!" he tells me. . . .
"It's the paddy-wagon!" So I say to myself: "Just
what I'm looking for." And I get on the bus.

Once in the courtroom, the poor fool is mistaken for a
criminal and browbeaten into confessing that he has
murdered his aunt by moonlight, cut off her left breast,
and eaten it (a neat bit of absurdity in itself). His confession will take him to the guillotine unless the President
of the Republic listens to his pleas, and we have no reason
to suspect that he will. Here is a situation that, for all its
black humor, exemplifies the observation of Jean Cassou
that there is a streak of cruelty in Feydeau's whimsical
handling of his characters. Life itself, so seemingly arbi-
trary in its treatment of man, is not very different:

[Feydeau's] mathematics goes hand in hand with
cruelty. . . . It is inexorable. Going to the very
limit of itself, it cannot help letting out a muted
little snicker. It realizes, most likely, how closely
it resembles the logic of real, human affairs. This
logic of the artist and man of the theater knows
itself to be the same as the logic that governs the
designs and actions of human society.[43]

It is no surprise that this cruelty can have near-tragic
overtones. With a shift of emphasis many a Feydeau hero

43. Cassou, "Le Génie systématique de Feydeau," *Cahiers de la
Compagnie Madeleine Renaud–Jean-Louis Barrault,* January 1956,
p. 60.

would feel uncomfortably at home in Artaud's "Theater of Cruelty" and its present-day descendants.

Nor are the harassed heroes of Feydeau's late plays any less representative of this wholly gratuitous suffering left unresolved. As each of the husbands bursts out of his marital bedlam—Follbraguet and several unfortunates like him —there is no evidence to make us believe that things will be better tomorrow, or, if they are, that they will be for long. What have they done to earn their fate? No more than the innocent Champignol or Barillon. They exist, and that is enough. They must be prepared for whatever frustrations a willful creator imposes upon them for his own, and our, amusement. After all, it's happening to them, not to us. And so we laugh the laughter of superiority, the laughter tinged with that satanic pleasure that Baudelaire saw in man's amusement at his fellow's plight. But it is not a laughter without afterthought. For, as we watch the mounting frustrations that lead Follavoine, Follbraguet, *et al.* out their respective doors, we perceive, however dimly, that it is no great step from such humorous agonies to the suffering of an innocent Humanity beyond the bounds of theatrical fantasy.

Perhaps the most innocent victim in all of Feydeau's repertory is Follbraguet's patient, Vildamour. Trapped in the dentist's chair, he can only grunt and groan as Follbraguet, drill in hand, vents the emotions that have been building within him. And when husband, in one final confrontation with wife, flings down his instruments and storms out of the room, Vildamour, in panic, is left still bound and gagged in the chair, helpless victim-once-removed of another man's convulsion.

Vildamour is also, in a sense, victim of something else, something much more concrete. As he sits there immobilized, abandoned, watching Follbraguet's tempestuous exit, we see him, in the few moments before the curtain, falling prey to a mass of apparatus. It is as if the dentist's chair and all its trappings—saliva pump and tubes and such—were so many malevolent objects, agents of the author's capricious design. Here is another link between Feydeau and the modern Theater of the Absurd, in which objects so often play a fundamental role in the drama of man against the inexplicable. A maze of blankets turns the stage into a jungle in Arrabal's *Le Labyrinthe*. A mysterious lift takes food from a still more mysterious cellar in Pinter's *The Dumbwaiter*. A tree, a rope, a pair of scissors—a whole spate of objects—obligingly descend from nowhere, offering themselves to the trapped hero of Beckett's *Acte sans paroles I* ("Act without words I"), only to taunt him when he tries to put them to use. And how many of Ionesco's plays pit man against thing, against the constant proliferation of matter, all of which—as in *Le Nouveau Locataire* ("The new tenant"), for example—seems bent on encroaching upon him in some absurd manner and to some absurd end?

True, Feydeau's décors are all perfectly realistic. As I have said, there are no expanding bodies or the like to confront and confound his heroes. But there is all the same in his comedies an insistence on material objects; on props, which, however plausible and believable, are made to do their part in carrying out the will of the creator against his creations. There is no dearth of examples. Feydeau reflects the abundant technology of his age. Like many humorists of the period—one thinks immediately of Alphonse Allais—he is a fanciful inventor. Witness the *fauteuil extatique* in *La Dame de chez Maxim*, a kind of electric chair whose current transfixes the occupant and any others in contact with him, and projects one and all into a beatific slumber. When Dr. Petypon proudly shows off this extravagant therapeutic device to his colleague Mongicourt, Feydeau is having a good time at the expense of serious science, poking mild fun at the unbridled optimism engendered by technological gadgetry.[44] But he is also putting on stage an object that will be capable, mere thing though it be, of carrying out its role in the imbroglio about to envelop his flesh and blood characters. Matter against man. And, of course, the *fauteuil* does just that, indiscriminately putting to sleep anyone who comes along at the wrong—or right—moment.

We need not, however, look only to the many inventions and mechanical devices of Feydeau's theater to find evidence of the power of objects. In *On purge Bébé* you will see even a pair of everyday chamber pots seemingly endowed with a malicious mind of their own, bent on the embarrassment of their manufacturer, the hapless Follavoine. And while reading the opening scene, try to keep a mental eye on Julie's recalcitrant stockings. Watch them as they seem to act as they please, adding their little bit to Follavoine's growing frustration. Or the ubiquitous *Figaro* in *Un Fil à la patte*, which keeps popping up throughout the first act at the most inopportune times. Who will deny that it too appears almost to be playing with a flustered Bois-d'Enghien, and enjoying its mischief? Ordinary objects one and all, and many others like them— essential parts of the machinery that subjects Feydeau's characters to his brand of "absurdity."

It would be hazardous to claim Feydeau's proto-absurd as a direct influence on any of today's "absurdist" playwrights, and especially so in the case of Ionesco. Not that it hasn't been done. One writer, in a humorous allusion to Ionesco's Balkan background, credits him with having "cooked up Labiche and Feydeau and Monnier in a tartar sauce." [45] And this, despite the fact that the author had

44. See my article "Georges Feydeau et le fauteuil extatique," *Revue d'histoire littéraire de la France*, October–December 1960, pp. 557–559.

45. Philippe Sénart, *Ionesco* (Paris: Editions Universitaires, 1964), p. 14.

never even known Feydeau's theater until well after his
own early successes, when so many critics confidently announced that he had been influenced by him.[46] Nevertheless, Ionesco is quick to admit that, once having read him,
he was "astonished to see that there was a great resem-
blance between Feydeau and myself . . . not in the themes,
not in the subjects; but in the rhythm and structure of the
plays." [47] He goes on to explain that it is the mounting
madness and dizzying acceleration of pace in a Feydeau
play—he uses *La Puce à l'oreille* as an example—that he
finds very much akin to his own "obsession with proliferation." And his observation is quite accurate. A play like
La Cantatrice chauve ("The bald soprano"), where the
"proliferation" is one of language, not of matter, builds
itself up little by little to a fever pitch in much the same
way and with much the same rhythm as a typical Feydeau
comedy. We may not understand every sentence that the
characters say, or every phrase, or even every word. But
we are aware of a crescendo of intensity in the situation
that gives rise to their utterances, however absurd, just as
we are, for example, in the imbroglio of *Un Fil à la patte*
or the frenzy of *On purge Bébé*. In other words, the bricks
may be different, but the mortar is very similar indeed.
It is easy to imagine that Ionesco had Feydeau's kind of
comedy in mind when he indulged in the following re-
flexions on the nature of the theater he would champion:

> And so, if the theater's value lay in the exaggera-
> tion of effects, these had to be exaggerated still
> more; they had to be emphasized and accentuated
> as much as possible. To push the theater beyond
> that middle zone that is neither theater nor litera-

46. Claude Bonnefoy, *Entretiens avec Eugène Ionesco* (Paris:
Editions Pierre Belfond, 1966), pp. 57–58.
47. Eugène Ionesco, *Notes et contre-notes* (Paris: Gallimard,
1962), p. 204.

ture is to restore it to its proper framework, its natural boundaries. The strings, rather than being hidden, had to be made still more visible, intentionally obvious, with a plunge into the grotesque, into caricature, beyond the pallid irony of witty drawing room comedies. No drawing room comedies. Instead, farce, and the extreme exaggeration of parody. Humor, to be sure, but with the tools of burlesque. Comedy that would be tough, unsubtle, exorbitant. And no dramatic comedies, either. A return to the unbearable. Everything pushed to paroxysm, to the very sources of the tragic. A theater of violence: violently comic, violently dramatic.[48]

Early in Feydeau's career, in a review of *Le Mariage de Barillon* in fact, one critic, commenting on his mad inventiveness, flippantly predicted that the young author was destined to end his days at Sainte-Anne, a Paris mental hospital.[49] He erred only in detail. Georges Feydeau died in 1921 in a sanitarium at Rueil, some five years after that moment when he pushed poor Follbraguet to the very brink of madness. Maybe he was a little mad himself even then. It would not be hard to see him as the victim of the undeserved, unpredictable—absurd?—fate of his hero. Perhaps he had long been just a trifle mad, even at the height of his career. If not, how was he so able to seize upon, and magnify so mercilessly, that grain of folly in us all, that absurdity in our actions and in our very existence? Perhaps his final submission suggests that when we can

48. Ibid., pp. 12–13.
49. Lucien Muhlfeld, in *Revue d'art dramatique*, 15 March 1890, p. 386.

no longer laugh at the madness within and without us, we risk falling victim to it.

Whether we choose to see Georges Feydeau as a commentator on the absurd in man's life or merely as an extremely agile constructor of farce at its best, it will be obvious to anyone who has ever seen his plays performed —and well performed, as they must be—that he is a master of his medium. It is not rare to see an audience literally doubled-up, breathless with laughter under the repeated blows of his attack. Admittedly, the printed text is a second-best to the living stage—especially here, where the reader must keep track of so many visual effects, all of which, sooner or later, come home to roost. As Bergson has suggested, it is hard to guffaw in the privacy of an armchair. Admittedly too, a translation is not the original. Still, I hope that through the present translations the American reader may come to appreciate, at least in some measure, the genius of a towering comic giant.

Wooed and Viewed

Par la fenêtre

CHARACTERS

HECTOR
EMMA

Illustration: Feydeau as a young man

A well-furnished drawing room. Upstage, a door leading to the hall. Down right, a window. Close to it, a chair. Up left, a fireplace and mantel-piece appropriately decorated. Up right, a door leading to HECTOR's *study. Center stage, a table set for lunch. Chairs and occasional furniture* ad lib.

At rise, HECTOR, *in shirtsleeves and apron, has just finished setting the table.*

HECTOR, *alone.* There! Not bad for a beginner, if I do say so myself! (*He looks down at his apron.*) Lucky I'm alone . . . If anyone saw me like this, who knows what they'd take me for? (*He flares out his apron and makes a mock curtsy.*) Well, they'd be wrong! Believe it or not, I'm a lawyer . . . Really! Not that I ever had much to say about it, heaven only knows . . . My mother's the one who decided it all. One day, there I was with my governess . . . I'll never forget, I was just eight months old . . . Anyway, there we were. Mother took one look at me, up and down, and all of a sudden it came to her: "He's going to be a lawyer!" . . . So now I'm a lawyer. It was as easy as that . . . It was the same thing when I got married. You think I had anything to say about it? Not a bit. It was Mother again . . . She's the one who decided it all. "Hector, I have just the girl for you! Just the girl!" And that's how it was . . . Now, don't misunderstand. I'm not complaining, mind you. My wife couldn't be prettier . . . Really . . . (*Reflecting.*) Of course, she's not exactly perfect. Once in a while she . . . (*Becoming more confidential with the unseen audience.*) Well, frankly, she's jealous. But when I say "jealous" . . . Take yesterday, for example. I was talking to Rose . . . She's our maid . . . I mean, she was our maid . . . But I'll come to that . . . Anyway, I was telling Rose to go do something or other, and all of a sudden my wife gets all red and begins to make a scene. Why? Because I was looking at Rose

3

while I was telling her what to do . . . Just looking at
her, understand? . . . Talk about being jealous! . . .
Well, a little later on, when I wanted my slippers, I
looked straight at my wife . . . straight at her . . . and
I said to Rose . . . she was standing behind me . . . I
said: "Go get my slippers!" I figured that way my wife
wouldn't say I was looking at Rose again. Well, she was
fit to be tied . . . my wife, that is. What a scene! She
said I was ordering her around in front of the help. So
she fired Rose on the spot and went running back to
her mother's. And that's how I happen to be home all
by myself . . . Well, not exactly by myself. Our downstairs neighbor, Madame Scandale, probably hasn't
closed her eyes for a minute, just so she can tell my
wife every move I make. (*He looks down toward the
floor and addresses the unseen neighbor.*) Sorry to dis-
appoint you, you old windbag! Wish you had something to tell, don't you! (*To the audience.*) There hasn't
been a soul in here but me, and I haven't stepped outside since she left. (*Thumbing his nose at the floor.*)
So there! . . . And now I'm going to have my lunch
. . . without my wife. (*Defensively.*) Well, so what? I
love her . . . Of course I do . . . I'd do anything for
her . . . I'd lay down my life. Still, I don't want to
starve to death waiting for her to come back. At least,
not on an empty stomach. (*The doorbell rings.*) Ah!
speak of the devil . . . (*Another ring.*) I'd know her
ring anywhere. (*Several more rings.*) All right, Antoinette! I'm coming!

> *He leaves upstage. A moment
> later* EMMA *enters through
> the same door, in great
> excitement.*

EMMA, *with a Latin accent.* Well, it's about time! Didn't
you hear the bell?

HECTOR, *following her, replying as graciously as possible.*

Why yes, Madame, but—

EMMA, *mocking.* "Why yes, Madame, but . . ." But what, imbecile?

> *She strides down right and peers out the closed window.*

HECTOR, *taken aback.* I beg your pardon, but—

EMMA, *without turning to look at him.* Come, come! Announce me!

HECTOR. Announce you?

EMMA. To your employer, of course!

HECTOR. My employer? . . . But I am my employer . . . I mean—

EMMA, *still looking out the window.* What are you talking about? Stop mumbling! Are you an idiot?

HECTOR, *removing the apron and putting on his coat.* No, my good woman, I'm a lawyer!

EMMA, *finally turning around.* A lawyer?

HECTOR. Exactly!

EMMA. You . . . you mean . . .

HECTOR. Precisely!

EMMA. Oh, Monsieur! What can I say? . . . And here I was, calling you an idiot, and thinking you were the . . . Oh!

HECTOR, *courteously.* Please, think nothing of it. After all, it's hard to tell when you don't know someone.

EMMA. But you will accept my apologies . . .

HECTOR, *bowing.* Really, you needn't give it another thought, I assure you . . . (EMMA *regains her composure.*) Now then, Madame, is there something I can do for you?

EMMA. Yes, Monsieur, there is. In fact . . .

> *She removes her hat and coat, and places them on a chair.*

HECTOR, *aside.* Good God! She's planning to stay! And there's my lunch getting cold!

EMMA, *nervously*. Monsieur . . .

HECTOR. Madame?

EMMA. Are you . . . Monsieur, are you . . . how shall I say . . . (*Emphasizing.*) noble?

HECTOR. Am I . . .

EMMA. Noble.

HECTOR. Well really, Madame, with a name like "Hector Bouchard" I'm hardly what you would call . . . Of course, I do have an aunt who once married a duke, but she—

EMMA. No, no, no! You don't understand. When I say "noble" I mean . . . I mean spiritually.

HECTOR. Oh? Well, spiritually . . . I suppose I'm as noble as anyone else. (*Aside.*) Now what on earth is she getting at?

EMMA. Fine! Then I'm going to ask a favor of you.

HECTOR. A favor?

EMMA. A big favor. (*She moves very close to him.*) A very big favor.

> *She moves still closer.*

HECTOR, *withdrawing before her advances, aside.* If Antoinette could see me now!

EMMA. You see, Monsieur, I'm a married woman . . .

HECTOR. Yes, I see . . . I see. (*He offers her a chair.*) Won't you have a seat?

> EMMA *sits down by the table.*
> HECTOR, *heaving a sigh of relief, sits across from her.*

EMMA. Yes, Monsieur, I have a husband . . .

HECTOR. Naturally.

EMMA. What do you mean, "naturally"?

HECTOR. Well, I mean . . . naturally. You said you were married, so I assumed . . . (*Aside.*) She has to spoil my lunch to tell me that?

EMMA, *continuing.* Yes, Monsieur, I have a husband . . . a jealous, jealous husband! A husband who never gives

me a minute's peace. A husband who suspects every
move I make . . . every move—

HECTOR, *a look of comprehension suddenly lighting his
face.* Ah, now I understand!

EMMA. You do?

HECTOR. Of course. Why didn't you say so in the first
place? (*Assuming a professional tone.*) You've come to
seek my assistance.

EMMA. Exactly!

HECTOR. Ah, well . . . Wait here, I'll just be a moment.
> *He leaves up right and re-
> turns immediately carrying
> a large, legal-looking volume.*

EMMA. Monsieur?

HECTOR, *blowing the dust off the book.* I'll be only too
happy to represent you. (*He begins leafing through the
volume.*) Now then, Madame, have you any reason to
suspect your husband's fidelity? Perhaps you have some
letters? Anything we might use in our case against
him . . . Any evidence?

EMMA. Evidence? Against him? What on earth for?

HECTOR, *still in a very official tone.* Well, Madame, I . . .
I assume you wish to seek a separation. And, as your
lawyer, I—

EMMA. My lawyer? A separation? Me? . . . Why, I never
said anything of the kind! (*Becoming aggressive.*) I'll
have you know I love my husband! I adore him!

HECTOR. Oh? That's very nice . . . I . . . But . . . Precisely what was it you had in mind? Just what is the
nature of your grievance against the gentleman?

EMMA. My "grievance"? Why, I just told you. He is a
jealous, jealous man. He makes my life miserable!

HECTOR. But my dear woman, there's not very much I can
do about that!
> *He looks at the audience and
> shrugs his shoulders.*

EMMA, *getting up and addressing him indignantly*. But he has no right to be, don't you understand? No right at all! (*She begins backing him into the corner, up right.*) You can say what you want about me, Monsieur! You can say anything you like. But as far as *that* goes, my conscience is clear!

HECTOR, *recoiling, losing his aplomb*. But my dear woman, I haven't said a word about you . . . or your husband!
He mops his brow.

EMMA, *walking over to the window, dramatically*. Me . . . unfaithful! Me! How could he even bring himself to think such a thing? Me? The very idea . . . saying I don't love him! And the scenes he makes! Oh!

HECTOR, *aside, going over to the table*. How do I get rid of her? I'm starving!

EMMA, *moving over to him resolutely, as if to announce an important decision*. Monsieur, I have come to you because you are my neighbor. I live just across the way.

HECTOR. Delighted, I'm sure. (*Aside.*) Is she making the rounds of the neighborhood?

EMMA, *sitting down near the window*. And now, Monsieur, you will please make love to me!

HECTOR. What? (*He looks at the audience, dumbfounded.*) I beg your pardon . . . Did I hear you say . . . you want me to . . .

EMMA, *getting up and moving toward him, very matter-of-fact*. Yes, if you don't mind . . . Of course, first I should tell you exactly how I feel about you.

HECTOR, *bowing fatuously*. Oh, Madame! Really . . . (*Aside.*) What a romantic young thing! A Juliet looking for her Romeo!

EMMA, *graciously, but somewhat embarrassed*. Monsieur, I think you are ugly . . .

HECTOR, *taken aback*. What?

EMMA, *even more graciously*. No, don't interrupt! You're ugly, you don't seem very bright, you are . . . well

. . . a little on the chubby side. In fact, you're perfectly
ordinary in every way. There's not a thing about you
that appeals to me . . . not a thing. Absolutely nothing!

HECTOR, *aghast*. But . . . but . . . (*He stands agape for a
moment, finally regaining his composure.*) You're really
much too kind! (*Aside.*) Her compliments do have a
style all their own, I must say!

EMMA, *still as gracious as can be*. In a word, Monsieur,
that is how I see you.

HECTOR, *sarcastically*. Thank you for the portrait. You
don't believe in unnecessary flattery, do you!

EMMA. Oh well, I just paint what I see . . . I'm an impres-
sionist, you might say. Besides, I'm sure you understand . . . I'm telling you all this so you won't get the
idea that I'm interested in you.

HECTOR. Why, the thought never entered my mind!

EMMA, *looking toward the window*. After all, you men do
get such foolish ideas . . . (*With a sigh of determination.*) Well, now that all that is taken care of . . . Now
that you know just where I stand . . . Let's begin:
come, make love to me!

She sits down again.

HECTOR. Look, if this is your idea of a joke . . .

EMMA. A joke? I beg your pardon!

HECTOR. You mean to sit there and try to make me believe that . . . that . . . No! What do you take me for?
(*Impatiently.*) Come now, tell me what you want!

EMMA. What I want? But I told you. I want you to make
love to me . . . Right here!

She points to her chair.

HECTOR. But . . . but . . . my good woman, I'm not the
slightest bit interested in you!

EMMA, *getting up and moving toward him, sharply*. And I
couldn't care less about you! I thought I explained all
that!

HECTOR. I don't even know you. I——

EMMA. I don't know you either.

HECTOR. Besides, I'm married.

EMMA. Well? So am I.

HECTOR, *losing his patience.* Now look! Really, this has gone far enough!

> *He moves behind the table.*

EMMA, *crossing down left.* But Monsieur . . . I'm not asking you the impossible. Don't you see? I want to teach my husband a lesson. I want to punish him for all the terrible things he suspects me of . . . for all those horrible scenes he makes. You can help me, Monsieur. Now do you understand?

HECTOR. I can . . . You want . . . No, not a word!

> *He snatches a slice of bread and devours it on the sly.*

EMMA, *aside.* Oh, these men! If they're not jealous, they're stupid! (*Aloud.*) Well, never mind. Let's begin anyway. Here, come over by the window.

> *She opens the window wide.*

HECTOR, *moving briskly stage left.* Wait a minute! What are you doing?

EMMA. What does it look like I'm doing? I'm opening the window.

HECTOR. But it's freezing outside!

EMMA. Then go fix the fire. (*Pointing to the fireplace.*) Can't you see it's out?

HECTOR. The fire? The fire's been out since yesterday . . . And besides, what's the good of lighting it if you've got the window wide open! It's like the North Pole in here. For heaven's sake, close it! (*Aside.*) She's out of her mind . . . absolutely out of her mind!

EMMA, *pointing to the apartment across the way.* What do you mean, "close it"? How can I close it? If I close it, how will Alcibiades see us?

HECTOR. Alcibi . . . Who?

EMMA. Alcibiades.

HECTOR. Alcibiades the Greek?

EMMA. What Greek? My husband isn't Greek!

HECTOR. I don't give a damn about your husband!

EMMA, *scandalized, moving toward him with fire in her eyes.* Oh! You forget, Monsieur, that you are speaking to his wife!

HECTOR, *thoroughly confused.* What? Who? Whose wife? . . . Oh, you mean Alcibiades' wife . . . I see! . . . Fine! Now close the window!

EMMA, *aside.* He's out of his mind!

> *She goes back to the window.*

HECTOR, *aside.* She's crazy . . . There's no other explanation. (*In a commanding voice.*) Now look here! Either you close that window or, I'm warning you, I'll . . . I'll . . . (*Sheepishly, withering before* EMMA's *menacing gaze.*) I'll catch cold.

EMMA. That's all right . . . I'll give you a handkerchief. Now then, let's begin.

> *She pulls* HECTOR *by the sleeve over to the window, despite his muttered imprecations.*

HECTOR, *breaking loose.* Wait a minute! It's freezing over here!

EMMA. Here, take my coat. (*She envelops him in her fur.*) There! Now please, it's getting late. We must begin. (*She sits down.*) Make love to me.

HECTOR, *falling onto a chair by the table.* "Make love to me . . . Make love . . ." On an empty stomach?

> *He snatches another piece of bread.*

EMMA, *getting up.* What? You mean you haven't eaten yet? Oh, Monsieur, why didn't you say so? (*Passing in front of the table.*) Of course, I should have realized!

11

The table is set, and . . . Oh my, how could I be so stupid? What can I say? . . . (*Suddenly.*) All right then, let's eat!

> *She sits down at the table.*

HECTOR, *incredulous, mechanically repeating her invitation.* "Let's eat!" . . . (*Getting up.*) I beg your pardon, Madame, but—

EMMA. What?

HECTOR. I said . . . I beg your pardon, but . . . I don't recall inviting you . . .

EMMA, *graciously.* Bah, don't let that bother you. I'm not offended . . . Now then, you sit over here, on my right . . . like the guest of honor.

HECTOR, *sitting down, taken aback.* "Guest of honor!" (*Aside.*) In my own house!

EMMA, *pointing to the table.* Oh look, there's only one setting. Call your servant, will you?

HECTOR. My servant? . . . But I am my servant . . .

EMMA. What? I thought you said you were a lawyer.

HECTOR. Of course I'm a lawyer. I'm a lawyer by profession . . . and a housekeeper by necessity. My wife fired the maid yesterday.

EMMA. You don't say! Why, what a coincidence. I just fired my maid too. Isn't it a small world!

HECTOR, *aside.* Not small enough!

EMMA. Well, since you are keeping house yourself . . . Go set the table for one more.

HECTOR. What? Since when—

EMMA. Go on, go on! You don't expect me to do it, I'm sure! I haven't the vaguest idea where anything is kept . . . Well, what are you waiting for? Go on!

> *She stamps the floor with her foot, in a gesture of impatience.*

HECTOR, *aside.* Now she's gone too far! (*Aloud.*) Not in a million years!

EMMA. What did you say?

> *She stamps again, harder.*

HECTOR, *aside.* Good God! Madame Scandale! (*Aloud.*) All right, all right! I'm going!

> *He leaves through the door, up right, casting angry glances in* EMMA's *direction and muttering under his breath.*

EMMA, *getting up and walking over to the window.* And as for you, Alcibiades . . . Oh! I'll teach you to be jealous! I'll teach you to suspect a wife who has always been a model of virtue! . . . So, you think I'm cheating on you? . . . Well, I'll show you! Before I get through, you'll see plenty to be jealous about . . . and it will serve you right! Yes, it will serve you right! It will! It will!

> *She stamps again and again, even harder.*

HECTOR, *entering and setting another place at the table.* There! (*Shivering.*) This place is like an ice box!

EMMA. Come here, will you? I need your help.

> *She takes one end of the table.*

HECTOR. With what?

EMMA. With this table. We're going to move it over by the window.

HECTOR. Oh no we're not, damn it! That's the last straw! There's no rhyme or reason . . . Whoever heard of anyone eating next to an open window in the middle of February? It's insane! You're insane! This whole damn thing is abso . . . abso . . . (*He tries to repress a sneeze.*) absolutely insane! (*He sneezes.*) There! I hope you're happy. Now I've got a cold.

EMMA. God bless you.

HECTOR, *aside.* God damn you!

EMMA. Monsieur Bouchard, I would like to point out to

you that if you hadn't put up such a silly fuss, we would have been finished long ago.

HECTOR, *speaking through his nose.* Madame Whoever-you-are, I'd like to point out to you that . . . (*He sneezes.*) that . . . (*Sneeze.*) that . . . (*Sneeze.*) Fine! Now I've really got it!

> *He places his napkin around his head and knots it under his chin like a kerchief.*

EMMA. Well, you can do what you like. But let me warn you . . . Unless you cooperate and do what I ask, I'll tell your wife that you've been making love to me. So there!

HECTOR. What? You'll tell my wife . . . Oh no, you couldn't . . . You wouldn't do such a thing! You . . . You . . .

> *He sneezes again.*

EMMA, *coaxingly.* I won't if you say you'll help me.

HECTOR. But really, my good woman . . . You're asking me . . . Just think—

EMMA. I have thought, Monsieur! My husband has the audacity to think that I'm unfaithful, and now he's going to pay for it. That's all. He must be punished . . . and by his own jealousy, too! That will be my revenge!

HECTOR. Yes, but have you thought what might happen?

EMMA, *very matter-of-fact.* Oh, I know what will happen. He'll kill you.

HECTOR, *recoiling.* What? He'll . . . Just like that? . . . And what am I supposed to be doing in the meantime?

EMMA. Oh, he'll kill you all right . . . Unless, of course, you . . . Oh no! I hope you wouldn't have the nerve to kill my Alcibiades!

HECTOR. But . . .

EMMA. It's bound to be a duel to the death. It always is. And of course, it will be the kind of duel that we have in our country . . . with hand drills.

She makes the gesture of turning a hand drill.

HECTOR, *appalled.* Hand drills?

EMMA. Yes, Monsieur, hand drills. That's how we fight duels in Brazil.

HECTOR. But . . . that's disgusting!

EMMA. Disgusting?

HECTOR. It's . . . it's revolting!

EMMA. You mean, you disapprove?

HECTOR. Of course I disapprove! . . . Hand drills! Ugh!

EMMA, *with disdain.* I see. In other words, Monsieur, you are afraid!

HECTOR. No . . . But for heaven's sake, I don't know the first thing about carpentry! I can't even hammer a nail!

He paces up and down.

EMMA, *still disdainfully, moving stage left.* Oh, these Frenchmen are all alike!

HECTOR. Now look . . . Let me suggest something else. Take my advice and file suit for a separation. It's much easier and . . . much less dangerous for everybody!

EMMA, *with fire in her eyes.* Separation! (HECTOR *draws back as she advances, menacingly.*) What kind of revenge is that? I told you, I love my husband! I adore him! I want revenge, not a separation.

HECTOR, *near the window.* But my dear woman—

EMMA, *following him.* No, that's not what I want at all! (*Forcing him onto the chair by the window.*) Come now, sit down and make love to me.

HECTOR. No! No! No!

EMMA. Look, I'm warning you . . .

HECTOR. For goodness' sake, be reasonable. You don't just walk into somebody's house and . . .

While he continues mumbling his objections, EMMA *looks out the window toward her own apartment.*

15

EMMA, *suddenly aghast.* Oh, my God! My God in heaven!
Is it possible? . . . Alcibiades . . . with a woman! Oh,
that beast! That good-for-nothing! That monster! Oh,
that . . . (*To* HECTOR.) Quick, my coat! My coat!
Where's my coat?

> *She runs round the table
> looking for her coat.*

HECTOR, *following her and joining in the search.* Her coat!
Where's her coat?

EMMA, *noticing it on* HECTOR's *shoulders.* You have it on,
you idiot! Give it to me!

HECTOR. Oh, so I do!

> *He gives her the coat, which
> she puts on in a flurry of
> excitement, along with her
> hat.*

EMMA. I'll . . . I'll scratch her eyes out, that's what I'll
do! I'll tear her to pieces . . . I'll . . .

> *She leaves through the hall
> door. A moment later the
> outer door is heard to slam
> behind her.*

HECTOR, *falling into an armchair, heaving a sigh of relief.*
Gone at last! What a woman! My God, what a woman!
I'm worn out! . . . Believe me, if she comes back, she
can knock, and kick, and ring the bell to her heart's
content . . . She won't get me to open that door. I've
had enough. I've had it up to . . . to . . . to . . .
(*Just as he fits the gesture to the word, raising his hand
to eye level, he has a sneezing fit.*) to here! (*Sneeze.*)
And I had to catch a cold in the bargain! (*Sneeze.*)
Damn! (*Sneeze.*) Well, she won't mind if I close the
window now! (*He gets up and walks over to the window. Suddenly his eye is caught by something across
the way.*) What? . . . Oh no! . . . I don't believe
it! . . . It can't be! . . . But that dress . . . It's An-

toinette's. It's her orchid dress . . . her famous orchid dress. I'd know it anywhere . . . Good God! My wife . . . with that Brazilian! Oh, the snake-in-the-grass! The . . . the . . . (*Sneeze.*) And all the time I thought she was at her mother's! Just what does she take me for? Well, she won't get away with this! I'll show her! I'll . . . I'll . . . (*Sneeze.*) I'll fight if I have to . . . even with hand drills! I don't care . . . I'll take lessons . . . I'll practice, I'll train . . . In two weeks I'll be able to . . . (*Suddenly struck by an idea.*) No, wait . . . I have a better idea. I'll get even with her . . . Oh, yes . . . but not that way! No . . . (*He begins pacing back and forth.*) Oh, if only that mad woman would come back now! If only she'd come back! . . . Oh, how I wish she'd come back! . . . (*The doorbell rings.*) Aha! Maybe . . . maybe . . . (*He runs out through the hall door. Offstage he is heard greeting* EMMA.) Come in! . . . Yes, please . . . Come right in!

EMMA enters.

EMMA, *laughing.* Ah, Monsieur Bouchard . . . You'll never guess . . .

HECTOR, *following closely on her heels.* Please, Madame, this is no time to be laughing. We have serious business, you and I.

EMMA. We do?

HECTOR. We certainly do!

EMMA. Why, what on earth is the matter?

HECTOR. The matter, my dear woman . . . The matter is that . . . You remember what you wanted me to do a little while ago? Well, now I accept . . . and with pleasure! Come over here, by the window.

EMMA. Oh, that! But I don't want to any more.

HECTOR. What? You don't want to? . . . But I do! I want to! I insist! Don't you understand? Now I'm the

17

one who's looking for revenge. An eye for an eye! A tooth for a tooth! A wife for a wife! . . . A hand drill for a hand drill!

EMMA. But, Monsieur . . .

HECTOR, *moving toward her with determination.* Come to the window. Come, let me crush you in my arms. Let me smother you with kisses. Let me . . . let me make love to you!

EMMA, *drawing back.* Whatever has come over you? Are you out of your mind?

HECTOR, *at the window.* Out of my mind? Ha ha ha! You mean to stand there and tell me you don't know about my wife? You don't know she's two-timing me? . . . At this very moment! . . . And with your husband, no less! Your Alcibiades!

EMMA. Your wife and my . . . Why, that's absurd!

HECTOR, *growing more and more excited.* Oh, it's absurd, is it? Then tell me I didn't see her over there! Tell me I don't recognize her orchid dress when I see it! Tell me—

EMMA. Her orchid dress? . . . Her . . . Oh, but you can't be serious! (*Laughing.*) You must have seen our new maid!

HECTOR. Come now, you can think up a better one than that!

EMMA. But I assure you . . . In fact, you must know her. Her name is Rose, and she used to work for you.

HECTOR. Rose? She . . . You mean, our Rose? The same Rose my wife fired yesterday?

EMMA. Exactly.

HECTOR. But . . . That's impossible . . . She . . . Is it really?

EMMA. None other. And since I was out, my husband let her in, and he was talking to her. That's all. Now do you believe me?

HECTOR, *sitting down by the table, with a sigh.* Oh, thank

heaven! You don't know how relieved I am! Here I was, all ready to think that my dear, sweet Antoinette . . .

EMMA. Yes, I know. You men are all alike, always getting jealous for no reason at all.

HECTOR, *suddenly jumping up.* Wait a minute! What about that dress? If that was Rose, why was she wearing my wife's . . . (*He stops short, mouth open, struck by a thought.*) Of course! (*Falling onto the chair.*) Now that's a good one for you! How did I ever forget that? . . . Antoinette gave her that dress a couple of days ago. Of course!

EMMA. You see?

HECTOR. What a relief! . . . Oh, what a relief! . . . And to think I could suspect her of . . . Oh, my! How can I ever make it up to her? . . . I'll beg her to forgive me, that's what I'll do. I'll throw myself at her feet . . .

EMMA. That's precisely what you should do, Monsieur. In fact, that's what my Alcibiades did just a few moments ago. And I forgave him!

HECTOR. You mean you're not out for revenge any more?

EMMA. Absolutely not! Although, now that you mention it, he did see us over here, you know.

HECTOR, *suddenly terrified.* He did?

EMMA. Oh yes! He even asked me who was that funny-looking little old lady I was talking to!

HECTOR. Little old . . . You mean, he thought . . .

EMMA. And so I told him you were the mother-in-law of an old schoolfriend of mine. How do you like that!

HECTOR. Mother-in-law? Me? A mother-in-law! (*Laughing.*) That's a little hard to take! But I suppose it's better than hand drills at twenty paces!

EMMA. And now, Monsieur, if you don't mind, I'll be on my way. I only came back to thank you for being so uncooperative.

HECTOR. For being so—

EMMA. Uncooperative.

19

HECTOR. How's that?

EMMA. Why yes. After all, if you hadn't been so very . . . how shall I say . . . ungentlemanly, I would have had my revenge on Alcibiades, and the poor dear would never have begged me to forgive him.

HECTOR, *laughing.* I guess you're right.

EMMA. Well, Monsieur . . . Maybe some other time . . .

HECTOR. Any time at all. Always happy to be of service! (*Bowing.*) Madame!

EMMA, *nodding, about to leave.* Monsieur! (*Several loud knocks are heard on the ceiling.*) My goodness, what on earth . . .

HECTOR. Oh, don't mind that. It's just the upstairs neighbor. She's cracking walnuts. (*Aside.*) That does it! First thing tomorrow, I look for another place! (*Aloud.*) Madame!

EMMA. Monsieur!

CURTAIN

On the Marry-go-wrong

Le Mariage de Barillon

GEORGES FEYDEAU AND MAURICE DESVALLIÈRES

CHARACTERS

BARILLON
JAMBART
BRIGOT
PLANTUREL
PATRICE
FLAMÈCHE
TOPEAU
A TELEGRAPH BOY

MADAME JAMBART
VIRGINIE
JOSÉPHINE

*Witnesses, relatives,
and wedding guests*

Illustration: Feydeau in 1904

ACT ONE

*Marriage chamber at the city hall. Up center, a raised platform
for the mayor, with table and chair. On either side of the
platform, two large doors. The one on the right leads off to
the other offices of the city hall; the one on the left leads
outside. Down left, another large door. Right, a bay window
occupying the entire side. Facing the platform, back to audience, two armchairs to be used by the bride and groom. A
few feet below these armchairs, also facing the platform, a
little bench covered with velvet. On each side of the armchairs, two rows of small chairs for the guests. On the
mayor's table, a number of official registers, books, etc.*

FLAMÈCHE, *standing on the platform, a feather duster in
his hand, singing at the top of his voice from the final
scene of* Lucia di Lammermoor.

> O my Lucy, my beloved,
> My Lucy, my beloved,
> I'll follow you,
> I'll follow you, in death!
>> *He stabs himself with the
>> feather duster.*

TOPEAU, *entering right, listening to the last few bars, and
applauding.* Bravo! Bravo!

FLAMÈCHE. Oh, Topeau! You were listening?

TOPEAU. Ah, Flamèche! I don't listen to you, I . . . I
drink you in! I breathe in every golden note! What a
voice!

FLAMÈCHE. Do you really think so?

TOPEAU. Do I think so? Do I . . . When it comes to voices,
believe me, I know. Music? I was brought up on it. I
drank deep . . . deep, at my father's bosom.

FLAMÈCHE. Your father?

TOPEAU. My father.

FLAMÈCHE. You mean he was a musician?

TOPEAU. An organist.

23

FLAMÈCHE. Oh? In a church?

TOPEAU. In the park. He had a little monkey, and every day—

FLAMÈCHE. Ha! Tell me another!

TOPEAU. But seriously, with a voice like yours how come you've never tried to make a career of it? Why don't you go to the Observatory?

FLAMÈCHE. The Observatory . . . ?

TOPEAU. Of music.

FLAMÈCHE. Oh! The . . . Yes, well, as a matter of fact I did go to the Conservatory once. I even got to sing for the director. Fine chap, too. He was speechless, absolutely speechless.

TOPEAU. I'm not surprised.

FLAMÈCHE. But then he said: "Look, in the theater it takes time. Nobody gets to the top just like that. You have to work at it. Start at the bottom."

TOPEAU. That's right.

FLAMÈCHE. So he got me a job here, in the city hall, sweeping floors.

TOPEAU. Well, that's no reason to stop dreaming of success.

FLAMÈCHE. Oh?

TOPEAU. After all . . . "To sweep . . . to sweep, perchance to dream . . ."

He laughs.

FLAMÈCHE. I'll get to the top, you'll see! I have the inspiration, the calling. Listen, I'll sing you a bacchanale.

TOPEAU. Don't bother. If it's in a foreign language I won't understand it.

FLAMÈCHE. No, no. A bacchanale. A drinking song. (*Singing.*)

> Wine, wine,
> Juice of the vine
> Nectar divine
> Beautiful wine . . .

TOPEAU. Stop! No drinking songs! Sing all the bac . . .
baccha . . . whatever you call them, but no drinking
songs!

FLAMÈCHE. Why not?

TOPEAU. Because I don't even want to hear the word
"drink." I'll run away!

FLAMÈCHE. You? Run away from a drink? Don't you have
your directions mixed?

TOPEAU. It's for my own good. You know, by nature I'm
something of a . . . a . . .

FLAMÈCHE. A boozer?

TOPEAU. Well, no, but . . . You know, it doesn't take
much to get me a little . . . confused. And when I
am . . . Well, I just can't see straight. And in a job
like this, you can imagine!

FLAMÈCHE. You mean you get into trouble?

TOPEAU. Do I! You don't know! Like yesterday, for example. Why do you suppose the mayor was foaming at
the mouth?

FLAMÈCHE. Why?

TOPEAU, *laughing at the thought of what he is about to
relate.* Well, you remember that fellow who came in
looking for a birth certificate? Something about an
inheritance?

FLAMÈCHE. Yes.

TOPEAU. What do you suppose I gave him? A death certificate!

FLAMÈCHE. You didn't?

TOPEAU. I can just see the expression on his face when he
went to collect! "Sorry, it's a rule: you have to be
alive to get the money!"

FLAMÈCHE. Naturally. No breath, no heir! Get it? No
breath—

TOPEAU. I get it!

FLAMÈCHE, *arranging the chairs.* Yes, you do have troubles, don't you!

TOPEAU. And just think, yesterday it was only half a bottle.

FLAMÈCHE. No! Only a half?

TOPEAU. Of cognac.

FLAMÈCHE. I don't believe it!

TOPEAU. I'm telling you. So now you know why I don't even want you to sing about it. Of course, if you know any other tunes . . .

FLAMÈCHE. Well, as a matter of fact, you can do me a favor. Help me learn this duet. (*He goes to pick up the score.*) Here . . . I'm Romeo, you're Juliet.

TOPEAU, *sitting down.* I'm Juliet?

FLAMÈCHE. That's right.

TOPEAU. But I don't know the part.

FLAMÈCHE. Never mind, just read what's written.

> *He begins to sing.*

O hark, Juliet, my darling!
Hear the lark's tender call: he announces the day.
(*Speaking.*) Go ahead, that's your cue.

TOPEAU. My cue? But I don't know the tune.

FLAMÈCHE. What do you mean? The notes are right in front of you.

TOPEAU. Yes, I can see the notes, but I can't find the tune.

FLAMÈCHE. All right, never mind. Just sing any tune at all. I'll start again. (*Singing.*)

O hark, Juliet, my darling!
Hear the lark's tender call: he announces the day.
(*Speaking.*) Well?

TOPEAU. Well?

FLAMÈCHE. I said sing any tune you want, as long as you get all the words. Here, skip all this part and start over here.*

---

* It has been necessary to alter the original here slightly. The duet from act 4 of Gounod's *Roméo et Juliette* contains a sizable passage omitted by Feydeau in this mock rendition.— Trans.

TOPEAU, *trying to sing the words to the tune of "Alouette."*

> Ah, it is true, 'tis day.
>
> Fly! You must forsake me my beloved.

BRIGOT, *entering, down left.* Excuse me, can you tell me where the Barillon wedding is taking place?

FLAMÈCHE, *singing, unaware of* BRIGOT'*s presence.*

> No, no, it is not the day.

BRIGOT. What? I thought for sure . . .

TOPEAU. Shhh! Be quiet and listen!

FLAMÈCHE, *still singing.*

> It is not the lark's singing
>
> 'Tis the sweet nightingale . . .

BRIGOT. Listen, you and your nightingales, how much more of this squealing do I have to listen to?

FLAMÈCHE *and* TOPEAU. Squealing?

BRIGOT. I ask you a simple question: "Where's the Barillon wedding?" And you tell me it's not the day.

FLAMÈCHE. I beg your pardon, I was singing.

BRIGOT. Singing, talking, what's the difference? That's what you said, isn't it?

TOPEAU, *aside.* Pleasant chap!

BRIGOT. Where's my nephew Barillon? Hasn't he shown up yet?

FLAMÈCHE. I'm sorry, Monsieur. No one has arrived. But the ceremony isn't for at least an hour.

BRIGOT. You mean he isn't here yet? What's the matter? Doesn't he love his wife?

FLAMÈCHE. Really, how should I know?

BRIGOT. Well, I know, and I'm only a witness! How do you like that? Of all the . . . I leave the hospital just for him—

TOPEAU. The hospital?

BRIGOT. Yes, the animal hospital.

FLAMÈCHE. That's no surprise.

BRIGOT, *tipping his hat.* I'm a veterinarian, my good man, from Troyes—

FLAMÈCHE. Oh, are you the one who takes care of the horse?

BRIGOT. The horse? What horse?

FLAMÈCHE. The Trojan horse! Get it? Troyes . . . Trojan horse—

BRIGOT. I get it! I get it! What an ass!

FLAMÈCHE. You wouldn't be trying to drum up business, would you, doctor?

BRIGOT. Very funny! (*Changing the subject.*) What the devil is that nephew of mine up to? Where do you suppose they can be?

FLAMÈCHE. What's your hurry? I told you, the wedding isn't until noon.

BRIGOT. And it's already eleven! I don't know about you, but I like to be punctual. Promptness in person, that's me. I always get everywhere an hour early. No matter who I have to meet, I give them a half-hour, and if they don't show up I leave.

FLAMÈCHE. You must miss a lot of appointments.

BRIGOT. Ninety out of a hundred. No one knows how to be on time any more. I don't know what it is. That imbecile—

FLAMÈCHE. Who?

BRIGOT. My nephew! He's getting married in an hour and he's not even here yet. Not like his uncle, I'll tell you! When I got married I was two months ahead of time. Seven months married and I was a daddy. Didn't waste any time.

TOPEAU. Oh, really? You mean—

BRIGOT, *to* TOPEAU. And who asked for your two cents' worth? (TOPEAU *leaves in a huff.*) Come on, let's go find him.

FLAMÈCHE. Who?

BRIGOT. Who do you think? The mayor. What's he doing?

I'll tell you what he's doing. He's getting fat on the taxpayers' money, that's what. Where is he?

FLAMÈCHE. I don't know. He's usually here by now. Like yesterday, for example—

BRIGOT. Yesterday? Who gives a damn about yesterday? Can't you shut up for a minute? Talk, talk, talk!

FLAMÈCHE, *aside*. He's lucky his patients are animals. He'd starve to death if he had to wait for human beings!

> FLAMÈCHE *leaves, up right.*

BRIGOT, *catching sight of* BARILLON, *entering*. Well, well! There he is. And it's about time!

BARILLON. Hello, Uncle. You haven't seen my fiancée, by any chance? Or my mother-in-law?

BRIGOT. Of course I haven't seen them. Why should I see them? Am I their bodyguard?

BARILLON. Then why the devil aren't they here yet? Unless . . . Do you suppose they didn't know enough to come directly to the city hall?

BRIGOT. What? You mean to say you weren't even going to call for them? Very nice! On your wedding day! If your mother-in-law lands on you it'll serve you right!

BARILLON. Lands on me? My mother-in-law? I can see you don't know her. She's as meek as a lamb, the slobbering old goat!

BRIGOT. Slobbering old goat?

BARILLON. That's right. She's got the kissing bug. Can't stop. Every minute of the day, that's all she does.

BRIGOT. Nothing wrong with that!

BARILLON. Thanks, just the same! You can have my share. I'm telling you, she's unbearable. Always on my neck. Until today I've put up with it. After all, tact, you know. But just wait. As soon as I say "I do" she'll have to find someone else to drool on!

BRIGOT. Still, that's no reason to keep them waiting.

BARILLON. Who?

BRIGOT. What do you mean, "Who"? Who do you think?

Your wife and your mother-in-law, that's who!

BARILLON. Of course, of course! I don't know what's the matter with me. I can't think straight today.

BRIGOT. Maybe you should take something. You don't look too well either, if you don't mind my saying so. What have you been up to?

BARILLON. Nothing. I just didn't sleep last night, that's all. You know how it is, the night before your wedding. I was out to supper with some friends . . . Jojo, Zizi, Froufrou . . .

BRIGOT, *aside*. Zizi? Froufrou?

BARILLON. Well, one thing led to another. Here a bottle, there a bottle . . . It didn't take me long to feel it, believe me!

BRIGOT. You mean you were drunk!

BARILLON. In a word. And you know, when you're drunk you can do all kinds of funny things. Anyway, after supper I was walking downstairs, and all of a sudden this other fellow passes me on the stairs. A total stranger. Just minding his own business, didn't say a word. So I grab him and yell at him: "You look like Louis-Philippe! Long live Poland!"

BRIGOT. What? That doesn't make sense.

BARILLON. I know. But when you've had a few too many . . . So anyway he says to me: "Get out of my way, you're drunk!" Well, I wasn't going to stand for that, so I slapped him, hard. And now—

BRIGOT. Let me guess. And now you have a duel on your hands!

BARILLON. Well, yes and no.

BRIGOT. What are you talking about, yes and no? You either have a duel or you haven't.

BARILLON. It's like this. If I want a duel I have one. If I don't, I don't.

BRIGOT. You lost me. Start again.

BARILLON. It's very simple. You see, the argument suddenly sobered me up and I began to think straight. So naturally, when we exchanged cards I didn't give him one of my own.

BRIGOT. Oh?

BARILLON. No. I gave him one of Dartagnac's cards. You know, Alfonso Dartagnac, the famous fencing champion.

BRIGOT. You gave him Dartagnac's card?

BARILLON. Sure, it never fails. Only two things can happen. Nine times out of ten the other fellow takes one look and apologizes on the spot, so nothing ever comes of it. Or else he doesn't . . .

BRIGOT. And then?

BARILLON. Nothing can come of it anyway.

BRIGOT. Pretty clever! But if Dartagnac ever finds out . . .

BARILLON. What?

BRIGOT. That he has a duel!

BARILLON, *with dignity*. Come now! Is he the kind to back out of a duel?

BRIGOT. No, I guess you're right, now that you mention it. By the way, who is the other fellow?

BARILLON. I don't know. I lost his card. Oh, was I drunk!

FLAMÈCHE, *entering on the mayor's platform, addressing* BARILLON. Excuse me, are you here for the wedding?

BARILLON. What wedding?

FLAMÈCHE. The Barillon wedding.

BARILLON. My God, that's right! (*To* BRIGOT.) That's a good one! He wants to know if I'm here for my own wedding! (*To* FLAMÈCHE.) I should say I am! In fact, I'd better hurry and get the bride.

FLAMÈCHE. Yes, on your wedding day she's a nice person to have around!

> BARILLON *leaves, down left.*
> *A moment later* PATRICE
> *enters, up left, obviously*
> *dejected, trailing a long rope*
> *behind him.*

31

BRIGOT, *noticing* PATRICE. Well, now. Who's that? Don't tell me that's the mayor. He's still wet behind the ears!

PATRICE, *dramatically, with a whimper in his voice.* Oh, faithless woman! Marrying another! It's too cruel, too cruel!

He looks toward the ceiling.

BRIGOT, *to* FLAMÈCHE. What's he looking for?

FLAMÈCHE, *to* PATRICE. What are you looking for?

PATRICE. A nail. I'm going to hang myself.

FLAMÈCHE. You're going to . . . Oh no! Not in this office!

PATRICE. I'll leave you the rope. It brings good luck, you know.

BRIGOT. What's he babbling about?

PATRICE, *still in grandiloquent fashion.* She's forsaken me, the heartless woman! Forsaken me for another! Ah, but she'll be sorry! As soon as they pronounce those fateful words, the words that separate us forever, I want her to see my body swaying in the breeze.

FLAMÈCHE. Hm, that's a pretty thought!

BRIGOT. Aha! Now I understand. You must be in love!

PATRICE. Desperately!

FLAMÈCHE. Poor boy!

BRIGOT, *making him sit down on the bench.* Well now, son. Tell me all about it. I'll be your confessor. After all, a doctor, a confessor . . . It's all the same.

PATRICE. Are you a doctor?

BRIGOT, *tipping his hat.* I'm a veterinarian. (*To* FLAMÈCHE.) You, leave us alone. I want to confess my sinner in private. (FLAMÈCHE, *very moved, leaves, up right.*) Now then, tell me, what's it all about?

PATRICE. Oh, please, you will see her, won't you? You will tell her that I loved her to the last, and that I'm dying for her!

He gets up.

BRIGOT. Now, now! Is that any way to talk? People don't come here to hang themselves. They might put a rope around their neck for life, but they don't hang themselves.

PATRICE. Oh, I can see you've never been in love!

BRIGOT. Me? Never been in love? Of course I have! And I'll tell you, she was something too. A real doll!

PATRICE. Really?

BRIGOT. Well, of course, that was a few years ago. Today she must be fifty-two or three.

PATRICE. Some doll!

BRIGOT. But what a face, what features! They used to say she had a kind of strained beauty.

PATRICE. Strained? Don't you mean restrained?

BRIGOT. No, strained. Her face was covered with little pockmarks. It gave her a certain . . . something.

PATRICE. I should imagine.

BRIGOT. Well anyway, to make a long story short, she went and married someone else. But don't think for a moment I was fool enough to do what you're doing! Oh no! Not a chance! I thought to myself: "Go ahead, let her marry the old bat. They haven't seen the last of me!" And sure enough, two weeks after she married him, thanks to me he was wearing the nicest pair of horns!

PATRICE. Really?

BRIGOT. Absolutely. Now you go do what I did. Wait until she's married and then . . . (*He gives himself a pair of horns with his fingers, and winks broadly to* PATRICE.) Get me?

PATRICE, *shaking* BRIGOT's *hand.* Oh, thank you, Monsieur. Thank you for such comforting advice. I'll do it! I'll do just what you say!

BRIGOT. Fine! The husband is some poor fool, I suppose?

PATRICE, *with conviction.* He is! He is! Somebody by the name of Varillon . . . or Marillon, or something.

BRIGOT, *leaping up.* Barillon? My nephew, Barillon?

PATRICE, *shrinking back.* Your nephew? Your . . . You mean—

BRIGOT. Yes, you idiot! (*Suddenly punching* PATRICE *in the stomach, almost knocking him over.*) You'll make a fool of my nephew, will you!

PATRICE. But—

BRIGOT, *punching him again.* You think you'll play around with his wife, do you? And you have the nerve to boast about it? And to me, his uncle!

PATRICE. But, but—

BRIGOT, *beating him.* Well, just try! Just you try! Believe me, there's more where that came from!

PATRICE. But, but . . . I won't . . . I won't . . .

> BRIGOT, *still threatening* PATRICE, *backs him up against the bay window, stage right.*

BARILLON'S VOICE. This way, Mother.

BRIGOT. See! Here he comes! Now I dare you, tell him what you told me! I dare you!

PATRICE. Leave me alone! Leave me alone!

> BARILLON *enters, down left, followed by* MADAME JAMBART *and* VIRGINIE.

BARILLON. This way . . . (*To* BRIGOT.) Well, here we are!

VIRGINIE, *catching sight of* PATRICE. Patrice!

PATRICE. Virginie!

BRIGOT, *to* BARILLON. Aha! I'm glad you're back. (*Pointing to* PATRICE.) You see him?

BARILLON, *cheerfully, to* PATRICE. How do you do! The pleasure is all—

BRIGOT. He's going to sleep with your wife!

BARILLON, *suddenly changing his expression.* What?

BRIGOT. That's what I said. In two weeks you'll be the talk of the town.

BARILLON, *approaching* PATRICE *with fire in his eyes.* Did you say that?

PATRICE, *protecting himself.* No, no! I didn't! I didn't!

VIRGINIE, *frightened.* Mother!

BARILLON, *shaking* PATRICE. So you're going to sleep with my wife, are you!

MADAME JAMBART, *pulling* BARILLON *away.* Please, son. Calm yourself.

BARILLON, *shaking her off.* Out of my way. (*To* PATRICE.) Make me the talk of the town, will you?

PATRICE, *pulling away.* Don't you touch me!

BARILLON. You're going to get out of here if I have to throw you out, understand?

PATRICE, *to* BRIGOT. See what you started, you and your stories!

BRIGOT. No one's asking you! Go on, get out! Out!

PATRICE, *in a sudden show of courage.* Listen, you, I'll go when I'm good and ready! You can't order me around!

BARILLON, *approaching* PATRICE. What did you say, you little—

VIRGINIE, *to* PATRICE. Oh please, Patrice, for my sake! Please, my darling!

BARILLON. What? "My darling"? (*Taking* PATRICE *by the collar.*) Get out, you swine! Out!

PATRICE. Now look! I've taken enough of this!

> He pushes BARILLON *vigorously onto the bench.*

BARILLON. Oh! You . . . you . . .

MADAME JAMBART, *to* PATRICE. Please! Please, you'd better go!

VIRGINIE. Please!

BARILLON, *getting up.* I'll kill him! I swear I will!

MADAME JAMBART, *holding him back, maternally.* Now, now!

BRIGOT, *to* MADAME JAMBART. Leave him alone. He's going to kill him.

VIRGINIE, *frightened.* He's going to kill him!

MADAME JAMBART, *still standing in* BARILLON's *way*. Now just control yourself! (*To* PATRICE.) Really, you'd better go!

PATRICE, *about to leave, down left*. All right! I'm going! But you haven't heard the last of me!

BARILLON, *shaking his fist at him over* MADAME JAMBART's *shoulder*. You show your face . . . You dare show your face, and I'll . . .

MADAME JAMBART. Barillon! Barillon!

BRIGOT, *laughing*. My God, what a wedding! What a wedding!

PATRICE *leaves*.

MADAME JAMBART. Now please, son, try to control yourself.

BARILLON, *thoroughly exhausted, falls onto the bench*. MADAME JAMBART, *in a flurry of emotion, throws her arms around his neck*.

BARILLON. Oh no! For God's sake, leave me alone! None of that! (MADAME JAMBART *withdraws a few steps*.) Oh! Can you believe it? She loves that fool! She actually loves him!

MADAME JAMBART. Don't worry son, she'll get over it once you're married.

BRIGOT, *facetiously*. What are you complaining about? After all, when you get married you want an affectionate wife, don't you? Well, if she loves him, that proves she's affectionate.

BARILLON. Oh, I see! You think so, do you? Hm! (*Gradually becoming calmer.*) Who is he, anyway, that . . . that . . .

MADAME JAMBART, *to* VIRGINIE. Yes, darling, who is the young man?

VIRGINIE. You remember, Mother. His name is Patrice Surcouf. I met him at the President's Ball.

MADAME JAMBART. Oh, is that the young man? I didn't realize. Really, Barillon he's a very nice chap. Fine family, too.

BARILLON, *angrily.* Very nice? He's absolutely charming!

VIRGINIE. And then I saw him every day after that.

MADAME JAMBART. You did? Where?

VIRGINIE. At my music lesson. He learned to sing, just so we could be together.

MADAME JAMBART, *delighted at such a romantic notion.* Well, what a gallant young man!

BARILLON, *storming.* Oh, don't stop now! Tell us everything! Don't mind me, after all!

VIRGINIE. And then he asked me to marry him. He said he would wait forever if he had to.

BARILLON. Of course! Tell us more! We're all ears!

BRIGOT, *to* BARILLON. Relax!

MADAME JAMBART. That's right, relax! (*Chucking him under the chin.*) He's so precious when he's angry! (*She throws her arms around his neck and plants a resounding kiss on his cheek.*) There!

BARILLON. That's lovely! Just lovely! (*Aside.*) Slobbering old—

MADAME JAMBART. Really, Barillon, you don't realize what a prize you're getting. What a girl! It makes me think of the first time I got married. (*To* VIRGINIE.) To your father, darling. (*To the others.*) Monsieur Pornichet . . . What a gentleman! I must say, I made him very happy.

BARILLON. I'm glad for him.

MADAME JAMBART. And believe me, I can say the same for my second husband, Monsieur Jambart. I made him happy too. I made all my husbands happy!

BARILLON. Fine! Lucky men!

MADAME JAMBART, *pointing to* VIRGINIE. And she'll be just the same. She'll make all her husbands happy. Won't you sweetheart?

BARILLON, *with a grimace.* What?

VIRGINIE. I'll do my best, Mother dear.

BARILLON. Those are pretty thoughts to be putting into her head. All her husbands!

MADAME JAMBART. I didn't mean it that way! Oh no! After all, I want her to have better luck than I had. God only knows I wouldn't want to see her a widow for anything.

BARILLON. Neither would I!

MADAME JAMBART. You can't imagine how hard it is sometimes, being a widow. I never dreamed . . . After all, Jambart was strong as an ox, never sick a day in his life. (*Sighing.*) It was his profession that took him from me.

BRIGOT. His profession?

MADAME JAMBART. Yes, he was a fisherman. (*Without thinking.*) Oh, Barillon! Take my advice, never marry a fisherman.

BARILLON. Not damn likely!

MADAME JAMBART. The day after our wedding he heard that the fish were running off the coast of Newfoundland. He couldn't resist. That very day he left.

BRIGOT. To try to fish up something better!

MADAME JAMBART, *sighing.* That was two years ago. The boat went down, and . . . and he's never been heard from since.

BARILLON, *anxious to change the subject.* How did we get off on this? For God's sake, I'm here to get married. What are we waiting for? (*He sees* FLAMÈCHE *entering, up right, carrying a large register.*) Ha! There's the clerk. (*To* FLAMÈCHE.) Say, you, where's the mayor?

FLAMÈCHE. I wish I knew. He should have been here long ago. I wonder if anything could have happened to him.

BRIGOT. No one's asking you what you think! Always gabbing, that's you!

FLAMÈCHE, *aside.* What a delightful individual!

PLANTUREL'S VOICE, *in the wings.* Flamèche! Flamèche!

FLAMÈCHE. There he is now. (*Into the wings.*) Yes, Your Honor!

> *The others gradually move toward the mayor's platform, making appropriate remarks such as: "It's about time," "Finally," etc.*

BARILLON. So, we're going to get a look at this famous mayor, are we?

PLANTUREL, *entering, up right, carrying a number of swords under his arm.* Has anyone been asking for me?

BARILLON, *with a start.* My God! My duel! It's him . . . the man on the stairs!

> *He dashes through the row of chairs, jumping here and there, and disappearing, down left, in a flash.*

MADAME JAMBART *and* BRIGOT. Where is he going?

> *During the following dialogue everyone passes quickly in front of PLANTUREL and FLAMÈCHE, who watch them in amazement as they rush off after BARILLON.*

BRIGOT, *to* PLANTUREL *as he passes in front of him.* He's sick! All mixed up! We'll get him.

MADAME JAMBART. Come back, son! Come back! (*To* VIRGINIE.) Virginie, come with me!

VIRGINIE. I'm coming, Mother dear.

> *They all leave one after another, down left.*

PLANTUREL. Now what was that all about?

FLAMÈCHE. I don't know. If you ask me, they're all crazy. I've had to put up with them for an hour already. They're here for the wedding at noon.

PLANTUREL, *moving down from the platform and placing his swords on the chair nearest the audience.* They are? Well, they'll just have to wait. I have other fish to fry. Tell me, has anyone come to see me about Alfonso Dartagnac?

FLAMÈCHE. No, Your Honor. But this letter came for you.

PLANTUREL, *reading the letter.* Oh no! That . . . that drunkard Topeau has been at it again!

FLAMÈCHE. Again?

PLANTUREL, *calling.* Topeau!

FLAMÈCHE. Topeau! Topeau!

TOPEAU, *entering.* Your Honor?

PLANTUREL. Do you know what you've done?

TOPEAU. Me, Your Honor?

PLANTUREL. How much more do you think I can take? (*Waving the letter in his face.*) Here's a nice complaint for you! This man asks for a copy of his birth certificate so he can get married, and you make it out to the wrong sex!

TOPEAU. Me? Did I do that?

PLANTUREL. Now I'm warning you. One more trick like that and out you go!

TOPEAU. Yes, Your Honor.

PLANTUREL. And don't forget it, you idiot!

TOPEAU, *leaving right center.* A pleasant bunch, these teetotalers!

PLANTUREL. Oh, Flamèche. (FLAMÈCHE *moves down from the platform and joins him.*) If two gentlemen come to speak to me about a duel, please let me know immediately.

FLAMÈCHE, *surprised.* A duel, Your Honor?

PLANTUREL. Yes, but I'd rather not spread it around. I can tell you, but please don't tell anyone else. The fact is, I have a duel.

FLAMÈCHE. You mean, you're going to fight.

PLANTUREL. I don't know if I'm going to fight or not. All

I know is I have a duel, and with Alfonso Dartagnac.

FLAMÈCHE. No!

PLANTUREL. Yes! It all happened last night, in the restaurant. Some stranger had the gall to stop me and tell me I looked like Louis-Philippe, and "Long live Poland," or something like that.

FLAMÈCHE, *shocked.* Oh!

PLANTUREL. You can just imagine how I lost my temper. I couldn't stop myself. So bang! He slapped me right in the face!

FLAMÈCHE. No! I can't believe it!

PLANTUREL. And who does it turn out to be? Alfonso Dartagnac! But please, I have to insist, don't tell a soul. And if anyone comes, let me know immediately, understand? (*He steps up to the platform and is about to leave, but returns suddenly.*) Oh, I almost forgot . . . I sent for a fencing master.

FLAMÈCHE. A fencing master?

PLANTUREL. Yes, I want him to show me a trick or two. You understand, I'm not exactly an expert! Maybe he can teach me a few passes, or something. Anyway, be sure to tell me when he gets here.

FLAMÈCHE. Of course, Your Honor. But what about the wedding? Those people—

PLANTUREL. They have plenty of time. It isn't even noon yet.

He leaves, up right.

FLAMÈCHE. Plenty of time? Oh well, why should I worry? (*He begins to hum a tune to himself.*) Ah, there they are!

MADAME JAMBART enters,
down left, dragging BARILLON
behind her.

MADAME JAMBART. For heaven's sake! Come on now, be a dear.

BRIGOT, *pushing him from behind, followed by* VIRGINIE.

Let's go.

BARILLON, *resisting.* No, damn it! Stop pushing! I tell you I've got my reasons. If you'd only listen to me.

BRIGOT. All right, we're listening. What? What's the matter?

BARILLON. Nothing! (*He looks around, then addresses* FLAMÈCHE.) He isn't here? He's gone out . . . my . . . the . . . the . . .

BRIGOT. What? Your . . . the . . . who?

BARILLON. No, I mean the mayor . . . the mayor.

FLAMÈCHE. His Honor? He's in there, in his study.

BARILLON. He is? Oh, my God! Come on everyone, we can't stay here another minute!

MADAME JAMBART. Why not?

BRIGOT. What the devil are you raving about? The mayor—

BARILLON, *moving quickly behind the bench.* Shh! Not so loud!

MADAME JAMBART. What is all this?

BARILLON, *in a whisper, so that* FLAMÈCHE *cannot hear.* Nothing! Nothing! Listen, for God's sake, whatever you do, don't anyone call me Alfonso Dartagnac.

MADAME JAMBART. Don't call you what?

BRIGOT. He's cracked.

MADAME JAMBART, *sitting on the chair on which* PLANTUREL *has placed his swords, and leaping up.* Owww! (*Taking the swords.*) What on earth . . . What are these doing here, of all places?

FLAMÈCHE. Those? Oh, those belong to His Honor. He has a duel with Alfonso Dar—

BARILLON, *jumping over the bench.* It's not me! It's not me!

MADAME JAMBART *and* BRIGOT. What?

FLAMÈCHE. What's wrong with him?

> *He goes up onto the platform.*

BARILLON, *taken aback and laughing stupidly.* Ha ha! That was a good one, wasn't it!

BRIGOT. Absolutely out of his mind!

BARILLON, *aside*. Watch! With my luck I've probably run up against Monte Cristo! (*Aloud, to* FLAMÈCHE.) I suppose he's pretty good with the sword?

FLAMÈCHE. Who?

BARILLON. The mayor.

FLAMÈCHE, *sarcastically*. Oh, you can say that again! A real genius!

BARILLON. That's what I thought! (*To everyone but* FLAMÈCHE.) Now, listen, let's talk seriously. (*They all come closer.*) Damn it, let's get out of here!

BRIGOT, MADAME JAMBART, *and* VIRGINIE. What? What?

BARILLON, *moving far right*. That's what I said. We can't stay here another minute. I don't want that mayor to marry us. He has the evil eye!

BRIGOT, MADAME JAMBART *and* VIRGINIE. What?

BARILLON. Absolutely! (*Going up to* FLAMÈCHE.) Young man, isn't there another mayor in the building?

FLAMÈCHE. No, Monsieur. I'm sorry, he's the only one we have!

BRIGOT, *going around to the other side of* FLAMÈCHE. What kind of a question . . . Do you think they stock them in different shapes and sizes?

BARILLON. Only one? How about the deputies?

FLAMÈCHE. The first one isn't here. He's doing his military service.

BARILLON. And the second?

FLAMÈCHE. He isn't here either. He's having a baby.

BRIGOT. He's what?

FLAMÈCHE. Well, I mean, his wife—

BARILLON. Listen, I have a wonderful idea. Let's skip this and just have the church wedding?

BRIGOT. Now I know you're crazy! Enough of this nonsense. (*To* FLAMÈCHE.) Go call the mayor.

BARILLON. No, for God's sake!

PLANTUREL, *appearing at the doorway, up right, but without moving on stage.* Oh, Flamèche, Flamèche!

BARILLON, *leaping at the sound of* PLANTUREL's *voice.* It's him! Let me out of here! (*He dashes across the rows of chairs, upsetting everything, grabs* VIRGINIE *by the hand as he passes, and drags her off with him, down left.*) Come on! Come on!

> *They leave.*

MADAME JAMBART. What? Not again?

BRIGOT, *moving toward the door through which* BARILLON *and* VIRGINIE *have just disappeared.* Again?

MADAME JAMBART, *about to rush off in pursuit.* Here, you take these!

> *She hands* BRIGOT *the swords she has been holding for the last few moments and leaves, down left.* FLAMÈCHE *leaves up right.*

BRIGOT. I'm through! I've chased that fool enough for one day!

> *He absentmindedly begins fencing with his shadow on the wall.*

PLANTUREL. Now what's gotten into them? (*He suddenly notices* BRIGOT.) Ah! The fencing master. (*To* BRIGOT.) I say, there you are! I've been waiting for you.

> *He comes down from the platform and joins* BRIGOT, *stage left.*

BRIGOT. You've been waiting for me! That's a good one! I've been here for an hour already.

PLANTUREL. Now then, let's not waste any time. Take off your coat.

BRIGOT. What?

PLANTUREL, *impatiently.* I said, "Take off your coat."

BRIGOT. Take off my—

PLANTUREL. Go on, go on! See, I'm taking mine off.

He removes his coat.

BRIGOT. Oh?

He puts down the swords and complies with PLAN-TUREL's *command.*

PLANTUREL, *taking one of the swords.* There! Now we can begin.

BRIGOT, *turning toward the door, down left.* Good! Just a minute, I'll go call the others.

PLANTUREL. Who? What others?

BRIGOT. Why, the wedding party, who else?

PLANTUREL. Don't be absurd! We don't need them!

BRIGOT, *aside.* Is this the damnedest wedding!

PLANTUREL, *pointing to a sword.* Now then, take your sword.

BRIGOT. My sword? I don't need a sword!

PLANTUREL. Of course you do! You don't think I'm going to fence with myself? Ready? En garde!

He assumes the stance.

BRIGOT, *assuming the same position, thoroughly confused.* My God! He's out of his mind too! It must be catching!

PLANTUREL. Now, what do we do?

BRIGOT, *crossing swords with* PLANTUREL, *then doing an abrupt about-face toward the door, down left.* Now we go call the bride and groom, that's what we do!

PLANTUREL. No, no, no! (*Aside.*) It's an obsession. Some people just have to have an audience. (*Aloud.*) You stay right here.

BRIGOT, *at a loss.* If you say so.

They cross swords.

PLANTUREL. And now, show me a move I can use.

BRIGOT. A move? (*Striking* PLANTUREL's *sword.*) Listen here, how much more of this game are we going to play? I didn't exactly come here to fence with you, you know!

He puts his sword on the bench.

PLANTUREL. You didn't? But . . .

BRIGOT. I came here to be a witness in a wedding. And I'll tell you, it's the damnedest—

PLANTUREL. What? You mean you aren't the fencing master?

BRIGOT. Me? Hardly! (*Tipping his hat.*) I'm a veterinarian, from Troyes.

PLANTUREL. Oh my! You aren't the one I was expecting at all! (*Putting an arm around his neck, confidentially.*) You see . . . I can tell you, but please don't tell anyone else. I don't want it to get around. I have a duel!

BRIGOT. Really? Congratulations! (*Aside.*) Big day for duels!

PLANTUREL. That's why I wanted you to show me a move or two, something I could use.

BRIGOT. Me, show you a move? That's a good one! Of course, I used to know some, but that was a long time ago.

PLANTUREL, *still holding his sword.* You did? Oh, please! If you could only think of one!

BRIGOT. Well, just a minute now. Let me see if I can remember. There used to be one . . . I think . . . Yes, that's right, you stand this way.

PLANTUREL, *pointing to one of the other swords.* Here, take your sword.

BRIGOT. I really don't need it.

PLANTUREL. Yes you do. I'll understand it better.

BRIGOT, *taking the sword.* All right, if you insist. Now look, you stand over here.

PLANTUREL, *crossing swords with* BRIGOT. Right. Now what?

BRIGOT. Once in position, you move to one side.

PLANTUREL, *complying.* Like that?

BRIGOT. And then, at the word "fire"—

PLANTUREL. What? At what word "fire"? What are you talking about, "fire"?

BRIGOT. That's what I said. The only dueling move I know is with a pistol.

PLANTUREL. Then what on earth are you doing with your sword?

BRIGOT. Well, I told you I didn't need it, didn't I? (*Losing patience.*) And besides, I'm not here to give you lessons!

PLANTUREL. But Monsieur—

BRIGOT, *putting on his coat.* Don't "but Monsieur" me! I came here to marry off my nephew. Now look, it's already noon. I'm going to call the bride and groom.

PLANTUREL, *aside.* Damn his old bride and groom! (*To* BRIGOT.) All right, all right! Let me know when they're here. I have to go get ready.

> *He goes off, up right, carrying his coat and swords.*

BRIGOT. Damn it! How long do I have to hang around this place? (*Calling to the others in the wings.*) Come on, all of you! Let's go! Let's go!

> VIRGINIE *enters, followed by* MADAME JAMBART.

MADAME JAMBART. Come now, son. Does the thought of getting married frighten you that much?

BARILLON, *entering, followed by the entire wedding party: witnesses, guests, etc.* Please, you'll have to excuse me. Nerves . . . that's all, nerves. (*Aside.*) What can I do? I'll have to go through with it!

VIRGINIE. But Mother dear, I don't want to marry Monsieur Barillon. I don't love him.

MADAME JAMBART. Don't be silly, darling. I'm sure you can love him if you try hard enough. Now be a dear and try.

BRIGOT, *aside.* That's what I call getting off to a good start!

MADAME JAMBART, *to* VIRGINIE. And besides, it's too late now. The mayor is all ready to marry you.

BARILLON, *hearing the last few words, aside.* My God, that's right! The mayor . . . If he recognizes me I'm finished! Now what?

FLAMÈCHE, *entering, up right.* Ladies and gentlemen, His Honor is about to arrive. Will you please take your places.

BARILLON. Our places? What places?

FLAMÈCHE. For the ceremony.

BARILLON, *wiping his face feverishly with his handkerchief.* Oh! I can't get out of it! It's all over! Finished!

FLAMÈCHE, *pointing out each person's place.* The bride sits here. And the groom here.

> BRIGOT *escorts* VIRGINIE *to her seat;* BARILLON, *before taking his place, shows* MADAME JAMBART *to hers.* BRIGOT *sits next to her. The other guests take their places.* FLAMÈCHE *opens the door, up right, and announces the arrival of the mayor.*

Ladies and gentlemen, His Honor!

BARILLON. My God!

> *He wraps his handkerchief around his face.*

MADAME JAMBART, *watching him in amazement.* What on earth . . . ?

BARILLON. It's nothing . . . nothing! I have a toothache, that's all . . . a toothache!

> PLANTUREL *enters, up right, wearing his official garb.*

FLAMÈCHE, *to the company.* You will please rise.

> *Everyone gets up.*

PLANTUREL, *on the platform.* Be seated.

> *They sit down.*

BARILLON. Hm! Hardly worth the trouble!

PLANTUREL, *aside, to* FLAMÈCHE. Now look, if two men

come to talk about a duel, be sure to let me know immediately, understand?

FLAMÈCHE. Very good, Your Honor.

> FLAMÈCHE *leaves, up right.*

PLANTUREL, *to the company.* This is the Barillon wedding, isn't it?

> *The members of the wedding party mutter various forms of assent: "Yes, Your Honor," "It is," "That's right," etc.*

BARILLON, *in a high, falsetto voice.* Yes, yes!

PLANTUREL, *pointing to* BARILLON. Is this gentleman the bridegroom?

BARILLON, *same voice.* Yes, Your Honor, I am!

PLANTUREL. Is anything wrong, Monsieur Barillon? Aren't you feeling well?

> *The others of the group look at one another quizzically, asking such questions as: "What's the matter?" "What's wrong with him?" etc.*

BARILLON, *same voice.* It's nothing! Just my tooth! I caught a cold in my tooth, that's all!

PLANTUREL, *aside.* Hm! If they ever have a family it won't be his fault!

BARILLON, *aside.* I'm dying!

PLANTUREL. I will now read you the marriage contract. (*Reading.*) "In the year eighteen hundred and eighty-nine, on this, the first day of April, at twelve o'clock noon, appearing before us, Mayor and duly authorized Registry Officer of the Eighth Precinct of the City of Paris, and in the offices of said Precinct, to be united in matrimony, Monsieur Jean-Gustave Barillon, residing in the Eighth Precinct of the City of Paris, of legal age,

being born in the City of Paris on the eighth day of
March in the year eighteen hundred and forty-nine,
legitimate son of Anatole Barillon and of—

FLAMÈCHE, *entering, up right, and whispering to* PLAN-
TUREL. Your Honor! There are two people who want
to see you right away.

PLANTUREL, *putting down the register abruptly.* My God!
The seconds! (*To the company.*) I beg your pardon!
You must excuse me, I'll just be a moment.

> *He dashes off, up right.*
> *The company look at one*
> *another, muttering such*
> *questions as, "Where is he*
> *going?" "What's the mat-*
> *ter?" etc.*

BRIGOT. Is he sick?

FLAMÈCHE, *trying to quiet them down.* Ladies and gentlemen! Please! (*He moves up to the mayor's platform and*
stands behind his desk.) Let me have your attention!

MADAME JAMBART. Quiet everyone! Shhh! He's going to
tell us something.

> *The general confusion*
> *subsides.*

FLAMÈCHE. Thank you, ladies and gentlemen. (*He clears*
his throat.) As you all know, there are numerous oc-
casions, like weddings, for instance, when it's customary
to present a concert of vocal or instrumental music—

> *The general conversation*
> *begins again, with such re-*
> *marks as "What?" "What's*
> *he talking about?" etc.*

BRIGOT. Now what?

FLAMÈCHE, *shouting above the company.* Of course, ladies
and gentlemen, it isn't always easy to find the right
talent for the occasion. Now, I don't want you to think
I'm trying to sell anyone, but just as a sample I'd like
to sing a little number for you.

BRIGOT. What a wedding!

> *Once again the company*
> *manifest their surprise and*
> *impatience with appropriate*
> *comments, which continue*
> *while* FLAMÈCHE *sings, try-*
> *ing to be heard above the*
> *general disapproval.*

FLAMÈCHE, *singing.*

The shades of night again enfold the earth,
The nightingale begins his silver song . . .

> PLANTUREL *finally reappears,*
> *up right, and the company*
> *murmur their approval with*
> *such comments as "Ah, there*
> *he is," "He's back," "Here's*
> *the mayor," etc. After a*
> *few seconds, order is*
> *restored.*

PLANTUREL, *going to his position.* I'm back. Please forgive the interruption. (*To* FLAMÈCHE.) You idiot! Why did you tell me they were the seconds? Seconds my foot! They were a couple of wet nurses looking for a license!

FLAMÈCHE, *to* PLANTUREL. But I didn't say anything about seconds. I said there were two people out there, that's all.

PLANTUREL, *to* FLAMÈCHE. All right, all right! Forget it! (FLAMÈCHE *leaves, up right.*) Now then, where were we? I've read the marriage contract, haven't I?

BRIGOT *and* MADAME JAMBART, *seconded by an affirmative mumble from the rest of the company.* Yes, yes! You have!

PLANTUREL. Good! I will now read the respective rights and obligations of the husband and wife. (*Reading.*) "Article two-hundred twelve of the Civil Code: The husband and wife are bound to one another by bonds of mutual fidelity and assistance. Article two-hundred

51

thirteen: The husband is obliged to protect his wife and provide for her needs. The wife is obliged to follow and obey the dictates of her husband. Article two-hundred fourteen . . ."

FLAMÈCHE, *running in.* Your Honor, Your Honor—

PLANTUREL, *leaping up from his seat.* Are they here? I'm coming! (*To the company.*) Please, I'll only be a moment! Excuse me, excuse me!

> *He leaves in a great hurry, up right. The company once again voice their disapproval: "Oh, no!" "Not again?" "What's the matter with him?" etc.*

BRIGOT. Really, it must be something he ate!

FLAMÈCHE, *standing once again at the mayor's desk.* I will now sing for you a more spirited number from my repertory. (*Singing.*)

> Soldier boy, beat the drum,
> Rum-tum-tum, rum-tum-tum.
> Soldier boy, beat the drum,
> Rum-diddle-um-tum-tum!

> *During this rendition the company object vociferously: "That's enough!" "Quiet!" "Go home!" etc. A moment later PLANTUREL reappears.*

BRIGOT, *noticing him.* It's about time!

PLANTUREL, *to* FLAMÈCHE. Again, you fool! This time two people who wanted to be vaccinated! You can bet I took care of them!

BRIGOT, *sarcastically, to* PLANTUREL. Pardon me, Your Honor, but is Your Honor sure that Your Honor is absolutely ready?

PLANTUREL. Yes, yes! I beg your pardon! You must excuse me! Really, I've been on edge all morning. (*Bending over confidentially to the company, all of whom turn an ear to listen.*) You understand, of course, this is in the strictest confidence . . . I'd rather no one else knew about it. I can tell you, but please, don't spread it around. You see, I have a duel!

BARILLON, *aside, turning a terrified face to the public.* Good God!

MADAME JAMBART. A duel?

> *The other members of the company mutter appropriate comments: "A duel?" "Really?" etc.*

PLANTUREL. So you understand, I've been expecting a visit from my opponent's seconds any minute. I keep thinking they've arrived.

> BARILLON *makes another grimace, as the company once again respond, sotto voce: "Oh, that explains it," "Now I understand," etc.*

BRIGOT. Fine! Now let's get on with this wedding.

PLANTUREL. Very good, let's proceed with the business at hand. (*To the company.*) You will please rise. (*Everyone stands.*) Monsieur Jean-Gustave Barillon, do you take—

PATRICE, *entering in a whirlwind, down left.* Stop! Stop!

> *Everyone looks toward* PATRICE *in great surprise, with such questions as: "What is it?" "Who's he?" "What's the matter?" etc.*

BARILLON. Him again?

PLANTUREL, *in the midst of the general tumult.* My good man, what's the meaning of this?

PATRICE, *far left.* I object to this marriage!

PLANTUREL. You do?

PATRICE. The lady cannot marry this gentleman!

PLANTUREL, *still trying to be heard above the noise of the crowd.* And why not?

PATRICE. Because I love her and she loves me!

BARILLON, *about to leap at* PATRICE, *but held back by the persons around him.* You . . . you . . . Let me get my hands on him!

> PATRICE, *seeing* BARILLON'*s intention, moves quickly to the other side of the stage, The general comments have, in the meantime, subsided.*

PLANTUREL. But, young man, these are hardly sufficient grounds for lodging an objection. After all, the bride is free to refuse.

> *Approval from the company: "Of course," "He's right," etc.*

PATRICE. But I tell you—

PLANTUREL, *to* BARILLON, *ignoring* PATRICE. Jean-Gustave Barillon, do you take this woman—

> *The rest of the sentence is completely drowned by the shouts which follow, in rapid succession.*

PATRICE. No, no, no! Never! Never!

BRIGOT, MADAME JAMBART, *and the members of the wedding party.* Yes, yes! He does!

BARILLON. I do, I do! Of course I do!

> *It is essential that, at this moment, the noise be as loud as possible and that it last long enough to allow* PLAN- TUREL *to ask the traditional question in such a way that the spectators know what he is saying, but without being able to hear a word. The noise and confusion will continue until* PLANTUREL *raps violently for order.*

PLANTUREL, *rapping.* Silence! Silence! Must I remind you

that this is a wedding? (*To* BARILLON.) Do you consent?
(*Affirmative gesture by* BARILLON.) Good! (*To* VIR-
GINIE.) And do you—

> He repeats the question to
> VIRGINIE; *but once again,
> although it is obvious what
> he is saying, his voice, as
> before, is completely obliter-
> ated by the rapid-fire shouts
> of* PATRICE *and the others.*

PATRICE, *far right.* Say no! Say no!

BARILLON. Will you shut up!

BRIGOT, MADAME JAMBART, *and the others.* Quiet! All of
you! Quiet!

PLANTUREL, *managing to be heard above the crowd.* . . .
take this man as your lawfully wedded husband?

PATRICE. No, no, no!

BRIGOT, MADAME JAMBART, *and the others.* Yes, yes!

PLANTUREL. Silence! For the last time, will you all be
quiet!

BRIGOT, *aside.* My God! What a wedding! What a wedding!

PLANTUREL, *to* VIRGINIE. Then you consent?

VIRGINIE, *dolefully.* I do, Your Honor.

PATRICE, *in a rage, while the rest of the company voice
their approval with joyous interjections.* Oh!

PLANTUREL. By virtue of the authority vested in me, I
pronounce you man and wife.

BARILLON. Finally!

PATRICE, *in despair.* Finished! It's all over!

FLAMÈCHE, *to the bride, the groom, and the several witnesses.* Will you please sign here.

BARILLON. I should say we will!

> *Everyone signs as the guests
> file out, down left, leaving
> only the principals on stage.*

PLANTUREL, *aside, while they are signing.* Twelve-thirty,
and still no sign of his seconds! I almost wonder if

they're going to show up at all. It wouldn't surprise me if they didn't. After all, maybe he was so drunk he forgot all about it.

BARILLON, *moving menacingly toward* PATRICE, *who has fallen despondently onto a chair, far right.* And now I'm going to take care of him! (*To* PATRICE.) You've had this coming to you for a long time. Stand up!

PATRICE, *rising to his feet.* You don't frighten me!

> *They begin fighting as everyone crowds around. In the ensuing uproar one can hear such shouts as "Stop them!" "He'll kill him!" "Mother!" "Lowlife!" etc. While fighting,* BARILLON *and* PATRICE *move in front of the mayor's platform.*

PLANTUREL. Enough! Enough! Separate them, somebody! Separate them!

> FLAMÈCHE *rushes between the two combatants and tries to separate them. As he does so, however,* BARILLON *loses the handkerchief that he has had tied around his face.*

PATRICE, *as he is pulled away by* FLAMÈCHE. I'll get you, just wait! I'll get you!

BARILLON, *not realizing that he has lost his handkerchief, and still with his back toward* PLANTUREL. What are you waiting for? Here I am! Come and get me!

PLANTUREL, *coming down from his desk and moving toward* BARILLON. Come now, come now. Let's be reasonable.

BARILLON, *turning to answer* PLANTUREL's *remarks.* Me? Be reasonable? But he's the one—

PLANTUREL, *recognizing* BARILLON, *with a start.* Alfonso Dartagnac!

> *He dashes off, up right.*

BARILLON, *leaping over and through the chairs, toward the door, down left.* He recognized me! (*To* VIRGINIE.) Come on! Let's get out of here!

VIRGINIE *and* BRIGOT. What?

MADAME JAMBART. But . . . but . . .

BARILLON, *tugging at* MADAME JAMBART. Come on! Come on! Everyone!

BRIGOT. But where are we going?

BARILLON. We're going home!

MADAME JAMBART, *struggling to free herself.* Will you let go of me! My shawl . . . I have to get my shawl!

BARILLON, *letting her go, almost causing her to fall backward.* We can't wait! Meet us later! (*To* BRIGOT.) Let's go! Let's go!

BRIGOT. All right, all right, all right! My God! What a wedding!

> BARILLON, BRIGOT *and*
> VIRGINIE *leave, down left.*

MADAME JAMBART, *running to get her shawl.* Wait! Wait for me!

PLANTUREL, *returning, up right.* But how can he be Alfonso Dartagnac? If he was Dartagnac he couldn't get married under the name of Barillon, could he? Hmmm! I wonder . . . (*To* MADAME JAMBART, *as she is about to leave.*) I beg your pardon, Madame, before you go—

MADAME JAMBART. Your Honor?

PLANTUREL. Your son-in-law is gone, isn't he?

MADAME JAMBART. Yes, yes. He just left. I don't know what it was all about. He seemed to be running away from someone.

PLANTUREL. Yes, didn't he! That's just how it looked to me too! Now tell me, just between you and me, has his name ever been Alfonso Dartagnac?

MADAME JAMBART. My son-in-law? Why, of course not! You know perfectly well his name is Barillon. Why should it be Dartagnac?

PLANTUREL, *aside.* Just as I thought! A trick! (*To* MADAME JAMBART.) Well, you can just tell Monsieur Barillon that he was in such a hurry to leave that he forgot to pick up his marriage booklet. Here, you can give it to him. (*Aside.*) The faker!

> *He hands her the open booklet.*

MADAME JAMBART. Oh? What are all these spaces for?

PLANTUREL. Those are for the names of their children.

MADAME JAMBART. They leave them plenty of room, don't they!

PLANTUREL, *turning the page.* And on the next page there's a copy of the official marriage certificate. You see? This makes it all legal. (*He begins reading over the document rapidly.*) ". . . Jean-Gustave Barillon, son of . . . so-and-so and so-and-so . . . and Hildegarde-Augustine . . ."

MADAME JAMBART, *correcting him.* No, you mean Virginie-Ernestine . . . Virginie-Ernestine Pornichet.

PLANTUREL. I beg your pardon! Look for yourself. "Hildegarde-Augustine, formerly the widow Jambart . . ."

MADAME JAMBART. What did you say? Widow . . . Widow Jambart? But that's me!

PLANTUREL. You? You? Then . . . but . . . your daughter?

MADAME JAMBART. My daughter is Virginie Pornichet! You just married her to Monsieur Barillon!

PLANTUREL. No, no, no!

MADAME JAMBART. Yes, yes, yes!

PLANTUREL. Now just a minute. I'll prove it. Flamèche, bring me the marriage contract. (FLAMÈCHE *brings the register from the mayor's desk.*) Here, you'll see! (*Scanning it.*) Oh no! My God! No! No!

MADAME JAMBART. What is it? What is it? (PLANTUREL *is on the verge of collapse.*) Help! Catch him!

FLAMÈCHE, *holding him up.* Your Honor!

PLANTUREL, *choking with anger.* It can't be! That . . .
that . . . He did it again! That idiot! That drunkard!
That . . . that . . . (*Calling.*) Topeau! Topeau!

TOPEAU, *appearing, up right, completely drunk.* Whaz-
zamatter?

PLANTUREL. You . . . You . . . You're fired! Get out! Do
you hear me? Out! Out!

FLAMÈCHE *and* MADAME JAMBART. What did he do?

PLANTUREL. What did he do? What did he . . . Look for
yourself! He put down the mother's name instead of
the daughter's!

FLAMÈCHE. What?

PLANTUREL. I've just married the groom to his mother-in-
law!

MADAME JAMBART. What? You . . . me . . .

PLANTUREL. Yes!

MADAME JAMBART. Oh, my God! I've married my son-in-
law! I've married my son-in-law!

> *She collapses into the arms
> of* TOPEAU, *who, completely
> out of his senses, plants a
> huge kiss on her cheek, while*
> PLANTUREL, *in a position of
> utter despair, falls into the
> arms of* FLAMÈCHE.

ACT TWO

*A drawing room. Upstage center, a door leading to the vesti-
bule. On each side of this door, a console table. Up right, set
at an angle, a door leading to* BARILLON's *room. Up left,
a corresponding door leading to the dining room. Down left,
another door; down right, a window. Up right, a wicker
dummy displaying* VIRGINIE's *wedding dress. Between the
window and the dummy, a full-length mounted mirror. Down*

*right, near the window, a couch covered with cushions. In a
similar position, down left, a table and chair.*

At rise, JOSÉPHINE, *wearing a crown of orange blossoms, is
posing, simpering and parading before the mirror.*

JOSÉPHINE, *with a coquettish curtsy.* "Yes, Your Honor!
I do, Your Honor! . . ." Oh! Wouldn't that be something! And just think! If only Anatole was a gentleman,
or even Maximilien! If either one of them wanted to
do right by me, after all these years! I could be wearing
one of these things too, only I'd put on twice as much,
because I need it more! (*Making a curtsy.*) "Yes, Your
Honor! . . ." And then, in church, everyone would
look at me and push and try to see me better. "Oh, look
at the pretty bride!" (*Trying to put on an air.*) "Ah,
Duchess darling! Isn't it all simply charming? Have
a look at that bride, darling! What a simply charming
bride! Really, darling, she's simply a doll!" Blah, blah,
blah!

> *She continues her gestures
> and her curtsies in silence.*

BARILLON, *appearing at the vestibule door, with* VIR-
GINIE, *and observing* JOSÉPHINE'*s actions.* Oh!

JOSÉPHINE, *unaware of their presence, continuing to pose.*
"Oh, Duchess darling! I never got married before. Isn't
it simply charming?"

BARILLON. Are you through making a fool of yourself?

JOSÉPHINE, *jumping at his voice.* Oh, Monsieur! Mademoiselle!

VIRGINIE. Really, Joséphine!

> *She removes her hat, placing
> it on one of the console
> tables, and moves to the
> table, far left.*

BARILLON. "Oh! Duchess darling! I never got married
before!" . . . Now just what are you up to?

JOSÉPHINE. I . . . I was only fixing—

BARILLON, *impatient.* What? What were you fixing? And who told you to put those flowers on your head? Take them off, do you understand?

JOSÉPHINE. Yes, Monsieur.

> *She removes the crown and replaces it on the dummy.*

BARILLON. You, playing with orange blossoms! That's a laugh!

JOSÉPHINE. I was only trying them on, Monsieur.

BARILLON. Ha! Only trying them on! You! (*Pointing to the crown.*) Like Lucrezia Borgia trying on Joan of Arc's halo!

JOSÉPHINE. Monsieur?

BARILLON. Never mind, it's too complicated. You can go now.

> *He points to the vestibule door.*

JOSÉPHINE, *aside.* Hm! Sounds like he's had one wedding too many!

> *She leaves.*

BARILLON, *behind the couch.* What a nerve! (*Moving around the couch and addressing* VIRGINIE, *far left, with a sudden change of tone.*) Virginie!

VIRGINIE. Yes?

BARILLON. Virginie, this is the first time we've been alone together.

VIRGINIE. Oh? So?

BARILLON, *taken aback.* What do you mean: "Oh? So?"

VIRGINIE, *somewhat at a loss.* Well, I mean . . . What do you mean, "What do you mean?"

BARILLON. What do I mean? This is the first time we've been . . . (*Emphasizing.*) alone! That's what I mean!

VIRGINIE. Oh well! Don't let that bother you. Don't mind me!

BARILLON, *going over to* VIRGINIE. Mind you? Don't mind

you? Of course I mind you . . . I mind you very much!
I mind you here . . . Here! (*He clutches at his heart.*)
I'm not made of stone, you know! I . . . I . . . I love
you!

VIRGINIE. Oh no! No! Please! Let's not get onto that subject!

BARILLON. That subject? But what other subject . . .
You're my wife!

VIRGINIE. Well, whatever you have to tell me can just wait
until Mother gets here.

BARILLON. I beg your pardon! Never in a million years!

VIRGINIE. What?

BARILLON. What does she have to do with this?

VIRGINIE. If what you have to say is honorable, Mother
has a right to listen.

BARILLON. Never! Never!

VIRGINIE. And if it's not honorable I don't want to hear it.

BARILLON. But . . . Good God in heaven! Of course it's
honorable!

VIRGINIE, *sitting in the chair, far left.* Oh, what language!

BARILLON. I said: "It is honorable!" Of course it's honorable. But that's no reason for your mother . . . After
all, lots of things are "honorable," but don't think I plan
to invite your mother to our . . . to . . . Well, I mean,
after all!

VIRGINIE. And besides, what do you have against my
mother?

BARILLON. Me?

VIRGINIE, *getting up.* Oh, I know. You hate her, don't you?

BARILLON. No! No! What are you—

VIRGINIE. I can tell. I've seen the face you make every
time she kisses you. I can tell.

BARILLON. Well who the devil asks her to kiss me every
second? (*Becoming angry.*) Who asks her to shove her
whiskers in my face? Who? Who?

VIRGINIE. Her whiskers!

BARILLON. Yes, damn it! Why can't she shave? I shave, don't I?

VIRGINIE, *moving stage right.* Oh! Now you're just being vulgar! I'll have you know my mother needs affection. She's very effusive, that's all.

BARILLON. Well let her go "effuse" on someone else, damn it!

VIRGINIE. And you've never shown her the slightest respect.

BARILLON. What?

VIRGINIE. Just now, for example, at the city hall. You didn't even wait for her. No! You had to run out like a madman!

BARILLON. You can say that again! (*Remembering his ordeal.*) Whew! "I now pronounce you Alfonso Dartagnac!" No thanks! (*Taking* VIRGINIE *by the hand and leading her over to the couch to sit down beside him.*) And besides . . . (*Romantically.*) I couldn't wait to be alone with you . . . to tell you everything I've been wanting to tell you . . .

               He embraces her.

VIRGINIE, *trying to free herself.* I thought I told you—

BARILLON. I don't care what you told me! You're my wife. My wife! Nothing can take you away from me! You're mine, and I love you!

               He kisses her passionately.

MADAME JAMBERT, *appearing at the vestibule door, and uttering a scream as she notices* BARILLON *and* VIRGINIE. Stop! Stop!

BARILLON *and* VIRGINIE. What? What is it?

MADAME JAMBART. Oh, my dears! If you only knew what's happened. Oh! Let me catch my breath! (*She places her hat on one of the console tables.*) Virginie, darling, kiss me! You're saved!

VIRGINIE *and* BARILLON. What? Saved?

MADAME JAMBART, *to* VIRGINIE. You never really wanted to marry Monsieur Barillon, did you? It was all against your will, wasn't it? Well, everything is all right. It's all been fixed.

VIRGINIE, *rising, along with* BARILLON. What?

MADAME JAMBART. You're not his wife any more darling! And he's not your husband!

BARILLON. What are you babbling—

MADAME JAMBART, *throwing her arms around* BARILLON's *neck.* Precious!

BARILLON, *freeing himself.* Let go of me!

MADAME JAMBART. I just want to kiss everyone, I'm so happy!

BARILLON. Will you please tell us what this is all about?

VIRGINIE. Yes, Mother dear, please.

MADAME JAMBART, *controlling her enthusiasm.* Well, you remember the contract?

BARILLON *and* VIRGINIE. The contract?

MADAME JAMBART. The marriage contract.

BARILLON. So?

VIRGINIE. What about it?

MADAME JAMBART. They made a mistake. It's all too wonderful!

BARILLON *and* VIRGINIE. A mistake?

MADAME JAMBART. They didn't put down Virginie's name at all! They put down someone else's name instead.

BARILLON. Someone else's?

MADAME JAMBART. Yes! . . . And so, instead of being married to Virginie, you're really married to . . . Guess!

> She chucks him under the chin.

BARILLON. Who? My God! Who?

MADAME JAMBART, *opening her arms, and in a lyrical tone.* Come, kiss your wife, darling!

BARILLON, *choking.* What? You don't mean . . . You can't mean . . . Who? Who?

MADAME JAMBART. Me!

BARILLON. What? I . . . They . . . You . . .

MADAME JAMBART. Me!

> BARILLON *lets forth a horrible moan and runs frantically around the room, pursued by* MADAME JAMBART. *Finally he lets himself fall in a heap onto the couch, his head in his hands.*

VIRGINIE, *frightened.* Oh!

MADAME JAMBART, *about to throw her arms about* BARILLON'*s neck.* Barillon!

BARILLON. Don't come near me! (*Bellowing.*) I'm married to my mother-in-law! I'm married to my mother-in-law!

MADAME JAMBART. Please, Barillon! Darling!

BARILLON, *seizing a cushion from the couch and threatening her with it.* Don't say that!

MADAME JAMBART. He's out of his mind. (*To* BARILLON.) Control yourself! Virginie, please, you tell him.

VIRGINIE. Yes, for heaven's sake, control yourself!

BARILLON. Control myself? Control myself? Ha ha ha! One minute I'm married to a beautiful young woman. The next minute she's turned into . . . (*Pointing to* MADAME JAMBART.) into that! That!

MADAME JAMBART. Barillon!

BARILLON, *threatening her with the cushion.* Don't come near me!

JOSÉPHINE, *appearing at the vestibule door.* His Honor, Monsieur Planturel.

BARILLON, *furious.* Oh, by all means! By all means! Show him in! (*As* PLANTUREL *enters,* BARILLON *throws himself at him, menacingly.*) You! In this house! You dare—

PLANTUREL, *pushing him aside.* Shhh!

BARILLON. What do you mean. "Shhh! Shhh!" A nice mess you've got me into!

PLANTUREL. Shhh!

BARILLON. Don't tell me "Shhh!" You don't think I'm going to let you get away with this, do you?

PLANTUREL, *pushing him suddenly onto the couch.* Shhhhh!

VIRGINIE *and* MADAME JAMBART. Oh!

PLANTUREL, *aside.* I may as well put on a good show!

BARILLON. That's too much! Just because you have a license to marry people, that's no reason to go around marrying them to their mother-in-law!

PLANTUREL. All right, I admit it. It was a mistake.

BARILLON. A mistake? I'll say it was a mistake! Why didn't you marry her yourself? Ha! Not damn likely!

MADAME JAMBART, *to* BARILLON. You aren't being very nice, you know.

BARILLON. I don't give a damn what I'm being! (*To* PLANTUREL.) You'll see, I haven't even begun with you!

PLANTUREL. Fine! Take me to court! I suppose you were planning to have the marriage annulled?

BARILLON. Of course!

PLANTUREL. And what makes you think you'll be able to?

BARILLON. What?

PLANTUREL. Well, really now, who's to blame for all this? I'll tell you who. You are!

BARILLON. Me?

PLANTUREL. Absolutely! You were at the city hall, weren't you? You signed the marriage contract, didn't you? When I asked you if you took the widow Jambart for your lawfully wedded wife, what did you say? I'll tell you what you said. You said "I do," that's what you said.

VIRGINIE. He's right.

BARILLON. Now just a minute. I said "I do." Of course I said, "I do"! But everyone was yelling and screaming. And my ears were covered, remember? I couldn't hear a word.

66

PLANTUREL. Well, that's just too bad! You shouldn't go around saying "I do" unless you can hear straight. Whose fault is that?

MADAME JAMBART. Absolutely!

PLANTUREL. In fact, do you want to know something? I'll tell you! The courts will find you guilty, my friend, not me.

BARILLON. Me?

PLANTUREL. Yes, you! Because I can take you to court for attacking my honor, Alfonso Dartagnac!

BARILLON. We'll see! Go ahead and take me to court. I don't give a damn! I'll still have this marriage annulled. Just wait! And as for you . . . By the time I'm through with you, you'll be looking for another job!

PLANTUREL. Oh, you think so? You're absolutely determined to break up this marriage?

BARILLON. Of course I am!

PLANTUREL. All right, my friend. I'm going to tell you just how to go about it, and without going to court either.

BARILLON, *seeing a ray of hope.* You are?

PLANTUREL. Yes, I am. You challenged me to a duel, remember? All right, then, I'm going to kill you.

BARILLON, *with a start.* Kill me?

MADAME JAMBART. Don't forget, darling, he's an expert!

PLANTUREL. My seconds will visit you in the morning.

BARILLON. But wait a minute! Wait!

PLANTUREL. There's nothing more to say.

BARILLON. But there is! There is. (*Amiably.*) Let's talk it over.

PLANTUREL. Are you determined to go through with an annulment and make me the laughingstock of my profession?

BARILLON. But . . . but . . . (*Pointing to* MADAME JAMBART.) I can't stay married to her!

MADAME JAMBART, *with a pout.* Oh, darling! Why not?

BARILLON. Ha!

PLANTUREL. Of course, there's always divorce.

BARILLON, *hopefully*. There is? (*Pointing to the couch.*) Well now, let's talk about this.

> *They both sit down on the couch.*

PLANTUREL. Yes. And besides, a divorce wouldn't take any longer than an annulment. And that way, at least, you'd be like everyone else. You wouldn't be a freak! Married to your mother-in-law. Think of the publicity!

BARILLON, *with a grimace*. I'm thinking!

PLANTUREL. You'd be ridiculous. Whereas this way, if you get a divorce . . . (*Getting up.*) Well, then you're just another husband who doesn't get along with his wife. It happens every day.

MADAME JAMBART. And what makes you think I'll give him a divorce?

PLANTUREL. Well, I thought—

BARILLON, *to* MADAME JAMBART. What? Of course you will! Who was I supposed to marry in the first place, you or your daughter?

PLANTUREL. But after all, she is much too young for you.

BARILLON, *angrily*. Oh is she? Well, that's my business, thank you!

PLANTUREL. People will think you're her father.

VIRGINIE. That's right, I'm only eighteen.

MADAME JAMBART. But I'm forty-two. And you . . . you're forty.

BARILLON. So?

MADAME JAMBART. Well, there's not nearly so much difference between us. We're just right for each other.

BARILLON, *sarcastically*. I like your reasoning!

PLANTUREL, *anxious to get off the hook*. Well then, is it all settled?

BARILLON, *seeming to weaken*. But . . . Oh . . . I suppose . . . (*He turns around and loses courage at the sight of* MADAME JAMBART, *who is smiling at him lovingly.*) I can't! I can't! It's bigger than I am! I can't do it!

MADAME JAMBART *and* VIRGINIE. Oh!

PLANTUREL. All right, then. That's that. I'll have to kill you. There's no other way out.

BARILLON. What? No! I mean . . . (*Weakening.*) Oh! . . . All right! All right! Have it your way!

> He falls in a heap onto the
> chair, far left.

MADAME JAMBART *and* VIRGINIE, *triumphant.* Ah!

PLANTUREL. I knew you'd listen to reason.

MADAME JAMBART, *ecstatic.* Oh Barillon, darling! (*To* VIRGINIE.) Virginie, come kiss your stepfather.

> VIRGINIE *approaches.*

BARILLON, *to* VIRGINIE, *who is about to embrace him.* Stepfather? Oh no! That's too much!

PLANTUREL, *shaking* BARILLON'*s hand as he moves to leave.* I'm happy to see how well everything has turned out. You owe it all to me! (*Bowing to* MADAME JAMBART.) Madame Barillon!

> He leaves, up center.

BARILLON, *despondently.* Madame Barillon!

MADAME JAMBART, *jumping for joy.* He called me Madame Barillon!

BARILLON, *still sitting dejectedly in the same place.* Madame Barillon! That's Madame Barillon! I have a mother-in-law for a wife, and a wife for a stepdaughter!

MADAME JAMBART, *prancing over to the mirror and looking at her reflection.* I'm a bride! I'm a bride!

VIRGINIE, *to* BARILLON. Thank you! Thank you for making Mother so happy!

BARILLON, *angrily.* Oh, think nothing of it! If you think I'm doing it for her . . .

MADAME JAMBART. Tra la la la! I feel like a schoolgirl. (*Moving toward* BARILLON.) This will add ten years to my life.

BARILLON, *between his teeth*. That's right, rub it in!

MADAME JAMBART, *putting her arms around* BARILLON, *who is still seated, and crushing him under her bulk*. You'll see how happy we'll be, just the three of us.

VIRGINIE, *on the other side of the table, taking* BARILLON's *hand*. Oh yes! You'll see! We'll be so happy!

BARILLON, *to* VIRGINIE. Happy? When I'm losing you?

VIRGINIE. But you're gaining Mother.

BARILLON. Thanks! I wasn't looking for quantity.

VIRGINIE. And besides, you're not losing me.

MADAME JAMBART. We're just playing different parts, that's all.

VIRGINIE. You'll see how wonderful it's going to be, Monsieur Barillon.

MADAME JAMBART, *to* VIRGINIE. Oh darling! You shouldn't call him Monsieur Barillon. He's your stepfather now. Call him Daddy.

BARILLON, *leaping up*. Daddy!

VIRGINIE. Oh yes! Yes! Daddy dear!

BARILLON, *beside himself, moving stage right*. No, no! Please! Not that!

PATRICE, *entering briskly, upstage center*. Ah! Monsieur Barillon, there you are!

VIRGINIE. Patrice!

BARILLON. You! You dare . . . You! In this house! Get out! Get out!

PATRICE. But I only wanted—

BARILLON. Out!

PATRICE, *waving a white handkerchief*. Just let me explain.

MADAME JAMBART. Give the poor boy a chance to talk.

BARILLON. All right, what is it?

PATRICE, *moving downstage*. I just wanted to tell you that

I've been to the city hall and that I've found out all
about the . . . the . . . Well, all about what happened.

BARILLON. What? Who told you?

PATRICE. The clerks. It's all over town. Oh, Monsieur!
Please let me tell you how sorry I am for making such
a scene this morning.

BARILLON, *with dignity*. Oh, really?

PATRICE. Yes! It was unforgivable. But you understand,
the thought of losing Virginie . . . I didn't know what
I was doing. You do understand, don't you? You will
forgive me? Please?

BARILLON, *gradually relenting*. Oh, for heaven's sake! . . .
Yes, I forgive you!

PATRICE. And now I want you to know that I wish you
and your new bride every happiness.

BARILLON, *in a sudden rage*. What?

MADAME JAMBART. Isn't he sweet!

PATRICE, *pointing to* MADAME JAMBART *and putting his
arm around* BARILLON. Madame Jambart is just the
woman for you. You couldn't have made a better choice.
She'll make a wonderful wife and mother.

BARILLON. Oh, really! You think so, do you?

PATRICE, *taking a pair of white gloves from his pocket
and putting them on*. And now, Monsieur . . . Now that
your position has changed . . . Now that you're her
father and not her husband . . .

BARILLON. What?

PATRICE. I have the honor of requesting the hand of your
stepdaughter, Mademoiselle Virginie Pornichet, in marriage.

BARILLON. What? What did you say?

PATRICE. I said: I have the honor of requesting the hand
of your stepdaughter—

BARILLON. I heard you! I heard you! So, you're in on this
little game too, are you? Well, I'll teach you—

He begins to run after
PATRICE, *who moves around*
the couch and stops far right.

PATRICE. Game? What game?

BARILLON. Is this your idea of a joke? Coming here to rub salt in my wounds?

MADAME JAMBART. What wounds?

BARILLON. Well, just you listen to me, young man! You can't have her!

PATRICE. Oh!

VIRGINIE, *pleading.* Daddy! Daddy dear!

BARILLON. Never! You can "Daddy dear" from now till doomsday! Never! Understand? So! I'm Daddy now, am I? Fine! Then I'm the boss, right? And what I say goes! (*To* PATRICE.) Before I give her to you I'll marry her myself!

PATRICE. What?

BARILLON. Sure! I'm in no hurry . . . I can wait.

VIRGINIE *and* MADAME JAMBART. What?

BARILLON. Now get out, all of you. I want to be alone!

MADAME JAMBART, *pouting.* Me too?

BARILLON, *threatening her with a cushion.* Especially you! Get out of here, all of you!

MADAME JAMBART, *to* PATRICE. You can't talk to him now. He's not in a good mood.

PATRICE. But . . . but . . . Is there any chance—

MADAME JAMBART. Yes, yes. Don't you worry. Just come along.

PATRICE, *to* BARILLON. Good afternoon, Monsieur!

He leaves with MADAME
JAMBART *and* VIRGINIE, *up*
left.

BARILLON, *alone.* Something's going to snap. I know it is! I can't take much more of this! I'm going mad, that's what! God in heaven, what happened? Here I am, in love with a girl I can't marry, and married to a . . . to a woman I can't love. It's too much!

JOSÉPHINE, *entering up center and approaching* BARILLON, *down right.* There's a letter for Monsieur . . .

BARILLON, *angrily.* All right then, give it to me. (JOSÉPHINE *hands him the letter, which he opens.*) Hm! It's from Brigot.

JOSÉPHINE. Who's Brigot, Monsieur?

BARILLON. Is that any of your business?

JOSÉPHINE. But Monsieur just said: "It's from Brigot."

BARILLON. I wasn't talking to you. (*Reading.*) "My dear nephew. Urgent business has obliged me to return to Troyes." (*Speaking.*) Good riddance! (*Reading.*) "I will be back for a visit in about two weeks, next time I come to Paris. Best wishes to your pretty little wife." (*In a rage.*) My pretty little wife!

He rips up the letter.

JOSÉPHINE. Oh, by the way, Monsieur, I heard the good news.

BARILLON. Good news? What good news?

JOSÉPHINE. Why, about Madame Jambart and Monsieur.

BARILLON, *with a sarcastic little laugh.* Oh? Thank you! Thank you very much!

JOSÉPHINE, *following* BARILLON *as he moves stage right.* Oh yes! Monsieur did a smart thing to change his mind. We all knew that Mademoiselle was too young.

BARILLON. That's fine! Thank you!

JOSÉPHINE. But with Madame . . . Well, Monsieur and Madame make such a nice couple.

BARILLON. All right! All right! That's enough!

JOSÉPHINE. We're all very happy about it in the kitchen.

BARILLON, *finally exploding.* Will you get out of here? Out! Out!

JOSÉPHINE. But, Monsieur, the help wanted me to be sure and give Monsieur their best wishes.

BARILLON. Well you can take back their goddamn best wishes! Now get out of here!

> JOSÉPHINE *moves toward the vestibule door. At this moment the* TELEGRAPH BOY *enters through the same door, a youngster of about eight.*

TELEGRAPH BOY, *entering.* Hello, nobody home?

BARILLON. What are you talking about, "Nobody home?" What do I look like?

TELEGRAPH BOY. Telegram for Madame Jambart.

BARILLON, *taking it.* You can leave it here.

TELEGRAPH BOY. Yes, Monsieur. Oh, by the way, Monsieur, everyone at the telegraph office asked me to congratulate you on the good news—

BARILLON, *beside himself.* What? You too? . . . You . . . Get out of here! Get out!

TELEGRAPH BOY. What about my tip?

BARILLON. Your tip? Your . . . You'll see what kind of a tip I give you! (*He lifts the boy bodily and hands him to* JOSÉPHINE.) Here! Get rid of this for me!

TELEGRAPH BOY, *while* JOSÉPHINE *carries him off.* Nyaa! Nyaa! It serves you right, you old cradle robber!

> JOSÉPHINE *and the* TELEGRAPH BOY *leave by the center door.*

BARILLON, *nervously bunching up the telegram, without realizing what he is doing.* Cradle robber? What kind of a conspiracy is this? Are they all trying to drive me out of my mind?

> *He throws the crumpled telegram on the floor and falls despondently onto the couch.*

MADAME JAMBART, *entering stage left, wearing an elegant nightgown and with her hair down her back, like a young girl.* Oh, I'm so excited . . . just like the first time! Now where is he? (*She looks around the room*

and notices BARILLON.) Oh, I do hope he won't be
disappointed with me.

BARILLON, *on the couch, with his back turned toward*
MADAME JAMBART, *dreaming.* Ah, Virginie! Virginie!
(MADAME JAMBART *bends over and kisses him.*) Vir-
ginie! (*He turns around and discovers* MADAME JAM-
BART.) Oh no! No!

MADAME JAMBART. I just couldn't resist, darling!

BARILLON, *getting up.* You couldn't let me forget this . . .
this catastrophe! You couldn't just let me sleep . . .
forever!

MADAME JAMBART. Sleep? On your wedding day?

BARILLON, *moving stage left.* Ha! We'll see if I sleep or
not!

MADAME JAMBART. Don't I make as pretty a bride as
anyone else? (*She goes to the dummy and takes the
crown of orange blossoms, puts it on her head, and
flits around the room in an attempt at grace.*) See!

BARILLON. Take that thing off.

MADAME JAMBART, *prancing over to* BARILLON, *clapping
her hands.* Oh! I'm so happy!

BARILLON. That's nice! Just stop jumping around like a
trained seal!

MADAME JAMBART. Me?

BARILLON. Yes! For heaven's sake, if you could only see
yourself!

MADAME JAMBART. Barillon, why are you so cold to me?
I'll have you know I made all my husbands very happy!

BARILLON, *moving stage right, muttering between his teeth.*
I knew that was coming!

MADAME JAMBART, *following him.* Go ask Pornichet, God
rest his soul! Ask him if he ever had any reason to
complain.

BARILLON. Thanks, I'd rather not!

MADAME JAMBART. And Jambart, poor dear. Go ask him.
We were only married one day . . .

BARILLON, *aside.* Lucky devil!

MADAME JAMBART. But even so, at least he had a taste of happiness before the sea swallowed him up. Go ask him!

BARILLON. Go ask him yourself, why don't you?

MADAME JAMBART. Ah, Barillon! You'll see. I'll make you happy too, as sure . . . (*She notices the crumpled telegram on the floor.*) as sure as that scrap of paper is lying on the floor over there.

BARILLON. Paper? What paper? (*He looks at the telegram.*) Oh, that! I almost forgot. It's for you . . . a telegram. It just came.

MADAME JAMBART. A telegram? For me? Be a dear and give it to me, will you?

BARILLON, *pushing the crumpled ball toward her with his foot.* Here, take it yourself.

MADAME JAMBART. Oh, Barillon! Please be a gentleman.

BARILLON, *picking it up and muttering, aside.* Hm! She's gone and tied herself up so tight she can't even bend over. (*To* MADAME JAMBART.) Here!

> *He hands it to her.*

MADAME JAMBART, *reading the address.* "Madame Jambart, Avenue Marceau . . . Try Rue de la Pompe . . . Try Avenue des Ternes . . . Try Rue Caumartin . . . Try . . ." Why, it's been to every one of my addresses for the last two years! Whoever could it be from? (*She opens it up and looks at the name.*) Oh! My God!

> *She falls onto the couch, in*
> *a faint.*

BARILLON. What is it? What's the matter? Oh, for heaven's sake! Virginie! Virginie!

> VIRGINIE *comes running in,*
> *up left, followed by*
> PATRICE.

VIRGINIE, *running to* MADAME JAMBART. Mother! Mother!

PATRICE. What is it?

BARILLON. What's the matter?

MADAME JAMBART, *coming to her senses.* Oh, Barillon!

BARILLON, VIRGINIE *and* PATRICE. What? Tell us!

MADAME JAMBART. It's Jambart! Jambart! He's alive!

VIRGINIE *and* PATRICE. What?

BARILLON, *choking.* Jam . . . Jam . . . Jambart . . . What did you say?

MADAME JAMBART. The telegram! It's from him! He's . . . he's coming back!

> *She swoons again.*

BARILLON. Oh!

> *He falls onto the couch beside her.*

VIRGINIE. My God! They've fainted! (*To* PATRICE.) Help me! Help me!

> PATRICE *moves behind the couch and rubs* BARILLON's *hands while* VIRGINIE *does the same to* MADAME JAMBART. *The two figures on the couch are in such a position that their heads are at the extremes while their knees are almost touching.*

MADAME JAMBART *and* BARILLON, *moaning, still in a faint.* Oh!

> *In a simultaneous movement both let their heads fall forward in such a way that* BARILLON's *head rests on* MADAME JAMBART's *bosom.*

MADAME JAMBART, *semiconscious.* Oh! . . . Oh! . . .

> *Suddenly she emits a strident shriek that brings* BARILLON *to his senses and forces him to his feet.*

BARILLON, VIRGINIE *and* PATRICE. What is it?

MADAME JAMBART, *getting up.* God in heaven! If he's alive . . . then he's my husband too!

BARILLON, VIRGINIE *and* PATRICE. That's right!

MADAME JAMBART. Then I'm . . . I'm a . . . a . . . biga-mistress!

BARILLON, VIRGINIE *and* PATRICE, *horrified.* Oh!

BARILLON, *suddenly, after a second of reflection.* And what does that make me?

MADAME JAMBART. You! Never mind you! You only have one wife!

BARILLON, *in despair.* One wife . . . and one husband!

MADAME JAMBART. What are we going to do? They'll drag us through every court!

BARILLON. We could run away . . . to Mongolia!

MADAME JAMBART. Oh, Barillon! What are we going to do?

PATRICE. Wait a minute, everybody. How do we know the telegram was really from Jambart?

VIRGINIE. That's right.

PATRICE. Maybe it's just someone playing a joke on you.

BARILLON. That's right.

PATRICE. After all, what day is today? It's April first, isn't it?

VIRGINIE. He's right!

BARILLON. It's an April Fool joke!

VIRGINIE *and* PATRICE. Of course! April Fool! April Fool!

MADAME JAMBART, *relieved.* Oh, my heavens! What a fright!

BARILLON, *delighted, goes so far as to embrace* MADAME JAMBART, *slapping her on the back.* What a foolish trick to play on us! And to think, we were silly enough to think he was still alive.

PATRICE, *embracing* VIRGINIE *in similar fashion.* Of course! After two years, he would have come back by now.

MADAME JAMBART. Besides, everyone knows his boat went down. The whole crew was swallowed up.

BARILLON. That's right. He was eaten alive by the fish.

MADAME JAMBART. Absolutely! He was eaten alive!

> *Everyone, in almost a frenzy of joy, dances around chanting: "He was eaten alive! He was eaten alive!"*

JOSÉPHINE, *entering up center.* Monsieur Jambart.

MADAME JAMBART. Jambart?

> *They stare at one another for a moment, looking for a way of escape, each one shouting louder than the next: "Jambart! Jambart!"* VIRGINIE *rushes off, down left.* MADAME JAMBART *and* BARILLON, *each running toward the center of the stage, collide. They both change direction simultaneously and run around the couch, once again bumping into each other.* BARILLON, *doing an about-face, dashes off, up right.* MADAME JAMBART, *running off, up left, collides with* PATRICE. *Then both dash out through the door, up left.*

JOSÉPHINE, *amazed to see them all leave.* Now where are they all off to?

> JAMBART *appears, up center. He is a large, hearty-looking seaman.*

JAMBART. Did you tell them?

JOSÉPHINE, *startled.* Oh!

JAMBART. What's the matter, sweetie-pie? Did I frighten you?

> *He advances toward her, almost menacingly.*

JOSÉPHINE. Oh no! Not at all, Monsieur!

> *She backs up toward the
> couch and moves all around
> it, trembling.*

JAMBART. Well, here I am. Me, Jambart! They all thought
I was dead and gone. Well, I ain't, not by a long shot!

JOSÉPHINE. You mean you're not dead?

JAMBART. Ha, ha! You're a funny one, you are! (*Moving
toward her.*) Do I look dead to you? Look close! Just
see if I ain't still got some life in me!

> *He embraces her passion-
> ately.*

JOSÉPHINE. Oh, Monsieur!

JAMBART. Well I'll be scuttled! There's a maid for you.
She ain't no lady, but she's lots of woman! And when
you've been on a desert island . . .

JOSÉPHINE. Of course I'm a woman! What did you think?

JAMBART. You sure are, sweetie-pie! You sure are! Now
tell me, where's my wife?

JOSÉPHINE. Your wife?

JAMBART. My wife. Madame Jambart, my better half.

JOSÉPHINE. Hm! Your better quarter!

JAMBART, *puzzled.* What? You mean she's half the size.
Shriveled up with grief?

JOSÉPHINE. That's right, with grief. (*Aside.*) Why should
I be the one to tell him?

JAMBART. Poor Hildegarde! Couldn't stand being without
me. (*To* JOSÉPHINE.) By the way, be a good girl, will
you? Run down and pick up my gear. It's all at the
foot of the stairs. You'll see it. There's a couple of
bags, some guns, and . . . Loulou.

JOSÉPHINE. Loulou?

JAMBART. My seal.

JOSÉPHINE. Your seal?

JAMBART. That's what I said. Me and Loulou was ship-
wrecked together. If he calls you "Mamma" don't get
scared. I trained him to do all kinds of little things.

JOSÉPHINE. A seal? But where on earth can I put him?

JAMBART. Oh, just stow him in the bathtub, in a little seawater. He'll be all right.

JOSÉPHINE. Seawater?

JAMBART. Sure. Ain't you got no seawater here?

JOSÉPHINE, *sarcastically.* Well, no Monsieur. They haven't put it in yet!

JAMBART. Never mind, sweetie-pie. Just toss in a little salt. He ain't fussy. He'll never know the difference.

JOSÉPHINE. No?

JAMBART. And anyway, he's in the big city now. May as well get used to phony stuff, don't you think?

JOSÉPHINE. Yes, Monsieur. (*She moves toward the door, up center.*) I'll go take care of it right away.

JAMBART. That's a good girl. (JOSÉPHINE *leaves.*) Ah! It does the old bones good to be back! I can hardly wait to see the look on Hildegarde's face when she sees me! And little Virginie! (*He begins pacing up and down.*) I wonder where in thunder they are. Maybe I'll take me a look around the place.

> *He goes to the door, up right, and begins to open it.*
> BARILLON, *whose hand is visible, pulls it quickly shut.*

BARILLON'S VOICE. Don't come in!

JAMBART. Sorry, sorry! . . . (*Aside.*) Must be the bathroom.

> *He goes over to the door, up left, and begins to open it.*

MADAME JAMBART'S VOICE. No! Don't come in!

JAMBART. There she is! That's her voice! Hildegarde, open up! Open up! (*He pushes the door open. A scream is heard from* MADAME JAMBART. JAMBART *backs out of the doorway, his arms extended toward his invisible wife.*) Hildegarde, it's me, Jambart!

MADAME JAMBART, *appearing.* Emile?

JAMBART. Sweetie-pie! I'm home! (*He crushes her in a*

passionate embrace for a moment. Then, taking her hands in his, steps back to look at her.) Let me get a good look. (*Aside, during another embrace.*) Hm! She ain't no younger!

MADAME JAMBART, *upset.* Is it . . . Is it really you?

JAMBART. Is it me? I'll say it is! Surprised you, didn't I? I can hardly believe it myself, after everything I've been through.

MADAME JAMBART. But . . . but they said you were eaten alive by the fish.

JAMBART. No! But I came mighty close, I'll tell you! There I was in the water. First thing I know, there's this shark making eyes at me. So I says: "Think you're going to make a meal out of me, do you?" And just then, when he turns around to see who I was talking to, I grabs him with my bare hands and chokes him to death. Good thing I did, too. All the other sharks took one look and said to each other: "Don't tangle with that cookie! He's a tough one!"

MADAME JAMBART. Did they really?

JAMBART. Sure, I'll tell you all about it some day. (*He moves behind* MADAME JAMBART, *taking her around the waist and speaking into her ear.*) But there's other things to talk about now. You just don't know how much love I've got stowed away, sweetie-pie. And I brought it all back, just for you.

MADAME JAMBART. Oh?

JAMBART. Every bit of it!

MADAME JAMBART, *disturbed.* It was nice of you to think of me.

JAMBART. Hildegarde!

> *He begins to embrace her.*

MADAME JAMBART, *aside, looking toward the door, up right, and resisting* JAMBART. Oh, my God! The other one . . . the other one is in there.

JAMBART. Hey, what's the matter with you?

MADAME JAMBART. Me?

JAMBART. Two years on a desert island and I can't even get a peck. What's the matter? Don't you love me no more?

MADAME JAMBART, *hesitating.* Yes . . . of course I do!

JAMBART. We've got to make up for lost time, you and me! You've got to do twice as much loving as before.

MADAME JAMBART, *moving stage left.* Yes, don't I!

JAMBART, *aside.* Cold as a clam! (*Suddenly noticing the wedding dress.*) Say, what's that?

MADAME JAMBART. That? Why . . . why, it's a wedding dress.

JAMBART. I know, but . . . (*With a sudden realization.*) Oh, of course! Why didn't you say so? Virginie! Little Virginie is getting married.

MADAME JAMBART. That's right! That's right! Today—

JAMBART. And where's the little sweetie? I bet she's all grown up. (*Calling.*) Virginie! Virginie!

MADAME JAMBART, *aside.* My God! How can I tell him?

JAMBART, *going to the door, down left, and calling.* Virginie! Where are you? (VIRGINIE *appears at the door.*) There she is. There's the little darling. Virginie!

> *He holds out his arms to embrace her.*

VIRGINIE, *kissing him with affected enthusiasm.* Oh! Is it possible? Is it really you?

JAMBART, *accompanying* VIRGINIE *center stage.* Well blow me down if it ain't. (*Admiring* VIRGINIE.) Just look at her, will you! And to think she's getting married today. I got here just in time, didn't I?

> MADAME JAMBART *signals* VIRGINIE *to say yes.*

VIRGINIE. Me? Married?

> MADAME JAMBART *signals more frantically.*

JAMBART. Sure! I know all about it. (*To* MADAME JAM-

BART, *as he catches her signals.*) What's all this business?

> *He waves his hands about*
> *his head, duplicating*
> MADAME JAMBART's *gestures*
> *to* VIRGINIE.

MADAME JAMBART. Why . . . I was only—

JAMBART, *to* VIRGINIE. It's true, ain't it? You are getting married?

VIRGINIE. Well, the fact is . . . I was at the city hall this morning, but—

MADAME JAMBART, *cutting in.* But the church wedding hasn't taken place yet!

JAMBART. Wonderful! I'll be there. I wouldn't miss it for anything. (*To* VIRGINIE.) And who's the lucky devil?

VIRGINIE. Monsieur Barillon, but—

MADAME JAMBART, *frantically.* But . . . but he's the only one!

JAMBART, *surprised.* What?

MADAME JAMBART. I said: "He's the only one!"

JAMBART. What are you talking about, "the only one"? You want her to marry a whole boatload?

MADAME JAMBART. No . . . no . . .

JAMBART, *aside.* I'll be scuttled if the old girl ain't been blowed off her course! (*Aloud.*) Well let's have a look at this Barillon. Where's he at?

MADAME JAMBART, *pointing to the door, up right.* In there. (*Aside.*) Oh well, he'll have to find out sooner or later. Let Barillon tell him.

JAMBART, *moving to the door and calling.* Barillon! Barillon! (*Trying to open the door.*) Open up!

BARILLON'S VOICE. No! Go away! Go away!

JAMBART, *pulling the door open.* There we go!

BARILLON, *appearing, obviously disconcerted.* Ugh!

JAMBART, *pulling* BARILLON *by the hand despite his efforts to resist.* Come on, matey, you're one of the family now.

They arrive center stage.

BARILLON. What? You mean—

JAMBART. Sure, I know all about it.

BARILLON. You . . . You know? (*To* MADAME JAMBART.) You told him?

MADAME JAMBART. Well, yes and no.

JAMBART, *to* MADAME JAMBART. What do you mean, yes and no? (*To* BARILLON.) Sure she did. She told me all about the wedding. (*To* MADAME JAMBART.) Didn't you?

MADAME JAMBART. Yes.

BARILLON. And . . . and you didn't mind?

JAMBART. Me . . . mind? Why should I mind? I'm tickled pink! Always nice to have another one in the family.

BARILLON, *aside.* Now that's damn broad-minded of him!

JAMBART. You'll see what a fine little crew we'll all be! Give a little, take a little . . . and everybody's happy. Right?

BARILLON. Of course! Of course! And besides, it won't be for long.

JAMBART. What?

BARILLON. Well, you see, I married her, but . . . Don't worry, we'll get a divorce as soon as possible.

JAMBART. Divorce? Divorce? What are you raving about? Married this morning and you already want a divorce?

BARILLON, *aside.* He wants me to keep her?

JAMBART. Virginie'll make a wonderful little wife. Couldn't ask for any better!

BARILLON. Who?

JAMBART. Virginie! Your wife. Who do you think?

BARILLON. Oh, my God, he doesn't know! (*Aside, to* MADAME JAMBART.) I thought you told him.

MADAME JAMBART. I tried, really I did. It just wouldn't come out.

JAMBART, *puzzled.* Hey, you two, what's going on?

MADAME JAMBART, *aside to* BARILLON. Go ahead, be brave. Tell him!

BARILLON. What? You want me—

MADAME JAMBART, *to* JAMBART. Monsieur Barillon has something very important to say.

BARILLON. Oh, there's no hurry!

MADAME JAMBART, *aside to* BARILLON. Go on, now's the time!

JAMBART. What is it? I'm listening.

BARILLON. Well, it's like this. In life . . . The . . . There . . . We . . . (*Abruptly.*) Tell me, did you have a pleasant trip?

MADAME JAMBART *and* VIRGINIE. What?

JAMBART. That's all you wanted to say?

BARILLON. Yes, yes.

JAMBART. Hm! Very important!

MADAME JAMBART, *to* BARILLON. Go on!

BARILLON, *aside to* MADAME JAMBART. Leave me alone. I'm working up to it gradually.

JAMBART. You want to know about my trip? Well, it was some adventure, I'm telling you!

BARILLON. Fine! Tell us about it. Go ahead, go ahead. Take your time!

MADAME JAMBART, *aside to* BARILLON. But when are you going to tell him?

BARILLON, *aside to* MADAME JAMBART. Later . . . Soon . . . You'll see. I'm waiting for the right moment. You don't just go up to someone like that and tell them: "Oh, by the way, I married your wife!" There's a right way to do everything. (*To* JAMBART.) You were saying . . . about your adventure . . .

JAMBART, *straddling the chair, down left.* Well, you know how it began . . . Just another fishing trip, like all the others. But during the trip we lost our ship—

BARILLON, *laughing foolishly.* Ha ha! That's nice!

JAMBART, *surprised.* What?

BARILLON. I mean, it's like a poem. "During the trip, we lost our ship!"

JAMBART. Hm! (*Aside.*) He's balmy, this son-in-law of mine! (*Continuing.*) Anyway, there we were. I'll never forget it. All of a sudden, there's a crash, and then everybody yelling from all sides.

VIRGINIE *and* MADAME JAMBART, *horrified.* Oh!

JAMBART. And then, water . . . water everywhere!

BARILLON, *smiling stupidly.* It must have been the ocean.

JAMBART. That's right! (*Aside.*) Absolutely balmy! (*Continuing.*) I was sinking, sinking . . . down, down, down . . . And then, what do you know . . . There I was going up again, up to the surface. I looked all around. The water was still there—

BARILLON. Oh? It was still there?

JAMBART. Yes, matey, it was still there, churning up like a tea kettle, believe me! Waves everywhere . . . everywhere! And nothing left of the boat. There I was, all alone in the middle of the ocean. What a spot to be in! For a minute I just stood still, tearing my hair . . .

BARILLON. You were standing on something?

JAMBART. Of course not! I was in the middle of the damn ocean!

BARILLON. Oh, I thought . . . You said you stood still, tearing your hair, and I thought . . .

JAMBART. I was floating, matey . . . I was floating and tearing my hair at the same time.

BARILLON. Oh, I see! Of course! (*To* MADAME JAMBART.) You see, he was floating, but every once in a while he would stop and tear his hair. I see.

JAMBART. I swum for an hour, at least. Believe me, I was getting mighty sick of all that water! Then out of nowhere, I see this desert island, a good twenty miles away.

MADAME JAMBART. How could you tell it was a desert island?

JAMBART, *as if it were`the most obvious answer in the world.* There wasn't nobody on it. (*Continuing.*) So I says to myself: "That's for me!" And I sets my course for dry land. But first I stops for a minute because my clothes and everything is so wet—

BARILLON. Was it raining?

JAMBART. Raining? No! I'm in the water, remember?

BARILLON. Oh, I see. They were on you . . . I see . . .

JAMBART, *aside*. Where'd she ever dig him up? (*Continuing.*) And so I stops for a minute and rips off my clothes.

MADAME JAMBART, *suddenly*. Oh, of course! That explains everything. That's why they thought you drowned.

JAMBART. What?

MADAME JAMBART. Your clothes and all your papers were washed up on the coast of Newfoundland.

JAMBART. Really? Well, lucky for them! If I knew that I never would have left them!

BARILLON. Well anyway, there you were . . .

JAMBART. There I was, headed for the desert island. Exactly seven hours later, by the clock . . .

BARILLON, *aside, puzzled*. Clock? What clock?

JAMBART. . . . I was dragging these old bones up on the beach.

> *He gets up and replaces the*
> *chair against the table.*

MADAME JAMBART. You were saved!

JAMBART. Saved! But that was only the beginning. Two years on the island, all alone, no food, no shelter . . . I damn near starved to death!

MADAME JAMBART. How horrible!

BARILLON. Absolutely horrible! Two years without food? (*To* VIRGINIE.) Go get Monsieur Jambart something to eat.

JAMBART. No, no. Don't bother, I'm fine—

VIRGINIE, *leaving up left*. I'll see what I can find.

BARILLON. Yes, anything. Any old scraps. Anything at all.

JAMBART, *continuing his story*. Ah! I'm telling you, it

wasn't easy. Two years like that! But the toughest part was being alone. Oh, Hildegarde . . . Hildegarde . . . Just you and me, we could have filled that island up in no time. All by myself, I couldn't do much about it!

BARILLON. Of course!

JAMBART. But all that's over now. I'm back! (*He stretches out his arms toward* MADAME JAMBART.) Sweetie-pie!

He embraces her.

BARILLON, *aside.* And what am I suposed to do?

JAMBART, *to* MADAME JAMBART. By the way, I forgot to ask you. Do we have a baby?

MADAME JAMBART. No.

JAMBART. Too bad! Misdeal! We'll have to try again.

BARILLON. Try again?

MADAME JAMBART, *aside to* BARILLON. For goodness' sake, this can't go on! You'll have to tell him!

BARILLON, *aside to* MADAME JAMBART. But . . . but . . . Just like that?

MADAME JAMBART, *aside to* BARILLON. You must!

BARILLON, *aside to* MADAME JAMBART, *determined.* You're right, I must! (*He approaches* JAMBART.) Monsieur Jambart!

JAMBART. What is it matey?

BARILLON, *laughing foolishly.* Ha ha ha!

JAMBART. What is it? What's so funny? (*Aside.*) He's a pleasant one! Looney, but pleasant.

BARILLON. Well, I was just thinking. What if . . . Well, I mean, you came back so unexpectedly . . . What if . . . After all, it would be possible . . . Wouldn't it?

JAMBART. What? What?

BARILLON. If . . . if your wife . . . After all, she didn't know. She thought you were dead, didn't she? So, I was thinking, what if she . . . What if you came back and she was married to someone else? What would you think about it?

JAMBART, *giving him a good-natured tap in the stomach.*

Ha! That's a good one. You are a joker after all!

BARILLON. Ha ha!

JAMBART. What would I think about it? Well, I'll tell you. I wouldn't think twice—

BARILLON, *delighted.* You wouldn't? You mean—

JAMBART. I wouldn't think twice about it matey. Whichever one came my way first, I'd slice 'em up into little bits and feed 'em to the sharks!

MADAME JAMBART *and* BARILLON, *instinctively withdrawing.* What?

BARILLON, *to* MADAME JAMBART, *pushing her ahead of him.* You . . . You go first! You—

JAMBART. And I'd boil the other one in oil!

BARILLON, *cringing.* Oh, my God!

JOSÉPHINE, *at the vestibule door.* His Honor, Monsieur Planturel.

BARILLON, *shaking.* The mayor? I've gone out! I'm not at home!

MADAME JAMBART. No! We're not in!

> *They move upstage.*

JAMBART. What?

PLANTUREL, *entering, up center.* What do you mean, you're not in?

BARILLON *and* MADAME JAMBART, *pushing him out.* No! No! Go away!

PLANTUREL, *forcing his way in.* For heaven's sake, let me in!

BARILLON. Well! My, my! What a nice surprise! Good of you to stop by. Too bad you can't stay. Come again soon.

> *He tries unsuccessfully to push* PLANTUREL *out the door.*

PLANTUREL. I beg your pardon!

BARILLON, *aside to* PLANTUREL. Shhh! (*To* JAMBART, *taking his arm.*) Come, let's go for a walk!

PLANTUREL. Now just a minute! Just a minute! I have to talk to you about the wedding.

BARILLON, *shouting over his voice.* Yes, yes! (*Forcing a laugh, very loud.*) Ha ha ha!

PLANTUREL. No matter what we do, we can't avoid the scandal. Everyone is talking about it!

JAMBART. What scandal?

BARILLON, *aside.* Won't he shut up?

MADAME JAMBART. I'm going to faint!

PLANTUREL. So the best thing is to go right ahead and get an annulment.

BARILLON. Of course, of course. That's fine. Let's leave it at that. Good-bye!

PLANTUREL. What do you mean, "Let's leave it at that"?

JAMBART. Annulment? Whose annulment?

PLANTUREL, *pointing to* MADAME JAMBART. Hers, of course! I married her this morning . . .

JAMBART. What?

PLANTUREL. . . . to Monsieur Barillon.

JAMBART. Barillon!!!

> *He emits a savage roar.*
> BARILLON *and* MADAME JAM-
> BART *look at each other,*
> *terrified.*

PLANTUREL, *to* JAMBART. What's the matter?

JAMBART, *going up to* PLANTUREL, *who shields himself with the dummy.* You! You married my wife to Barillon? (*Going over to* BARILLON, *who crawls under the table.*) You married my wife? (*Going up to* MADAME JAMBART, *who tries to hide behind the couch.*) You married Barillon? . . . I'll kill you all! I'll kill you! Every one of you!

> *Another roar.*

BARILLON, MADAME JAMBART *and* PLANTUREL, *aghast.* Ohhh!

> *At that moment* JOSÉPHINE
> *enters, carrying the seal in*

her arms. JAMBART, *still
roaring, grabs it by the tail,
striking out blindly with it
in all directions, as the
animal cries "Papa,
Mamma."* VIRGINIE *appears,
up left, carrying a tray of
food, and terrified by the
sight, drops everything to the
floor. The curtain falls on a
scene of wild confusion.*

ACT THREE

*The drawing room of a country house, at Bois-Colombes, deco-
rated in pseudo-Japanese style. Upstage center, a pair of
French doors leading onto the garden. Down right,* BARIL-
LON's *room; down left,* JAMBART's. *Up right, a door leading
to the rest of the house. Up left,* MADAME JAMBART's
*quarters. On each side of the French doors, a bamboo chair.
To the right of the French doors, a bamboo table; to the left,
a Japanese console table. Occasional tables ad lib., set with
various Japanese furnishings, lamps, etc. Downstage, in
front of the footlights, on both sides of the stage, a pair of
bamboo armchairs.*

PLANTUREL, *entering from the garden, preceded by* JO-
SÉPHINE. You say they're not at home?

JOSÉPHINE. No, Monsieur. Madame and her husbands
have gone out for the evening.

PLANTUREL. Hm! That is annoying! Oh, by the way, you
didn't receive a telegram for me, by any chance?

JOSÉPHINE. Here, Monsieur? At Bois-Colombes?

PLANTUREL. Yes, I knew I was coming here so I gave this
address.

JOSÉPHINE. No, Monsieur. No telegrams.

PLANTUREL. Damnation! Then that means the case didn't come up today.

JOSÉPHINE. What case, Monsieur?

PLANTUREL. The annulment. It was supposed to be acted on this afternoon.

JOSÉPHINE. Oh, I think Monsieur is mistaken. I heard them say it isn't coming up for another week at least.

PLANTUREL. Another week? Oh, my! (*He begins pacing back and forth.*) Tell me, whatever made them move way out here? You're a hundred miles from nowhere!

JOSÉPHINE. Really, Monsieur, it wasn't my idea.

PLANTUREL, *sitting in the armchair, stage right.* No, I don't suppose it was. Whoever heard of such a thing? Coming way out to the country in the middle of April! And in this weather! Why, it's freezing out here!

JOSÉPHINE. But Monsieur, we had to go somewhere! We couldn't stay in Paris. They were making our life miserable.

PLANTUREL. Who? What do you mean?

JOSÉPHINE. Well, when Monsieur Jambart came back, you remember . . . When he found out about his wife and Monsieur Barillon—

PLANTUREL. He wanted to kill everybody, I remember!

JOSÉPHINE. That's right. Well, his bark was worse than his bite. He didn't kill anybody at all. He calmed down quick enough and they all decided to sit back and wait for the annulment. So, that's what they're doing, all three of them.

PLANTUREL. All three of them? You mean they're all living together?

JOSÉPHINE. Yes, Monsieur. Only it isn't like it sounds. They've got rules.

PLANTUREL. I see! Of course that still doesn't explain what you're all doing out here in the country.

JOSÉPHINE. I told you, Monsieur. We just couldn't stay in Paris another minute. As soon as everybody in the neighborhood found out about Madame and her two husbands . . . Well, take the grocer, for instance. I was talking to him the very next day, and he says to me: "You know, it's disgusting, that's what it is!"

PLANTUREL. No! The grocer said that?

JOSÉPHINE. Yes! And then one fine day the landlord says we have to move. He says he's not going to rent his apartment to a pack of Orientals.

PLANTUREL. Well, I suppose things are better out here.

JOSÉPHINE. Better? Ha! We've been here a week, and already they're pointing at us. Wherever they go, Madame and her husbands, all the little children follow them around. They've even made up a song about them.

PLANTUREL. A song?

JOSÉPHINE. Yes, it goes like this: (*Singing.*)

> A lady in town, so they claim,
> Is living in sin and in shame.
> Two husbands she weds,
> So she straddles two beds.
> "Colossus of Rhodes" is her name!

PLANTUREL, *getting up, laughing.* Not bad!

JOSÉPHINE. I'm telling you, Monsieur, everybody's singing it. It's even worse than Paris! Believe me, I'm fed up. I'm going to find a decent job somewhere.

PLANTUREL. And how is Madame Jambart taking all this? Having two husbands, I mean.

JOSÉPHINE. Her? You can imagine! She has two husbands, but she might as well have none, for all the good it does her! She can't be a wife to either one of them!

PLANTUREL. You mean Jambart hasn't insisted on . . . on his rights?

JOSÉPHINE. How can he? Those are the rules. After all, Monsieur Barillon has "rights" too. She's married to both of them, isn't she? (*Putting her hands on her hips.*) If she goes to . . . If she lets . . . Well, I mean, where would that put the other one?

PLANTUREL. Right behind a pair of horns!

JOSÉPHINE. You see what I mean, Monsieur!

PLANTUREL, *beginning to pace back and forth again, looking at his watch.* Well, all this is very interesting, I'm sure, but I do wish they'd hurry up. Where did you say they were?

JOSÉPHINE. They went to the theater. There's a show in town and the director sent Madame some tickets. He's the first gentleman we've met the whole time we've been out here.

PLANTUREL. Will it be over very late?

JOSÉPHINE. Oh no, Monsieur. They should be back any minute. (*Tinkle of the bell.*) See! There they are now. I'll go let them in.

JOSÉPHINE leaves, up right.

PLANTUREL, *following* JOSÉPHINE *with his eyes as she opens the unseen door offstage.* Hm! I guess not!

JOSÉPHINE, *entering with* BRIGOT. No, Monsieur. They're not here.

BRIGOT. Of all the luck! And I've come all this way just to see them.

JOSÉPHINE. But they won't be long. (*Pointing to* PLANTUREL.) Monsieur is waiting for them too.

BRIGOT, *recognizing* PLANTUREL. Well, Your Honor! This is a surprise! (JOSÉPHINE *leaves, up right.*) So we meet again!

PLANTUREL, *nodding politely to* BRIGOT, *but without recognizing him.* Monsieur!

BRIGOT. I take it you've been well since I saw you last?

PLANTUREL. Fine! Fine! (*Aside.*) Who the devil is he?

BRIGOT. You don't recognize me, do you?

PLANTUREL, *sitting down.* Of course, of course! (*Aside.*) My tailor? . . . My grocer? . . .

BRIGOT. The last time you asked me to show you . . . (*He makes a few quick passes with an imaginary sword.*) some moves . . . Remember?

PLANTUREL, *misunderstanding, aside.* Some shoes? Hm! Must be my shoemaker. (*To* BRIGOT.) Yes, my good man. Of course!

BRIGOT, *punctuating his question with the same imaginary passes.* Well, is everything . . . all right?

PLANTUREL, *aside.* Poor chap! What a strange tic! (*Aloud.*) I beg your pardon?

BRIGOT, *same as before.* I said: "Is everything all right?"

PLANTUREL. Well, as a matter of fact, I'm very glad to run into you.

BRIGOT. Oh?

PLANTUREL. Yes. First of all, I'm sure I ordered them in calfskin, but they're in kid. (*Pointing to his shoes.*) See?

BRIGOT. Hm! You don't say! (*Aside.*) Now what's that supposed to mean?

PLANTUREL, *standing, and making* BRIGOT *feel his shoes.* And besides, just feel this instep.

BRIGOT, *recoiling slightly.* Really, I'd rather not, if it's all the same.

PLANTUREL. Go ahead. You'll see what I mean.

BRIGOT, *aside.* If it makes him happy! (*Touching* PLANTUREL's *shoe. Aloud.*) Yes, I see! Very interesting! You know, it's funny, with me it's never the instep. It's always the toe that's too tight.

PLANTUREL, *moving upstage.* Oh, you! Who cares about *your* shoes!

BRIGOT, *aside, moving stage left.* That's a good one! And I'm supposed to give a good goddamn about his!

PLANTUREL. My maid will bring my shoes around in the morning.

BRIGOT. Fine! (*Aside.*) Better humor him!

> JOSÉPHINE *enters, as* PLAN-
> TUREL *moves to leave.*

JOSÉPHINE, *to* PLANTUREL. Are you leaving, Monsieur?

PLANTUREL. Yes, I'll go meet them at the theater. (*To* BRIGOT.) Good night. You will take care of it first thing, won't you?

BRIGOT, *as if to humor him.* Of course! Of course!

PLANTUREL. Thank you.

> *He leaves, up right.* BRIGOT *watches him go, scratches his head for a moment, then shrugs his shoulders.*

BRIGOT, *to* JOSÉPHINE. Say, you! Tell me something. How are the newlyweds getting along?

JOSÉPHINE. The newlyweds, Monsieur?

BRIGOT. Yes. They've been married now for three weeks, and I haven't heard a word from them.

JOSÉPHINE. Who, Monsieur?

BRIGOT. Why, my nephew and his pretty little wife.

JOSÉPHINE, *half aloud and half to herself.* Pretty little wife!

BRIGOT. That's what I said! And I suppose you don't think Virginie is as pretty as they come?

JOSÉPHINE. Oh yes, Monsieur! She's pretty all right!

BRIGOT. Well, then, what are you talking about? . . . And how's he getting along with her mother?

JOSÉPHINE. Who, Monsieur?

BRIGOT. My nephew, Barillon! Is he satisfied with her?

JOSÉPHINE. With her mother, Monsieur?

BRIGOT. Yes, Virginie's mother.

JOSÉPHINE. Oh, then you do know all about it! Well, they don't get along as good as they should . . .

BRIGOT. Hm! Just what I thought. It's always the mother that makes all the trouble.

JOSÉPHINE. For example, Monsieur, they sleep in different rooms.

BRIGOT. Who?

JOSÉPHINE. Monsieur Barillon.

BRIGOT. And Virginie?

JOSÉPHINE. Oh no, Monsieur. Her mother.

BRIGOT. Her mother! Well, I should hope so! That's all they need!

JOSÉPHINE. Maybe you think so, Monsieur, but I don't think it's very nice. If I was her I wouldn't like it one bit!

BRIGOT, *aside, moving stage right.* Talk about the help you get nowadays! (*Aloud.*) Tell me, is my room ready?

JOSÉPHINE. Not yet, Monsieur.

BRIGOT, *moving upstage.* Well, what are you waiting for? I might not look it, but I'm dead on my feet!

JOSÉPHINE. Oh yes, Monsieur. You look it!

BRIGOT. What?

JOSÉPHINE. Nothing, Monsieur. I'll go get your room ready. If you want to lie down, Monsieur, there's a couch in there.

> *She points to the door, down left.* BRIGOT *leaves by the same door.* JOSÉPHINE *is about to leave too when* PATRICE *enters from the garden.*

PATRICE. Pssst! Pssst!

JOSÉPHINE. Monsieur Patrice! What are you doing here?

PATRICE. They're out tonight, aren't they?

JOSÉPHINE. Yes, but—

PATRICE. I must see Mademoiselle Virginie!

JOSÉPHINE. But . . . you can't. She's asleep. She has a headache.

PATRICE. That's all right. Show me where her room is.

JOSÉPHINE. But Monsieur—

PATRICE. And don't argue with me! I've come all this way and I'm going to see her. It's my last chance!

JOSÉPHINE. But Monsieur Barillon said that if you ever showed your face here we should throw you out the window, head first!

PATRICE. Oh he did, did he? Well, he doesn't frighten me! I don't care what he said! (*At that moment a general uproar is heard outside, followed by several desperate peals of the garden bell.*) My God, what's that?

JOSÉPHINE. It sounds like they're back. I'd better go open up.

She leaves, upstage center.

PATRICE. They're back? Oh! Where can I hide?

He rushes offstage, down right. For a moment the stage remains empty. Outside the crowd can be heard singing the song about MADAME JAMBART, *of which the last line particularly is clearly audible: "Colossus of Rhodes is her name!" At that moment* BARILLON, JAMBART *and* MADAME JAMBART *enter frantically from the garden, one after another, their clothing in disarray. They stand for several moments in the center of the stage, trying to catch their breath.*

BARILLON, *to* JOSÉPHINE, *as she enters.* Joséphine! Shut the gate! Shut the gate!

JAMBART. Batten down the hatches! Hurry it up! Step lively!

JOSÉPHINE. I'm going! I'm going!

She leaves once again, upstage center.

MADAME JAMBART. Oh my, my, my! What a night! My God! What a night!

BARILLON. It's a disgrace!

JAMBART. Worse than in Paris!

99

BARILLON. Just look at us!

MADAME JAMBART, *moving upstage and removing her hat.* They would have cut us to ribbons!

BARILLON. And did you see all those apples? You go try to buy some and the grocer never has any. Never mind! They found plenty to throw at us.

JAMBART, *to* BARILLON. A fat lot of complaining you should be doing! Who told you to take them damn tickets in the first place?

BARILLON. Me? Sure, blame it on me! You were the one who kept saying, "Let's go! Let's go!"

JAMBART. Sure, because you said you wanted to. I thought I'd be nice to you.

BARILLON. Very nice! Thank you! God, what a night!

MADAME JAMBART. And imagine that director. (*To* BARILLON.) I hope you'll give him a piece of your mind! What a nerve, writing on all those posters: "Added Attraction, Tonight Only, the Bigamist of Bois-Colombes."

BARILLON. I should hope I'll go give him a piece of my mind!

JAMBART. Both of us, matey. We'll each give him half a piece.

MADAME JAMBART. "The Bigamist of Bois-Colombes"! If I knew that, we never would have gone.

BARILLON. And we wouldn't have missed anything. A nice reception they gave us when we came in: "There they are! Kick 'em out! Kick 'em out!" And all those things they began throwing . . . chairs, oranges . . .

JAMBART. And damn rotten ones to boot!

BARILLON. It's a disgrace! Don't they have any police here?

JAMBART. Police? Who do you think was heaving all them apples?

BARILLON. No!

MADAME JAMBART. And that song! Oh, that horrible song!

JAMBART. I thought them brats would never shut up.

> JOSÉPHINE *enters up right*
> *and begins placing a table*
> *cloth on the bamboo table.*

BARILLON. A nice thing for Hildegarde to have to listen to!

JOSÉPHINE, *singing to herself without realizing it.* "Colossus of Rhodes is her name!"

MADAME JAMBART. Fine! Now we're even singing it ourselves. (*To* JOSÉPHINE.) What are you doing?

JOSÉPHINE. May I serve the chocolate, Madame?

MADAME JAMBART. Oh, I should say so! After all I've been through I can use it. And bring the tea, too, if its ready.

> JOSÉPHINE *leaves, up right.*

BARILLON. And what about me? You think I'm enjoying this?

JAMBART. Damn lucky it'll all be over in a week!

MADAME JAMBART. Patience, patience. (*Noticing* JOSÉPHINE *enter with a tray.*) Ah! (*To* BARILLON *and* JAMBART.) Bring over the table, will you?

JAMBART, *to* BARILLON, *without moving.* The table!

BARILLON, *to* JAMBART. That's right. Go get it.

JAMBART. Go get it yourself!

BARILLON. Why me?

JAMBART. All right! We'll both get it.

> *They carry the table down-*
> *stage, placing it between the*
> *two armchairs at the edge of*
> *the stage.* MADAME JAMBART
> *moves upstage and gets a*
> *chair, which she brings over*
> *to the table.*

MADAME JAMBART, *to* JOSÉPHINE. You can leave the tray right here.

JOSÉPHINE. Yes, Madame.

> *She puts down the tray,*
> *then goes upstage and brings*
> *another chair to the table.*

> MADAME JAMBART *and the*
> *two men sit in the arm-*
> *chairs;* JAMBART *is stage left*
> *of the table,* BARILLON *stage*
> *right, both seated in profile.*
> MADAME JAMBART *sits facing*
> *the audience, next to*
> JAMBART, *with a space*
> *next to her for* VIRGINIE.

Now I have to tell Madame that Madame will have to find someone else. I'm giving my notice.

JAMBART *and* BARILLON. What?

MADAME JAMBART. Aren't you happy here?

JOSÉPHINE. It's not that, Madame . . . You understand. I'll be wanting to get married some day, and . . . I've got to watch out for my reputation, that's all.

MADAME JAMBART, *preparing to pour the tea.* So?

JOSÉPHINE. Well, Madame, I was talking to some of my relatives, and . . . Well, they don't think it's such a good idea to stay in a place where all three of you . . . You see what I mean, don't you Madame?

MADAME JAMBART. Why, I never . . . You, of all people! I've known you to have three or four affairs going at the same time!

JOSÉPHINE. That's right, Madame, but mine weren't legal.

BARILLON. Charming!

MADAME JAMBART. All right! We accept your notice. Now go tell my daughter we're back.

JOSÉPHINE, *leaving up right.* Very good, Madame.

MADAME JAMBART, *after* JOSÉPHINE's *exit.* Isn't that lovely! Even the help is deserting us.

JAMBART. Hey, where's the chocolate?

BARILLON. Right in front of you.

> JAMBART *takes the pitcher*
> *of chocolate, holding it in*
> *his hand during the next*
> *few replies.*

VIRGINIE, *entering up right.* Good evening, Mother. (*She*

kisses MADAME JAMBART.) Did you all have a pleasant time?

BARILLON. Ha! She should only know!

VIRGINIE, *going over to* JAMBART *and offering a cheek.* Good evening, Daddy! (JAMBART *kisses her affectionately without replying. She then moves around the table to* BARILLON, *offering the same cheek that* JAMBART *has just kissed.*) Good evening, Daddy!

BARILLON, *about to kiss her, but changing his mind.* No! That's Jambart's cheek.

> He kisses her on the other cheek.

MADAME JAMBART, *to* VIRGINIE, *who sits down beside her.* What would you like, darling, tea or chocolate?

VIRGINIE. Tea, please.

> MADAME JAMBART *pours the tea for herself and* VIRGINIE. JAMBART, *still holding the pitcher of chocolate, serves himself as slowly and deliberately as possible, stopping every few seconds to smell the chocolate, in an attempt to frustrate the obviously impatient* BARILLON.

BARILLON, *folding his arms, to* JAMBART. Let me know when you're through sniffing the chocolate!

JAMBART, *looking up, unruffled.* When I'm through? Is this a race or something? You want to make a pig of yourself?

BARILLON. Never mind! Just hurry up!

> Seeing that JAMBART is still procrastinating, he takes a piece of bread, rips it in half, and begins to butter it.

JAMBART, *putting down the pitcher silently and picking up a piece of bread, which he then proceeds to break in two.* And look who was in such a damn hurry for the chocolate, will you! Been standing there for an hour and he don't even take it! Just wanted to pick on me!

MADAME JAMBART. Now, now! Boys!

BARILLON. Well I can't do two things at once, can I?

> JAMBART, *who has finished breaking his bread, reaches with his knife to pick up a pat of butter in the butter dish.* BARILLON *does likewise, simultaneously reaching for the same pat.*

JAMBART. Well, make up your mind. Which one do you want? Do you have to go sticking your knife in every blooming piece?

MADAME JAMBART. Boys, please!

BARILLON, *to* MADAME JAMBART. But Hildegarde, every time I reach for a piece he takes it off my knife.

JAMBART. Go on! Choose! . . . You can't say I ain't trying to be reasonable.

BARILLON, *angrily pushing aside the butter dish with his knife.* Here, damn it! Take it all!

MADAME JAMBART. Oh, these meals! These meals! And they say three people can live together under one roof!

JAMBART, *tasting the chocolate and making a grimace.* Pouah! That stinks!

> *He pours what is left in his cup into the pitcher.*

BARILLON, *who has stood up and watched the action with amazement.* Now that's what I call fine manners!

JAMBART. What's the matter? Ain't you got yours yet?

BARILLON, *showing his empty cup.* What do you think? And even if I had! Do you always pour your drinks back after you taste them?

JAMBART. So what? You think I'm a leper or something?

BARILLON. God! Where was he brought up? (*To* MADAME JAMBART.) I'll have tea!

MADAME JAMBART, *to* VIRGINIE. Pour the tea, darling.

VIRGINIE, *serving* BARILLON. It's really very good. I know you'll like it.

MADAME JAMBART. The grocer said it was the very best. It's called "Desert Fragrance."

> BARILLON *sips the tea.*

JAMBART. That's just because it tastes like camel—

BARILLON, *spitting a mouthful back into the cup.* Pouah! (*He slams the cup down on the table in disgust.*) Now look, just because you don't like it do you have to spoil it for everyone else?

MADAME JAMBART, *in a commanding tone.* Please! These meals are absolutely impossible! Can't we talk about anything else?

VIRGINIE, *coming to the rescue with another subject of conversation.* Did you all sleep well last night?

BARILLON. Who?

JAMBART. Like a top.

BARILLON. Ha! Speak for yourself! I didn't shut my eyes. That damn seal of yours kept me up with his yapping. All night: "Papa, Mamma, Mamma, Papa." That's all I heard.

JAMBART. Well, what do you expect from him, a lecture?

BARILLON. No, I don't expect anything! I just expect him to shut up and let me sleep! That's what I expect!

JAMBART, *to the others.* See, always thinking of himself!

> *Everyone rises from the table.*

MADAME JAMBART, *to* JOSÉPHINE, *who has just entered up right.* Take this away, Joséphine.

JOSÉPHINE. Yes, Madame.

> *She leaves by the same door, taking with her the tray and its contents wrapped in the tablecloth.*

MADAME JAMBART, *to the two men.* The table, please.

> *The two men look at each
> other.*

JAMBART, *to* BARILLON, *with a gesture.* The table.

BARILLON, *same gesture.* That's right. You heard her.

JAMBART. Why me?

MADAME JAMBART, *to* JAMBART. Go ahead, Emile, you be
the sensible one.

JAMBART. We'll both take it.

> *They pick up the table, each
> by an end. After a few
> steps* BARILLON *drops his
> end.*

JAMBART. Well?

BARILLON. I always have to do everything around here.
You do a little work for a change!

> JAMBART *grudgingly takes
> the table back to its original
> position upstage, while*
> BARILLON *lights his cigarette.*

MADAME JAMBART. Virginie, come be a darling and help
me out of these clothes.

> MADAME JAMBART *and*
> VIRGINIE *leave, up left.* JAM-
> BART, *noticing that* BARILLON
> *has begun to smoke, sniffs
> the air as if to find fault
> with the odor.* BARILLON
> *intentionally blows a few
> puffs his way.*

JAMBART, *coughing.* Hum! Hum!

BARILLON. What's the matter? Did you catch cold?

JAMBART, *taking a clay pipe from his pocket and putting
it in his mouth.* No. It's just that damn oriental junk
you're smoking. It makes me sick.

> *He takes a tobacco pouch
> from his other pocket and
> fills the pipe.*

BARILLON. Then why are you smoking, may I ask?

JAMBART. To get rid of the smell.

BARILLON. Very smart! I thought you didn't like the smoke.

JAMBART, *packing down the tobacco.* Oh, with me it's different. At least this is French tobacco I'm smoking. Good patriotic tobacco.

BARILLON, *sitting in the armchair, down right.* Of course!

JAMBART, *moving upstage.* Damn right! You don't see me making them Turks rich.

BARILLON. Ha! That's a good one! Do I look like a man who's making the Turks rich? Do I?

JAMBART, *ignoring the question.* Nothing like a good pipe and lots of fresh air.

> *He opens the French doors*
> *and lights his pipe.*

BARILLON, *suddenly chilled.* What are you doing? It isn't summer, you know!

JAMBART. Us sailors like plenty of fresh salt air. Gives you good strong lungs. (*He takes several deep breaths at the open doors.*) Nothing like that clean salt air!

BARILLON, *getting up and going over to close the doors himself.* Sure! Do you know where you are? A fat lot of salt air you're going to get out here!

JAMBART, *moving down left.* All right! You can go choke in this hole if you want to. I'm going to bed. See! I'm always giving in!

BARILLON. That's right, you go to bed. (*Aside, between his teeth.*) And don't bother to get up!

JAMBART. After I eat I just got to go to sleep.

> *He goes to his room.*

BARILLON. And after he sleeps he's just got to eat! (*He sniffs the air, disgustedly.*) Ugh! That damn pipe of his!

> *He opens the French doors.*

MADAME JAMBART, *entering up left in a dressing gown, followed by* VIRGINIE. What on earth are you doing?

BARILLON. I'm opening the doors. It's that other husband

of yours and his damn pipe! You can hardly breathe
in here.

MADAME JAMBART. Really, why are you always picking on
Emile?

VIRGINIE. Be careful! You know, he won't stand for it
much longer.

BARILLON. Oh, is that so? He's just a blowhard and you
know it. He was going to kill me, remember? Sure!
He's all wind, that's all. I'm not afraid of him!

JAMBART'S VOICE, *coming from his bedroom.* Hey! What
in the name of—

BARILLON, VIRGINIE, MADAME JAMBART. What is it?

> JOSÉPHINE *enters, up right.*

JAMBART, *rushing onstage in a flurry, reaching extreme
stage right.* A man! There's some damn man in my
bed!

MADAME JAMBART. A man?

JOSÉPHINE. Oh, I forgot to tell you, Madame. It's Monsieur
Brigot.

VIRGINIE. Uncle Brigot?

BRIGOT, *entering down left, in his underwear and shirtsleeves.* All right! Who's the damn fool that woke me
up? (*Noticing* BARILLON.) Oh, you're back? How are
you?

BARILLON, *flustered.* Fine, fine! But . . . just look at you!

MADAME JAMBART *and* VIRGINIE. Really!

BRIGOT. Oh! I'm sorry! I . . . I jumped right out of bed
. . . I didn't have time . . . (*Bowing ceremoniously to
the group.*) Ladies . . . gentlemen . . . if you'll excuse
me, I'll go get dressed.

BARILLON. Yes, by all means!

MADAME JAMBART. Joséphine, show Monsieur Brigot to the
guest room.

> BRIGOT *and* JOSÉPHINE
> *leave, up right.*

BARILLON, *to* JAMBART, *mockingly.* Now that's what I call

a real brave man! He finds my Uncle Brigot in his room
and he comes running out scared half to death! I could
find a dozen men in my room . . . A dozen! It wouldn't
scare me a bit! (*Pushing the door of his room open,
with bravado.*) Ha! That's a good one!

> *He enters his room, down
> right.*

JAMBART, *shrugging his shoulders.* All wind, that's him!

BARILLON, *rushing headlong from his room, to the middle
of the stage.* Help! Help! There's . . . there's a man in
my room!

MADAME JAMBART *and* VIRGINIE, *drawing back.* In your
room? Who?

BARILLON, *petrified.* I . . . I don't know!

JAMBART, *approaching* BARILLON. A dozen men, huh? Ha
ha ha!

BARILLON, *with sudden self-possession.* That's right, a
dozen! (*Shaking with fear once again.*) But one? My
God! (*Pleading with* JAMBART.) Emile . . . you . . .
you come with me.

JAMBART, *none too anxious.* Oh, all right. Come on.

BARILLON, *following him and addressing* MADAME JAMBART
and VIRGINIE. I'm telling you, he was a giant!

JAMBART, *to* BARILLON. Sure he was! Sure!

> *They get to the door, each
> one backed up against the
> wall on either side.*

BARILLON, *calling into the room.* Come out, whoever you
are!

> PATRICE *comes out of the
> room.*

MADAME JAMBART. Patrice!

BARILLON, *taken aback.* You?

JAMBART, *puzzled.* Who's this bird?

PATRICE, *unruffled, pointing to* VIRGINIE. Monsieur, I have
the honor of requesting the hand of your stepdaughter—

BARILLON. Again? Don't you ever give up? I told you once!
Never! Understand? Never! (*To* VIRGINIE.) Virginie,
leave us alone!

VIRGINIE, *leaving, up right.* Oh!

BRIGOT, *arriving by the same door, in dressing gown and
nightcap.* What's all the commotion?

> *He moves between* BARILLON
> *and* PATRICE.

BARILLON. This . . . this gentleman has the nerve to chase
Virginie all the way out here!

BRIGOT, *recognizing* PATRICE. Him! (*To* BARILLON.) But
he's the one . . . I told you, he said he was going to
sleep with your wife, but you wouldn't listen!

PATRICE, *to* BRIGOT. What are you talking about? His
wife? How can she be his wife when he's been living
with her mother?

BRIGOT. What? Her mother? (*To* BARILLON.) You're living
with her mother?

JAMBART. Not for long, believe me!

BRIGOT. My God! He's having an affair with his mother-in-
law! It's revolting!

BARILLON. My mother-in-law? What are you talking about?
My mother-in-law is dead.

BRIGOT, *looking at* MADAME JAMBART. Your mother-in-
law—

MADAME JAMBART. You mean my mother? Of course, she
passed away years ago.

BRIGOT. They're out of their minds!

JAMBART, *to* PATRICE. And what's your name, matey?

PATRICE. Patrice Surcouf.

JAMBART, *his face lighting up.* Surcouf? Did you say
Surcouf?

PATRICE. That's right.

JAMBART. Same as Robert Surcouf?

BARILLON. Who?

JAMBART. The famous privateer!

PATRICE. Yes, Monsieur. He was my grandfather.

JAMBART, *slapping him on the back.* Well, matey, that's good enough for me! Virginie is yours! And a fine couple you'll be!

PATRICE. Oh, Monsieur!

BARILLON. Now just a minute! (*To* JAMBART.) You can't do that! What right do you have? (*To* BRIGOT.) What right does he have to do that?

BRIGOT. That's what I want to know. Who the hell is he anyway?

BARILLON. Nobody! . . . That is, he's my wife's husband.

BRIGOT. Virginie's husband?

BARILLON. No, no! Madame Jambart's husband!

BRIGOT. You mean he's your father-in-law?

BARILLON, *exasperated.* What are you talking about? She's my wife! And . . . Oh! Forget it!

BRIGOT. All right! Forget it! I give up!

> *He leaves, thoroughly*
> *confused, up right.*

BARILLON, *returning to* PATRICE. Never, my friend! You understand? Never!

PATRICE, *between* BARILLON *and* JAMBART. But, Monsieur—

JAMBART, *to* PATRICE. Leave it to me, matey. You come back tomorrow. We'll fix it. She's as good as yours!

PATRICE. Good-bye. I'm leaving . . . (*Dramatically.*) with hope in my heart!

BARILLON. Never mind, just leave! That's all! And don't come back!

> *Everyone except* BARILLON
> *accompanies* PATRICE *to the*
> *door, up right, shaking his*
> *· hand and congratulating him.*

JAMBART, *returning downstage.* What a match! A Jambart and a Surcouf!

BARILLON. Oh, you think so, do you? Well, we'll see! I'm her stepfather and I refuse, absolutely!

JAMBART. Oh do you now? And how about me? I'm her stepfather too, you know! And I was her stepfather before you even showed up!

MADAME JAMBART. He's right.

BARILLON. Maybe, but as long as I'm one of Virginie's stepfathers, nobody's going to marry her but me!

JAMBART, *becoming angry.* Over my dead body!

BARILLON. With pleasure!

JOSÉPHINE, *entering with* PLANTUREL, *up right.* His Honor, Monsieur Planturel.

> *She leaves by the same door.*

BARILLON. You?

PLANTUREL. Yes, my friend, me! And I have wonderful news for all of you!

BARILLON, JAMBART, MADAME JAMBART. News? What news?

PLANTUREL. The annulment! It's official. Here's the telegram.

> *All three make a dash for
> the telegram.*

JAMBART, *reading.* "Marriage annulled. Decree to follow."

> *He moves upstage, his arms
> toward heaven in a gesture
> of gratitude, and returns
> down right.*

BARILLON, *to* PLANTUREL. Is it possible? (*To* MADAME JAMBART.) Hildegarde! (*Extending his arms, about to embrace her, then changing his mind. To* JAMBART.) May I?

JAMBART. Sure, go ahead.

> BARILLON *and* JAMBART
> *both embrace* MADAME
> JAMBART, *each kissing her
> on one cheek as she faces
> the audience.*

PLANTUREL, *aside.* Very touching! (*Aloud.*) You know, I didn't get the good news myself until just a few moments ago. The court must have decided to consider the case sooner than they expected. Anyway, all's well that ends well!

BARILLON. And now Emile . . . my good friend Emile, is back where he belongs! (*To* JAMBART, *nudging him knowingly.*) Know what I mean?

JAMBART. Ha ha! (*To* MADAME JAMBART, *with a passionate embrace.*) Sweetie-pie!

BARILLON. Isn't that nice! Come on, Planturel. You're the mayor. Let's marry them off in style!

PLANTUREL. But they're already—

BARILLON. So what? Come on!

JAMBART, *entering into the spirit.* Hildegarde, to the altar!

BARILLON. That's right! We're going to give you both a time you'll never forget. (*Calling.*) Joséphine! Brigot! (*Dramatically.*) Lights! Pomp! Splendor!

BRIGOT, *entering up right.* Again? And I was just falling asleep.

JOSÉPHINE, *entering a moment later.* Monsieur?

BARILLON, *to* JOSÉPHINE. Pomp, Joséphine, pomp!

JOSÉPHINE. Is there a fire, Monsieur?

BARILLON. What? . . . No, no, no! Pomp! Pomp! You know, lots of lights, candles, everything!

JOSÉPHINE leaves, up right.

BRIGOT. What on earth for?

BARILLON. Why, to celebrate the marriage of Hildegarde Jambart to her rightful husband, Emile Jambart! Understand?

BRIGOT stands scratching his head.

JOSÉPHINE, *entering with three candelabra, in time to hear* BARILLON's *last remarks.* Oh, you mean the marriage is annulled? Then I take back my notice.

She lights the candelabra.

BARILLON, *dramatically.* And now let us escort them to the nuptial chamber.

BRIGOT. Escort them . . . You? Her husband? Escort them . . .

BARILLON. No, no! (*Pointing to* JAMBART.) He's the husband. I'm a bachelor!

BRIGOT. A bachelor? (*Shrugging his shoulders.*) Very nice, now he's a bachelor!

> JOSÉPHINE *gives a candelabrum to* BARILLON, BRIGOT, *and* PLANTUREL. *The three men are standing in a line in front of the French doors with* BARILLON *in the middle, while* JAMBART *and* MADAME JAMBART *stand far right.*

BARILLON. Everybody! Ready?

> BARILLON *begins singing the melody of the Wedding March from* Lohengrin *and is soon joined by* PLANTUREL *and* BRIGOT. *During the singing* JAMBART *takes* MADAME JAMBART's *hand and they advance slowly. When they arrive before* BARILLON, *he steps out of line and precedes them into the room, up left.* PLANTUREL *and* BRIGOT *join the procession, and the whole group enters the bedroom, from which can be heard shouts of "Long live the bride and groom." After a few moments the garden bell rings.*

JOSÉPHINE, *just as she is about to enter the bedroom also, at the end of the procession.* At this hour? Who on earth—

> *She goes to open the door.*

BRIGOT, BARILLON, PLANTUREL, *returning from the bedroom.* Good night! Sleep tight!

JAMBART, *appearing at the threshold of the bedroom.* And listen, you! No tricks! It ain't the first time, you know.

BARILLON. Don't worry.

JAMBART. Good night.

> *He closes the door and the key can be heard turning.*

BARILLON, *shouting through the door with the mock solicitude of a father who has just married off a daughter.* Be good to her!

JAMBART'S VOICE. Leave that to me, matey!

BARILLON. Now another chorus, everyone.

> *While singing, they all cross over, up right, to leave.* BRIGOT *leaves, but the rest of the group is stopped in its tracks by* JOSÉPHINE, *who enters in a flurry of excitement.*

JOSÉPHINE, *waving an envelope.* Monsieur! Monsieur!

BARILLON. What is it?

JOSÉPHINE. There's a gentleman outside. He gave me this. He says it's very important.

BARILLON. Ah! It must be the decree . . . the decree that makes me a free man!

> *He kisses the envelope.*

PLANTUREL. That's what the telegram said. "Marriage annulled. Decree to follow."

BARILLON. Beautiful decree! Lovely decree! I'll have it framed. (*He opens it.*) That's what it is. "The Court . . . etc. etc. . . . Whereas . . . etc. etc. . . . Requesting annulment of marriage . . . etc. etc. . . . Therefore, the Court declares null and void the marriage contracted between Hildegarde Barillon and . . ." Good God!

PLANTUREL. What is it?

BARILLON, *choking.* Read it! Read it!

PLANTUREL, *taking the document.* "Between Hildegarde Barillon and Emile Jambart." What? They've annulled the wrong marriage!

BARILLON. That means she's still my wife! . . . And here I was just a minute ago . . . (*He makes a dash for the door, up left, followed by* PLANTUREL.) Open the door! Open the door!

JAMBART'S VOICE. Avast, mates! Leave us alone!

PLANTUREL. In the name of the law! Open this door!

JAMBART'S VOICE. Later!

BARILLON. Not later! Now! Now!

JAMBART'S VOICE. Not a chance, matey!

BARILLON *and* PLANTUREL, *shouting.* Help! Help!

> BARILLON *runs to the French doors, opens them wide, still shouting for help.*

BRIGOT, *entering up right.* This is the damnedest place to try to get some sleep.

BARILLON. Uncle! Help me, for heaven's sake! Jambart is in there with Hildegarde.

BRIGOT. So? What did you think he was going to do, play cards? You knew he was going to—

BARILLON. But you don't understand! He's in there with my wife!

BRIGOT. Your wife? Now she's your wife, is she? And who does that make him married to?

BARILLON. He's not married at all! (*To* PLANTUREL.) Go get an ax, or a hammer, or something! Quick!

PLANTUREL. Right away!

> *He runs out, up right.*

BARILLON, *to* BRIGOT. Help me break down the door!

> *They both throw themselves against the door.*

JAMBART, *appearing in shirtsleeves, with his sailor's jacket under his arm.* Now listen, I thought I told you—

BARILLON, *lunging at him and pulling him center stage.* That's enough! Never mind what you told me!

MADAME JAMBART, *entering in a dressing gown, her hair disheveled.* Is this your idea of a joke?

BARILLON. A joke? A joke? Read this if you think it's a joke. (*He hands the decree to her and* JAMBART.) It wasn't my marriage they annulled, it was yours!

JAMBART *and* MADAME JAMBART. What?

> MADAME JAMBART *falls into the armchair, down left, hiding her face in her handkerchief.*

BARILLON, *to* JAMBART. You're not her husband, I am!

JAMBART, *placing his jacket on the back of the armchair, stage right.* You? Then what about—

BARILLON, *suddenly, to* JAMBART. Emile! Please, tell me the truth. I know it's not your fault, but . . . was I . . . were we in time?

JAMBART. What?

BARILLON. I mean, did you . . . am I . . . (*Dramatically.*) Have I been . . . wronged?

JAMBART, *back to the audience, extending his right hand to* BARILLON *and speaking as if with difficulty.* Oh, matey, I'm sorry!

BARILLON, *with a grimace.* Oh!

> *Moment of silence.*

BRIGOT, *without understanding anything of what is going on.* Touching, aren't they?

JAMBART, *suddenly moving stage right.* Well, I guess I'd better pull up anchor and be on my way.

BARILLON, MADAME JAMBART *and* BRIGOT. What?

JAMBART, *contrite.* No, after this I can't stay under the same roof as the rest of you.

MADAME JAMBART. You mean you're leaving?

JAMBART. That's right, I'm moving on. Good-bye.

> *He puts on his cap and is about to leave.*

BARILLON, *in a voice trembling with emotion.* Jambart!

JAMBART. What?

BARILLON, *handing him his jacket.* Here, you'd better take this. It's cold out.

JAMBART. Thanks.

MADAME JAMBART. But where are you going?

JAMBART. Back to my island, I guess. But don't worry, you won't never be out of my mind.

BRIGOT. "Out of his mind" is right.

JAMBART. I won't forget you.

BARILLON, *going over to a little table between the two doors, stage right, and picking up a small framed picture of himself, handing it very emotionally to* JAMBART. Emile! Here, take this. It's a picture of me.

JAMBART, *no less emotionally.* Ah! Thanks, mate. (*He embraces him.*) I'll send you mine, first thing. (*To* MADAME JAMBART, *who has begun to weep at the touching scene.*) Now, now, Hildegarde. Dry them pretty eyes. Be brave.

MADAME JAMBART, *rushing into his arms, sobbing.* Emile! (*Between sobs.*) And . . . and . . . don't forget Loulou.

JAMBART. My seal? Keep him. He'll remind you of me.

BARILLON. No, no! Please, take him with you! Please!

JAMBART, *ignoring the plea.* But I ain't going till I kiss our little Virginie good-bye. Our . . . your . . . Well, anyway—

MADAME JAMBART. Virginie! Virginie!

VIRGINIE, *entering up right, followed by* PATRICE. Mother?

MADAME JAMBART. Say good-bye to your . . . to the captain.

> VIRGINIE *kisses* JAMBART
> *dutifully on the cheek.*

BARILLON, *to* PATRICE. You again? For God's sake, do you crawl through the woodwork?

PATRICE. I just had to tell her the good news myself. About her stepfather's consent, I mean.

JAMBART. It's all off sonny. I ain't her stepfather no more.

PATRICE. No! I don't believe—

BARILLON. That's right! I'm her stepfather now. And you can just go back the way you came, understand? I've had enough of you!

> *He begins chasing* PATRICE *around the stage. As they arrive in front of the door up right,* JOSÉPHINE *comes running in, almost knocking them over.*

JOSÉPHINE. Help! The mayor is out there fighting with a burglar or something!

PLANTUREL, *entering upstage right, dragging* TOPEAU *by the necktie.* Now I've got you! Try to break through the gate, will you? (*Suddenly recognizing him.*) My God! Topeau!

BARILLON *and* MADAME JAMBART. Topeau?

TOPEAU. That's right. Topeau!

BARILLON. What's all this about? Who sent you here?

PLANTUREL. Where did you come from?

TOPEAU. From the courthouse.

BARILLON. You mean the prison, don't you?

TOPEAU. No, no! From the Clerk's Office at the Appeals Court.

PLANTUREL. The Clerk's Office?

TOPEAU. Yes, I'm working there now. At least, I was. (*Confidentially.*) You see, I still like my liquor. That's why I'm here. I went and made a terrible mistake.

PLANTUREL, BARILLON *and* MADAME JAMBART. Again?

TOPEAU. I'm afraid so. You know that annulment decree? (*Sheepishly.*) Well, I put down the wrong name.

PLANTUREL, BARILLON *and* MADAME JAMBART. What?

TOPEAU. It wasn't the Jambart marriage they annulled. It was the Barillon marriage.

BARILLON, *while the others gasp in disbelief.* I don't believe it!

TOPEAU. Here's the note from the Chief Magistrate him-

119

self. (*Handing the note to* BARILLON, *and falling to his knees in front of him.*) You will forgive me, won't you?

BARILLON. Forgive you? (*He makes him rise.*) My God, I love you!

> *He embraces* TOPEAU
> *wildly.* BRIGOT, *at a loss,*
> *lifts his arms to heaven,*
> *moving upstage along with*
> PLANTUREL.

JAMBART, *embracing* MADAME JAMBART. Hildegarde!

PATRICE, *extending his arms to* VIRGINIE. Virginie!

VIRGINIE. Patrice, darling!

BARILLON. Just a minute, you two! None of that!

PATRICE. But it's all arranged, isn't it?

BARILLON. Not on your life! I'm taking her back!

VIRGINIE. Really, Monsieur Barillon, please believe me. You've never been, and never will be, anything more than a stepfather to me.

BARILLON. Hm! I see. So that's the way it is! (*Resigned.*) Well, at least don't call me Monsieur. Let me be just plain Barillon. (*To* BRIGOT.) I guess I'm still a bachelor after all.

> *He moves center stage.*

BRIGOT, *joining him.* Now just a minute! You? A bachelor? Then who's the husband in this mess?

BARILLON, *pointing to* JAMBART. The husband? He is!

BRIGOT. You mean everything is changed?

BARILLON *and* JAMBART. Yes. It's very simple.

> *Their next lines are uttered*
> *simultaneously, producing*
> *an almost unintelligible*
> *jumble.*

BARILLON. I married my mother-in-law, but they annulled the marriage, and so now he's her husband again.

JAMBART. My wife was going to be his mother-in-law, but now it's all off, and Patrice is going to marry Virginie.

BARILLON, *alone.* Understand?

BRICOT. Not a blessed word!

JAMBART. Well, anyway, that's what happened.

BARILLON. All right, everybody. Once again!

> *He begins singing the*
> *Wedding March and is*
> *immediately joined by the*
> *rest of the company, as*
> JAMBART, *taking* MADAME
> JAMBART's *arm, leads her*
> *once again offstage, amid*
> *appropriate shouts of*
> *joviality.*

CURTAIN

Not by Bed Alone

Un Fil à la patte

CHARACTERS

BOIS-D'ENGHIEN
BOUZIN
THE GENERAL
CHENNEVIETTE
FONTANET
FIRMIN
JEAN
ANTONIO
ÉMILE
LANTERY

LUCETTE
MADAME DUVERGER
VIVIANE
MARCELINE
MISS BETTING
NINI

*The janitor, domestics, the florist,
two policemen, a gentleman, a lady,
the bride, the groom, the bride's father,
members of a wedding party*

Illustration: Feydeau in his prime

ACT ONE

LUCETTE GAUTIER's *elegantly furnished drawing room. Set diagonally in the upstage right corner, a fireplace with mirror and various decorations. In the stage right wall, upstage, a pair of French doors leading to* LUCETTE's *bedroom. In the upstage wall, facing the audience, two pairs of French doors: one, almost center stage, leads to the dining room, its panels opening in toward the audience; the other, nearer the stage left wall, opens onto the hall, where a coat rack can be seen standing. In the dining room one can see part of a table, and a sideboard stacked with dishware. Another pair of French doors in the stage left wall, upstage. Downstage left, against the wall, a piano and stool. Downstage right, a console table and vase. Near the piano, but far enough to permit adequate passage, a sofa, its back toward the piano, almost perpendicular to the footlights. At the downstage end of the sofa, an end table; at the other end, a light chair. Downstage right, not far from the console table, a rectangular table with chairs to its right and left and behind; on the table is a folded copy of the* Figaro. *In front of the fireplace, a pouf; to its right, a chair, placed against the wall. Between the two pairs of French doors in the upstage wall, a small chiffonier. Knickknacks here and there, paintings on the walls, etc.*

At rise, MARCELINE *is standing at the fireplace, drumming impatiently as if waiting for someone. During this time,* FIRMIN, *in the dining room, has finished setting the table and looks at his watch as if to say, "What a fine time to be having lunch!"*

MARCELINE, *going to the sofa and sitting down.* Really, Firmin, if we don't eat soon I'm simply going to wither up and die!

FIRMIN, *entering from the dining room.* But Mademoiselle, you can hardly expect me to serve while Madame is still in her room.

MARCELINE, *moodily.* Oh! She can be a nuisance, that sister of mine! And just think, I was congratulating her only yesterday . . . I said: "Look, Lucette dear, I know your lover has given you up, and that you're terribly unhappy. But, my dear, at least you've been getting out of bed on time, and we can all eat at noon again!" Now it seems my congratulations were a little premature.

FIRMIN. Who can say, Mademoiselle? Perhaps Madame has found a successor to Monsieur Bois-d'Enghien.

MARCELINE. Lucette? Oh no! She could never do that. She takes after Father . . . She has principles, after all. And besides, if she had done anything of the kind I would have known about it for days.

FIRMIN. Oh? Well . . .

MARCELINE, *getting up.* And even so, that still wouldn't be an excuse for staying in bed until quarter past twelve! I know that love is supposed to make you forget what time it is, and all that, but . . . (*With a smirk.*) No, I just don't understand. I've never been up on such things.

FIRMIN. Never, Mademoiselle?

MARCELINE. No, Firmin, never.

FIRMIN. Oh really, Mademoiselle, you ought to be!

MARCELINE, *with a sigh.* I know, but what do you expect? I've never been married. After all, who wants to marry the sister of a nightclub singer? . . . And anyway, I don't care how mad a girl is about a man, I should think that by noon . . . Well, really! Take roosters, for example. They're not exactly backward lovers, but they're up at four in the morning, aren't they?

> *She sits down again on the sofa.*

FIRMIN. You are absolutely right, Mademoiselle.

LUCETTE, *dashing out of her room, up right, as* FIRMIN *moves upstage.* Oh, Marceline!

MARCELINE, *still sitting.* There you are! I must say—

LUCETTE. Quick, get me an aspirin!

MARCELINE, *getting up.* An aspirin? Aren't you feeling well?

LUCETTE, *radiant.* Not feeling well? Me? Don't be silly. It's for him! He has a splitting headache.

> *She sits at the table,*
> *downstage right.*

MARCELINE. Him? Who?

LUCETTE. Why Fernand, of course! He's come back!

MARCELINE. Monsieur Bois-d'Enghien? No!

LUCETTE. Yes!

MARCELINE, *speaking to* FIRMIN *while moving upstage to the chiffonier to get an aspirin.* Firmin, what do you think? Monsieur Bois-d'Enghien has come back!

FIRMIN, *wiping a plate which he has taken from the dining room table, and moving toward* LUCETTE. Monsieur Bois-d'Enghien? Really? Well, I hope . . . I mean, Madame must be quite pleased.

> *He moves back toward the*
> *dining room.*

LUCETTE, *getting up.* Pleased? I should say I am! You can just imagine how I felt when I saw him at the door last night. (*Taking an aspirin from* MARCELINE.) Thank you . . . (*Continuing.*) And you'll never guess. Here I've been, all this time, thinking such terrible things about him, and the poor boy has been in a dead faint for two weeks!

> *She moves down right.*

MARCELINE. No! Why, that's frightful!

> *She moves up left.*

LUCETTE. Let's not even talk about it. Just think, if he hadn't recovered, the poor dear . . . He's such an attractive thing, too! (*To* FIRMIN, *who is busy in the dining room.*) Don't you think so, Firmin?

FIRMIN, *who has not been following the conversation.* I beg your pardon, Madame?

LUCETTE. I say, don't you find Monsieur Bois-d'Enghien terribly attractive?

FIRMIN, *without much conviction.* Oh, yes indeed, Madame.

LUCETTE, *expansively.* I simply adore him!

BOIS-D'ENGHIEN'S VOICE. Lucette . . . Lucette . . .

LUCETTE. Ah! There he is now. (*To* MARCELINE.) Do you recognize his voice?

MARCELINE. How could I forget it?

LUCETTE, *moving to the bedroom door.* Here I am, dearest.

MARCELINE, *joining her at the door.* May I see him?

LUCETTE. Of course you may. (*Speaking through the door, to* BOIS-D'ENGHIEN.) There's someone here to see you, treasure. Marceline wants to say hello.

BOIS-D'ENGHIEN'S VOICE. Oh? Hello, Marceline!

MARCELINE. Hello, Monsieur!

FIRMIN, *moving behind* MARCELINE. How are you feeling, Monsieur?

BOIS-D'ENGHIEN'S VOICE. Is that you, Firmin? . . . Not too badly, thanks. Just a bit of a headache.

> MARCELINE *and* FIRMIN *voice their sympathy with such comments as "Shame," "Too bad," etc.*

LUCETTE, *entering the bedroom.* Come now, dearest, you must get ready. We're all going to have lunch.

> *She disappears as the doorbell rings.*

MARCELINE. Oh my, who can that be? (FIRMIN *goes out through the hall door to answer.*) Really, at this rate they're going to starve me to death!

FIRMIN, *reappearing at the door.* Monsieur de Chenneviette. (*To* CHENNEVIETTE.) May I ask, Monsieur, if you are staying for lunch?

CHENNEVIETTE. Why yes, Firmin, thank you.

FIRMIN, *aside.* That's no surprise!

CHENNEVIETTE. Hello, Marceline.

MARCELINE, *moodily*. Hello.

FIRMIN. Have you heard the news, Monsieur? He's come back!

CHENNEVIETTE. Who's that?

MARCELINE. Bois-d'Enghien!

CHENNEVIETTE. Bois-d'Enghien? No! I don't believe it!

FIRMIN. It's true, Monsieur. He arrived last night.

CHENNEVIETTE. That's the funniest thing I've heard yet.

FIRMIN. Yes, Monsieur, I quite agree . . . Please excuse me. I'll go tell Madame you are here.

CHENNEVIETTE. I must say, they're a changeable bunch!

FIRMIN, *knocking at* LUCETTE's *door while* MARCELINE *chats with* CHENNEVIETTE. Madame!

LUCETTE'S VOICE. What is it, Firmin?

FIRMIN. The gentleman has arrived, Madame.

LUCETTE'S VOICE. Gentleman? What gentleman?

FIRMIN. The father of Madame's child, Madame.

LUCETTE'S VOICE. Oh, him! Fine! Tell him I'll be right there.

FIRMIN, *to* CHENNEVIETTE. Madame will be here presently, Monsieur.

CHENNEVIETTE. Thank you, Firmin. (*To* MARCELINE, *as* FIRMIN *returns to the dining room*.) I still can't believe he's come back to her . . . And I suppose they've taken up again right where they left off?

MARCELINE. Well . . . (*Nodding in the direction of* LUCETTE's *room*.) It would seem that way!

CHENNEVIETTE, *sitting on the sofa*. Poor Lucette! When is she going to come down to earth? Bois-d'Enghien is a delightful fellow. I don't deny it for a moment. But after all, he's just not for her. Why, the chap doesn't have a penny to his name.

MARCELINE. I know. But to hear Lucette tell it . . . Well, it seems when you're in love, the more money a man has lost the better he is.

CHENNEVIETTE, *ironically*. Oh, really?

MARCELINE. Of course, I wouldn't know. I've never been married. These things are beyond me.

> *She sits down at the table,*
> *down right.*

CHENNEVIETTE, *teasing.* Obviously, my dear! . . . But tell me, where does this leave that South American chap? General . . . General . . . What's his name? *

MARCELINE. You mean General Irrigua y Gonzalez y Lopez y Morales y—

CHENNEVIETTE. Yes, that's the one.

MARCELINE. My goodness, I'm afraid he's been left out in the cold . . . Not that it matters. He's still got his names to keep him warm.

CHENNEVIETTE, *ignoring her last remark.* Now that's not very clever of Lucette! (*Getting up.*) Here she has the luck to meet a man with millions, one who's gone absolutely out of his mind for her . . . And a general, no less! . . . Of course, they're all generals where he comes from, but still . . .

MARCELINE, *getting up.* And such a charming gentleman, too. Why, just a few nights ago I saw him where Lucette was singing. The minute he found out I was her sister, he got himself introduced and sat there feeding me chocolates until I couldn't eat any more.

CHENNEVIETTE. And that's the kind of man she could have had! I don't understand it. Yesterday she seemed perfectly reasonable. It was all over between her and Bois-d'Enghien. In fact, she even said she was going to send a note to this General . . . General Moneybags, and arrange to meet him today. Now what? I suppose there's not a chance, now that . . . now that Lover-boy is back!

MARCELINE. It looks that way, doesn't it?

CHENNEVIETTE. It's absurd, absolutely absurd! Well, that's her business!

> *The bell rings.*

130

MARCELINE, *getting hungrier by the minute.* Oh no! Not another one!

> FIRMIN *enters through the hall door, followed by* NINI GALANT.

FIRMIN. They are in here, Madame.

MARCELINE. Why, it's Nini!

CHENNEVIETTE. Nini Galant!

NINI, *still at the door.* None other! And how are you all, darlings?

> *She puts her bag against the sofa and moves downstage.*

MARCELINE *and* CHENNEVIETTE. Fine, fine.

FIRMIN, *to* NINI. Have you heard the news, Madame?

NINI. What news?

FIRMIN. He's come back!

MARCELINE. That's right!

CHENNEVIETTE. What do you think of that?

NINI. Who, for heaven's sake? Who's come back?

FIRMIN. Monsieur Bois-d'Enghien, Madame.

MARCELINE. That's right!

CHENNEVIETTE. Bois-d'Enghien!

NINI. You're joking!

LUCETTE, *entering from her room and greeting her guests.* Why Nini, what a surprise! . . . (*To* CHENNEVIETTE.) And Gaston, you dear, how are you? (*Without giving them a chance to answer.*) Have you heard the news?

NINI. Yes, I just heard. Fernand is back.

LUCETTE. That's right, darling. Isn't it wonderful?

NINI. I'm so terribly happy for you, Lucette. Is . . . is he here now?

LUCETTE. Of course. Just a moment, I'll call him. (*She goes to the bedroom door and calls.*) Fernand! Nini is here. She wants to see you. (BOIS-D'ENGHIEN's *muffled*

131

voice is heard expressing a muted objection.) What?
. . . Oh, don't be silly, you can come just as you are.
We're all friends! (*To the others.*) Here he comes,
everybody!

> BOIS-D'ENGHIEN *appears,*
> *wrapped in a voluminous*
> *striped dressing gown, tied*
> *round the waist with a*
> *cord. In his hand is a*
> *hairbrush, which he has*
> *obviously not finished using.*
> *He moves downstage be-*
> *tween* FIRMIN *and* LUCETTE.

EVERYBODY. Hip hip, hurrah! Hip hip, hurrah! Hip hip,
hurrah!

BOIS-D'ENGHIEN, *bowing.* Why thank you . . . Ladies . . .
Gentlemen . . .

> *The ensuing dialogue must*
> *be spoken very rapidly, each*
> *line following on the heels*
> *of the last, until "Well*
> *anyway, he's back!"*

NINI. If it isn't the prodigal lover!

BOIS-D'ENGHIEN. What? . . . Why I—

MARCELINE. Naughty boy, playing hard to get!

BOIS-D'ENGHIEN, *protesting.* Not at all . . . You don't
really think—

CHENNEVIETTE. Delighted to see you back, old boy!

BOIS-D'ENGHIEN. Thank you, I'm sure—

FIRMIN. Madame really hasn't been herself since you left,
Monsieur.

BOIS-D'ENGHIEN, *shaking everybody's hand in turn.* Oh?
Well, she . . . I . . .

NINI. Well anyway, he's back!

> *The group echoes her re-*
> *marks with comments like*

> *"That's right," "He's back,"*
> *"Welcome home," etc.*

BOIS-D'ENGHIEN, *with a foolish little smile.* Yes, yes . . .
He's back! (*Moving down right, passing the brush
through his hair. Aside.*) He's back all right! . . . And
to think, I came here to tell her we were through forever!

> *He sits at the table.* FIRMIN
> *leaves through the hall door.*
> MARCELINE *has moved up-*
> *stage, as* LUCETTE *and* NINI
> *sit on the sofa next to one*
> *another.* CHENNEVIETTE *is*
> *standing behind the sofa.*

LUCETTE, *to* NINI. You're staying for lunch, aren't you?

NINI. Dreadfully sorry, darling. I really can't possibly.
That's what I came to tell you.

LUCETTE. You can't? You're sure?

MARCELINE, *getting hungrier all the time.* That's a shame.
I'll go tell Firmin you're not staying.

LUCETTE, *to* MARCELINE. While you're at it, you can tell
him to put the eggs on the table.

MARCELINE, *her eyes glazed with hunger.* The eggs? Yes,
of course! The eggs!

> *She runs out into the dining
> room.*

LUCETTE, *to* NINI. Now then, why can't you stay?

NINI. I'd love to, but I have another . . . (*Emphasizing.*)
engagement! That's what I wanted to tell you, darling.
Really big news. You'll never guess . . . I'm getting
married!

LUCETTE *and* CHENNEVIETTE, *in disbelief.* You?

BOIS-D'ENGHIEN. Married? (*Aside.*) I see I'm not the only
one!

NINI. Married! Little old me! Just like the best of them!

LUCETTE. Congratulations, dear.

CHENNEVIETTE, *moving center stage.* And who's the . . .
lucky young man?

NINI. Why, my lover, silly!

CHENNEVIETTE, *sarcastically.* You mean he's already your
lover, and still he wants to marry you? My God, what
on earth is he looking for?

NINI. What do you mean, "looking for"? I don't think
you're very funny.

LUCETTE, *ignoring* CHENNEVIETTE'*s remarks.* Which lover,
darling?

NINI. Which lover? How many do you think I have? Serious ones, I mean . . .

LUCETTE. Well . . .

NINI. One, that's all! The Duc de la Courtille! (*She notices
the look of consternation on the faces of* LUCETTE *and*
CHENNEVIETTE.) That's right, I'm going to be the
Duchesse de la Courtille!

LUCETTE. No!

CHENNEVIETTE. Wonderful idea!

LUCETTE. Oh, I'm simply delighted for you, Nini dear.

> *During the preceding ex-*
> *change,* BOIS-D'ENGHIEN *has*
> *been glancing casually at a*
> *copy of the* Figaro *lying*
> *on the table near him.*
> *Suddenly he jumps up*
> *with a start.*

BOIS-D'ENGHIEN, *aside.* Good God! My engagement! They've
announced my engagement in the *Figaro!*

> *He crumples up the paper,*
> *rolls it into a ball and puts*
> *it inside his dressing gown,*
> *against his chest.*

LUCETTE, *who, along with the others, has seen this maneuver, running over to him.* What on earth's the matter?

BOIS-D'ENGHIEN. Nothing, nothing! Just a nervous habit!
I . . . I . . .

LUCETTE. Fernand, you poor dear, you're not going to be sick again, are you?

BOIS-D'ENGHIEN. No, no! I'm fine, really! (*Aside, while* LUCETTE, *returning to* NINI, *explains to her that* BOIS-D'ENGHIEN *has been ill.*) No thanks! I can't very well throw my marriage in her face just like that . . . Not before I've prepared her for it.

CHENNEVIETTE. Oh, Lucette, that reminds me. Did you see that very nice article about you in the *Figaro* this morning?

LUCETTE. Why no, I didn't.

CHENNEVIETTE. Well, I'm glad I brought you a copy just in case. One second . . .

> *He pulls a copy of the*
> Figaro *from his pocket and*
> *opens it out.*

BOIS-D'ENGHIEN. What?

CHENNEVIETTE. There you are. If you'd like to take a look . . .

BOIS-D'ENGHIEN, *plunging toward the paper and ripping it from* CHENNEVIETTE'*s hands.* No, no! Not now!

> *He places this paper in*
> *the same place as the first.*

CHENNEVIETTE, *nonplussed.* I beg your pardon?

> *Everyone echoes* CHENNE-
> VIETTE'*s amazement with*
> *appropriate comments:*
> *"What on earth . . .?"*
> *"What's the matter?" etc.*

BOIS-D'ENGHIEN. No! We're going to eat. This is no time to be reading the paper! It's bad for the stomach!

CHENNEVIETTE. What's got into him?

MARCELINE, *entering from the dining room.* Let's eat, everybody. Everything's ready.

BOIS-D'ENGHIEN. There, you see? Everything's ready!

CHENNEVIETTE. He's out of his mind. That's all there is to it!

The bell rings.

BOIS-D'ENCHIEN, *moving toward the bedroom door, stage right.* Wait just a minute while I finish dressing. (*Aside, as he leaves.*) After all, no need to break the news to her before lunch.

He leaves.

FIRMIN, *entering from the hall.* Monsieur de Fontanet has arrived, Madame.

LUCETTE. My goodness, that's right. I'd forgotten all about him. Show him in, Firmin. And set a place for him, will you?

She gets up and moves right.

NINI, *moving toward her.* You mean you're having Fontanet for lunch? Oh, darling, I pity you!

LUCETTE. Why, for heaven's sake?

NINI, *laughing good-naturedly.* Why? . . . Have you ever smelled his breath?

LUCETTE, *laughing.* Oh, that! Well, I admit he does have a bit of a problem, but he's an awfully pleasant chap. He wouldn't harm a fly.

CHENNEVIETTE, *behind the sofa, laughing too.* No, not unless he got close enough to breathe on it!

NINI, *still laughing.* That's right!

LUCETTE, *going to the hall door to meet* FONTANET. I think you're both simply terrible!

> *During the preceding exchange,* FONTANET *is seen through the hall door, removing his coat, which* FIRMIN *places on the coat rack.*

FONTANET, *entering, to* LUCETTE. Ah, there she is, the star herself! Delighted to see you, my dear.

He kisses her hand.

LUCETTE. I'm so glad you could come. (*Nodding in* NINI's *direction.*) We were just mentioning your name.

FONTANET, *flattered by the attention, bowing.* Why thank
you! (*To* LUCETTE.) You see, it was a mistake to invite me. I always take people seriously when they invite me to lunch.

LUCETTE. I was hoping you would!

> *During the following ex-
> change,* NINI, *moving over
> to the table down right and
> sitting down, chats with
> MARCELINE, standing
> nearby.*

FONTANET, *shaking* CHENNEVIETTE's *hand, then moving
back to* LUCETTE. Well now, you must have been pleased
with that magnificent article in the *Figaro* this morning.

LUCETTE. Not really . . . As a matter of fact, I haven't
seen it yet.

FONTANET. You haven't? (*Taking a* Figaro *from his
pocket.*) Well, lucky I brought one along for you.
(*Opening it out.*) There you are.

BOIS-D'ENGHIEN, *entering from* LUCETTE's *room.* All right
everybody, I'm ready. Let's . . . (*Noticing the paper.*)
Another one? (*He rushes headlong between* LUCETTE
and FONTANET *and rips the paper from the latter's
grasp.*) I'll take that! Give it to me!

> FONTANET *stands agape.
> The others express their
> disbelief with appropriate
> remarks: "What?" "Again?"
> etc.*

FONTANET. What on earth—

BOIS-D'ENGHIEN. No, this is no time to be reading the
paper! We're going to eat!

> *He rolls the paper into a
> ball.*

LUCETTE. But for heaven's sake, there's an article in it
about me!

BOIS-D'ENGHIEN, *stuffing the paper into his pocket.* Don't

worry, I'll hold it for you. There! It's all put away. (*Aside.*) Does everyone read that damned paper?

FONTANET, *in an almost challenging tone.* Just one moment, Monsieur!

BOIS-D'ENGHIEN, *ready to accept the challenge.* Oh?

LUCETTE, *quickly stepping between them.* Monsieur de Fontanet, I'd like you to meet Monsieur Bois-d'Enghien, my . . . (*Emphasizing.*) friend.

FONTANET, *taken aback by* LUCETTE's *maneuver, but unable to ignore the ceremonial procedure.* Delighted to meet you.

BOIS-D'ENGHIEN. How do you do.

> *They shake hands.*

FONTANET, *rather pompously.* I congratulate you, Monsieur, on your good fortune. I too am one of Mademoiselle Gautier's most devoted admirers . . . platonic, to be sure! Her charm and talent have completely . . . (*Noticing that* BOIS-D'ENGHIEN *has been sniffing for a moment or two.*) I say, is something wrong?

BOIS-D'ENGHIEN, *simply.* No, no . . . It's just that smell. Don't you notice it?

> *The others try to keep from laughing.*

FONTANET, *sniffing.* Smell? . . . No . . . no . . . But then, that doesn't mean anything. I have a very poor sense of smell. People are always noticing odors that completely escape me.

> *He sits down on the sofa and begins chatting with* CHENNEVIETTE, *standing behind.*

LUCETTE, *whispering quickly to* BOIS-D'ENGHIEN. Be quiet, for goodness' sake! It's him!

BOIS-D'ENGHIEN. It's . . . Oh, I mean . . . (*Going over to* FONTANET, *naïvely.*) I'm awfully sorry, old boy, I didn't realize.

FONTANET. You didn't realize what?

BOIS-D'ENGHIEN. Oh . . . nothing.

> *He makes a grimace as if to say "What a smell!"*

FIRMIN, *entering from the dining room.* Luncheon is served.

LUCETTE. Good! Come, everybody. Let's all sit down and eat.

MARCELINE, *making a beeline for the dining room.* And not a minute too soon!

NINI. Well, Lucette darling, I'd better be going.

LUCETTE, *accompanying her toward the hall door.* Are you sure you won't stay?

NINI, *picking up her bag near the sofa.* No, darling, really . . .

LUCETTE, *while* NINI *says good-bye to* CHENNEVIETTE *and* FONTANET. All right. I won't insist this time. But I do hope that when you become the Duchesse de la Courtille you won't forget to come see us once in a while.

NINI. Why no, Lucette dear! I'll never stop visiting my ordinary friends.

LUCETTE, *bowing from the waist.* Thank you!

> *The others laugh.*

NINI, *realizing what she has said, and laughing along with the others.* Oh no, I didn't mean it that way!

MARCELINE, *reappearing at the dining room door.* Well? Where is everyone?

LUCETTE. We're coming. (*Showing* NINI *out.*) Good-bye, darling.

NINI. Bye bye!

> *She leaves through the hall door.*

CHENNEVIETTE, *sitting on the piano stool.* There goes the new Duchesse de la Courtille!

LUCETTE. Bah! She could marry every lord in England and still never be a lady!

FONTANET. Quite!

LUCETTE. Now then, let's eat! (*She steps back to let* BOIS-D'ENGHIEN *and* FONTANET *go into the dining room first, then moves over to* CHENNEVIETTE, *still sitting on the stool, seemingly lost in thought.*) Well, aren't you coming?

CHENNEVIETTE. Yes . . . Only . . . I wanted to have a word with you first, if you don't mind.

> *He gets up and moves downstage a bit, as* LUCETTE *follows.*

LUCETTE. What is it?

CHENNEVIETTE. It's . . . it's about the child. His allowance is due, you know, and—

LUCETTE, *simply.* Is that all? I'll give it to you after lunch, all right?

CHENNEVIETTE, *laughing rather sheepishly.* Look, I hate to have to ask you for it. I . . . I wish I could take care of it myself, but . . . Things aren't going too well, you know.

LUCETTE, *good-naturedly.* I know. Only this time try not to lose your son's allowance at the races!

CHENNEVIETTE. Please Lucette! You keep throwing that up to me! I told you what happened the last time. I never would have lost if not for that tremendous tip I got.

LUCETTE. Oh yes! A fine tip it turned out to be!

CHENNEVIETTE. Well, what could I do? The owner of the horse took me aside himself and said to me: "Look, my horse is the favorite, but don't bet on him. It's all fixed. I've told the jockey to hold him back."

LUCETTE. So?

CHENNEVIETTE. So? He didn't hold him back, that's all. The horse came in first . . . (*With conviction.*) Well, is it my fault if the jockey was a crook?

FIRMIN, *entering from the dining room.* Mademoiselle

Marceline has asked, Madame, if you and Monsieur de Chenneviette would be kind enough to come have lunch.

LUCETTE, *a little impatient.* Oh my, that's all she thinks about! Food! (FIRMIN *returns to the dining room.*) Come, let's be kind to my sister's delicate stomach. (*The bell rings.*) And for goodness' sake, let's not even wait to see who that can be!

> *They enter the dining room and are greeted with an "Ah!" of satisfaction as they close the doors behind them. A moment later* FIRMIN *enters through the hall door, followed by* MADAME DUVERGER.

FIRMIN. But I don't think she can see you now, Madame. She and her guests are at lunch.

MADAME DUVERGER. That is unfortunate! I really must see her as soon as possible.

FIRMIN. Well, Madame, I shall do my best. Who shall I say is calling?

MADAME DUVERGER. Oh, Mademoiselle Gautier wouldn't know me by name. Just tell her I've come to ask if she would be willing to sing at a party I'm giving.

FIRMIN. Very good, Madame. (*He points to a chair, near the table, and invites her with a gesture to sit down, as he walks toward the dining room. Just then the bell rings again.* FIRMIN *stops short and moves toward the hall door.*) Excuse me, Madame.

> *He goes out.* MADAME DUVERGER *sits down, looks around casually for a moment, then reaches into her bag and takes out a copy of the* Figaro, *unfolding it slightly as if she does not intend to sit reading long.*

141

MADAME DUVERGER, *running her eyes over several columns of the paper.* Oh, how nice! An announcement of Viviane's marriage to Monsieur de Bois-d'Enghien.

> *She scans the announcement with frequent nods of approval. Her reading is interrupted by the arrival of* BOUZIN, *coming in from the hall, followed by* FIRMIN.

BOUZIN. But . . . at least you can ask her if she'll see me. You won't forget the name . . . Bouzin.

FIRMIN. Yes, Monsieur. I'll try.

BOUZIN. It's about a song I sent her not long ago. You won't forget?

FIRMIN. No, Monsieur . . . If you will wait here just a moment . . .

BOUZIN, *nodding politely to* MADAME DUVERGER. How do you do.

> MADAME DUVERGER *returns his nod silently and goes back to her paper. Just then a bell rings, though one can tell by its sound that it is not the bell to the apartment that has rung several times before.*

FIRMIN, *aside.* Oh my, now what can they want in the kitchen? (*Looking askance at* MADAME DUVERGER *and* BOUZIN *as if to say:* "I'll never get round to announcing them!")

> *He leaves through the hall door.* MADAME DUVERGER *continues reading.* BOUZIN, *after putting his hat on the sofa and his umbrella in the corner near the piano, sits*

142

*down on the chair at one
end of the sofa. After a
moment of silence he begins
looking around aimlessly.
Finally he notices the paper
which* MADAME DUVERGER
*is reading, stretches his
neck to see, then gets up
and walks over to her.*

BOUZIN. I say, is that the *Figaro* you're reading?

MADAME DUVERGER, *looking up.* I beg your pardon?

BOUZIN. Your paper . . . Is it the *Figaro?*

MADAME DUVERGER, *somewhat taken aback.* Why yes, it is.
She continues reading.

BOUZIN. Awfully good paper, don't you think?

MADAME DUVERGER. Oh?

BOUZIN. Yes, awfully good! . . . You know, there's quite
an announcement on page four. I don't know if you've
come to it yet . . .

MADAME DUVERGER, *wholly unconcerned.* No, I'm afraid
I haven't.

BOUZIN. You haven't? Oh, well . . . Do you mind? (*He
takes the paper and unfolds it before the astonished
gaze of* MADAME DUVERGER.) There! In the theatrical
section. It's really very interesting . . . See . . . (*Reading.*) "Every evening this week, at the Alcazar, Mademoiselle Maya will perform her new number: 'I Play
Footsie, Footsie, Footsie With My Little Tootsie-
Wootsie . . .' " (*He hands the paper back to her,
smiling with an air of satisfaction, as if he has proved
a point.*) Here, you can read it for yourself.

MADAME DUVERGER, *taking the paper.* I beg your pardon,
my good man, but precisely what makes you think I
care whether Mademoiselle What's-her-name plays
footsie, footsie, footsie with her little tootsie-wootsie?

143

BOUZIN. What?

MADAME DUVERGER. It's obviously another one of those asinine songs.

BOUZIN. Oh no!

MADAME DUVERGER. No?

BOUZIN, *simply.* You see, I wrote it.

MADAME DUVERGER. Oh, I see. (*Sarcastically.*) You must excuse me. I had no idea you were a composer.

BOUZIN, *on whom the sarcasm is evidently lost.* Why yes . . . That is, I'm a composer by nature . . . and a notary's clerk by profession.

> FIRMIN *reappears, carrying a magnificent bouquet.*

MADAME DUVERGER, *to* FIRMIN. Well, can she see me?

BOUZIN. And me?

FIRMIN. I'm sorry. I haven't been able to announce either of you yet. I was called to the kitchen for these flowers.

MADAME DUVERGER. Oh.

> *She takes up her paper again.*

BOUZIN, *pointing to the flowers.* I say, that's quite a bouquet! Do you get a lot like that?

FIRMIN, *simply.* Yes, Monsieur, *we* get quite a few.

BOUZIN. Some millionaire must have sent that one, right?

FIRMIN, *indifferently.* I really couldn't say, Monsieur. There's no card with the flowers. They are from an anonymous admirer.

> *He places the bouquet on the piano.*

BOUZIN. Anonymous? Now isn't that silly! To go to all that expense and not even say who you are!

MADAME DUVERGER, *to* FIRMIN. Will you please announce me?

FIRMIN, *moving toward the dining room.* Immediately, Madame.

BOUZIN, *running over to him.* And you won't forget my name, will you?

FIRMIN. No, I won't forget, Monsieur Bassoon.

BOUZIN. No, no! Bouzin! B–O–U—

FIRMIN. Of course, Monsieur! Bouzin!

BOUZIN. Just a moment, I'll give you my card.

> *He looks through his wallet*
> *for a calling card.*

FIRMIN. There's really no need, Monsieur. I'll remember. Your name is Bouzin and you wrote a song for Mademoiselle Gautier.

BOUZIN. Right! (FIRMIN *begins moving toward the hall door.* BOUZIN *follows close on his heels.*) But I still think if I gave you my card . . . (FIRMIN *ignores his objections and leaves.*) I'm sure he's going to get my name all wrong. (*He puts his card back into his wallet and moves toward the sofa, looking admiringly at the bouquet.*) What a bouquet!

> *He is just about to replace*
> *his wallet in his pocket when*
> *suddenly an idea hits him.*
> *He makes certain that*
> MADAME DUVERGER *is not*
> *looking, then takes out his*
> *card and places it among*
> *the flowers.*

After all, somebody may as well get some good out of it.

> *He puts the wallet back in*
> *his pocket. After a moment*
> *or two of silence, he sud-*
> *denly begins to laugh.*
> MADAME DUVERGER *looks*
> *up quizzically.*

Oh, I was just thinking about my song. I can't help laughing!

> MADAME DUVERGER *ignores*
> *his remarks and continues*

> *reading. A moment later*
> BOUZIN *laughs again.*

You must be wondering what my song is like!

MADAME DUVERGER. Not in the least!

> *She returns to her paper.*

BOUZIN, *moving over to her.* Oh, I don't mind if you're curious. You see, it's a song I wrote especially for Lucette Gautier. Everybody kept saying: "Why don't you write a song for Lucette Gautier?" And naturally, I was sure she'd be happy to sing something of mine . . . So I wrote it. Listen, I'll sing you the chorus just to give you an idea . . . (MADAME DUVERGER, *resigned to her fate, folds her paper and places it on the table.* BOUZIN *sings.*)

> I love my baby for her cake
> And for her casserole,
> But most of all I love her
> For her jolly jelly roll.
> Take a look,
> She's my cook,
> And I love her, yes I do!

> *He smiles, waiting for*
> *congratulations.*

MADAME DUVERGER, *without conviction.* Yes . . . Very nice, I'm sure.

BOUZIN. I knew you'd like it!

MADAME DUVERGER, *not knowing quite what to say.* Yes . . . Yes . . .

BOUZIN. Of course, it's not exactly for little girls!

MADAME DUVERGER. No . . .

BOUZIN. But then again, even little girls . . . If they don't understand it, it doesn't teach them much. And if they do understand it, they don't have much to learn!

MADAME DUVERGER. Yes . . .

BOUZIN, *abruptly, after looking her over for a moment.*

146

Excuse me if I ask you something, but haven't I seen
you somewhere? Don't you sing at the Eldorado?

MADAME DUVERGER, *repressing a laugh as she stands up.*
No, my good man, I'm afraid not. I'm not . . . in the
theater. (*Introducing herself.*) I am the Baroness
Duverger.

BOUZIN. Oh? Then it must be someone else. (*He moves
upstage just as* FIRMIN *comes back in from the hall,
carrying a large sheet of paper.* BOUZIN *anxiously goes
to speak to him.*) Did you tell her I was here?

FIRMIN. Yes, Monsieur.

Uncomfortable silence.

BOUZIN. Well, what did she say?

FIRMIN. Mademoiselle Gautier said that your song was
asinine, Monsieur, and asked me to give it back to
you.

He gives him the song.

BOUZIN, *suddenly changing his expression.* She said . . .
(*In a fit of pique.*) I see! Of course, it doesn't surprise
me in the least! (*Sarcastically.*) I could hardly expect
her to like anything a little different from those everyday songs she sings!

FIRMIN, *good-naturedly.* If you would take my advice,
Monsieur . . . (BOUZIN *takes his hat from the sofa.*)
Next time, before you decide to write something for
Mademoiselle Gautier, come speak to me first.

BOUZIN, *disdainfully.* You?

FIRMIN. Yes, Monsieur. The fact is, Monsieur, I've seen
so many of the songs people have written for her that I
know exactly what she wants.

BOUZIN, *still full of contempt.* Thank you! You're much
too kind! But I never work with a collaborator! . . .
(*Ready to leave.*) I'll take my song to someone who
has more taste . . . and talent!

FIRMIN. As you like, Monsieur.

BOUZIN, *mumbling, almost to himself.* Asinine, is it? Ha! (*To* FIRMIN, *pointing to the bouquet.*) And to think I . . . (*He picks up the bouquet and carries it a few steps toward the door, then apparently changes his mind.*) No! . . . No! . . . (*He replaces it on the piano and addresses* FIRMIN *with a sneer.*) Good day!

FIRMIN. Good day, Monsieur.

> BOUZIN *leaves through the hall door.* FIRMIN *watches his petulant exit with a knowing shake of the head.*

MADAME DUVERGER, *moving toward* FIRMIN. Now then, did you announce me?

FIRMIN. Yes, Madame. But as I suspected, Mademoiselle Gautier is unable to leave her guests. She suggests, Madame, that if you wish to discuss business arrangements, you may return a little later this afternoon.

MADAME DUVERGER. That is a nuisance! But if I must . . . It's just that there's so little time. You see, I want her to sing at my daughter's engagement party this evening.

FIRMIN. Yes, Madame.

MADAME DUVERGER. Well then, you may tell her I'll come back within the hour.

FIRMIN. Very good, Madame. (*He shows her to the hall door.*) This way, Madame.

> MADAME DUVERGER *leaves, followed by* FIRMIN, *who closes the French doors behind him. At the same moment* CHENNEVIETTE *opens the dining room doors a crack and pokes his head through.*

CHENNEVIETTE, *opening the doors wide.* Everybody's gone, we can come out now!

> LUCETTE, CHENNEVIETTE, BOIS-D'ENGHIEN *and*

> FONTANET *enter, voicing
> appropriate expressions of
> satisfaction, each holding a
> cup of coffee.* CHENNEVIETTE
> *stands by the fireplace.*
> FONTANET *sits at the table,
> stage right.* LUCETTE *and*
> BOIS-D'ENGHIEN *come down-
> stage left.*

LUCETTE, *after a moment, putting down her cup, to* BOIS-D'ENGHIEN. Is something wrong, dearest? You seem so unhappy.

BOIS-D'ENGHIEN. Wrong? Why no, not a thing! (*Aside.*) How do I tell her?

> *He goes to the sofa and
> sits down.*

LUCETTE, *moving behind the sofa and throwing her arms around his neck just as he is about to swallow a mouthful of coffee.* Love me?

BOIS-D'ENGHIEN. Of course . . . I'm crazy about you! (*Aside.*) How do I break the news?

> LUCETTE *moves around the
> sofa and plants herself, on
> her knees, next to him.*

FONTANET, *suddenly noticing the bouquet.* My, what lovely flowers!

LUCETTE, *her back turned toward the bouquet.* Flowers?

FONTANET, *pointing.* Over there, on the piano.

> CHENNEVIETTE *and* BOIS-
> D'ENGHIEN *mutter a word
> or two of admiration:
> "Superb," "Lovely," etc.*

LUCETTE. Now who do you suppose could have sent them?

CHENNEVIETTE, *taking the bouquet from the piano and carrying it downstage.* Look, here's a card. (*Reading.*) "Camille Bouzin."

LUCETTE, *taking the bouquet.* Bouzin? . . . You mean . . .

Oh my! And to think how terribly I treated him just now! But that song . . . (*To* FONTANET.) That was his song I showed you all at lunch.

FONTANET. Oh, that!

LUCETTE, *carrying the bouquet toward the fireplace.* But really, why did he have to write such an impossible song? If only it could be fixed up somehow . . . (*Smelling the flowers.*) Oh, they're lovely! (*Suddenly.*) Why, what on earth . . . Look, there's something else . . .

> *She takes a little jewel box from among the flowers and places the bouquet in a vase above the fireplace. Everyone looks on curiously, asking such questions as "What is it?" "What can it be?" etc.* LUCETTE *opens the box and stands for a moment, dumbfounded.*

Oh no, I . . . I can't believe it! This . . . this is too much! Look, a ring!

> *She places the ring on her finger, holds out her hand for all to see, and goes over to the table, where she puts the jewel box as she sits down. The others voice their surprise and admiration with expressions like "A ring?" "Isn't it beautiful!" etc.*

And these diamonds . . . And this ruby . . . They're real, I'm sure of it! Just look at them! I . . . I don't understand . . .

CHENNEVIETTE, *moving over toward* LUCETTE. And you mean to say that Bouzin fellow sent it?

BOIS-D'ENGHIEN. He must have money to burn!

LUCETTE. My goodness, you'd certainly never think so to

look at him. The way he dresses . . . You feel like putting a handful of change in his hat!

CHENNEVIETTE. Well, he's a millionaire all right to be able to send gifts like that.

FONTANET. He's a millionaire . . . And what's more, I'd say he's in love!

LUCETTE, *laughing.* Do you think so?

BOIS-D'ENGHIEN, *who has moved stage left, aside.* Now there's a thought . . . If I can push this Bouzin off on Lucette . . . That could just get me off the hook, couldn't it!

LUCETTE. But that awful song . . . Really! There must be something we could do to change it around a little . . .

FONTANET. Wait, I have an idea. Why couldn't you turn it into one of those singing advertisements . . . for a pastry company, or something?

CHENNEVIETTE, *at the table, near* LUCETTE. How, for example?

FONTANET. Oh, you know the sort of thing . . . Perhaps something like this. (*Singing.*)

> You love your baby for her cake
> And for her casserole,
> But most of all you'll love her
> If she serves our jelly roll!

(*Speaking.*) Then you throw in the name of the company, with a "cha-cha-cha" or two, and there you have it!

CHENNEVIETTE, *laughing.* Not bad!

BOIS-D'ENGHIEN. I think he's got something!

LUCETTE. Wonderful idea! I'll suggest it to him.

She gets up.

FONTANET, *modestly.* Oh well, ideas aren't hard to get. I have plenty of them. It's carrying them out that bothers me.

BOIS-D'ENGHIEN, *moving beside him.* That's the way with most of us!

FONTANET. I did try to write a song once . . . a silly sort

of thing . . . (*Speaking right in* BOIS-D'ENGHIEN's *face.*)
It was called "Ha Ha Ha, Ho Ho Ho!"

> BOIS-D'ENGHIEN *recoils, then
> smiles immediately to cover
> his displeasure, and moves
> far left.*

LUCETTE, *to* FONTANET. Did you have much success?

FONTANET, *still very modestly.* Oh . . . I wouldn't say it
exactly took my breath away!

BOIS-D'ENGHIEN, *with conviction.* No . . .

> CHENNEVIETTE *and* LUCETTE
> *burst out laughing.*

FONTANET, *laughing with them but without knowing why.*
I say . . . Did I say something funny?

LUCETTE, *laughing, pointing to* BOIS-D'ENGHIEN, *who has
sat down on the sofa, doubled up with laughter.* No,
no . . . It's just Fernand. He's in one of his silly moods.
He gets that way!

FONTANET, *catching the contagious laughter more and
more.* Oh! . . . But I still can't imagine what I could
have said . . .

LUCETTE, *struggling to speak between spasms of laughter.*
Nothing . . . Really! You . . . you didn't say a thing!
(*Still laughing, but trying to change the subject.*) Now
then, let's talk about something serious. Tell me, will
you be in the audience tonight?

FONTANET. No, not tonight, I'm afraid. I'm going to a
party.

LUCETTE, *dominating her laughter little by little.* Oh . . .
Well, I don't know why I bothered to ask. I'm not
singing this evening anyway. It's my night off.

FONTANET. Just as well. I would have hated to miss you.
But I do have to spend the evening at the home of a
very dear friend, the Baroness Duverger.

BOIS-D'ENGHIEN, *suddenly stops laughing and jumps to his
feet, a pained expression on his face. Aside.* Good God!
My mother-in-law!

FONTANET. There's going to be a reception for her daughter. She's marrying some chap by the name of . . . by the name of . . . Now what is his name? It's on the tip of my tongue. (BOIS-D'ENGHIEN *is close to panic.*) It's something like . . .

> *He probes his memory*
> *without success.*

BOIS-D'ENGHIEN, *coming between* LUCETTE *and* FONTANET. Forget it! Forget it! We're not interested!

FONTANET, *persistent.* Just a moment . . . It's . . . It's a name like yours, I think.

BOIS-D'ENGHIEN. No it's not! It can't be! There aren't any!

LUCETTE, *to* BOIS-D'ENGHIEN. What on earth are you so excited about?

BOIS-D'ENGHIEN. Excited? I'm not excited! It's just . . . It's like these people who tell you: "Listen, it's a name that begins with a W"—

FONTANET, *quickly.* I've got it!

BOIS-D'ENGHIEN. Schmidt!

FONTANET. No, no . . . Oh, now I've lost it again.

BOIS-D'ENGHIEN. Besides, who cares what his name is? We don't know him, do we?

> *The bell rings.*

CHENNEVIETTE. He's right.

BOIS-D'ENGHIEN. Of course I'm right. Forget it!

LUCETTE, *to* FIRMIN, *who has entered, and who is looking for something behind the various pieces of furniture.* What is it, Firmin?

FIRMIN, *with a note of disdain in his voice.* Nothing at all, Madame. It's merely that gentleman . . . Monsieur Bouzin. He says he left his umbrella.

> *Everyone repeats the name*
> *"Bouzin" with surprise.*

LUCETTE, *moving upstage.* Oh, how nice! Show him in, Firmin. By all means!

FIRMIN, *surprised.* Oh?

LUCETTE, *going to the hall door.* Why, come right in,

Monsieur Bouzin! (*Introducing him as he enters.*)
Monsieur Bouzin, I'd like you to meet my friends.

> BOIS-D'ENGHIEN, FONTANET
> *and* CHENNEVIETTE *welcome
> him with "Ah, Monsieur
> Bouzin!" "How do you do!"
> etc. At the same time* FIRMIN
> *leaves through the hall door.*

BOUZIN, *surprised at the reception, bowing rather sheepishly.* How . . . how do you do. Excuse me, but I . . .
I think I must have left my—

LUCETTE, *solicitous.* Do sit down, Monsieur Bouzin.

> *Everyone brings him a chair,
> with the result that, before
> he knows what has happened, four chairs are lined
> up behind him. The others
> all echo* LUCETTE's *invitation: "Do sit down!" "Won't
> you have a chair!" etc.*

BOUZIN, *sitting half on one, half on another, finally settling
tenuously on the chair offered by* LUCETTE. But . . .
but . . . I . . .

> LUCETTE *and* BOIS-D'ENGHIEN
> *sit on either side of him,
> with* FONTANET *and* CHEN-
> NEVIETTE *standing by the
> table.*

LUCETTE. There! Now I'm going to scold you, you
naughty boy! Why ever did you go running off with
your song that way?

BOUZIN, *with a bitter smile.* Why, indeed! After that . . .
that domestic of yours said you thought it was asinine!

LUCETTE, *protesting.* Asinine? Your song? Oh no, he
must have misunderstood what I said!

> *The others take up her remark, assuring* BOUZIN *with*

> *shouts of "He misunder-*
> *stood!" etc.*

BOUZIN, *his face brightening.* Oh? Well, of course, I was
sure he must have . . .

LUCETTE. But before you say another word, you must let
me thank you for your magnificent flowers.

BOUZIN, *confused.* Flowers? . . . Oh yes, my flowers! . . .
Please, don't mention it. It was nothing, really.

LUCETTE. What do you mean, don't mention it! Why, I
don't know how to thank you. It was a perfectly
charming gesture.

FONTANET. I should say!

BOIS-D'ENGHIEN *and* CHENNEVIETTE. Perfectly charming!

LUCETTE, *suddenly, showing off her ring.* And the ring!
Did you see the ring I'm wearing?

BOUZIN. Your ring? Why yes . . . yes . . .

BOIS-D'ENGHIEN. It's lovely!

FONTANET *and* CHENNEVIETTE. Simply lovely!

LUCETTE, *coyly.* You see, I've put it on my finger.

BOUZIN, *still confused.* Yes, so it seems . . . (*Aside.*) Now
what is that supposed to mean?

LUCETTE. The ruby is absolutely exquisite!

BOUZIN. The ruby? . . . (*Looking more closely at the
ring.*) Oh yes, that's what it is all right. (*After a short
pause.*) And just imagine how much a thing like that
costs!

> *Everyone looks at one*
> *another, amazed, not*
> *knowing what to say.*

LUCETTE, *taken aback.* I'm sure . . . But believe me, I
certainly appreciated it.

BOUZIN. You might not think so, but a ring like that costs
a small fortune.

CHENNEVIETTE, *moving behind the table.* It does?

LUCETTE, *to* CHENNEVIETTE. Certainly it does. That doesn't
surprise me in the least.

> CHENNEVIETTE *gradually moves over to the sofa.*

BOUZIN. Of course! You could feed a family for two years on what that costs.

> *The others look at one another in astonished horror.* BOIS-D'ENGHIEN *looks squarely at* BOUZIN *as if to say "What kind of a man are you?"*

BOIS-D'ENGHIEN, *aside to* CHENNEVIETTE. I think this is the most disgusting display I've ever seen.

CHENNEVIETTE, *aside to* BOIS-D'ENGHIEN. He's absolutely offensive!

> *He moves upstage.* BOIS-D'ENGHIEN *gets up and replaces his chair by the sofa.*

LUCETTE, *still trying to be pleasant.* Anyway, that just proves that the person who gave it was terribly generous.

BOUZIN. You can say that again! (*Aside.*) He was an idiot, if you ask me! (*Aloud.*) Now to get back to my song . . .

LUCETTE. That's right, your song . . .

FONTANET, *getting up and replacing his chair beside the table.* Well, my divine diva, I see you have work to do. I'll be on my way.

LUCETTE, *getting up.* Oh? Well, if you must . . . Let me see you to the door.

> *She replaces her chair in its original position near the table.*

FONTANET. Please, don't bother . . .

LUCETTE, *following him out through the hall door.* Don't be silly. It's no bother at all. (*To* CHENNEVIETTE, *over her shoulder.*) Why don't you come with me. I'll give you that . . . that little something for the child. You can send it right off.

CHENNEVIETTE. Fine!

> BOUZIN, *without getting up,*
> *has followed all this activity,*
> *pivoting in his chair until*
> *he is facing upstage.*

LUCETTE. You will excuse me, Monsieur Bouzin . . . I'll just be a minute.

> *Everyone leaves except*
> BOIS-D'ENGHIEN *and* BOUZIN.

BOIS-D'ENGHIEN, *who has watched their exit, pacing back and forth, suddenly stopping in front of* BOUZIN, *who has got up to take his chair over to the table.* You know what I think? You're in love with Lucette, that's what!

BOUZIN, *amazed.* I'm what?

BOIS-D'ENGHIEN. Absolutely! Don't try to hide it . . . You're in love! And I say bravo! Go to it! You've got to strike while the iron's hot, you know!

BOUZIN. What?

BOIS-D'ENGHIEN. If you're any kind of a man, Lucette is already as good as yours.

BOUZIN. That's very nice, but—

BOIS-D'ENGHIEN, *quickly.* Shhh! Here she comes! Remember, not a word about it today. You make your first move tomorrow!

> *He moves stage left, hands*
> *in pockets and whistling, in*
> *an attempt to appear casual.*

BOUZIN, *aside.* Of all things . . . Whatever makes him think I'm in love with Lucette Gautier?

LUCETTE, *entering, to* BOUZIN. There! I hope you'll excuse me for running out like that . . .

BOUZIN. Perfectly all right . . . (*Aside.*) I'm not the least bit in love with her!

LUCETTE, *sitting stage left of the table.* Now we can have our little chat in peace. Where were we?

BOUZIN, *sitting at the table, facing the audience.* You were saying . . .

LUCETTE. Oh yes, your song . . . Why, it's delightful!
There are no two ways about it. It's simply delightful!

BOUZIN. Thank you! (*Aside, putting his hat under the
table.*) And that fool thought she said it was asinine!

LUCETTE. Still, you know . . . It's all well and good to
say "Let well enough alone!" Your song . . . As I
said, it's delightful, but . . . It could use a little more
. . . more character, I think.

BOUZIN, *protesting mildly.* Well, I—

LUCETTE. Yes, that's what it needs. I'm sure you don't
mind my speaking frankly. It's terribly clever, but . . .
but that isn't everything you know.

BOUZIN, *speechless.* But—

LUCETTE, *to* BOIS-D'ENGHIEN, *who is leaning against the
fireplace, at a discreet distance.* Don't you agree?

BOIS-D'ENGHIEN. Of course! Of course! (*He moves over
to the table and sits down.*) And something else, if you
don't mind my saying so . . . There's something about
the form that bothers me a little.

LUCETTE. I know, but that goes without saying. The form
does leave a lot to be desired, but I'm not even talking
about that.

BOIS-D'ENGHIEN. And then too, it's . . . it's a little flat,
don't you think? I mean, there's not much to it.

LUCETTE. Yes, I suppose you're right. You do rather get
the feeling that the song was composed by someone
awfully clever, but . . . but . . . someone awfully
clever who . . . who . . .

BOIS-D'ENGHIEN, *coming to the rescue.* Who had someone
else write it for him!

LUCETTE. Exactly!

BOUZIN, *nodding.* Really? (*After a brief pause.*) Well anyway, aside from that, you did like it, didn't you?

LUCETTE. Oh yes! Very much!

BOIS-D'ENGHIEN. Very much indeed!

LUCETTE, *changing her tone.* Now then, here's what we
had in mind. Do you have the song with you?

BOUZIN. No, I left it at home.

LUCETTE. Too bad!

BOUZIN. But I can get it. I live just around the corner. I can run right over.

He gets up.

LUCETTE, *getting up.* Fine! If you're sure you don't mind. That way we'll be able to do some work on it.

BOUZIN. Mind? Why, not a bit. After all . . . (*He moves quickly toward the hall door.*) I'll be back in no time.

LUCETTE, *following him, pointing to his umbrella.* Don't forget your umbrella!

BOUZIN, *excitedly.* No, no! Thank you!

*He takes the umbrella from
behind the piano and leaves.*
LUCETTE *accompanies him.*

BOIS-D'ENGHIEN, *alone, moving stage left.* There! At least I've got things started as far as this Bouzin character is concerned. Now to get down to business. No more dilly-dallying! We're signing the marriage contract to-night, after all. I'll just have to come right out with it and tell her we're finished.

LUCETTE, *entering from the hall and speaking to the invisible* BOUZIN. Yes, that's right! And do hurry, won't you?

BOIS-D'ENGHIEN, *sitting on the sofa, aside.* My God, how do I begin?

LUCETTE, *moving behind the sofa and throwing her arms around* BOIS-D'ENGHIEN's *neck.* Love me?

BOIS-D'ENGHIEN, *without conviction.* I'm mad about you.

LUCETTE. Darling!

*She moves round the sofa
and joins him.*

BOIS-D'ENGHIEN, *aside.* There must be a better way to begin.

LUCETTE, *sitting next to him.* Oh, Fernand, I'm so happy! I can still hardly believe my eyes. You naughty thing, you! If you only knew how miserable I've been without you. I thought everything was finished between us!

BOIS-D'ENGHIEN, *protesting hypocritically*. Finished?

LUCETTE, *passionately*. Fernand, dearest . . . Tell me I've really got you back again.

BOIS-D'ENGHIEN. Of course you have. You've really got me back again . . . (*Aside.*) Back against a good old wall, that's where you've got me!

LUCETTE, *overhearing a word or two.* What?

BOIS-D'ENGHIEN. I said: You've really got me back again . . . for good and all!

LUCETTE, *looking deeply into his eyes*. And tell me you're my very own, and that you won't ever belong to anyone else.

BOIS-D'ENGHIEN. I'm your very own . . . and I won't be long! . . . I mean, I won't belong to anyone else. There!

LUCETTE, *drawing his head against her chest*. Nannikins!

BOIS-D'ENGHIEN. Lulu!

> *She forces him into a most uncomfortable position on her lap, his head cradled in her arms.*

LUCETTE. There!

BOIS-D'ENGHIEN, *aside*. I think I got off on the wrong foot.

LUCETTE. See how nice and comfy I am!

BOIS-D'ENGHIEN, *aside, obviously very uncomfortable*. Wonderful!

LUCETTE, *languidly*. I could stay this way for twenty years! Wouldn't that be nice, darling?

BOIS-D'ENGHIEN. It might be a little long, don't you think?

LUCETTE. You would be my "Nannikins" and I would be your "Lulu" . . . and we would just let the rest of the world go trotting by.

BOIS-D'ENGHIEN, *aside*. What fun!

LUCETTE, *sitting up, allowing* BOIS-D'ENGHIEN *to sit up too*. What a shame we have to be realistic! (*She gets*

*up, goes around the sofa, suddenly addressing him
again.*) Love me?

BOIS-D'ENGHIEN. I'm mad about you.

LUCETTE. Darling!

> *She continues her circuit
> around the sofa, moving
> toward center stage.*

BOIS-D'ENGHIEN, *aside.* This is definitely not the way!

LUCETTE, *center stage, with a provocative look and a
voice full of innuendo.* Then . . . come help me dress,
dearest.

BOIS-D'ENGHIEN, *a little sullen.* No, not just now, Lucette.

LUCETTE, *surprised, moving toward him.* Why? What's
bothering you?

BOIS-D'ENGHIEN. Bothering me? Nothing!

LUCETTE. There must be something. You look so unhappy.

BOIS-D'ENGHIEN, *standing up, ready to take the bull by
the horns.* All right! If you really want to know what's
bothering me . . . It's this . . . this whole situation.
It . . . it can't go on any longer, that's all!

LUCETTE. Situation? What situation?

BOIS-D'ENGHIEN. Our situation. I mean you and me.
(*Aside.*) Ayayay! (*Aloud.*) I was going to have to
tell you sooner or later. I may as well face up to it and
get it over with. Lucette, we can't keep seeing one another.

LUCETTE, *choking.* What?

BOIS-D'ENGHIEN. It's just impossible! (*Aside.*) Ayayay!

LUCETTE, *with a sudden intuition.* My God! You're getting married!

BOIS-D'ENGHIEN, *hypocritically.* Me? Why . . . don't be
absurd! Whatever gave you that idea?

LUCETTE. Then why? Why?

BOIS-D'ENGHIEN. It's . . . it's just that . . . the way things
are now . . . with me, I mean . . . Well, I can't treat

161

you the way you deserve to be treated, that's all, and . . . and . . .

LUCETTE. Is that all that's bothering you? (*She bursts out laughing, letting herself fall in a heap on his lap.*) Ha ha ha! You silly goose, you!

BOIS-D'ENGHIEN. What?

LUCETTE, *holding him in her arms, tenderly.* You know how happy I am, just the way things are.

BOIS-D'ENGHIEN. Yes, but . . . but my pride . . . my dignity!

LUCETTE. Bah! Forget about your dignity! What does anything matter as long as you know I love you? (*Breaking away, passionately.*) Oh yes, darling, I do love you!

BOIS-D'ENGHIEN, *aside.* I'm doing better all the time!

LUCETTE. Just the thought that you could be getting married, and I . . . (*She embraces him as if she were about to lose him.*) Darling! Tell me that you'll never get married! Never!

BOIS-D'ENGHIEN. Me? Of course not!

LUCETTE, *gratefully.* Oh, thank you! (*Breaking away.*) Besides, if you ever did, I know what I would do.

BOIS-D'ENGHIEN, *uneasy.* What's that?

LUCETTE. Oh, it wouldn't take long, you can be sure of that! One bullet in the brain, that's all!

BOIS-D'ENGHIEN, *his eyes popping out of their sockets.* My God! Whose?

LUCETTE. Mine, of course!

BOIS-D'ENGHIEN, *reassured.* Oh . . . Oh, I see.

LUCETTE, *approaching the table, nervously fingering the* Figaro *left there by* MADAME DUVERGER. No, believe me! I wouldn't be afraid to . . . to end it all. The minute I found out . . . (*Rattling the paper.*) The minute I read it in the paper . . . No, I wouldn't be afraid!

162

BOIS-D'ENCHIEN, *terrified, but without moving. Aside.* God in heaven! The newspaper!

LUCETTE, *becoming more calm.* See how silly I can be! There I go getting all upset over nothing.

> *She throws the* Figaro *on the table and moves down right. While her back is turned* BOIS-D'ENCHIEN *pounces on the paper and stuffs it inside his coat.*

BOIS-D'ENCHIEN, *aside, with a sigh of relief.* They must grow these things here!

> LUCETTE *has turned round at the noise.* BOIS-D'ENCHIEN *tries to cover up his move with a foolish little smile.*

LUCETTE, *throwing herself into his arms.* Love me?

BOIS-D'ENCHIEN. I'm mad about you.

LUCETTE. Darling!

> *She moves back upstage.*

BOIS-D'ENCHIEN, *aside.* Now I can never tell her . . . Not after that! Never!

> *He goes over to the sofa and lets himself fall dejectedly.* CHENNEVIETTE *enters from the hall, holding an envelope which he has just finished sealing.*

CHENNEVIETTE, *to* LUCETTE. There! The letter is ready. You wouldn't happen to have a stamp, would you?

LUCETTE, *moving toward her room.* Just a moment . . . I'll go look.

CHENNEVIETTE, *reaching into his pocket.* Here . . . I think I've got the right change.

LUCETTE, *good-naturedly.* For a stamp? Don't be silly . . . I don't need the money.

CHENNEVIETTE, *a little annoyed.* Well neither do I, thank you! I'm not looking for charity, you know!

LUCETTE. If you feel that way about it . . .

> *She takes the money and
> enters her room.*

CHENNEVIETTE, *to* BOIS-D'ENCHIEN. It's funny. There are some things women just don't understand.

BOIS-D'ENCHIEN, *preoccupied.* Yes . . . yes . . .

CHENNEVIETTE. What's the trouble, old man? You look a little out of sorts.

BOIS-D'ENCHIEN. Out of sorts? Ha! That's putting it mildly. I'm at the end of my rope!

CHENNEVIETTE. My goodness! What's wrong?

BOIS-D'ENCHIEN, *getting up and moving toward him, a glimmer of hope in his eye.* You know, maybe you can help me at that! Maybe . . . You see, there's something I've got to tell Lucette, but I just don't know how. I can tell you, after all . . . You are her . . . Well, I mean, you're . . . you're practically her husband . . . and . . . Well, the fact is, Lucette and I are going to have to call it quits.

CHENNEVIETTE, *dumbfounded.* What? Did you say what I think you said?

BOIS-D'ENCHIEN. Yes, you heard me. I've got to give her up.

CHENNEVIETTE. But . . .

BOIS-D'ENCHIEN. Don't you understand? I'm getting married!

CHENNEVIETTE. You?

BOIS-D'ENCHIEN. Exactly! And we're signing the marriage contract tonight!

CHENNEVIETTE. Good God in heaven!

BOIS-D'ENCHIEN, *taking him by the arm, and in his most persuasive tone.* You know perfectly well it's the best thing that could happen to her.

CHENNEVIETTE. Oh, you don't have to convince me, old

man. In fact, she has a tremendous fish nibbling at the hook right now. If she only wanted to pull him in!

The bell rings.

BOIS-D'ENGHIEN. Then tell her, for heaven's sake! Tell her! She'll listen to you . . .

CHENNEVIETTE. Ha! You think so?

FIRMIN, *appearing at the hall door.* General Irrigua!

CHENNEVIETTE, *aside.* Speak of the devil! (*To* FIRMIN.) Show him in! By all means . . . (*Suddenly calling* FIRMIN *back before he disappears.*) No, wait!

FIRMIN. Monsieur?

CHENNEVIETTE. You'd better wait until we've gone. (*To* BOIS-D'ENGHIEN.) Come on, let's get out of here!

BOIS-D'ENGHIEN. But . . .

CHENNEVIETTE. Let's go! We'll only be in the way!

BOIS-D'ENGHIEN, *suddenly understanding.* Oh! . . . You mean he's the—

CHENNEVIETTE. Right! The big fish!

BOIS-D'ENGHIEN. Then what are we waiting for? Come on, let's let him nibble in peace!

They steal away furtively through the dining room doors.

MARCELINE, *entering through the French doors in the stage left wall, just as* FIRMIN *is about to show* THE GENERAL *in.* Who was that at the door, Firmin?

FIRMIN. General Irrigua, Mademoiselle.

MARCELINE. The General? Oh my! Quick! . . . Show him in and go tell my sister!

She moves between the piano and sofa.

FIRMIN, *showing him in.* This way, Monsieur. Won't you come in.

THE GENERAL, *with a thick Spanish accent.* Bueno! I come een!

He enters, followed by ANTONIO, *who is carrying*

*two bouquets. One of them
is immense; the other, a
tiny one, which he holds
behind his back.*

MARCELINE, *bowing.* General!

THE GENERAL, *recognizing her.* Ah! The seester! Mamoiselle, I keess your hand. (*He carries out the gesture with great aplomb, then calls to* FIRMIN.) Garçonne! (*As* FIRMIN *fails to reply, he calls still louder.*) Garçonne! . . . Boy! . . . Valé dé pié!

FIRMIN, *approaching.* I beg your pardon, Monsieur. Do you mean me?

THE GENERAL. But of course I mean you! Who you theenk I mean? I no mean me! (*Aside.*) Qué bruta este hombre! (*Aloud.*) Go tell your meestress I am arrive!

FIRMIN. Very good, Monsieur. (*He begins walking stage right just as* LUCETTE *enters from her room.*) Ah! Here she is now, Monsieur.

> FIRMIN *leaves through the
> hall door.*

THE GENERAL. Ah! Ees her! (*To* LUCETTE, *who stops short in surprise.*) Madame! Thees ees most beauteeful day of my life!

LUCETTE. Monsieur?

MARCELINE, *introducing.* Lucette, this is General Irrigua—

THE GENERAL, *bowing.* Heemself!

LUCETTE. Oh, General, I beg your pardon . . . I didn't realize—

THE GENERAL. Ees nothing!

LUCETTE, *nodding toward* ANTONIO, *who has remained upstage.* Monsieur!

THE GENERAL. Ees my interpreter.

LUCETTE. I'm perfectly delighted to meet you, General.

THE GENERAL. Ah! Delighted ees for me, Madame! (*To* ANTONIO.) Antonio, las flores, por favor . . . (ANTONIO

166

hands LUCETTE *the large bouquet without revealing the small one.*) Please to permeet I geeve leetle flowers, Madame.

LUCETTE, *taking the bouquet.* Why General . . .

THE GENERAL, *taking the small bouquet from* ANTONIO *and presenting it to* MARCELINE. And . . . I have theenk also of seester.

MARCELINE, *taking the flowers.* For me? Oh, General . . .

THE GENERAL, *to* MARCELINE. Ees smaller than other one, but ees easier to carry. (*To* ANTONIO.) Antonio, you go now wait for me een hall, yes?

ANTONIO. Bueno, mi general!

> *He leaves.*

LUCETTE. You're really much too kind, General. I simply adore flowers!

THE GENERAL, *gallantly.* Ees pleasure!

MARCELINE, *to* THE GENERAL, *smelling her bouquet, with a little smirk.* So do I. I simply adore them!

THE GENERAL. Sí, but ees for Madame I speak.

LUCETTE, *spreading out the flowers to show them off.* Look, Marceline! Aren't they magnificent!

THE GENERAL. Are your slaves I put at your feet!

LUCETTE, *laughing.* My slaves?

THE GENERAL, *trying to express himself more clearly.* Bueno! . . . I put these bosoms at feet of queen of bosoms! (LUCETTE *and* MARCELINE *look at one another and burst out laughing.*) For why you laugh? (*To* LU-CETTE.) Ees true. For me you are queen of bosoms!

LUCETTE, *controlling herself.* Blossoms, General . . . Blossoms!

THE GENERAL. Ees what I say, no?

MARCELINE. You're terribly flattering, General!

> THE GENERAL *bows deeply*
> *from the waist.*

LUCETTE, *to* MARCELINE. Marceline, be a dear and run along, would you?

MARCELINE. Me?

THE GENERAL, *with a grand gesture.* Sí, run along, seester!

MARCELINE. What . . .

THE GENERAL, *very polite, but firm.* You go now, yes?

MARCELINE. Yes, I'm going . . . I'm going! (*Aside.*) Barbarian!

> *She leaves up left, while* LUCETTE *puts the flowers in a vase on the console table, down right.* THE GENERAL, *moving toward the sofa, waits for* MARCELINE *to leave.*

THE GENERAL, *suddenly, as* LUCETTE *moves over to the table.* Ees you! You! And ees me, here, weeth you . . . alone!

LUCETTE, *sitting at the table.* Won't you sit down, General?

THE GENERAL, *passionately.* I no can seet!

LUCETTE, *surprised.* You can't sit down?

THE GENERAL. I no can seet! I am too much een fever! Ah! When I receive letter from you . . . Letter who say "Sí," ees all right I come for veeseet you . . . Ah! Caramba! Caramba! (*Unable to express what he feels.*) Oh, I no can say eet . . .

LUCETTE. Why General, what's the matter? You seem all upset?

THE GENERAL. Oh, sí! Sí! Ees true! Ees becose I . . . Ees becose I see ees me, here, weeth you . . . alone! (*Becoming more daring.*) Lucette! Ees becose I love you!

LUCETTE, *quickly getting up and moving around the table.* Not so fast, General! That's dangerous ground you're treading on!

THE GENERAL. Danger? Ha! For me ees no afraid of danger! Een my country ees I was meeneester of war!

LUCETTE. You?

THE GENERAL, *bowing*. Heemself!

LUCETTE. Well, this is an honor, General! You, the minister of war!

THE GENERAL, *correcting her*. No, no . . . Ess . . . Ess . . .

LUCETTE, *without understanding*. "Ess"? What do you mean, "ess"?

THE GENERAL. Ess-meeneester. I no more meeneester now.

LUCETTE, *with an almost sympathetic tone*. Oh? That's too bad. What are you now?

THE GENERAL. Now? Een my country? I am preesoner.

LUCETTE, *recoiling*. What?

THE GENERAL. Sí! Eef I go back, they keel me.

LUCETTE. You?

THE GENERAL, *with a reassuring gesture*. Sí! But ees nothing . . . Ees becose I come here, en Francia, for to buy sheeps for my government.

LUCETTE. Sheep?

THE GENERAL. Sí. Two battlesheep, three cruiser, and five deestroyer.

LUCETTE. Oh, I see. But why . . .

THE GENERAL. Bueno! I lose them all een game of roulette!

LUCETTE. You lost them at roulette? (*With a tone of reproach in her voice.*) But how, General?

THE GENERAL, *as if it were really nothing at all*. Ees I have no luck, never! Ees always same theeng. Eef I bet eight, ees come out nine. So ees why I lose always much money!

LUCETTE, *sitting down at the table*. Why General, that's terrible!

THE GENERAL, *still very casually*. Oh, for me ees nothing! Ees always more plenty. Ees always enough for geeve to you.

LUCETTE. To me?

THE GENERAL, *in the grand manner.* Everytheeng!

LUCETTE. But . . . what for?

THE GENERAL, *passionately.* For so ees I can love you . . . Sí, ees becose I love you! Ees becose I see ees me, here, weeth you . . . alone! Ah! Lucette . . . Ees too leetle my heart for so much love I have for you! Ees so beeg your beauty . . . Ees I am . . . I am . . . (*Dropping his poetic tone for a moment.*) Un momento . . .

>> *He moves upstage.*

LUCETTE, *aside.* Now what?

THE GENERAL, *opening the hall door.* Antonio!

ANTONIO, *appearing at the door.* Sí, mi general?

THE GENERAL. Cómo se dice "subjugar"?

ANTONIO. "Subjugate," mi general.

THE GENERAL, *waving him away.* Bueno! Gracias, Antonio!

ANTONIO. Bueno, mi general!

>> *He leaves.*

THE GENERAL, *to* LUCETTE, *suddenly reassuming his passionate tone.* Ees I am subjugate by you. Everytheeng I have I geeve to you. My life, my money . . . Sí, I geeve you everytheeng. I geeve you shirt off my back . . .

LUCETTE, *aside.* Thank you!

THE GENERAL. I go hongry for you. But I no mind. I like, becose ees for you!

LUCETTE, *nodding doubtfully.* You, General, go hungry? I don't think you know what the word means.

THE GENERAL, *moving down left.* Oh, sí! Sí! I know! I no always be reech. Before be general een army, I no have money. No, no! Much time I spend be poor professor. Much time I have to go leeve een other people houses . . . where I geeve French lesson.

LUCETTE, *trying to repress a laugh.* French lessons? You mean, you used to be able to speak it?

THE GENERAL. Sí, sí!

LUCETTE. Whatever happened?

THE GENERAL, *naïvely.* I tell you. Een my country I know how speak French very good. Ees when I come here, en Francia, for some reason, I no speak so good. You see?

LUCETTE, *laughing.* Yes, I see!

THE GENERAL. Sí!

LUCETTE. Sí! (*Anxious to change the subject.*) Won't you sit down, General?

THE GENERAL, *excited.* I no can seet! Here, weeth you . . . alone . . . Eef I seet, ees at your knees I must seet. (*He kneels down before her.*) Ees you are goddess for to kneel down, saint for to worsheep . . .

LUCETTE. Really, General . . .

THE GENERAL, *very matter-of-fact.* Where eet ees your bedroon?

LUCETTE, *taken aback.* What?

THE GENERAL, *passionately.* I say, where eet ees your bedroon?

LUCETTE, *regaining her composure.* Why General, what a question!

THE GENERAL. Ees love . . . love who speak weeth my mouth. Ees becose I like to leeve there! Ees becose bedroon of beauteeful woman you love, ees like . . . ees like . . . (*Getting up.*) Un momento!

LUCETTE, *aside, with a note of good-natured sarcasm.* Here we go again!

THE GENERAL, *at the hall door.* Antonio!

ANTONIO, *appearing.* Sí, mi general?

THE GENERAL. Cómo se dice "tabernáculo"?

ANTONIO. "Tabernacle," mi general.

THE GENERAL. Bueno! Gracias, Antonio!

ANTONIO. Bueno, mi general!

He leaves.

THE GENERAL, *silently returning to his knees before* LU-CETTE, *making certain that he is just as he was before, then exclaiming.* Ees like taberlac . . . Place for where to worsheep goddess!

*He takes her left hand in
his hands.*

LUCETTE, *placing her right hand, the one with the ring,
over both his hands.* I must say, General, your flattery
covers a multitude of sins!

THE GENERAL, *without understanding.* Sí, sí! (*Getting
up.*) Oh, ees you have reeng on feenger, yes?

LUCETTE, *getting up.* My ring? Oh, that! Yes ! . .

THE GENERAL. Ees very preetty, yes?

LUCETTE, *very casually, moving stage right.* It's really
just a trinket.

THE GENERAL. Ees treenket? What means treenket?

LUCETTE. You know. A trifle . . . a mere bauble, that's
all.

THE GENERAL. Un mirboble . . . Sí, sí! (*Changing his
tone.*) Un momento! (*Going to the hall door and calling.*) Antonio!

ANTONIO, *appearing.* Sí, mi general?

THE GENERAL. Que significa "mirboble" en español?

ANTONIO. Mirboble? (*Looking toward* LUCETTE, *puzzled.*)
Mirboble?

LUCETTE. No, no . . . I was telling the General that something was . . . (*Enunciating.*) a mere bauble.

ANTONIO, *understanding.* Ah! A mere bauble. Sí, sí! (*To*
THE GENERAL.) La señora le dice a Usted que es . . .
es poca cosa.

THE GENERAL, *repeating the new word with obvious pleasure.* Ah! Sí, sí! Un mirboble! Sí, sí! (*To* ANTONIO,
waving him away.) Bueno, bueno, bueno! Gracias, Antonio!

ANTONIO. Bueno, mi general!

He leaves.

THE GENERAL, *joining* LUCETTE, *stage right.* Sí, sí! Un
mirboble!

LUCETTE. You understand . . . I'm attached to it for sen-
timental reasons.

THE GENERAL, *touched*. Ah! Sí, sí! I am so happy, Lucette!

LUCETTE. It used to belong to my mother.

THE GENERAL, *suddenly excited*. Qué dice? Ees was for who? You say . . . You say . . .

LUCETTE, *surprised at his reaction*. General?

THE GENERAL. Ees fron me, thees reeng, fron me! I send thees morneeng weeth flowers!

LUCETTE. You?

THE GENERAL. But of course!

LUCETTE, *crossing left, very confused*. But then . . . but . . . but . . . You?

THE GENERAL. Sí! Sí!

LUCETTE, *aside*. And Bouzin? . . . Oh no, really! How could he have the nerve to . . . Oh no! . . . And that song! . . . Well, we'll see about that! The very idea!

THE GENERAL, *noticing her agitation*. For why you so deesturb?

LUCETTE. It's nothing . . . nothing at all! What were you saying, General?

THE GENERAL, *with a tinge of irony*. So ees no fron mother, the reeng?

LUCETTE. The ring? The ring? Oh no! Certainly not! I thought you were talking about another ring . . . Not this one. Oh no! But I had no idea that I had you to thank for it.

THE GENERAL, *modestly*. Ees notheeng! (*Moving right with a grandiose gesture.*) Ees mirboble! (*Returning to* LUCETTE.) And now I geeve bracelet for to keep heem company.

> He takes a jewel box from
> his pocket and hands it to
> LUCETTE.

LUCETTE. Oh, General! I don't know what to say. Whatever did I do to deserve all these beautiful things?

THE GENERAL, *very simply*. Ees I love you! That ees all!

LUCETTE. You love me? (*With a sigh.*) Ah, General! Why must things be so . . . so . . .

THE GENERAL, *cutting her off, with irrefutable logic.* Becose ees so!

LUCETTE. No, no! Don't say that.

THE GENERAL, *coldly determined.* Sí, sí! I say eet!

LUCETTE, *handing back the jewel box.* Then I have no choice, General. I'm afraid you'll have to take back your presents. I really don't have the right to accept them.

THE GENERAL, *pushing aside the jewel box.* But for why? For why?

LUCETTE, *simply.* Because . . . I can never love you, General.

THE GENERAL, *with a leap.* What you say?

LUCETTE, *bowing her head.* I . . . I love someone else.

> She very casually puts the
> jewel box into her pocket.

THE GENERAL. Someone else? You? Ees some other man?

LUCETTE. Obviously.

THE GENERAL, *pacing back and forth.* Caramba! Who ees? Who ees thees man? Ees have to see heem! Ees have to know!

LUCETTE. Please, General, control yourself!

THE GENERAL. Ah, sí! Someone he tell me you have for lover, preetty man . . .

LUCETTE. Pretty? Well . . .

THE GENERAL. But I no believe eet, becose . . . becose I have receive your letter . . . Caramba! . . . So he exeest, thees man! . . . So he exeest! Oh! Who ees? Who ees?

LUCETTE. Please, General . . .

THE GENERAL, *with a frenzied roar.* Oh!

LUCETTE, *placing her hands gently on his shoulders.* Believe me, General, if only my heart were my own, you would be my very first choice.

THE GENERAL, *with restrained despair*. Ah! Lucette! You make me seeck . . . seeck een heart!

LUCETTE. But do try to understand, won't you? As long as I love him I can never love anyone else.

THE GENERAL, *struggling against his despair, with a note of resignation*. Bueno! And how long you need for thees?

LUCETTE, *with passion*. How long? Ah! I'll love him as long as he lives!

THE GENERAL, *determined*. Bueno! Now ees clear for me what I must do.

LUCETTE. What?

THE GENERAL. Notheeng! Ees clear. Ees clear.

> *A knock is heard at the dining room door.*

LUCETTE, *moving toward the table*. Come in.

BOIS-D'ENGHIEN, *opening the door a crack and disguising his voice, but without showing himself*. There's someone asking to see Mademoiselle Gautier for a moment.

LUCETTE, *recognizing his voice*. What? Oh yes, of course! I'll be right there. (*Aside.*) He could be more tactful!

> THE GENERAL *has moved stealthily behind the sofa and suddenly pulls the door open.*

THE GENERAL, *fiercely*. What you want, you? For why you here?

> BOIS-D'ENGHIEN *has been forcibly pulled into the room, his hand still on the door knob.*

BOIS-D'ENGHIEN, *rather pathetically, bowing several times in an effort to be agreeable*. Hello there!

LUCETTE, *aside*. My God! (*Quickly introducing* BOIS-D'ENGHIEN.) General, I'd like you to meet Monsieur Bois-d'Enghien, an old friend of mine.

THE GENERAL, *suspicious.* Ah?

BOIS-D'ENGHIEN. That's right . . . an old friend! That's all I am . . . just an old friend!

> *The bell rings.*

THE GENERAL, *still doubtful.* You old friend? That ees all?

LUCETTE. Why of course that's all, General . . .

BOIS-D'ENGHIEN. Less! Even less!

THE GENERAL. Bueno! Eef you old friend of Lucette . . .

> *He shakes his hand and moves downstage.*

FIRMIN, *entering from the dining room, to* LUCETTE. Madame?

LUCETTE. Yes, Firmin?

FIRMIN. It's that lady, Madame . . . the one who was here earlier asking if you would sing at her party this evening. I've asked her to wait in the dining room.

LUCETTE. Oh? Thank you, Firmin . . . I'll be right there. (FIRMIN *goes out through the hall door, leaving it open.*) If you'll excuse me, General . . . I'll just be a moment.

THE GENERAL. But of course!

> LUCETTE *moves upstage,* THE GENERAL *moves far left.*

BOIS-D'ENGHIEN, *following* LUCETTE, *in a quick aside to her.* Look . . . I have to be going, you know!

LUCETTE. Please! Wait just a little while. I'll only be a minute. In the meantime you can keep the General company.

BOIS-D'ENGHIEN. All right, but don't be long.

> LUCETTE *goes out through the dining room door. A few moments go by, during which* THE GENERAL *and* BOIS-D'ENGHIEN *exchange polite little smiles in the obvious absence of anything to say to one another.*

THE GENERAL, *breaking the silence.* Ees very . . . very
. . . (*Unable to find the right word, lapsing into Spanish.*) ambulatoria, no?

BOIS-D'ENGHIEN. I beg your pardon?

THE GENERAL. Mamoiselle Gautier . . . she no seet steel
een one place!

BOIS-D'ENGHIEN, *suddenly understanding.* Oh . . . No,
you're quite right, General.

THE GENERAL, *moving closer to him.* So . . . you seeng
een nightclub weeth Lucette, no? Een one same?

BOIS-D'ENGHIEN, *startled by* THE GENERAL's *supposition.*
What? (*Deciding that it will be easier to agree than
disagree.*) Oh, yes . . . yes! Exactly! In one same . . .
(*Correcting himself.*) I mean, in one the same. (*Aside.*)
Damn! (*Aloud.*) In the same one . . . the same one!

THE GENERAL, *categorically.* Ees you are tenor!

BOIS-D'ENGHIEN. Tenor? Why yes. You've put your finger
right on it! (*Aside.*) Why not, while I'm at it!

THE GENERAL. Sí! Een your face I see ees you are tenor!

BOIS-D'ENGHIEN. Oh, really? You're a good judge of faces!
(*Singing.*)
The shades of night again enfold the earth.
The nightingale begins his silver song . . .

THE GENERAL, *aside, grimacing.* Ugh! Thees ees man for
to seeng een nightclub?

BOIS-D'ENGHIEN, *coughing and clearing his throat.* Hum!
Hum! Terrible season for colds, isn't it!

THE GENERAL, *motioning him to approach.* You tell me,
Monsieur Bodégué . . .

BOIS-D'ENGHIEN, *correcting him.* Excuse me, it's "Bois-
d'Enghien."

THE GENERAL. Bueno! Ees what I say, no? "Bodégué."
(BOIS-D'ENGHIEN *shrugs his shoulders in resignation.*
THE GENERAL *takes his arm in a confidential manner.*)
You good friend weeth Lucette, no?

BOIS-D'ENGHIEN, *noncommittal.* Well, in a way.

THE GENERAL. Then you tell me. Ees true she have lover?

BOIS-D'ENGHIEN. What?

THE GENERAL, *releasing his arm.* Sí! I know. She tell me everytheeng.

BOIS-D'ENGHIEN. She did? Oh well, in that case . . . (*Aside.*) And here I am acting like an idiot to keep him from finding out!

THE GENERAL. Sí. Ees very preetty man, no?

BOIS-D'ENGHIEN, *coyly.* Well really, General . . . I'm hardly in a position . . .

THE GENERAL. But I no see here preetty man who eet can be.

BOIS-D'ENGHIEN, *aside.* Much obliged!

THE GENERAL. Bueno! So you tell me, no? Who ees thees man?

BOIS-D'ENGHIEN, *aside.* Why not? (*Aloud.*) Do you really want me to tell you, General?

THE GENERAL. Oh, sí! Sí! Por favor!

BOIS-D'ENGHIEN, *fatuously.* Well, it's none other than . . . (*Laughing.*) Ha ha ha! You're going to be surprised!

THE GENERAL, *laughing along with him.* Ha ha ha!

BOIS-D'ENGHIEN. You really want to know? (*Still laughing.*) Ha ha ha!

THE GENERAL. Sí, sí! Ha ha ha! (*Suddenly serious.*) Becose I want to keel heem!

BOIS-D'ENGHIEN, *swallowing what he was about to say, moving far right.* Good God! (*Forcing a nervous little laugh to hide his panic.*) Ha ha ha! That's a good one! Ha ha ha!

THE GENERAL. Sí! (*Approaching him and joining in, to be polite.*) Ha ha ha!

> *During the preceding exchange* LUCETTE *and* MADAME DUVERGER, *unseen by the two men, appear momentarily at the open hall door.*

LUCETTE, *in the hall, addressing* MADAME DUVERGER, *who is now out of sight.* Right! Then I'll see you this evening. Good afternoon, Madame.

> *She can be heard closing the outside door, invisible to the audience.*

THE GENERAL, *soberly returning to his obsession.* Bueno! So you tell me who ees?

BOIS-D'ENGHIEN, *catching sight of* LUCETTE *in the hall.* Shhh! Not now! Just a minute!

THE GENERAL. Bueno, bueno!

> *He moves stage left.* BOIS-D'ENGHIEN *shudders, as if to say: "That was close!"*

LUCETTE, *entering and moving toward her room.* There! That didn't take too long, I hope. I'm going to be singing at a party tonight . . . And a very fashionable one, too! (*To* THE GENERAL.) Now if you'll excuse me for just another moment, General . . . I'll be right with you.

THE GENERAL, *bowing.* But of course.

LUCETTE, *just as she is about to enter her room, to* BOIS-D'ENGHIEN. Oh, while I think of it, you wouldn't like to come hear me, would you? I have a few invitations.

BOIS-D'ENGHIEN. No, I . . . I . . . Not tonight, thanks. (*Aside.*) I already have an engagement!

LUCETTE. What about you, General?

THE GENERAL. Oh, sí! Weeth pleasure!

LUCETTE. Fine! Here's an invitation.

> *She hands him an invitation, which he places in his pocket.*

THE GENERAL. Muchas gracias!

LUCETTE. Now I'll just be a minute.

> *She enters her room.* BOIS-D'ENGHIEN, *visibly shaken by the ordeal he has had to*

179

> *suffer in silence, moves*
> *down right and stands by*
> *the table.*

THE GENERAL, *joining him.* Bueno! Now you tell me, yes? What ees her name?

BOIS-D'ENGHIEN. Her name? Whose name?

THE GENERAL. Name of man!

BOIS-D'ENGHIEN, *mortified.* Man? . . . Man? . . . What man?

THE GENERAL, *disregarding his attempt to hedge.* Ees preetty man?

BOIS-D'ENGHIEN, *nervously picking up the jewel box which had contained the ring and which had been left on the table, playing with it unconsciously.* Why . . . Well, that is . . . (*Suddenly inspired, as he looks at the jewel box, exclaiming.*) Bouzin! His name is Bouzin!

THE GENERAL. Poussin?

BOIS-D'ENGHIEN. That's right! Bouzin!

THE GENERAL. Bueno! Poussin es un hombre muerto! I keel heem!

> *He stalks far left as if*
> *contemplating murder.*
> BOIS-D'ENGHIEN *shudders*
> *and mops his brow. At that*
> *moment the bell rings.*

FIRMIN, *at the hall door, announcing.* Monsieur Bouzin.

THE GENERAL, *surprised.* Cómo?

> BOIS-D'ENGHIEN *looks up in*
> *stark horror as* BOUZIN
> *enters, in obvious good*
> *spirits.*

BOUZIN, *placing his umbrella against the chair near the sofa.* I'm back, everyone, and I've brought the song. (*He looks around.*) Oh, isn't Lucette . . . (*Correcting himself.*) Isn't Mademoiselle Gautier here?

> THE GENERAL *moves toward*
> *him.*

BOIS-D'ENGHIEN, *rushing between them*. What? No . . . Yes . . . That is . . .

> *During the ensuing dialogue,* BOIS-D'ENGHIEN, *terrified, tries to come between the two men.* BOUZIN, *on the other hand, does his best to approach* THE GENERAL *and carry on a friendly conversation.*

THE GENERAL, *to* BOUZIN. Monsieur Poussin, no?

BOUZIN, *very agreeable*. Why yes, Monsieur . . .

BOIS-D'ENGHIEN. That's right! He's Bouzin! He is! He is!

THE GENERAL. Ees I am so happy to meet you.

BOUZIN. Thank you. The pleasure is mutual, I—

THE GENERAL, *in a peremptory tone*. Geeve to me your card!

BOUZIN. My card? Why, certainly . . .

> *He reaches into his pocket with one hand, and with the other pushes aside* BOIS-D'ENGHIEN *in order to approach* THE GENERAL.

BOIS-D'ENGHIEN, *resigned, moving out of the way. Aside.* Oh my!

THE GENERAL. Here, I geeve you mine.

> *He hands* BOUZIN *his card.* BOUZIN *gives him one of his own.*

BOUZIN, *reading*. General Irrigua—

THE GENERAL, *bowing*. Heemself!

BOUZIN, *bowing*. General . . .

THE GENERAL. Now you tell me, yes . . . You no be beezy tomorrow, een morneeng?

BOUZIN, *thinking*. Busy? Tomorrow? . . . No, no . . . But, why . . .

THE GENERAL, *gradually losing his temper*. Becose I want

181

to take you on field of honor. Becose I want your head!
(*Seizing him by the collar.*) Becose I want to keel you!

BOUZIN. My God! What did he say?

BOIS-D'ENGHIEN, *pleading.* General . . .

THE GENERAL, *shaking* BOUZIN *like a fruit tree.* Becose I
no like someone he get een my way. When anytheeng
een my way, I no go jump over eet. I get reed of eet!

> *He turns* BOUZIN *about
> several times, still holding
> him by the collar.*

BOUZIN. Ah! For God's sake! Let me go! Let me go!

BOIS-D'ENGHIEN, *trying to separate them.* General,
please . . .

THE GENERAL, *pushing away* BOIS-D'ENGHIEN *with his right
hand while still shaking* BOUZIN *with his left.* Ees no
your beezness, Bodégué! (*To* BOUZIN, *still shaking him.*)
And you . . . You no preetty at all, onderstand? No
preetty at all!

BOUZIN. Help! Help!

> *General confusion, shouts,
> etc.*

LUCETTE, *running in at the noise.* What's the matter? What
on earth . . .

> THE GENERAL *releases*
> BOUZIN, *pushing him away
> as* LUCETTE *enters.*

BOUZIN, *regaining his balance.* Why, this . . . this . . .
this gentleman . . .

LUCETTE, *to* BOUZIN. You? You had the nerve to come
back? (*Pointing to the door, angrily.*) Monsieur Bouzin . . . Get out!

BOUZIN, *taken aback.* But . . . but . . . I brought the song.

LUCETTE. Oh you did, did you? Well, you can just take
your song right back, because your song is asinine, do
you understand?

BOIS-D'ENGHIEN, *echoing.* Asinine!

THE GENERAL, *with conviction, as if he knew what it was*

all about. Sí! Ees asinine! Your song ees asinine!

LUCETTE, *pointing.* There's the door, Monsieur Bouzin! Now will you kindly leave!

BOUZIN, *helplessly, at a loss.* But . . . but . . .

BOIS-D'ENGHIEN. You heard what she said. Get out!

THE GENERAL. Sí! Get out, Poussin! Get out!

> *They all crowd round him and push him toward the hall door with shouts of "Out! Out!"*

BOUZIN, *leaving, in a daze.* It's a madhouse, that's what it is!

LUCETTE, *moving near* BOIS-D'ENGHIEN, *center stage.* The very idea! What does that man take us for?

THE GENERAL, *joining them.* Gracias, Lucette! For me you have do thees!

LUCETTE. What?

THE GENERAL. For me you have get reed of thees man!

LUCETTE. Oh? Well, if that's all you want, you can be sure he'll never come back!

THE GENERAL, *kissing her hand.* Gracias!

> *During this exchange* BOUZIN *has tiptoed back to get his umbrella. In his nervousness, however, he gets tangled up in the furniture and knocks over the chair against which the umbrella is resting.*

LUCETTE *and* BOIS-D'ENGHIEN, *turning round at the noise.* You again?

BOUZIN, *in a voice choked with terror.* My umbrella! I forgot my umbrella!

> *He dashes out as the others follow him menacingly with shouts of "Get out, Bouzin!" "Out, out!" etc.*

183

MADAME DUVERGER's *lavishly furnished bedroom, opening out onto the drawing room by means of a four-paneled door in the center wall. Through the open door one can see the fireplace in the drawing room. In the stage right wall, upstage, a door. In the stage left wall, downstage, another door. Stage right, center, the canopy of a four-poster. The bed itself has been removed for the occasion and has been replaced by an armchair. Next to the canopy, on its downstage side, an occasional chair. Attached to the wall, under the canopy, an ornate light fixture which would ordinarily be used for reading in bed. Against the center wall, on the stage right side of the drawing room door, a large and elegant closet, with double doors, empty. On the other side of the door, a lady's dressing table, with all its appurtenances, almost entirely hidden by an elaborate six-paneled screen, the last panel of which is fixed to the corner of the set. In front of the screen, a square table and a chair. Chairs placed on each side of the door, down left. Right center, a chaise longue placed almost perpendicular to the footlights, its head away from the audience, slightly raised. At the foot of the chaise longue, a small end table on which there is an electric button. In the middle of the room, a chandelier, lighted. Throughout this act the characters are dressed in evening clothes, unless otherwise indicated.*

At rise, VIVIANE *is standing next to the end table, right center.* MISS BETTING, *in street clothes, is kneeling in front of her, putting the finishing touches on* VIVIANE'S *evening gown. In all of their conversation,* VIVIANE *accompanies her spoken dialogue with deaf-and-dumb hand language, so that* MISS BETTING, *a deaf-mute, may understand.*

VIVIANE. Are you almost finished, Miss Betting? (MISS BETTING *communicates something in sign language.*) You say you need another pin? (MISS BETTING *nods assent.* VIVIANE *hands her a pin from the end table.*)

184

You don't want my fiancé to stick himself, do you? (MISS BETTING, *with a half amused, half scandalized look, again says something with her hands.*) Why, there's nothing shocking about that, Miss Betting!

> *She laughs.* MISS BETTING
> *joins in, silently.*

MADAME DUVERGER, *entering from the drawing room.* Viviane, aren't you ready?

VIVIANE. Just a moment, Mamma. Miss Betting hasn't finished pinning me up. (*Laughing.*) I don't know what she has against my fiancé . . . but I'm going to have more points sticking out of me than a barbed-wire fence! (*Innocently.*) You'd think she was afraid he might go climbing!

MADAME DUVERGER, *taken aback.* Viviane! What a comparison!

VIVIANE, *naïvely.* Did I say something wrong, Mamma?

MADAME DUVERGER. No, darling. Not at all. (*Aside.*) Innocent as a lamb, poor child!

VIVIANE, *suddenly changing her tone.* Oh, Mamma . . . Please be a dear and tell Miss Betting to stay for the party.

MADAME DUVERGER. Why of course! Doesn't she want to?

VIVIANE. No! And I did so hope she could meet my fiancé.

MADAME DUVERGER, *to* MISS BETTING, *standing up, in a tone of goodnatured reproach.* Now then, what's all this? Of course you'll stay, won't you? (MISS BETTING *shakes her head quizzically, as if to say she doesn't understand.*) I said: "Of course you'll stay for the party!" (*Same response from* MISS BETTING.) Party . . . To-night . . . Dancing . . . (*Enunciating.*) Dancing . . . (*She executes a dance step or two while* MISS BETTING *looks on, smiling but puzzled.*) It's no use. I keep forgetting she can't hear a word I say. Viviane, darling, you tell her.

VIVIANE, *still accompanying her words with appropriate sign language*. Mother insists, Miss Betting. You'll simply have to stay for the party!

> MISS BETTING, *suddenly understanding, directs a rapid volley of sign language at* MADAME DUVERGER.

MADAME DUVERGER, *who has watched intently, nodding her head as if she understood*. Yes, yes . . . (*To* VIVIANE.) What did she say, darling?

VIVIANE. She said she was terribly sorry, because she would have loved to meet my fiancé, but that her mother is sick and she has to spend the evening with her.

MADAME DUVERGER, *to* MISS BETTING, *solicitously*. Oh, of course! Of course! Mother . . . sick . . . sick . . .

> MISS BETTING *lets loose another volley of sign language*.

MADAME DUVERGER, *nodding*. Yes . . . Yes . . .

VIVIANE. She says that at her mother's age the least little thing can be dangerous.

MADAME DUVERGER. Yes . . . Yes . . .

> MISS BETTING, *smiling sheepishly, continues her manipulations*.

VIVIANE, *to* MISS BETTING. Oh, that's all right.

MADAME DUVERGER, *to* VIVIANE. What did she say?

VIVIANE. She says you should forgive her, but she keeps forgetting that you can't understand a word she says.

MADAME DUVERGER. Oh, well . . .

VIVIANE, *to* MISS BETTING, *changing the subject*. Are you almost finished? (MISS BETTING *indicates with a gesture that the dress is ready*.) There! (*She takes a few steps toward the center so that her mother and* MISS BETTING *may admire the dress*.) What do you think, Mamma?

MADAME DUVERGER. Oh, Viviane, darling! It's simply lovely! I've never seen you look more beautiful!

VIVIANE. Do you like it, Miss Betting?

> MISS BETTING *answers in her sign language, obviously enthusiastic.*

MADAME DUVERGER. What did she say?

VIVIANE. She said it's simply lovely and that she's never seen me look more beautiful.

MADAME DUVERGER, *somewhat startled.* Oh?

> *Another rapid communication from* MISS BETTING.

VIVIANE. And now she wants to know if she may go.

MADAME DUVERGER. Why yes, if she must. Only, before I forget, tell her to be here early tomorrow. I shan't be able to take you to your singing lesson with Professor Capoul, and I want her to go with you instead.

VIVIANE, *to* MISS BETTING, *still duplicating her words with signs.* Mother says you may go if you must, but that you should be here early tomorrow to take me to my singing lesson with Professor Capoul.

> MISS BETTING *addresses a reply to* MADAME DUVERGER.

MADAME DUVERGER. What did she say?

VIVIANE. She said she'll be delighted. (*She sits down on the foot of the chaise longue as* MISS BETTING, *moving upstage, waves "good-bye" to her.* VIVIANE *responds in kind.*) Good-bye.

> MISS BETTING, *almost at the drawing room door, waves "good-bye" to* MADAME DUVERGER.

MADAME DUVERGER, *moving toward the door and awkwardly imitating her gesture.* Good-bye! Good-bye! (*Aside, moving downstage.*) I'm beginning to pick up a few words. (MISS BETTING *leaves.* MADAME DUVERGER *approaches* VIVIANE, *looks at her tenderly for a moment, then kisses her and sits down next to her on the chaise longue.*) Well, darling! The great day is here at last!

VIVIANE, *rather indifferently.* Yes, I guess it is . . .

MADAME DUVERGER, *putting her arm around* VIVIANE'*s waist.* And you're very happy to be marrying Monsieur de Bois-d'Enghien, aren't you?

VIVIANE. Happy? Oh . . . I don't know that I much care, really.

MADAME DUVERGER, *stunned.* You . . . You don't know that you much care?

VIVIANE, *quite categorical.* No. He's only becoming my husband, after all.

MADAME DUVERGER. But . . . I should think that would be enough for you! Why do you think anybody ever gets married?

VIVIANE. Oh? To be like everyone else, I suppose. There comes a time . . . Well, it's like going from a nurse-maid to a governess, I imagine. There comes a time when you have to go from a governess to a husband.

MADAME DUVERGER, *shocked beyond words.* Oh!

VIVIANE. Yes . . . A husband is just a sort of lady's maid . . . Only he's a man, that's all.

MADAME DUVERGER, *speechless.* But . . . But . . .

VIVIANE. Is something wrong, Mamma?

MADAME DUVERGER. But that's *not* all, Viviane!

VIVIANE. It isn't?

MADAME DUVERGER. Motherhood, darling! How do you feel about becoming a mother?

VIVIANE. Oh, I think that would be very nice, Mamma . . . But what does a husband have to do with that?

MADAME DUVERGER. What . . . What does a husband have to do—

VIVIANE, *cutting her off.* Yes! After all, there are lots of single girls who have children, and lots of married

women who don't. If it were only up to the husbands . . .
Well . . .

> MADAME DUVERGER *is about*
> *to reply, but finding no*
> *suitable answer, gets up*
> *and moves stage left,*
> *shaking her head in*
> *resignation.*

MADAME DUVERGER, *to* VIVIANE, *who has risen also.* But
darling, what can you possibly dislike about Monsieur
de Bois-d'Enghien? He's from a fine family . . . He's
good-looking . . .

VIVIANE, *moving behind the chaise longue, with a note of
disdain.* Oh! For a husband I suppose he'll do. In any
marriage the husband is never as good-looking as the
. . . the other man.

MADAME DUVERGER. The other man! What makes you think
there has to be another man? When you get married
you may as well find a husband who has all the qualities
you're looking for. That way there's no need to go making up the difference!

VIVIANE, *joining her, stage left.* Yes, Mamma, but that's
just the trouble. I could never marry a man who had
the qualities I'm looking for.

MADAME DUVERGER. And why not, for goodness' sake?

VIVIANE. Because . . . you would never let me. I would
have wanted someone very . . . well, someone very
prominent.

MADAME DUVERGER. Certainly. I can understand that. An
artist, for example.

VIVIANE. Oh no! A gigolo!

MADAME DUVERGER, *with a start.* Viviane!

VIVIANE. Yes! A man like Monsieur de Frenel, for instance.
(MADAME DUVERGER *cannot repress a gesture of horror.*) He's only one example. There are many others.

189

You remember him, don't you? We met last summer at Trouville. (*Enthusiastically.*) Oh yes! Monsieur de Frenel would have been simply perfect!

MADAME DUVERGER. But . . . You can't be serious! Why, that man has an absolutely scandalous reputation!

VIVIANE, *emphasizing the words.* Yes, Mamma, absolutely scandalous . . . I know! That's the sort of thing that makes a man stand out . . .

MADAME DUVERGER. Oh!

VIVIANE. A man with so many mistresses that they're on everybody's lips.

MADAME DUVERGER, *stunned.* "Mistresses!" Did you say . . . Viviane, where did you learn that word?

VIVIANE, *ingenuously.* In school, Mamma. In my history lessons. (*Reciting.*) Henry IV, Louis XIV, Louis XV, 1715 to 1774 . . .

MADAME DUVERGER. Imagine teaching such things to little girls!

VIVIANE. In fact, three of his mistresses even died for him!

MADAME DUVERGER. For Louis XV?

VIVIANE. No, no! For Monsieur de Frenel! Two of them shot themselves, and the third one died of indigestion.

MADAME DUVERGER. Oh?

VIVIANE, *carried away.* And . . . Why, every woman in Trouville was chasing him. Every one, Mamma!

MADAME DUVERGER, *holding her back as she is about to cross right.* But . . . You, Viviane! I still don't understand why *you* found him so attractive!

VIVIANE. But I just told you, Mamma. Because every woman in Trouville was chasing him! That's how it is with everything, isn't it? Why do we ever want anything? Because everybody else wants it, that's why. It's what they call "supply and demand" I think. Well, with Monsieur de Frenel . . .

MADAME DUVERGER. There was a big demand . . . I see!

VIVIANE. Exactly! That's when I said to myself: "There's

the kind of husband I want!" Because there's a lot of satisfaction in having a husband like that. It's like getting the Legion of Honor. You're proud of it for two reasons: first, for the prestige it brings you, but most of all, because it makes everyone else turn green with envy!

MADAME DUVERGER. But . . . That isn't love, darling! That's sheer vanity!

VIVIANE. Oh no, Mamma! Believe me, it *is* love! When you can say to yourself: "You see this man? Well, another woman would have given her right arm for him, but she'll never have him, because he's all mine!" (*She executes a little curtsy.*) That's love, Mamma!

MADAME DUVERGER, *moving downstage slightly, sighing.* I don't know where you get your ideas, Viviane.

VIVIANE, *moving behind her and taking her around the waist, lovingly.* You're just too young to understand.

MADAME DUVERGER, *laughing.* I'm afraid so!

She kisses VIVIANE.

VIVIANE. You see, that's the only fault I find with Monsieur de Bois-d'Enghien. He's very nice and all that . . . But he simply doesn't . . . stand out, that's all! He's never had even the least little woman kill herself over him . . .

MADAME DUVERGER. And you think that will keep him from making you happy?

VIVIANE, *letting go of her mother and moving right.* Oh, I suppose he'll make me happy enough . . . (*Rejoining* MADAME DUVERGER.) And anyway, even if he doesn't, nowadays, with divorce and all . . . It's so simple . . .

She moves right.

MADAME DUVERGER, *to the audience.* She certainly seems ready for marriage, I must say! (*Noticing that* ÉMILE, *the butler, has appeared at the drawing room door.*) Yes Emile? What is it?

ÉMILE. Monsieur de Bois-d'Enghien, Madame.

MADAME DUVERGER. Oh my . . . Show him in, won't you.

ÉMILE. Very good, Madame.

> *He leaves. A moment later*
> BOIS-D'ENGHIEN *enters, in*
> *lively and jocular mood,*
> *carrying a bouquet.*

BOIS-D'ENGHIEN. Hello, everyone! Mother! . . . Viviane, darling!

MADAME DUVERGER. Good evening . . . son!

VIVIANE, *smiling and taking the bouquet from* BOIS-D'ENGHIEN. More flowers? Again?

BOIS-D'ENGHIEN. For you . . . never too many! (*Aside.*) And besides, my florist gave me a flat rate from now till the wedding.

> VIVIANE *places the flowers*
> *in a vase on the end table.*

MADAME DUVERGER, *to* BOIS-D'ENGHIEN, *jovially.* Why son, aren't you even going to kiss her? Today you may, you know!

BOIS-D'ENGHIEN, *still in high spirits.* Of course I am, Mother! Just you watch! (*He fits the deed to the word, and in so doing pricks his finger on one of* VIVIANE's *many pins.*) Ouch!

VIVIANE. Careful . . . I'm full of pins.

BOIS-D'ENGHIEN, *sucking on his finger.* Thanks for telling me. I never would have noticed!

VIVIANE, *coyly.* That should teach you to keep your hands to yourself!

BOIS-D'ENGHIEN. All right . . . I've learned my lesson. See!

> *He kisses her again, this*
> *time with his hands behind*
> *his back.*

VIVIANE. Greedy!

MADAME DUVERGER, *approaching* BOIS-D'ENGHIEN *and extending her cheek to him.* And what about Mother? Doesn't she get one too?

BOIS-D'ENGHIEN, *making a face.* Of course she does! There!

(*He kisses her with his hands behind his back. Aside.*)
First the dessert, then the meat!

MADAME DUVERGER, *jokingly*. Oh, with me you don't have to watch your hands. I'm not full of pins!

BOIS-D'ENGHIEN, *aside*. Thank you!

MADAME DUVERGER. Now, son, I have some news that should make you very happy. We can't have the church on the day we had planned, so I've had to move the wedding ahead two days.

BOIS-D'ENGHIEN. Wonderful! Nothing could please me more. As a matter of fact, my florist was just saying he thought it was an awfully long engagement . . . (*To* VIVIANE.) Darling, I couldn't be more delighted!

MADAME DUVERGER, *behind* BOIS-D'ENGHIEN. And you will make her happy, won't you, son?

BOIS-D'ENGHIEN, *without thinking, turning around*. Who?

MADAME DUVERGER. Who? Who do you think? My little girl! Not the man in the moon!

BOIS-D'ENGHIEN, *recovering*. Of course . . . Of course I'll make her happy, Mother!

VIVIANE. And even if you don't . . . I was just saying to Mamma . . . There's always divorce, isn't there?

BOIS-D'ENGHIEN, *stunned*. There's always . . . Isn't it a little early to be thinking—

VIVIANE. I don't know . . . I think there's something very chic about being divorced.

BOIS-D'ENGHIEN. Oh?

VIVIANE. I think it would be much better than being a widow!

BOIS-D'ENGHIEN. So do I, believe me!

MADAME DUVERGER, *to* VIVIANE, *while taking* BOIS-D'ENGHIEN's *right hand in her left, and placing her right hand on his shoulder*. Besides, darling, with Fernand you'll never have to think about going to such extremes. He's a serious and settled young man, thank heaven!

VIVIANE, *with an almost inaudible sigh*. Yes, he is!

BOIS-D'ENGHIEN, *aside.* Well . . .

MADAME DUVERGER, *letting go of his hand.* Oh, I suppose he's sown a wild oat or two . . . like every young man . . .

BOIS-D'ENGHIEN, *the picture of injured innocence.* Never!

MADAME DUVERGER, *softly, to* BOIS-D'ENGHIEN, *delighted.* What? You mean not even the least little . . . little . . .

BOIS-D'ENGHIEN. Never! I don't know why you should even think . . . Of course, as a boy I used to see my friends running after girls all the time. But not me! In fact, I used to ask them what on earth they could find to do once they caught them!

VIVIANE, *plaintively, aside.* My oh my!

BOIS-D'ENGHIEN. No! There's only been one love in my life . . .

VIVIANE *and* MADAME DUVERGER, *simultaneously, the former as if to say "Impossible!," the latter as if to say "I knew it!"* Oh!

BOIS-D'ENGHIEN. My mother!

> VIVIANE, *who had moved toward him with a glimmer of hope in her eyes, moves back in disillusionment.*

MADAME DUVERGER, *touched.* That's very sweet!

BOIS-D'ENGHIEN. I always said I wanted to save myself . . . just for my wife.

MADAME DUVERGER, *to* VIVIANE, *while taking* BOIS-D'ENGHIEN's *hand.* You see, darling! Will you ever realize what a . . . what a gem of a man you're marrying?

VIVIANE, *aside, wryly.* A real gem!

BOIS-D'ENGHIEN, *pompously, still playing the part.* No . . . They'll never be able to say, the way they do about so many men, that I'm bringing into a marriage the sordid dregs of my bachelor life!

VIVIANE. Assorted dregs? What assorted dregs?

BOIS-D'ENGHIEN, *momentarily taken aback.* No, no! Sordid

. . . It's an expression . . . "The sordid dregs of my bachelor life." It's a figure of speech.

MADAME DUVERGER. That's right.

VIVIANE. Oh, I see.

BOIS-D'ENGHIEN, *to* VIVIANE, *resuming the self-righteous tone.* Yes, indeed! When you marry me it's almost as if you were marrying . . . Joan of Arc.

VIVIANE. Joan of Arc?

MADAME DUVERGER. Joan of Arc?

BOIS-D'ENGHIEN. Except that I'm a man, that's all.

VIVIANE. But . . . why Joan of Arc? Are you a national hero?

BOIS-D'ENGHIEN. No . . . I've never had the chance. (*Dramatically.*) What I mean is that . . . I'm coming to the end of my bachelor life with a heart as pure . . . as Joan of Arc's, when, at the end of her heroic campaign, she was captured and betrayed by the Bastard Lionel . . .

MADAME DUVERGER, *shocked.* Fernand! Such language, from you?

BOIS-D'ENGHIEN. What do you mean? That was his title . . . Lionel, the Bastard of Vendôme. I can't very well call him the Maharajah!

VIVIANE, *wryly.* He's right, Mamma.

MADAME DUVERGER, *laughing.* Oh, Fernand! You dear boy! You're a sheer delight!

VIVIANE, *aside.* He's even more incredible than I imagined!

BOIS-D'ENGHIEN, *aside, moving left.* This may not exactly be cricket, but it does make me look good.

> ÉMILE *appears at the*
> *drawing room door.*

MADAME DUVERGER. What is it, Emile?

ÉMILE. One of the guests has arrived, Madame.

MADAME DUVERGER. Already? My goodness! Who?

ÉMILE. Monsieur de Fontanet, Madame.

BOIS-D'ENGHIEN, *aside, with a start.* Fontanet! The one I met this morning!

MADAME DUVERGER, *noticing* BOIS-D'ENGHIEN'S *reaction.*

What's the matter, son? Do you know him?

BOIS-D'ENGHIEN, *quickly.* Me? No, not at all!

MADAME DUVERGER. Oh, I thought perhaps . . . (*To* ÉMILE.) Please ask Monsieur de Fontanet to join us here, Emile.

> ÉMILE *leaves.*

BOIS-D'ENGHIEN. Here? In your bedroom?

MADAME DUVERGER, *with a laugh.* Heavens, yeš! Fontanet is an old friend.

BOIS-D'ENGHIEN, *aside.* Good God! And there's no way I can possibly warn him! He's bound to blurt something out!

ÉMILE, *showing* FONTANET *in.* This way, Monsieur.

> *He leaves.*

FONTANET. Good evening, Baroness. What a pleasure—

BOIS-D'ENGHIEN, *rushing between* FONTANET *and* MADAME DUVERGER, *cutting him off.* Well hello there! What a wonderful surprise! And how is everything?

> *He pulls* FONTANET *downstage, almost to the footlights.*

FONTANET, *startled.* You . . . Here? But I didn't—

BOIS-D'ENGHIEN. Of course! Of course! Who else?

MADAME DUVERGER, *completely at sea.* But . . .

BOIS-D'ENGHIEN, *aside to* FONTANET, *quickly.* For God's sake, don't put your foot in it, whatever you do!

MADAME DUVERGER, *to* BOIS-D'ENGHIEN. You mean you do know him?

BOIS-D'ENGHIEN. Do I know him? Of course I know him!

MADAME DUVERGER. But just a moment ago you told me—

BOIS-D'ENGHIEN. Because I had no idea you meant *this* Fontanet! Why, of course I know Fontanet!

> *He shakes* FONTANET's *hand vigorously.*

FONTANET. I should say so! In fact, only today we had lunch together.

BOIS-D'ENGHIEN, *becoming unstrung.* Today? . . . Well, yes . . . Lunch . . . That is, not really very much . . . I wasn't very hungry . . . I mean . . .

MADAME DUVERGER. What a coincidence! Where, may I ask?

BOIS-D'ENGHIEN. Where? Where . . . what?

MADAME DUVERGER. Where did you have lunch?

BOIS-D'ENGHIEN. Oh . . . Out that way . . . You know . . . (*To* FONTANET, *gesturing.*) Where was it exactly?

FONTANET. We ate with our young star, you remember.

BOIS-D'ENGHIEN, *aside.* Idiot!

MADAME DUVERGER. Young star?

VIVIANE. What young star?

BOIS-D'ENGHIEN, *quickly.* You know! Young Star . . . Young Star . . . the Chinese restaurant!

FONTANET, *aside.* What?

BOIS-D'ENGHIEN, *to* MADAME DUVERGER *and* VIVIANE, *forcing a laugh.* You mean . . . You mean you've never heard of Young Star's famous Chinese restaurant?

MADAME DUVERGER *and* VIVIANE. Never!

BOIS-D'ENGHIEN, *to* FONTANET *laughing even harder to cover his confusion.* What do you think of that, Fontanet? They've never even heard of Young Star's restaurant!

FONTANET, *laughing along with him.* Ha ha ha! (*Suddenly changing his tone.*) Neither have I!

BOIS-D'ENGHIEN, *with an involuntary grimace.* Oh! (*Laughing again, but with less conviction.*) Neither have you! (*Pointing to* FONTANET.) That's a good one! Ha ha ha! He eats in a restaurant and he doesn't even know the name! (*Moving far left and pushing* FONTANET *along with him.*) Ha ha ha! Fontanet . . . Still the old joker! Never heard of Young Star's restaurant! (*Aside to* FONTANET, *quickly.*) For God's sake, will you be quiet!

MADAME DUVERGER, *who has been laughing along with*

them. And how did you find this . . . Young Star's restaurant?

BOIS-D'ENGHIEN. Find it? I didn't find it!

MADAME DUVERGER. What?

BOIS-D'ENGHIEN. Oh, you mean . . . (*To* FONTANET.) She wants to know how I found the restaurant . . .

MADAME DUVERGER. That's right . . . How did you find it?

BOIS-D'ENGHIEN. Of course! (*Aside.*) Whose damned idea was this?

VIVIANE. Well?

BOIS-D'ENGHIEN, *at a loss.* You know . . . It's . . . it's just on the other side of . . . (*Brief, embarrassing silence.*) Well, say you're standing near the Opera . . . You know where the Opera is?

MADAME DUVERGER. Of course!

BOIS-D'ENGHIEN. All right, then. You're standing in the safety zone . . . with the Opera in front of you and the avenue in back. Understand? . . . Good . . . (*He pivots around suddenly, as do the others.*) Then you do a sharp about-face . . . (*Calmly and precisely.*) so that the Opera is in back of you and the avenue in front . . .

MADAME DUVERGER. Just a moment. Wouldn't it have been easier to start that way?

BOIS-D'ENGHIEN. I . . . I suppose so. Only, I know this way better.

MADAME DUVERGER, *as* BOIS-D'ENGHIEN *is about to continue.* Besides, you know . . . It doesn't really make any difference to me where the restaurant is. I was just asking . . .

BOIS-D'ENGHIEN. Oh? (*Heaving a sigh of relief.*) Well, then, let's forget it!

FONTANET, *aside, looking at* BOIS-D'ENGHIEN. What on earth is bothering him?

MADAME DUVERGER, *to* FONTANET. The only thing that really matters is that you do know one another after all.

And I thought I was going to have to introduce you to Viviane's fiancé!

FONTANET. Viviane's fiancé? Who?

MADAME DUVERGER. Him, of course! Monsieur de Bois-d'Enghien!

FONTANET. What? You mean, he . . . (*Aside.*) But what about Lucette? . . . Aha! Now I understand . . . Young Star's restaurant indeed! (*Aloud, to* BOIS-D'ENGHIEN.) You mean you . . . (*Pointing to* VIVIANE.) . . . and she . . . Didn't I tell you this morning her fiancé had a name just like yours? Remember?

BOIS-D'ENGHIEN, *aside.* Swine!

> *At the end of his rope,*
> BOIS-D'ENGHIEN *stamps*
> *suddenly and sharply on*
> FONTANET's *foot with his*
> *heel, unseen by the others.*

FONTANET, *in pain.* Owwww!

MADAME DUVERGER *and* VIVIANE. What's the matter?

BOIS-D'ENGHIEN, *feigning ignorance, making even more noise than the others.* What's the matter? What is it? What's wrong with him? What is it?

FONTANET, *limping over to the chaise longue and sitting down.* My foot! . . . Oh! . . . My foot!

BOIS-D'ENGHIEN, *aside.* That should change the conversation!

FONTANET, *furious, to* BOIS-D'ENGHIEN. You . . . You . . . With that heel of yours!

BOIS-D'ENGHIEN. Me? Why . . . I beg your pardon!

FONTANET. Oh! And right on my corn!

BOIS-D'ENGHIEN, *seizing the new subject.* You have corns? (*To the others.*) He has corns! What a shame . . . There's nothing so unattractive!

FONTANET. Unattractive or not, when you step on them they hurt!

VIVIANE, *next to the chaise longue.* Does it still hurt, Monsieur de Fontanet?

FONTANET, *getting up and moving left, with obvious difficulty.* Oh! It's a little better, thank you. I'll be all right.

BOIS-D'ENGHIEN. Of course you will. At least it won't keep you from witnessing the marriage contract when Lantery gets here!

FONTANET, *rubbing his foot.* Oh, Is Lantery your notary?

MADAME DUVERGER. Yes, he is. He's one of the best, don't you think?

BOIS-D'ENGHIEN, *happy to have changed the subject.* I should say! (*To* FONTANET.) Don't you think so?

FONTANET. Yes . . . He has only one fault, poor man . . .

MADAME DUVERGER. Oh? What's that?

FONTANET. Have you ever stood close to him? (*The others exchange meaningful glances, which* FONTANET *misinterprets as looks of incomprehension.*) Well, I mean . . . He smells bad! (*The others, doing their best to repress a laugh, emit an "oh" or two.*) Haven't you ever noticed? (*Turning toward* BOIS-D'ENGHIEN *and exhaling in his face.*) Whew! Really, it's unbearable!

> *He moves far left.*

BOIS-D'ENGHIEN, *aside.* The pot calling the kettle black!

> ÉMILE *enters, moving downstage toward* MADAME DUVERGER, *carrying a little tray and a calling card.*

ÉMILE. Madame, there is a lady who says that Madame is expecting her. There is another lady and a gentleman with her.

> *He hands her the tray.*

MADAME DUVERGER, *reading the calling card.* Oh, yes . . . Fine! Tell her I'll just be a moment.

ÉMILE. Very good, Madame.

> *He leaves.*

BOIS-D'ENGHIEN. Anyone we know?

MADAME DUVERGER. Oh, just a little surprise I've planned for my guests.

FONTANET. Really?

BOIS-D'ENCHIEN. But you'll tell us, won't you?

MADAME DUVERGER. No, no! You'll see . . . I want it to be a surprise. I know you'll be delighted. (*To* VIVIANE.) Come along, darling.

VIVIANE. Yes, Mamma.

> MADAME DUVERGER *and*
> VIVIANE *leave through the*
> *drawing room door.* BOIS-
> D'ENCHIEN *accompanies*
> *them to the door, then re-*
> *turns downstage to*
> FONTANET, *quickly.*

BOIS-D'ENCHIEN. My dear fellow, do you have any idea what agony you've been putting me through?

FONTANET. Sorry, old boy! I finally understood, after a while. But how was I supposed to know that *you* were her fiancé, of all people? I mean, you . . . Lucette Gautier . . . I thought . . .

BOIS-D'ENCHIEN. No, no, no! That's been over for weeks!

FONTANET. But . . . just this morning . . . weren't you and she—

BOIS-D'ENCHIEN. So? What does that prove? This morning I was just . . . passing through to say good-bye, that's all. Just stopped in to have "one for the road," you might say!

> *He moves right.*

FONTANET. Oh?

BOIS-D'ENCHIEN, *returning quickly to* FONTANET. But please, whatever you do, if you happen to see Lucette, don't breathe a word about my marriage. She'll find out soon enough.

FONTANET. Of course, not a word! (*The sound of several voices is heard in the wings.*) Ah, that must be the Baroness.

BOIS-D'ENGHIEN, *indifferently.* With her big surprise, I
suppose.

FONTANET. I think I'll take a peek. (BOIS-D'ENGHIEN *remains downstage while* FONTANET, *at the drawing room
door, stops short for a moment in evident disbelief.*)
What? What is she doing here? (*Speaking into the
drawing room.*) You? But what on earth . . .

> FONTANET *disappears into
> the drawing room.*

BOIS-D'ENGHIEN, *curious.* "You" . . . "She" . . . Who, for
goodness' sake?

> *He moves to the door, looks,
> and recoils in terror.*

Good God in Heaven! Lucette!

> *He rushes headlong to the
> door, up right, but finds it
> locked. Wild-eyed, he looks
> around, not knowing which
> way to turn.*

Lucette . . . Here, in this house! But how . . . Who . . .
Who . . .

> *He is about to run to the
> other door, down left, but
> just as he reaches the draw-
> ing room door he stops in
> his tracks as he sees the
> others approaching. In
> desperation he runs to the
> closet along the center wall,
> opens the doors, and hides
> inside.*

God have mercy on my soul!

> *He shuts the closet doors
> in front of him.* FONTANET,
> MADAME DUVERGER, VIVIANE,
> LUCETTE, MARCELINE *and*
> CHENNEVIETTE *have ap-
> peared in the drawing room,*

*where they can be seen
through the open door.*

FONTANET. Yes, indeed! Talk about surprises . . . I should
say so! What a surprise!

MADAME DUVERGER. I knew you would be delighted! (*To*
LUCETTE, *pointing to the door.*) This way, Mademoiselle
Gautier . . . Right in here.

FONTANET, *aside.* My God! Bois-d'Enghien! (*He moves
quickly to the doorway and holds the others off. Aloud.*)
No, no! Not in here!

MADAME DUVERGER. What?

*The others look at one an-
other and make comments
like: "Why not?" "What's
wrong?" etc.*

FONTANET. Because . . . Because . . . (*He turns to take
a quick look around the room and sees that* BOIS-
D'ENGHIEN *is no longer there.*) Well, I mean . . . If
you want to come in . . . Why not? I mean . . .

MADAME DUVERGER, *as if to say "What a prank at your
age!"* Really, Fontanet!

*The others mumble
appropriately.*

FONTANET, *aside.* Thank heaven he got away!

*Everyone enters from the
drawing room.* VIVIANE *and*
FONTANET *move over by the
chaise longue, while* LUCETTE
and MADAME DUVERGER
come down center. MARCE-
LINE *and* CHENNEVIETTE
*stand over by the table,
stage left.*

MADAME DUVERGER, *to* LUCETTE. Now then, I hope this
room will suit you, Mademoiselle.

LUCETTE. Oh yes, Madame . . . Perfectly! It couldn't be
better!

MADAME DUVERGER, *to* MARCELINE, *who is carrying* LU-
CETTE'*s wardrobe box.* You there . . . You may put
Mademoiselle Gautier's things on the table. There's a
good girl . . .

MARCELINE, *aside, carrying out the instructions.* Good girl!
Who does she think she's talking to?

LUCETTE, *introducing* CHENNEVIETTE, *who is holding a
little handbag containing* LUCETTE'*s make-up, etc.* Madame, let me present Monsieur de Chenneviette, one of
my dearest friends and . . . something of a relative,
in a way. I took the liberty of asking him along . . .
He acts as my manager for all my private engage-
ments.

MADAME DUVERGER. Delighted, Monsieur!

> CHENNEVIETTE *bows.*

MARCELINE, *aside.* No danger of her introducing me!

MADAME DUVERGER, *to* LUCETTE. I think you should find
everything you need here, Mademoiselle. This is really
my bedroom, but I've had it specially arranged just for
this evening.

LUCETTE. Oh, I'm terribly sorry you've had to go to so
much trouble!

MADAME DUVERGER. Trouble? Not at all, my dear. I wanted
to give a performer of your talent a dressing room that
would be worthy of you.

LUCETTE. Why, thank you! (*Suddenly noticing the armchair under the canopy, stage right.*) My goodness,
what's that? A throne?

> *The others all peer at the
> armchair.*

MARCELINE *and* CHENNEVIETTE. A throne?

LUCETTE, *to* MADAME DUVERGER. Really, Madame, you're
very kind, but . . . You didn't have to . . .

MADAME DUVERGER. A throne? (*Suddenly understanding,
with a little laugh.*) No, no, my dear . . . That's not a
throne! It's the canopy to my bed. I had the bed removed and a chair put in its place for you.

LUCETTE, *a little piqued.* Oh, I see. Of course . . .

MADAME DUVERGER, *moving around the room to point things out, as* CHENNEVIETTE, *playing the role of manager, follows a few paces behind.* Now then, behind the screen you should find whatever toilet articles you need . . . (*Approaching the closet, as if to open it.*) As for your costumes and things, you may want to put them in this closet.

> *She leaves the closet and moves to the chaise longue,* CHENNEVIETTE *still following.*

LUCETTE. Fine!

MADAME DUVERGER, *pointing to the end table.* And if you should need anything at all, you may simply press this button on the table. Besides, this door . . . (*She goes to the door, up right, and tries to open it.*) My word, who could have locked it? (*To* VIVIANE, *who has moved in front of the closet with* FONTANET, *chatting with him.*) Viviane, be a dear, would you? Run round and open the door. It's locked from the other side.

VIVIANE. Yes, Mamma.

> *She leaves through the drawing room door.*

MADAME DUVERGER. As I was saying, this door leads to the servants' quarters and the pantry. If you should need anything, it might be even faster for your maid to run down and get it herself.

MARCELINE, *appalled.* Her maid? What maid?

MADAME DUVERGER *to* MARCELINE. Why, I thought you . . . Mademoiselle . . . Aren't you . . .

MARCELINE. Hardly, Madame! I am Mademoiselle Gautier's sister!

MADAME DUVERGER. Oh, my dear! I beg your pardon! I had no idea . . .

MARCELINE, *sullen.* It's quite all right! (*Aside.*) Her maid, indeed!

> *She moves to the table and begins opening the wardrobe box.*

VIVIANE, *entering up right.* There, Mamma. It's open.

> *She goes to the end table and takes her bouquet.*

MADAME DUVERGER, *to* LUCETTE. Now perhaps you would like to see where you are going to perform. You must want to make certain that everything is in order . . . The platform, the arrangement of the piano . . .

LUCETTE. Oh no, Madame. I leave all those details to my manager. (*Aside, to* CHENNEVIETTE.) It's all yours, darling!

CHENNEVIETTE, *aside to* LUCETTE, *giving her the handbag he has been holding.* Thank you! (*To* MADAME DUVERGER.) If you would be good enough to show me the way, Madame . . .

MADAME DUVERGER, *going toward the drawing room door.* Certainly . . . We'll go with you. (*To* FONTANET, *who has been pacing aimlessly in front of the closet.*) Coming, Fontanet?

FONTANET. After you, Baroness.

LUCETTE, *opening her handbag on the end table.* In the meantime, my sister will help me get things ready in here.

MADAME DUVERGER, *about to leave.* Very good . . . Come along, Viviane.

VIVIANE. Yes, Mamma.

MADAME DUVERGER, *to* VIVIANE, *as a sudden afterthought, as she joins her to leave.* My word, darling! Where on earth is your fiancé?

VIVIANE. I have no idea, Mamma. He must be out getting the fresh air.

> *She follows the three of them out, upstage, taking her bouquet with her.*

MARCELINE, *who has opened the wardrobe box and placed the cover upright on one of the chairs next to the table.* Very nice, I must say! Now they're taking me for your maid!

LUCETTE. Don't be silly. She had no way of knowing you were my sister. It's not written all over you, after all.

MARCELINE. No, but I know you! Nothing makes you happier than seeing someone make a fool of me!

LUCETTE. Marceline, for heaven's sake! Instead of standing there grumbling, I wish you would unpack my costumes and put them in the closet. They're getting all wrinkled in that box.

MARCELINE, *unpacking.* You'll see! Some day I'll . . . I'll do something rash. And it will be your fault!

LUCETTE. You? Do something rash? And what, for example?

MARCELINE, *moving center stage with one of* LUCETTE's *costumes over her arm.* I'll find myself a lover, that's what!

LUCETTE, *laughing.* You?

MARCELINE. Don't laugh . . . I can, you know!

> She fingers the costume
> nervously, without paying
> attention to what she is
> doing.

LUCETTE, *still laughing.* Ha ha ha! Of course you can, darling! Ha ha ha! A lover! (*Suddenly noticing that* MARCELINE *is wrinkling her costume, changing her tone.*) Marceline! Look what you're doing to my costume! (*Moving left while* MARCELINE *goes to the closet, grumbling.*) No! I should say you're not a maid . . . Because if you were a maid, you certainly wouldn't work for anyone very long!

MARCELINE. Certainly not for you, I'm sure! (*She tries unsuccessfully to open one of the doors of the closet.*)

Oh! What's the matter with this closet? I can't get it open.

LUCETTE, *behind the table, stage left, putting the cover back on the wardrobe box.* It must be locked, silly. Turn the key. Is that so hard?

MARCELINE. I'm turning it, can't you see? It still won't open.

LUCETTE. What do you mean, it won't open! (*Going to the closet, out of patience.*) Even a simple thing like opening a closet-door . . . Is there anything you do know how to do? Here, let me do it! (*She pushes* MARCELINE *out of the way and tries to open the door, without success.*) Hm!

MARCELINE. Well?

LUCETTE. It . . . It does seem to be sticking.

MARCELINE, *mockingly.* Is there anything you do know how to do?

LUCETTE, *ignoring her remark.* It's almost as if there were something holding it from the inside. (*To* MARCELINE.) Here, let's both give it a try. (MARCELINE *joins in the attempt.*) One, two, three!

> *At the count of three, the door yields, revealing* BOIS-D'ENGHIEN *who almost falls on top of them.* MARCELINE *and* LUCETTE *scream. They recoil in horror, not daring to look.*

BOIS-D'ENGHIEN, *regaining his composure in the closet, very calmly.* Well hello there!

LUCETTE. Fernand!

MARCELINE. Bois-d'Enghien!

LUCETTE, *still shaking from anger and fright.* What . . . What are you doing in there?

BOIS-D'ENGHIEN, *stepping out.* Me? Why . . . What do you think? I . . . I was waiting for you!

LUCETTE. In the closet?

BOIS-D'ENGHIEN. In the . . . Yes, in the . . . closet. (*Trying to appear rational and unruffled.*) You know . . . Life . . . Well, you know, there are times when a man just likes to be alone . . . (*Changing the subject, as if he had succeeded in giving a perfectly acceptable explanation.*) Well now, what's new since this afternoon?

LUCETTE, *still angry, not to be put off.* You . . . You frightened me half to death! Do you realize that?

MARCELINE. Only a lunatic would frighten anybody that way!

BOIS-D'ENGHIEN, *forcing a laugh to cover his confusion.* Ha ha ha! You mean I frightened you? Ha ha ha! I really did? You weren't just making believe?

LUCETTE. Did we look as if we were making believe?

BOIS-D'ENGHIEN. Ha ha ha! Then my little joke really worked?

LUCETTE. Little joke?

BOIS-D'ENGHIEN, *still laughing.* Of course! I said to myself: "She'll be here any minute . . . She opens up the closet, and there I am!" Ha ha ha! I thought it was a wonderful joke!

LUCETTE. Oh yes! Perfectly charming, your little joke!

MARCELINE. It was stupid if you ask me!

BOIS-D'ENGHIEN. Much obliged! (*Aside.*) My God! How can I keep the others away?

CHENNEVIETTE, *entering from the drawing room.* Everything's ready in there. (*Suddenly noticing* BOIS-D'ENGHIEN.) Bois-d'Enghien!

BOIS-D'ENGHIEN. Chenneviette!

CHENNEVIETTE. I say . . . What are you doing here?

BOIS-D'ENGHIEN, *trying to appear natural.* Oh . . . Just like that.

LUCETTE. And you'll never guess where I found him! In the closet!

CHENNEVIETTE. In the closet?

BOIS-D'ENGHIEN, *with a hearty but unconvincing laugh.* Yes! In the . . . Ha ha ha! Isn't that the funniest . . .

CHENNEVIETTE, *aside.* He's out of his mind!

> *During the preceding exchange,* MARCELINE *has been hanging* LUCETTE'*s things in the closet.*

MARCELINE, *to* LUCETTE, *carrying off the empty wardrobe box.* I'll take this out, all right?

LUCETTE. Yes . . . Please.

MARCELINE, *leaving up right, grumbling.* Through the maid's door!

> *She leaves.*

LUCETTE, *to* BOIS-D'ENGHIEN. Then you must know these people. I didn't realize . . .

BOIS-D'ENGHIEN, *with aplomb.* Of course! I've known them for years.

LUCETTE. Really?

BOIS-D'ENGHIEN. I've known Madame Duverger since she was a baby.

LUCETTE *and* CHENNEVIETTE. What?

BOIS-D'ENGHIEN. I mean . . . She's known me since I was a baby . . . So . . .

LUCETTE. That's funny . . .

BOIS-D'ENGHIEN, *doubling up with laughter and moving right.* It certainly is! Ha ha ha! I think so too!

LUCETTE, *to* CHENNEVIETTE, *watching* BOIS-D'ENGHIEN *in amazement.* What's got into him? All he can do is laugh!

BOIS-D'ENGHIEN, *suddenly becoming serious and almost lunging at* LUCETTE, *while* CHENNEVIETTE *moves down right.* And now you're going to do me a favor and refuse to sing in this house!

LUCETTE *startled.* Refuse to . . . What? Why on earth . . .

BOIS-D'ENGHIEN. Why? She wants to know why? . . . Because . . . Because . . . There's a terrible draft, that's why. You know how bad that is for your voice.

LUCETTE. A draft? Where?

BOIS-D'ENCHIEN, *hardly knowing what he is saying.* Everywhere, that's where! All around the platform! Everywhere!

LUCETTE. All around the platform? Well, I'll find out about that in a hurry. I'll speak to the Baroness.

> *She begins moving toward the drawing room door.*

BOIS-D'ENCHIEN, *pouncing on her and holding her back.* No, no, no! Not the Baroness . . . She . . . I . . . It will make an awful hubbub and . . . I wouldn't want her to know I told you!

LUCETTE, *breaking loose.* Don't be silly . . . I won't even mention your name. (MADAME DUVERGER *appears in the drawing room.*) Ah, there she is. This is the best time to find out.

BOIS-D'ENCHIEN, *dashing toward the door, down left, in a frantic effort to avoid* MADAME DUVERGER. Sorry! I've got to be going!

LUCETTE. Wait a minute!

BOIS-D'ENCHIEN, *at the door.* I haven't been here! You haven't seen me! You don't know where I am!

> *He disappears through the door.*

LUCETTE. What's got into him?

CHENNEVIETTE, *who has been witnessing this scene in utter amazement, aside.* I wish I knew what all this was about!

MADAME DUVERGER, *entering, speaking to herself.* I wonder where he can be, that son-in-law of mine.

LUCETTE, *going up to her.* Ah, Madame Duverger. I'm glad you're here . . . I wanted to speak to you. It seems there's a terrible draft in your drawing room.

MADAME DUVERGER, *with a start.* In my drawing room?

LUCETTE, *polite but firm.* Yes, Madame. That's what I've been told. You understand, of course . . . I can't sing a note when there's the slightest draft on my back.

MADAME DUVERGER, *not knowing what to say, or whom to appeal to, turning alternately to* LUCETTE *and* CHENNEVIETTE. But . . . but Mademoiselle! I don't know what you mean! A draft? In the drawing room? Why, there's not a word of truth . . . Monsieur . . . In my drawing room? Mademoiselle, believe me . . . A draft? Why, come see for yourself! There isn't the slightest breath of air!

LUCETTE. Yes, I would like to have a look . . . Because, you do understand . . . Under such conditions, after all, I really couldn't—

> *She approaches the drawing room door with* MADAME DUVERGER.

MADAME DUVERGER. Please! Come see for yourself! (*At the door.*) In my drawing room . . . A draft? . . . No, no! Absolutely not!

> *They leave, still talking back and forth.*

CHENNEVIETTE, *moving left.* Draft my foot! What's all this nonsense about a draft?

BOIS-D'ENGHIEN, *bolting into the room all out of breath, through the door up right.* Ah! You're alone!

CHENNEVIETTE, *surprised.* What? You . . . (*Pointing to the door, down left, through which* BOIS-D'ENGHIEN *had disappeared a moment before.*) I thought you went out—

BOIS-D'ENGHIEN. That's right! Out that door, and then . . .

> *He indicates with a gesture that he has run upstairs, crossed over, and come down on the other side.*

CHENNEVIETTE. But why? For goodness' sake, what's going on?

BOIS-D'ENGHIEN. What's going on? I'll tell you what's going on! I've got a five-story house hanging over my head, that's all! Lucette is here! Do you realize what that means? In a few minutes the notary will be here with the marriage contract. That's what's going on!

CHENNEVIETTE, *with a start.* No!

BOIS-D'ENGHIEN, *dejected.* Yes!

CHENNEVIETTE, *slapping his thigh and turning his back on* BOIS-D'ENGHIEN. Now how in thunder—

BOIS-D'ENGHIEN. Exactly! How in thunder! (*Putting his hands on* CHENNEVIETTE's *shoulder and turning him back around.*) And unless you help me get Lucette out of here, by hook or crook, that thunder is going to explode all over the place!

CHENNEVIETTE. But how?

BOIS-D'ENGHIEN. I don't know . . . You've got to, that's all!

CHENNEVIETTE, *with a half-turn, as before.* I'll do my best . . .

BOIS-D'ENGHIEN, *turning him back again.* Where is she? Where is she now, do you know?

CHENNEVIETTE, *losing patience at* BOIS-D'ENGHIEN's *maneuver, breaking loose.* She's with the Baroness, in the drawing room, looking into that . . . that silly draft of yours!

> *He moves upstage away*
> *from* BOIS-D'ENGHIEN.

BOIS-D'ENGHIEN. Oh God! Then everything's going to come down around my ears!

> *Voices in the wings.*

CHENNEVIETTE, *quickly.* Careful! Here they come!

> BOIS-D'ENGHIEN, *with a*
> *grimace, dashes toward the*
> *door, down left, just in*

> *time to bump into* VIVIANE
> *entering. They both utter
> an "oh" of surprise and
> pain, and stand for a
> moment rubbing their
> respective bruises.*

BOIS-D'ENGHIEN, *aside.* Damn! (*Aloud, forcing a laugh.*) Well, what a surprise! Where have you been?

VIVIANE. Me? . . . Where have *you* been? I've been looking everywhere!

BOIS-D'ENGHIEN. Why, so have I! So have I! (*Trying to pull her away.*) Come, now we can go look together!

VIVIANE, *holding him back.* Look for what? Here we are!

BOIS-D'ENGHIEN. Of course! Of course! (*Aside.*) I don't even know what I'm saying!

VIVIANE, *aside.* Idiot!

CHENNEVIETTE, *who has moved downstage, far right, aside.* He's babbling, poor chap!

> MADAME DUVERGER's *voice
> is heard in the wings.*

BOIS-D'ENGHIEN. There they are!

> *He moves stealthily toward
> the door, down left, trying
> to escape without being
> seen.*

MADAME DUVERGER, *to* LUCETTE, *entering from the drawing room.* You see, Mademoiselle, I was right.

LUCETTE. Yes . . .

MADAME DUVERGER, *just as* BOIS-D'ENGHIEN *is about to disappear.* Ah, Bois-d'Enghien! There you are!

BOIS-D'ENGHIEN, *stopping short and turning, with all the aplomb he can muster.* Oh! I was just . . . looking for you.

MADAME DUVERGER, *about to introduce* BOIS-D'ENGHIEN *to* LUCETTE. Mademoiselle . . .

BOIS-D'ENGHIEN, *aside, with a look of pained resignation.* God!

MADAME DUVERGER, *as* LUCETTE *nods to indicate that she already knows him.* You must let me introduce—

CHENNEVIETTE, *plunging between the two women and seizing* LUCETTE *by the hand.* No, no! Don't bother! She knows him! She knows him!

MADAME DUVERGER, *upset by the jostling she has received.* What?

> *A general uproar ensues, during which* MADAME DUVERGER *and* VIVIANE *express their surprise with comments like "What's the matter?" "I don't understand!" etc., as* LUCETTE *tries to free herself from* CHENNEVIETTE's *grip.*

LUCETTE. Let go of me!

CHENNEVIETTE, *dragging her toward the drawing room door.* Come on! You're coming with me!

LUCETTE, *struggling.* But where? Where . . .

CHENNEVIETTE. To find the draft! I know just where it is!

LUCETTE, *disappearing through the door, against her will.* No, no, no! Let go of me!

> MADAME DUVERGER *and* VIVIANE, *startled, have moved upstage to watch their hasty exit.* BOIS-D'ENGHIEN *remains down left.*

BOIS-D'ENGHIEN, *aside, happy to be delivered.* There's a good dog, Rover! Haul her off! . . . Ah! I could kiss him!

MADAME DUVERGER. What's the matter? Why is he dragging her away like that?

BOIS-D'ENGHIEN. Why? (*He strides up to the two women, stands between them, and, taking them both by the hand, pulls them downstage with similar giant strides, which they follow as best they can.*) Because . . . Because you were just about to make a terrible blunder, that's why!

MADAME DUVERGER, *on one side of him.* Me? A blunder?

VIVIANE, *on the other side.* What kind of a blunder?

BOIS-D'ENGHIEN, *to* MADAME DUVERGER. You were just about to say: "This is Monsieur de Bois-d'Enghien, my future son-in-law . . ." Or, "I'd like you to meet my daughter's fiancé . . ." Something like that, right?

MADAME DUVERGER. Naturally.

BOIS-D'ENGHIEN, *with an air of deepest mystery.* Well, that's exactly what you must never say. (*Pointing to the door through which* CHENNEVIETTE *and* LUCETTE *disappeared a moment before.*) He . . . That gentleman just told me all about it . . . That's why he was so anxious to get her out of here . . . You must never, never say the word "fiancé" or "son-in-law" or anything like that, in front of Lucette Gautier!

MADAME DUVERGER. Why not?

BOIS-D'ENGHIEN. Why not? Well . . . Because . . . It seems . . . That gentleman just told me all about it . . . It seems she once had a very unhappy love affair.

VIVIANE, *suddenly interested.* Really?

BOIS-D'ENGHIEN, *mournfully.* Yes . . . Some handsome, dashing young man that she was madly in love with, of course . . . They were supposed to be married. But unfortunately, he was weak . . . very weak. One fine day . . . (*Sighing.*) he succumbed . . .

MADAME DUVERGER, *touched.* Oh, poor thing! To what? Consumption?

BOIS-D'ENGHIEN. No, no! To a rich old widow who packed up and took him off to America . . .

MADAME DUVERGER *and* VIVIANE. Oh!

BOIS-D'ENGHIEN, *dramatically.* And so . . . The wedding? Pffft! Out the window! Lucette Gautier has never been the same. Now you understand . . . All you have to do

216

is mention the word "fiancé" or "son-in-law" or anything like that . . . That gentleman just told me all about it . . . And right away, she goes all to pieces . . . Hysterics, fainting spells, and all that sort of thing!

MADAME DUVERGER. Why, that's frightful! I'm so glad you warned me.

VIVIANE. It's a real love story! I like it!

BOIS-D'ENGHIEN, *to* MADAME DUVERGER. Well, if I hadn't warned you . . . And if that gentleman hadn't told me all about it . . .

MADAME DUVERGER, *while* BOIS-D'ENGHIEN *moves upstage to watch for* LUCETTE's *return.* Just think what might have happened. I'm certainly glad you warned me.

VIVIANE. Oh yes! So am I!

> LUCETTE *appears in the drawing room, talking to* FONTANET *and* CHENNE-VIETTE.

BOIS-D'ENGHIEN, *aside, noticing them.* My God, they're back! (*He dashes downstage like a streak, seizes* MADAME DUVERGER *and* VIVIANE *each by the hand, and pulls them toward the door, down left.*) Come on! We're getting out of here! Let's go!

MADAME DUVERGER *and* VIVIANE, *bewildered.* What? . . . What? . . . Why?

BOIS-D'ENGHIEN, *pushing them through the door, first* VIVIANE *then* MADAME DUVERGER. I've got something else to tell you . . . Something to show you . . . It's upstairs! . . . Upstairs! . . . Come on!

> *He pushes them out, despite their objections, and disappears with them through the door.*

LUCETTE, *to* CHENNEVIETTE, *who precedes her through the drawing room door.* Really, I don't know what gets into you. Of all the silly things to do!

CHENNEVIETTE, *moving toward the chaise longue, aside.* Thanks to that damned Bois-d'Enghien I have to go make myself look like an idiot!

FONTANET, *who has entered behind them.* I say, is this a private conversation?

LUCETTE. No, no. Not at all.

> *She sits down on the chaise longue.*

FONTANET. You're sure I'm not intruding?

LUCETTE, *looking at herself in a pocket mirror which she has taken from the end table, powdering her nose.* No, no. Really.

FONTANET, *moving down left.* Because, frankly, it's awfully dull in there. Everybody's run off and left me all alone, as if I had the plague or something.

LUCETTE. Poor Fontanet!

FONTANET. Well, it's not much fun!

ÉMILE, *announcing at the drawing room door.* General Irrigua.

> *He retires.*

LUCETTE. The General? Oh my, I almost forgot.

> *She replaces the mirror, etc., on the end table.*

FONTANET. Who's that?

CHENNEVIETTE. Don't tell me he's been invited!

LUCETTE. Yes, I asked him . . . (*To* THE GENERAL, *appearing at the drawing room door.*) Hello, General. Come right in, won't you?

THE GENERAL, *entering hurriedly with a bouquet in one hand and an opera hat in the other, approaching* LU-CETTE *with determination.* Oh! Ees I am so late! Ees very bad, no? For becose I lose so much time I could have spend weeth you!

LUCETTE. Why no, General, you're not late at all.

THE GENERAL, *nodding to* CHENNEVIETTE *and* FONTANET.

Buenos días! (*To* LUCETTE, *offering her the bouquet.*)
Now please to permeet, Mamoiselle, I geeve . . .

LUCETTE, *without taking them.* Oh! Wild flowers . . .
What a sweet thought!

THE GENERAL. Sí! I peeck weeth my own hands. Most of
all ees wild roses, full weeth throne . . . For becose
you are queen who seet on throne of museec! (*Waiting
for his compliment to take effect.*) Ees clever, no? You
like?

CHENNEVIETTE, *bewildered.* Throne?

THE GENERAL, *to* CHENNEVIETTE. Sí! You no like?

CHENNEVIETTE. I no understand!

LUCETTE. I think you mean "thorns," General.

THE GENERAL. Ah! Bueno! Ees full with thorn, for queen
of melodía, who seet on thorn and make such pretty
sound.

LUCETTE. That's a charming tribute. Thank you.

> CHENNEVIETTE *and* FONTA-
> NET *nod in hypocritical
> approval.*

THE GENERAL, *handing* LUCETTE *the bouquet, tied together
by a strand of pearls.* But eef bouquette ees leetle,
streeng ees beeg!

LUCETTE, *getting up, taking the bouquet and removing
the necklace with great surprise.* A string of pearls! Oh,
General . . . Really!

THE GENERAL, *in the grand manner.* Ees notheeng! Ees
mirboble!

FONTANET, *moving over to the group to admire the pearls.*
May I?

> LUCETTE, CHENNEVIETTE *and*
> FONTANET *voice their ad-
> miration with exclamations
> like "Aren't they beautiful!"
> "Perfectly lovely!" etc.*

219

LUCETTE, *while* CHENNEVIETTE *fastens the pearls around her neck.* I simply can't tell you, General, how happy I am. They're magnificent!

> *She places the bouquet in*
> *the vase on the end table.*

THE GENERAL, *reveling in his generosity.* Sí, sí!

FONTANET, *scrutinizing.* They're exquisite! (*To* THE GENERAL.) You must let me compliment you on your taste, Monsieur!

> THE GENERAL *bows,*
> *modestly.*

LUCETTE, *introducing* FONTANET *without moving from* CHENNEVIETTE, *as he finishes attaching the necklace.* General Irrigua, Monsieur Ignace de Fontanet.

THE GENERAL, *extending his hand.* Ees pleasure!

FONTANET. How do you do, General. I must say, it's refreshing to see that the spirit of chivalry is still very much alive. And in such good taste . . .

THE GENERAL, *sniffing.* Oh, ees notheeng!

FONTANET, *bowing and scraping before* THE GENERAL, *and finally backing him against the wall, far left.* There's something terribly nice about being a millionaire and a gentleman at the same time, when there are so many millionaires who aren't gentlemen and so many gentlemen who aren't millionaires!

THE GENERAL, *turning to escape, but followed persistently by* FONTANET. Sí, sí! (*Taking a little box from his vest pocket and offering it to* FONTANET.) Here! Please to take one, yes?

FONTANET. What's that?

THE GENERAL. Ees lozenge. I chew heem when I have smoke ceegar.

FONTANET, *bowing, and replying right in* THE GENERAL'*s face.* Ha! Thank you just the same, General, but I don't smoke.

THE GENERAL, *quickly raising his opera hat to his face, seemingly in a gesture of regret, but actually to shield himself.* Oh, I am sorry! (*Offering the box again.*) Please to take one anyway!

FONTANET. All right, if you insist.

THE GENERAL. Muchas gracias!

> *He moves far right.*

FONTANET, *still on his heels.* As I was saying, General . . .

THE GENERAL, *defending himself with his hat as best he can.* Sí, sí! (*Nodding rapidly several times in an attempt to end the conversation.*) Bueno, bueno! (*Suddenly noticing* MADAME DUVERGER *about to enter from down left.*) Ah! Pardon!

> *He moves quickly to greet her.*

MADAME DUVERGER, *entering.* No, really! Can you imagine? He makes us climb three flights, all the way to the attic, just to stand there and tell us that the house doesn't have a lightning rod! Of all things . . .

THE GENERAL, *nodding.* Madame!

> MADAME DUVERGER *greets his bow with a quizzical look.*

LUCETTE. Oh, Madame Duverger! Please let me introduce one of my dear friends, General Irrigua—

THE GENERAL, *bowing.* Heemself!

LUCETTE, *continuing.* . . . who was happy to accept one of the invitations you were kind enough to give me.

THE GENERAL, *showing the invitation to* MADAME DUVERGER. Sí! You want I geeve you teecket?

MADAME DUVERGER, *smiling.* That's hardly necessary, General. This is just a family affair, you know.

THE GENERAL, *very graciously, as if he were making the most polite remark possible.* Ees make no deefference to me. I come here only for Mamoiselle Gautier.

MADAME DUVERGER, *taken aback.* Oh? I see . . . (*Aside, while* THE GENERAL *speaks to* LUCETTE.) Well, at least he doesn't mince words!

VIVIANE, *entering down left, dragging* BOIS-D'ENGHIEN *by the hand.* But you've got to come in! Whatever's the matter with you?

BOIS-D'ENGHIEN. Nothing! Nothing at all! (*Catching sight of* THE GENERAL, *aside.*) Oh God, not the General too!

THE GENERAL, *turning around and recognizing* BOIS-D'ENGHIEN. Ah, bueno! Ees Bodégué! (*Addressing him.*) You are goeeng to seeng sometheeng for us, no?

LUCETTE. What?

> *The others reply to* THE
> GENERAL's *suggestion with*
> *comments like "Bois-*
> *d'Enghien, sing?" "Why*
> *should he sing?" etc.*

THE GENERAL. Sí, sí! For becose he ees tenor, Bodégué!

> *A unanimous "no" of dis-*
> *belief arises from the group.*

VIVIANE, *to* BOIS-D'ENGHIEN. I didn't know you could sing.

BOIS-D'ENGHIEN. Eh . . . Well, you know . . . Just a little . . . Not very much . . .

VIVIANE. I had no idea . . . Why, we'll be able to sing duets!

BOIS-D'ENGHIEN, *aside, to the audience.* I'm improving! I'm improving all the time!

ÉMILE, *announcing.* Monsieur Lantery.

> *He retires.*

MADAME DUVERGER. Ah, the notary. (*Going to greet him.*) Good evening, Monsieur Lantery.

LANTERY. Good evening, Baroness. Ladies . . . Gentlemen . . .

> THE GENERAL, *after turning*
> *upstage momentarily to*
> *examine the new arrival,*
> *moves over to chat with*

> CHENNEVIETTE, *on the far*
> *side of the chaise longue.*

MADAME DUVERGER, *to* LANTERY. Well, now that you're here, Monsieur, I suppose we may as well begin. Do you have the contract?

LANTERY. No I don't, Baroness. One of my clerks should be along with it any minute . . . In fact . . . (*Looking toward the drawing room.*) Yes, there he is now.

> BOUZIN *appears in the*
> *drawing room, talking to*
> ÉMILE.

MADAME DUVERGER. Splendid!

BOIS-D'ENGHIEN, *catching sight of* BOUZIN, *aside.* Good God! Bouzin! (*Crossing right, aside to* LUCETTE.) Pssst! Look . . . Bouzin!

LUCETTE, *aside to* BOIS-D'ENGHIEN. Bouzin? . . . Oh my! If the General ever sees him . . .

> *She tries to keep* THE
> GENERAL *occupied, talking*
> *to him with her back*
> *toward the audience, thus*
> *preventing him from turning*
> *in* BOUZIN's *direction. In*
> *the meantime* LANTERY *goes*
> *to join* BOUZIN.

MADAME DUVERGER, *following* LANTERY. This way, everybody. We're ready to listen to the contract.

FONTANET, *to* VIVIANE, *who has joined him.* After you, my dear.

> *They leave, as* BOIS-
> D'ENGHIEN *crosses left.*

MADAME DUVERGER, *from the drawing room.* Monsieur de Chenneviette, will you join us?

CHENNEVIETTE, *who has been talking to* THE GENERAL, *to* MADAME DUVERGER. I'll be delighted, Madame! (*To* THE GENERAL.) You will excuse me, General?

THE GENERAL. Ees pleasure, Cheviotte!

> *He continues chatting with*
> LUCETTE *as* CHENNEVIETTE
> *leaves.*

MADAME DUVERGER, *to* BOUZIN, *in the drawing room.* Why, it's the gentleman I met this morning!

BOUZIN, *recognizing her.* Oh, Madame . . . I mean, Baroness! I had no idea . . . I mean . . . (*Regaining his composure.*) Well, so we meet again.

MADAME DUVERGER. Yes, so it seems. (BOUZIN, LANTERY, VIVIANE, FONTANET, *and* CHENNEVIETTE *disappear into the wings, as* MADAME DUVERGER, *at the drawing room door, addresses* LUCETTE.) Wouldn't you like to join us too, Mademoiselle?

BOIS-D'ENGHIEN, *with a start.* What?

LUCETTE. That's very kind of you, Madame, but I'm afraid I'd better not. I really should begin getting ready.

> *She goes to the closet and*
> *takes out a blouse which*
> MARCELINE *had previously*
> *hung there.*

MADAME DUVERGER. Of course . . . Whatever you think best. (BOIS-D'ENGHIEN *heaves a sigh of relief.*) And you, General?

THE GENERAL, *bowing.* Muchas gracias! But no . . . I stay weeth Mamoiselle Gautier.

> *He moves down, far right.*

MADAME DUVERGER, *aside.* Naturally. (*Aloud.*) Well then . . . Come along, Bois-d'Enghien.

> *She disappears into the*
> *wings.*

BOIS-D'ENGHIEN, *anxious.* Coming, coming!

> *He makes a move for the*
> *door.*

LUCETTE, *moving toward the chaise longue, undoing the laces of the blouse she is holding. To* BOIS-D'ENGHIEN. You? You're not going in there, are you?

BOIS-D'ENGHIEN, *suddenly rooted to the spot.* Oh? Don't you think . . . I mean . . .

LUCETTE. Just to hear the notary read a silly old marriage contract?

BOIS-D'ENGHIEN, *affecting an air of supreme indifference.* Oh . . . Well . . .

LUCETTE. What difference does it make to you?

BOIS-D'ENGHIEN. Me?

> *He makes a gesture as if to say, "I couldn't care less!"*

THE GENERAL, *trying to present a conclusive argument.* Sí! For why you go? Ees I go? No! . . . Bueno!

BOIS-D'ENGHIEN, *in hypocritical agreement.* Bueno! Bueno! (*Aside, sarcastically.*) It's only my marriage contract, after all!

LUCETTE, *moving toward the closet.* Of course, if you really want to, you could go in at the very end, just to watch the signing . . .

BOIS-D'ENGHIEN, *enthusiastically.* Why not!

LUCETTE, *stopping at the closet.* With me . . .

BOIS-D'ENGHIEN, *aside, with a shudder.* Bueno! . . . Very bueno!

LUCETTE, *hanging up the blouse.* After I finish dressing.

> *The others, obviously be-
> coming impatient, shout
> BOIS-D'ENGHIEN's name
> several times from the wings.*

BOIS-D'ENGHIEN, *aside.* That's right, now it's their turn! (*Aloud, nervously.*) I'm coming! I'm coming!

LUCETTE, *returning to the chaise longue.* What on earth do they want you for?

BOIS-D'ENGHIEN, *forcing a little laugh.* I . . . I wish I knew!

> *All the others, except
> LANTERY, appear in the
> drawing room.*

MADAME DUVERGER, *taking a few steps into the room.*

Well, Bois-d'Enghien? What's keeping you? (*Pointing to* BOUZIN, *who has entered and stationed himself, through bureaucratic habit, behind the table, stage left.*) Monsieur is waiting for you so he can read the contract.

THE GENERAL, *recognizing* BOUZIN *and leaping forward.* Poussin!

BOUZIN. Good God, it's that madman! . . . Let me out of here!

> THE GENERAL *begins pursuing him round the table, back and forth, amid general confusion and consternation.*

THE GENERAL. Poussin! . . . Ees always Poussin! . . . Thees time, es un hombre muerto, Poussin! I keel heem!

> BOUZIN *finally escapes, down left, knocking over one of the chairs near the door in an attempt to stop* THE GENERAL, *close on his heels.* THE GENERAL, *jumping over the chair, reaches the door but is stopped by* BOIS-D'ENGHIEN, *who, running after him, holds him back by a coat tail. The following rapid exchange is almost drowned out by the accompanying tumult, becoming little more than pantomime.*

MADAME DUVERGER, *as* BOUZIN *dashes out.* Good heavens! What's the matter? Where are they going?

LUCETTE. It's nothing! We'll take care of it! (*To* CHENNEVIETTE, *who has taken a position next to her, near the chaise longue.*) Run after them! Do something! Stop them!

> CHENNEVIETTE *complies, reaching the door just as*

THE GENERAL *breaks away from* BOIS-D'ENGHIEN. *Pushing* BOIS-D'ENGHIEN *aside,* CHENNEVIETTE *dashes out in hot pursuit. By this time the others have entered from the drawing room.* MARCELINE *has moved to the far side of the chaise longue, with* FONTANET *behind it.* VIVIANE *has joined* MADAME DUVERGER *near the table, up left. After a moment of general confusion, the chase continues through the drawing room. First* BOUZIN *is seen streaking by the open door, closely followed by* THE GENERAL *and, finally,* CHENNEVIETTE.

MADAME DUVERGER, *crossing over toward* LUCETTE. Will you please tell me what this is all about? I mean, really! Pouncing on Monsieur Bouzin that way . . . What kind of friends do you have?

LUCETTE. Please, Madame . . . You must excuse him. You see—

MADAME DUVERGER, *indignant.* The very idea! . . . And in my house!

LUCETTE. Yes, but you see . . .

The two women continue speaking, both at once; LUCETTE, *to excuse* THE GENERAL, MADAME DUVERGER, *to express her irritation.*

MADAME DUVERGER, *authoritatively, after a moment or two of this double dialogue.* Enough of this! We're here to read a contract, not to play hide-and-seek! Bois-d'Enghien, give Viviane your arm, and follow me!

> *She moves toward the*
> *drawing room.*

LUCETTE, *suddenly suspicious.* But . . . Why Bois-d'Enghien?

MADAME DUVERGER, *still upset, without thinking.* Why? Because he's her fiancé, that's why!

LUCETTE. Her fiancé . . . Bois-d'En . . .

> *She utters a sharp cry and*
> *faints, falling in a heap into*
> MARCELINE's *arms, as the*
> *others excitedly shout "What*
> *happened?" etc.*

MARCELINE. Ah! My God! . . . Lucette! . . . Help! She's fainted!

> MADAME DUVERGER *and*
> VIVIANE, *having moved*
> *quickly downstage, remain*
> *motionless, rooted to the*
> *spot. All the others surround*
> *the unconscious* LUCETTE,
> *finally laying her down on the*
> *chaise longue.*

BOIS-D'ENGHIEN, *striding across to* MADAME DUVERGER, *with reproach in his voice.* There! Now you did it! You said that word "fiancé" . . . You see what happened?

MADAME DUVERGER. Me?

VIVIANE, *in an accusing tone.* Yes, you did! You did!

BOIS-D'ENGHIEN. And after I warned you!

> *He returns to* LUCETTE.

VIVIANE. After he told you never, never to mention that word in front of her!

> MADAME DUVERGER, *even*
> *more overwrought than*
> *before, throws up her hands*
> *in despair, as if to say, "How*
> *did I ever get mixed up in*
> *this?"*

THE GENERAL, *bursting in, up right, closely followed by* CHENNEVIETTE. There! Ees feeneeshed! I keeck heem out fron house, thees Poussin!

CHENNEVIETTE, *aside, wiping his forehead.* My God, what a night!

THE GENERAL, *suddenly noticing* LUCETTE. Ay, Dios! Qué es eso? . . . Lucette? Ees seeck? . . . (*Going over to her.*) Lucette?

BOIS-D'ENGHIEN, *clapping his hands in impatience.* Quick! Get the smelling salts . . . or some vinegar, or something!

> MARCELINE *runs out, up right, while* BOIS-D'ENGHIEN, MADAME DUVERGER *and* VIVIANE *go looking frantically for smelling salts on the dressing table, upstage. Meanwhile* FONTANET, CHENNEVIETTE *and* THE GENERAL *surround* LUCETTE, *trying to revive her.*

THE GENERAL, *rubbing* LUCETTE's *left hand while* CHENNEVIETTE, *on the other side, rubs the right.* Lucette! Lucette! For why you do thees theeng? Come back to me, Lucette! Come back!

FONTANET, *bending over* LUCETTE's *face from behind the chaise longue.* All she needs is a few deep breaths of fresh air.

BOIS-D'ENGHIEN, *returning from the dressing table.* That's right . . . Don't stand so close, for heaven's sake . . .

THE GENERAL. Sí, sí! Por el amor de Dios, go away fron her!

CHENNEVIETTE. Yes, give her room! Give her room!

BOIS-D'ENGHIEN, *quickly moving left, as* FONTANET *moves back from the chaise longue.* Let's all give her room! (*To* MADAME DUVERGER *and* VIVIANE.) Come on . . .

We can leave her with them for a minute while we go
sign the contract.

> *He begins leaving with the
> two women.*

THE GENERAL, *as they reach the drawing room door.*
Queeck! A key! Geeve to me a key!

BOIS-D'ENGHIEN, *excitedly running over to* THE GENERAL
*and giving him a key from his pocket, without wonder-
ing why.* A key? Here . . . Here's a key!

THE GENERAL. Gracias!

BOIS-D'ENGHIEN, *returning to the women, but suddenly
stopping and turning toward* THE GENERAL. What on
earth for?

THE GENERAL, *putting the key down* LUCETTE's *back.* For
thees!

BOIS-D'ENGHIEN, *running back to the chaise longue.* But
. . . Are you out of your mind? That's the key to my
apartment! What did you do that for?

THE GENERAL. Ees for to cure her.

BOIS-D'ENGHIEN. But that's only good for a nosebleed, you
. . . you . . .

THE GENERAL. Sí, but ees maybe same for thees, no?

BOIS-D'ENGHIEN, *beside himself.* No, is not same for this,
damn it!

MADAME DUVERGER, *impatiently, to* BOIS-D'ENGHIEN. Well?
Are you coming?

BOIS-D'ENGHIEN, *stamping about like a horse, not knowing
which direction to turn.* Yes, yes! I'm coming! (*Aside.*)
I'll go sign the contract and run right back.

> BOIS-D'ENGHIEN, MADAME
> DUVERGER *and* VIVIANE
> *leave, closing the four
> panels of the door behind
> them.*

THE GENERAL. Queeck, breeng water! Vinagre! . . . Sometheeng!

FONTANET, *going over to the dressing table.* There must be something over here.

CHENNEVIETTE. My God, what a night!

THE GENERAL. Dios mío! Lucette, come back to me! Lucette! . . . Ay!

FONTANET, *returning with a moistened napkin.* Here, this water may help bring her round.

THE GENERAL. Gracias! (*Mopping* LUCETTE's *brow.*) Lucette! Lucette! For why you no come back to me?

FONTANET, *behind the chaise longue.* Do you think, perhaps, if I blew a little air in her face—

THE GENERAL *and* CHENNEVIETTE, *together, pushing him briskly aside.* No! No!

FONTANET, *moving down center.* Poor child! She went all to pieces when she heard that Bois-d'Enghien was getting married. Quite a shock, I should think . . .

> CHENNEVIETTE *shudders, imagining what* THE GENERAL's *reaction is going to be.*

THE GENERAL, *still mopping* LUCETTE's *brow.* Heem? The tenor? For why she care eef he get marry?

FONTANET, *with a little laugh.* Why? Well, really . . . He is her lover, after all!

> CHENNEVIETTE *braces himself for the inevitable storm.*

THE GENERAL, *lunging at* FONTANET, *seizing him by the throat and shaking him vigorously.* What ees thees theeng you tell me? What ees thees theeng? Bodégué? Bodégué ees lover of Lucette?

> *In the meantime* CHENNE-VIETTE *has noticed the napkin covering* LUCETTE's *face, picked it up, and begun mopping her brow.*

231

FONTANET, *breathing in* THE GENERAL's *face.* Yes! Of course! (*Struggling.*) What's the matter with you?

THE GENERAL, *wincing and turning his head sharply to avoid* FONTANET's *breath, but without letting him go.* Ees lover of Lucette? Bodégué?

FONTANET, *choking.* Let . . . Let me go! What . . . What's the matter with you?

> *The two inner panels of the drawing room door fly open, and* BOIS-D'ENGHIEN *strides quickly in.*

BOIS-D'ENGHIEN, *center stage.* Well, is everything under control?

> THE GENERAL, *suddenly releasing* FONTANET, *who goes staggering about, then pounces on* BOIS-D'ENGHIEN, *seizing him by the throat.*

THE GENERAL, *as* BOIS-D'ENGHIEN *reels under his attack.* Ees true you lover of Mamoiselle Gautier?

BOIS-D'ENGHIEN, *stunned.* What? . . . . Who? . . . Who? . . .

THE GENERAL, *shaking him.* Ees true you lover? Ees true?

FONTANET, *aside, still recovering from his ordeal.* I seem to have started something.

> *He beats a strategic retreat, out the drawing room door, closing it behind him.*

BOIS-D'ENGHIEN, *struggling.* What . . . What do you think you're doing? Let me go!

CHENNEVIETTE, *trying to calm them, without leaving* LU-CETTE. General! Bois-d'Enghien! . . . Please! That's enough!

THE GENERAL, *pushing* BOIS-D'ENGHIEN *away, looking him up and down, scornfully.* So Bodégué! You theenk you be antelope, no?

BOIS-D'ENGHIEN. What?

THE GENERAL. Sí! You theenk maybe you go be antelope weeth Lucette, no?

BOIS-D'ENGHIEN. Elope with Lucette? Me?

THE GENERAL. You! (*Categorically.*) So I keel you!

> *He returns to* LUCETTE, *joining* CHENNEVIETTE *in an effort to revive her.*

BOIS-D'ENGHIEN, *in a rage.* Oh, I see! You're going to kill me! Just like that!

THE GENERAL, *returning to* BOIS-D'ENGHIEN, *shouting.* Sí! Becose I love her! Becose I no like someone he get een my way, you onderstand?

BOIS-D'ENGHIEN, *furiously, at the top of his voice.* In your way? How am I getting in your way? I'm getting married, in case you hadn't noticed! What on earth do you think I want with your Lucette? . . . I want you to take her off my hands, that's what I want!

THE GENERAL, *suddenly pacified.* Ees true? You no een love weeth Lucette?

BOIS-D'ENGHIEN, *still shouting.* I just told you . . . (*Accentuating each syllable.*) I am getting married!

THE GENERAL. Ah! Bodégué! You are my friend!

> *He takes* BOIS-D'ENGHIEN's *hands in his and shakes them warmly.*

CHENNEVIETTE, *who has continued to care for* LUCETTE. Look, she's opening her eyes.

> BOIS-D'ENGHIEN *and* THE GENERAL *run over to the chaise longue.*

THE GENERAL. Ah, sí! Sí! (*Jabbing* BOIS-D'ENGHIEN *jovially in the ribs.*) Ees key! Ees key!

BOIS-D'ENGHIEN, *without understanding.* What?

THE GENERAL. I tell you . . . Key ees no for noseblood only. Ees same for thees. (*He rubs* LUCETTE's *hands with renewed enthusiasm.*) Lucette! Lucette!

BOIS-D'ENGHIEN. Look, you two . . . Leave me alone with her for a few minutes, will you? I'm going to have to handle this myself. It's the only way.

THE GENERAL, *willing to consent to anything in his elation.* Bueno, bueno! We go. (*To* CHENNEVIETTE.) Come, Cheviotte. (*To* LUCETTE, *as they approach the drawing room door.*) Ah! Come back to heem, Lucette! Come back to heem!

> THE GENERAL *and* CHENNEVI-
> ETTE *leave.* BOIS-D'ENGHIEN
> *closes the door behind them.*

LUCETTE, *regaining consciousness.* Oh! What . . . what happened? Where am I?

BOIS-D'ENGHIEN, *falling to his knees beside her.* Lucette!

LUCETTE, *tenderly placing her hands on his shoulders, plaintively.* Is . . . Is that you, darling?

BOIS-D'ENGHIEN. Lucette! Forgive me! Please . . . It's all my fault! Say you forgive me!

> *At these words* LUCETTE's
> *expression changes abruptly,*
> *as she remembers what has*
> *happened.*

LUCETTE, *suddenly pushing him away, almost knocking him over.* You! You . . . Oh, don't you speak to me! I hate you!

> *She gets up and moves left.*

BOIS-D'ENGHIEN, *scuffling over to her on his knees.* Lulu! Lulu darling!

LUCETTE. So, it's true! You . . . That marriage contract . . . It was yours! You're getting married!

BOIS-D'ENGHIEN, *standing up, with a hypocritical tone of self-denunciation.* Yes! Yes, Lucette, I'm getting married.

LUCETTE. He's getting married! He admits it! (*Scornfully.*) Oh! You . . . you monster! You . . .

BOIS-D'ENGHIEN, *pleading.* Lucette!

234

LUCETTE, *with a bitter smile.* Well, there's only one thing left for me to do now.

> *She moves right with a grandiose, dramatic gesture as if to say, "The die is cast!"*

BOIS-D'ENGHIEN, *on edge.* What?

LUCETTE, *rummaging in her handbag.* Just what I said I was going to do!

BOIS-D'ENGHIEN, *aside.* What did she say she was going to do?

LUCETTE, *in a voice choked with tears.* My blood will be on your hands! (*She pulls a revolver from the handbag, sobbing.*) Good-bye! I hope you'll always be very happy!

BOIS-D'ENGHIEN, *lunging at her, pinning her arms to her sides.* Lucette! For heaven's sake, are you out of your mind?

LUCETTE, *struggling.* Let me go! Take your hands off me!

BOIS-D'ENGHIEN, *trying to take away the revolver.* Lucette! Please! . . . Think of what you're doing! . . . You can't! You . . . (*Desperate for a convincing argument.*) You're in someone else's house! It's not polite! It just isn't done!

LUCETTE. I don't care!

BOIS-D'ENGHIEN. Besides . . . I can explain everything. Please, you'll see. You'll understand if you just listen. But . . . but if you kill yourself you won't understand anything at all, understand?

LUCETTE, *breaking away.* All right! Go ahead, explain!

BOIS-D'ENGHIEN, *reaching quickly for the revolver.* First give me that gun!

LUCETTE, *eluding his grasp.* No, no! First you explain!

> BOIS-D'ENGHIEN *mops his brow in evident despair.*

235

MADAME DUVERGER'S VOICE, *from the wings.* Bois-d'Eng-hien! Bois-d'Enghien!

BOIS-D'ENGHIEN, *aside, moving upstage.* Oh, God! Now what? (*Aloud, opening one of the panels of the draw-ing room door and partly disappearing.*) Yes! What is it?

MADAME DUVERGER'S VOICE, *muffled.* Aren't you going to join us? All the guests are waiting for you.

> *In the meantime,* LUCETTE, *unnerved by the ordeal, has pulled on the barrel of the revolver, thereby drawing out a fan with which she fans herself nervously.*

BOIS-D'ENGHIEN, *attempting to be agreeable.* Yes, yes! Right away, Mother! Just a moment!

> *He shuts the door in obvious ill humor.*

LUCETTE, *closing the fan, aside, with the determination of someone making a decision.* "Mother" my foot! You're not married yet, my friend! Just wait!

> *She puts the revolver back in her handbag on the end table and moves to the far side of the chaise longue, kneeling beside it.*

BOIS-D'ENGHIEN, *going over to her, taking up where he left off.* Please, Lucette! I know how you feel, but . . . Try to be brave. For my sake . . . For the sake of . . . (*Dramatically.*) our love!

LUCETTE, *throwing her arms in the air, collapsing onto the chaise longue.* Our love! As if there were anything left of our love!

> *She leans on the back of the chaise longue, hiding her face in her arms, sobbing.*

BOIS-D'ENGHIEN, *crouching behind the chaise longue.* Any-

thing left? Why, what do you mean, "anything left"?
Silly!

LUCETTE, *raising her head, with little gasps of grief.* But
you're getting married!

BOIS-D'ENGHIEN. So? What does that prove? I can get
married and still love you at the same time. After all,
does the right hand have to know what the left hand is
doing?

LUCETTE, *kneeling on the chaise longue, replying with an
ingenuous little voice, as if thoroughly convinced by
his reasoning.* Really?

BOIS-D'ENGHIEN, *hypocritically categorical.* Of course!

> *He gets up and moves
> around the chaise longue.*

LUCETTE, *aside to the audience.* Snake in the grass!

BOIS-D'ENGHIEN, *aside.* Just watch me get rid of her once I'm
married! (*Aloud, sitting across from* LUCETTE, *his
back toward the audience.*) Lulu!

LUCETTE, *playing her little role.* Nannikins! Love me?

BOIS-D'ENGHIEN. I'm mad about you!

LUCETTE. Darling!

> *She rests her right hand
> casually on the end table,
> accidentally touching the
> bouquet as she does so.*

BOIS-D'ENGHIEN. See? Nothing has changed. Nothing at
all . . . Lulu!

> *During his protestations,
> LUCETTE has been fingering
> the flowers, behind his back,
> as if reflecting on a plan.*

LUCETTE, *aside to the audience, as an idea suddenly hits
her.* Ah! Just wait! (*Continuing her role, throwing her
arms around* BOIS-D'ENGHIEN's *neck. Aloud.*) Then you
mean, Nannikins, that we can go on just as we were?

BOIS-D'ENGHIEN. Why not, I'd like to know!

LUCETTE, *with feigned delight.* Oh! I'm so happy! And to

think . . . Here I was, telling myself . . . You'll never guess! . . . I was telling myself that we were finished! Through! I was telling myself . . . (*Dramatically.*) that our love was dead!

BOIS-D'ENGHIEN. You were? (*Hypocritically, as if finding it impossible to believe.*) No!

LUCETTE, *her left arm around his neck, pointing to the bouquet with her right hand.* Look! See these wild flowers? Do they remind you of anything?

BOIS-D'ENGHIEN, *sentimentally.* They . . . they remind me of the country.

LUCETTE, *with a sigh, raising her arms in the air as if to embrace the memories she is evoking, while* BOIS-D'ENGHIEN, *one arm around her waist, bows his head in simulated reverie.* Ah, yes! The country! Remember when we were students, darling? What wonderful times we had . . .

BOIS-D'ENGHIEN, *aside to the audience.* "Like lovebirds" . . . You'll see!

LUCETTE, *putting her face next to his and taking his chin in her left hand.* Just the two of us . . . Like two little lovebirds! (BOIS-D'ENGHIEN *gives a knowing nod to the audience.*) Remember how we used to lie in the grass, and how I used to tease you . . . (*She takes a flower from the bouquet and tickles his ear with it.*) And how angry you would always get when I put things down your back to tickle you . . .

> *Taking advantage of* BOIS-D'ENGHIEN's *position, his head bent forward, she thrusts the flower, thorns and all, down his back.*

BOIS-D'ENGHIEN, *with a sudden cry of pain.* Owww! What are you doing?

LUCETTE, *pushing the flower further down his back.* Down

. . . Down . . . (*Winking to the audience as if to say,
"Just watch!"*) Way down . . .

BOIS-D'ENGHIEN, *standing up, trying with appropriate con-
tortions to retrieve the flower.* Now look what you've
done. You and your little games! I can't reach the
damned thing!

> *He grimaces, in evident
> discomfort.*

LUCETTE, *still kneeling on the chaise longue, in a hypocritical little voice.* Does it bother you, darling?

BOIS-D'ENGHIEN, *still grimacing.* What do you think? It's
full of thorns!

LUCETTE, *with mock compassion.* Oh! (*Changing her
tone.*) Well then, why don't you get it out?

BOIS-D'ENGHIEN. "Get it out!" Don't you think I'm trying?
It's inside my underwear. I can't get it out.

LUCETTE, *in the most natural tone.* Then take your clothes
off.

BOIS-D'ENGHIEN, *furious.* Take my . . . Are you out of
your mind? Take my clothes off? Here? With my engagement party going on in the next room?

LUCETTE, *getting up and moving around the chaise longue.*
Oh really, darling, I don't see the harm. We'll just lock
the doors . . . (*She goes and locks the door up right,
then the drawing room door and the door down left,
finally returning down center.* There! If anyone comes
along they'll think that you've gone off somewhere and
that I'm getting dressed. It's perfectly natural. Now go
ahead, take your clothes off.

BOIS-D'ENGHIEN. No! Absolutely not!

LUCETTE, *lyrically.* Ah, you see! I knew it . . . You don't
love me any more!

BOIS-D'ENGHIEN, *losing patience.* I do! Of course I do!

LUCETTE. No, you don't! If you did, you wouldn't mind
undressing just because I'm here!

BOIS-D'ENGHIEN. Lucette, for heaven's sake . . . (*Still twisting and turning in his struggle with the flower.*) Owww! That thing hurts, damn it!

LUCETTE. Well then, don't be so stubborn. All you have to do is go behind the screen and get it out. It won't take a minute.

BOIS-D'ENGHIEN, *in a tone of angry resignation, taking off his coat and putting it on the chaise longue.* I suppose I'll have to, before it drives me crazy! (*He moves behind the screen, pulling the panels all around him so that he is completely hidden.*) Are you sure the doors are locked?

LUCETTE. Yes, yes! . . . Now go on . . . (*Aside to the audience, with a gesture of victory.*) Now I've got him! (*Aloud.*) In the meantime, darling, I'm going to get dressed for my numbers.

> *She moves quickly around the room, quietly unlocking all the doors, then goes to the closet, removes her costume, and returns to the chaise longue.* BOIS-D'ENGHIEN, *meanwhile, has taken off his shirt and draped it over one of the panels of the screen.*

BOIS-D'ENGHIEN'S VOICE, *behind the screen, grumbling.* Of all things for me to be doing at a time like this . . . Thanks to you!

LUCETTE, *taking off her skirt.* I don't see why you have to make such a fuss. A silly little flower happens to fall down your back. So you take it out, that's all.

BOIS-D'ENGHIEN'S VOICE. Oh, just like that! . . . In the first place, your "silly little flower" feels more like a porcupine . . . And it didn't just happen to fall down my back! (LUCETTE *gives the audience a knowing wink.*) There! I've got it.

LUCETTE, *still next to the chaise longue, with mock passion.* You've got it? Oh, please . . . Let me have it!

BOIS-D'ENGHIEN'S VOICE. What on earth for?

LUCETTE. I want to keep it. It's been next to your heart!

BOIS-D'ENGHIEN, *appearing hesitantly from behind the screen in his woolen undershirt, holding the flower in his right hand, and with his left trying to keep his pants from falling down.* Oh? (*Putting his right hand to his backside.*) Since when do I sit on my heart!

> *He turns as if to retreat behind the screen.*

LUCETTE. I don't care . . . Let me have it anyway!

BOIS-D'ENGHIEN, *taking it to her.* Here, if it means so much to you.

> *He tries to return to the screen, but* LUCETTE *has seized his hand, and with a sudden tug pulls him to her.*

LUCETTE, *with feigned admiration.* Oh, you beautiful man! Just look at you!

BOIS-D'ENGHIEN, *fatuously.* Well . . .

> *Once again he turns toward the screen, but again* LUCETTE *holds him back.*

LUCETTE. You handsome, handsome thing, you!

BOIS-D'ENGHIEN. Please, Lucette! If anyone saw me like this . . . You're sure the doors are locked?

LUCETTE. Yes, yes! Of course! (*Clutching him close to her.*) Oh! Just having you here, next to me . . . (*She clasps her right hand to her bosom, still holding him fast with the left.*) All mine! (*With exaggerated lyricism.*) My Romeo in underwear!

BOIS-D'ENGHIEN. Really, Lucette . . .

LUCETTE. And when I think . . . (*Waxing dramatic.*) When I think that all this will soon be taken from me . . . Oh no! No, I won't let them! I won't! (*She flings her arms madly around his neck and falls in a heap onto the chaise longue, in such a way that* BOIS-D'ENGH-IEN, *paralyzed by her grip, finds himself sitting on the floor unable to move.*) Oh, Fernand, darling! (*Raising her voice with each successive exclamation.*) I love you! I love you! I love you!

BOIS-D'ENGHIEN, *petrified.* For heaven's sake, not so loud! You'll have them all in here in a minute!

LUCETTE, *shouting.* I don't care! Let them come! Let them all see how much I love you! . . . Oh, Fernand, darling! (*With her right hand she presses the electric button on the end table, producing a number of loud, determined rings, during which she continues her vehement protestations.*) I love you! I love you! I love you!

BOIS-D'ENGHIEN, *during the commotion, getting to his knees, but with his head still firmly held by* LUCETTE. Oh, my God, now the telephone!

LUCETTE, *still shouting.* I love you! I love you! I love you!

BOIS-D'ENGHIEN, *in a panic.* Please, that's enough! They'll hear you!

LUCETTE, *more determined than ever.* I love you! I love you! I love you!

> *There are several sharp raps at the drawing room door, accompanied by shouts of "What's going on in there?" "What's the matter?" "Open the door!" etc.*

BOIS-D'ENGHIEN. No, no, no! You can't come in! (*To* LU-CETTE, *who is still shouting.*) For God's sake, will you stop that!

LUCETTE, *uttering one more triumphant shout.* I love you!

> *Suddenly the door flies open and everyone, including a number of hitherto unidentified guests, appears in the*

> *doorway. There is a general*
> *gasp of dismay and disbelief.*

BOIS-D'ENGHIEN, *getting up.* No, no, no! You can't come in! . . . I told you! You can't come in!

> MARCELINE *has moved up*
> *right.* CHENNEVIETTE *and*
> FONTANET *are behind the*
> *chaise longue.*

MADAME DUVERGER, *with one hand hiding* VIVIANE's *head against her bosom, with the other pointing to* BOIS-D'ENGHIEN. He . . . He's practically naked!

LUCETTE, *still on the chaise longue, in a distant voice, as if awaking from a dream.* Oh, what a man! No one makes love the way he does! No one!

BOIS-D'ENGHIEN, *beside himself.* What . . . What is she talking about?

> *Everyone gives* BOIS-
> D'ENGHIEN *looks of reproach.*

FONTANET. Scandalous!

CHENNEVIETTE. I should say!

MADAME DUVERGER. Here, in my house . . . Under my roof . . . (*To* BOIS-D'ENGHIEN, *summoning up all her dignity.*) Monsieur, I'll thank you to leave and never come back!

BOIS-D'ENGHIEN. But . . . Mother! (MADAME DUVERGER *shudders noticeably.*) The wedding . . . Viviane . . .

MADAME DUVERGER, *turning her back on him.* Never!

BOIS-D'ENGHIEN. But . . . But . . .

THE GENERAL, *who has just entered from among the guests in the drawing room, going up to* BOIS-D'ENGHIEN *with fire in his eyes.* So Bodégué! Tomorrow, een morneeng, on field of honor! For becose I keel you! Sí! I keel you!

BOIS-D'ENGHIEN, *not knowing which way to turn.* Good God in heaven!

ACT THREE

The set is divided into two parts. The larger, stage left, occupies about three quarters of the stage, and represents the third-floor landing of a fashionable house. Upstage, an elegant staircase rising from stage left to right. Facing the audience, against the enclosed stairwell, a bench. Down left, leading to BOIS-D'ENGHIEN's *apartment, a door, equipped with an electric button. This door locks from the inside. On the downstage side of the door, another bench similar to the first. Downstage, in the partition cutting the stage in two, just opposite the door to the apartment, another door, opening inward, leading directly into* BOIS-D'ENGHIEN's *dressing room. (This door also locks from the inside.) It is this room which occupies the remaining portion of the set, stage right. In the wall of the dressing room, right center, a two-paneled window, which opens inward. In the upstage wall, far right, a door opening out onto a corridor of the apartment. On the stage left side of this door, a large washstand with the usual toilet accessories: combs, brushes, assorted bottles, washcloths, towels, toothbrush, etc. Down right, a chair covered with various articles of gentleman's clothing, neatly folded. Next to this chair, upstage, an armchair. Between the armchair and the window, a coat peg with a lady's dressing gown hanging from it. On the floor, under the dressing gown, a pair of lady's slippers. Upstage, between the washstand and the partition, a coat rack.*

At rise, JEAN *is in the dressing room, near the armchair, polishing* BOIS-D'ENGHIEN's *shoes.*

JEAN. It's a disgrace, that's what it is! Last night he signs his marriage contract and this morning he still hasn't come home. And it's already ten o'clock! No . . . It's a disgrace, that's all! (*He puts down one shoe and begins polishing the other.*) Not that I'm telling anybody how to live, mind you . . . It's just that when you get engaged, it seems to me you should come sleep at home and not go running around . . . (*He breathes on the*

shoe to make it shine.) Or at least you should do what
I did . . . Go sleep with the girl you're going to marry
. . . But none of this running around!

> *During the preceding,* THE
> FLORIST *has come up the
> stairs with a basket of
> flowers on his head. He stops
> on the landing, looks at both
> doors, then rings the bell,
> stage left.*

Now who can that be? It's not Monsieur, he has his
key. (*Pointing up right, to the door which opens
onto the corridor of the apartment.*) Ha! If you think
I'm going to walk all the way around just to open the
door . . . (*He opens the dressing room door that opens
out onto the landing.*) Who is it? What do you want?

THE FLORIST, *coming over to him from the other side of
the landing.* Oh, excuse me . . . I'm looking for the
Brugnot wedding.

JEAN, *crossly.* Well keep looking. It's the next floor.

THE FLORIST. But . . . They told me downstairs that it
was two flights up.

JEAN. That's right. Two flights up from the mezzanine.

THE FLORIST. Oh, pardon me! I thought—

JEAN. Don't mention it! (*He slams the door shut.* THE
FLORIST *climbs the stairs, out of sight.*) That's the
sixth one today who's come looking for that Brugnot
wedding. It's a damned pain, that's what it is!

> BOIS-D'ENGHIEN *appears,
> looking tired and unkempt,
> coming up the stairs to the
> landing. His evening clothes,
> which can be seen under his
> coat, are in a state of dis-
> array: tie askew, shirt
> crumpled, etc.*

BOIS-D'ENGHIEN. God, what a night!

He rings long and loud.

JEAN. And there's number seven! (*Opening the dressing room door abruptly.*) It's not here! It's upstairs!

BOIS-D'ENGHIEN. What?

JEAN, *recognizing him.* Oh, Monsieur Bois-d'Enghien! . . . It's you!

BOIS-D'ENGHIEN, *entering and moving right, angrily.* Jean! Of course it's me! Who else would it be?

JEAN. But Monsieur . . . Ten o'clock in the morning! Is that a time to be coming home? And after your engagement party, no less!

BOIS-D'ENGHIEN, *between his teeth.* Did I ask for your opinion?

JEAN. No, Monsieur.

BOIS-D'ENGHIEN. Then keep it to yourself!

JEAN. Yes, Monsieur.

BOIS-D'ENGHIEN, *giving* JEAN *his coat and hat.* That's all I need . . . A few words of wisdom from you! (*Pacing up and down.*) Do you have any idea where I spent the night?

JEAN. No, Monsieur.

BOIS-D'ENGHIEN. In a hotel, that's where! And do you know whose fault it was?

JEAN. No, Monsieur.

BOIS-D'ENGHIEN. Well I'll tell you . . . It was your fault!

JEAN. Mine, Monsieur?

BOIS-D'ENGHIEN. Absolutely! If you had been here when I got home last night . . . But no, that's too much to expect! I rang the bell, I knocked, I did everything but break the door down . . .

JEAN. But Monsieur, you had your key, didn't you?

BOIS-D'ENGHIEN. My key? Ha! I had it when I went out all right, but I left it somewhere. (JEAN *gives him an inquisitive look.*) Down somebody's back, if you must know!

JEAN, *going over to the coat rack and hanging up the coat*

and hat. Really, Monsieur. You should be more careful where you leave things.

BOIS-D'ENGHIEN, *taking off his dress coat, vest, tie, and collar.* And besides, don't change the subject. You should have been here, that's all! Where the devil were you?

JEAN. Why Monsieur, you know perfectly well . . . I was with my wife. You always give me one night a week to . . . to pay my respects to Madame Jean.

BOIS-D'ENGHIEN. Yes . . . Well, let me tell you, you're getting to be a nuisance with your Madame Jean!

JEAN, *offended.* A nuisance . . . You mean for you, Monsieur!

BOIS-D'ENGHIEN. Of course I mean for me!

JEAN. Of course . . . Because, for Madame Jean, I assure you . . .

BOIS-D'ENGHIEN, *losing his patience.* Will you forget about Madame Jean! What difference does she make to me? I'm thinking about myself!

JEAN, *dryly.* Yes, Monsieur, I see . . .

BOIS-D'ENGHIEN, *still in a rage.* Besides, I'd like to know what makes that Madame Jean of yours so damned fascinating anyway!

JEAN. Well, Monsieur, you will excuse me if I omit the details . . . Just let me say, Monsieur, that since there is no little Jean running about as yet . . . Well, there are some things that no one else can do for you, Monsieur, and . . .

BOIS-D'ENGHIEN. All right, all right! I shouldn't have asked. I have other things to think about.

JEAN. Yes, Monsieur.

BOIS-D'ENGHIEN. Instead of standing here jabbering you should be making yourself useful.

JEAN. Yes, Monsieur.

BOIS-D'ENGHIEN. That key, for instance, now that I think of it . . . Why don't you go and—

JEAN, *interrupting.* And get it back, Monsieur? Right
away.

BOIS-D'ENGHIEN. No, no, no! Just a minute! That key can
stay right where it is. I want you to go find a lock-
smith and have him come put a new lock on the door
so the old key won't work any more.

JEAN. Ah, very good, Monsieur.

> *He moves toward the door,*
> *up right.*

BOIS-D'ENGHIEN, *pointing to the other door.* Here, don't
bother going down the back stairs . . . Go this way,
it's faster.

JEAN, *changing direction and about to go out.* I think
you'll find all your clothing in order, Monsieur, if you
wish to change.

BOIS-D'ENGHIEN. Fine, fine! Now go ahead and don't
waste any time.

JEAN. Yes, Monsieur.

> *He leaves without closing*
> *the door, and disappears*
> *down the stairs.*

BOIS-D'ENGHIEN, *sitting in the armchair and taking off his*
trousers. Good God, what a night! . . . No, that's one
night I won't forget in a hurry! I'm sure she must be
very pleased with her handiwork. Dragging my name
through the mud, getting me kicked out of that house,
breaking up my marriage . . . Oh yes, she must be
very pleased with herself. Well, believe me, I'll get
even! I don't know how, but I'll get even! (*He goes to*
the washstand, in his underpants, and turns the faucet
to fill the bowl.) And on top of everything, that hotel!
Imagine, spending a night in that hotel, sleeping in my
clothes . . . And no toothbrush, no razor, nothing . . .
No, that's one night I'll never forget!

> *He plunges his face in the*
> *bowl and scrubs vigorously.*
> *In the meantime, a lady and*

gentleman have come up the stairs and appear on the landing. THE GENTLEMAN *is about to go up another flight.*

THE LADY, *pointing to the door to* BOIS-D'ENCHIEN's *dressing room, still ajar.* No, no, dear. This must be it.

THE GENTLEMAN. Oh, do you think so?

THE LADY. Certainly. They've left the door open. See?

THE GENTLEMAN. Hm! . . . I suppose you're right. (*He strides into the room, followed by his wife.*) Funny . . . Are you sure this is it?

BOIS-D'ENCHIEN, *still upstage, his face dripping, towel in hand.* Who . . . What on earth do you want?

THE LADY, *moving far left under the impetus of her shock.* Oh!

THE GENTLEMAN. I beg your pardon!

THE LADY. He's naked!

She covers her eyes.

BOIS-D'ENCHIEN. Well? What do you want?

THE GENTLEMAN, *nonplussed.* Are you . . . Are we . . . I mean, isn't this the Brugnot wedding?

BOIS-D'ENCHIEN. Does this look like the Brugnot wedding? . . . It's upstairs, damn it! Upstairs!

THE GENTLEMAN. I beg your pardon!

BOIS-D'ENCHIEN. Very nice! . . . You just walk right in while I'm getting dressed . . . Very nice!

THE LADY, *moving toward the door with her husband, peeking at* BOIS-D'ENCHIEN *through her fingers.* But Monsieur, it's only common decency to close the door when one is . . . disrobing.

BOIS-D'ENCHIEN. Oh, of course! It's my fault! I suppose I asked you to come in? What do you think this is, a public waiting room? Get out! Go on . . . Get out!

He slams the door in their faces.

THE GENTLEMAN, *on the landing.* Barbarian!

BOIS-D'ENGHIEN, *returning to the washstand.* That's a good one!

> *He wipes his face.*

THE GENTLEMAN, *following his wife up to the next floor.* You see? I knew it was upstairs.

THE LADY. But dear, anyone can make a mistake.

> *They disappear up the stairs.*

BOIS-D'ENGHIEN. That's just what I need to make my day complete . . . Playing doorman along with everything else! That idiot Jean will never learn to shut the door when he goes out!

> BOUZIN *appears coming up the stairs and goes to the door, far left.*

BOUZIN. Bois-d'Enghien . . . third floor. This must be it.

> *He rings.*

BOIS-D'ENGHIEN, *who is preparing to brush his teeth.* Oh no, not another one so early in the morning! And just when Jean isn't here, naturally! Well, too bad . . . They can wait!

BOUZIN. Hm! Nobody home?

> *He rings again.*

BOIS-D'ENGHIEN. Again? . . . Well I certainly can't go to the door like this!

BOUZIN, *impatiently.* There must be somebody at home!

> *He rings again, much longer.*

BOIS-D'ENGHIEN, *opening his door a crack and poking his head out, careful to conceal his state of undress behind the door.* Who is it? What do you want?

BOUZIN, *crossing over, tipping his hat.* Ah, Monsieur Bois-d'Enghien, it's me.

BOIS-D'ENGHIEN. You! What are you doing here? I'm not at home!

> *He is about to slam the door.*

BOUZIN, *putting his foot in the door.* No, wait! I'll only

be a minute. Monsieur Lantery sent me . . . The notary . . .

BOIS-D'ENGHIEN, *trying to close the door*. No no no! For
heaven's sake, I'm getting dressed!

BOUZIN. I don't mind. You don't have to stand on ceremony with me.

BOIS-D'ENGHIEN, *relenting*. All right, come in . . . But
just for a minute . . . Now what do you want?

> BOUZIN *enters the dressing
> room and* BOIS-D'ENGHIEN
> *shuts the door.*

BOUZIN. Well, as I was saying, Monsieur Lantery sent me.
He wanted me to give you this copy of your marriage
contract.

> *He takes the folded docu-
> ment from his pocket.*

BOIS-D'ENGHIEN, *flaring up*. My marriage contract? Ha ha!
That's a laugh! You picked a nice time, I'll tell you!

BOUZIN, *baffled by the sudden explosion*. But—

BOIS-D'ENGHIEN. You know what you can do with that
contract, don't you?

BOUZIN. No, I—

BOIS-D'ENGHIEN. Well I'll tell you! You can take it and
rip it up into little pieces! That's what you can do with
it! . . . And that's not all!

BOUZIN. But—

BOIS-D'ENGHIEN. Where have you been anyway? Haven't
you heard? It's all off! All through! No wedding!
Nothing! (*He puts his toothbrush in his mouth and
takes the contract from* BOUZIN.) Here . . . Here's
what I think of your contract!

> *He rips it in half.*

BOUZIN. But . . . I was supposed to give you the bill . . .
For the notary's services . . .

BOIS-D'ENGHIEN, *with a bitter laugh, while* BOUZIN *picks
up the pieces*. The bill? Ha ha ha! That's the best one

yet! The bill! It's not enough that everything is finished . . . I'm going to have to pay for it too! Not damned likely!

BOUZIN. But . . .

> *During the preceding exchange,* THE GENERAL, *in an obviously angry mood, has come running up the stairs. He stalks up to the door, far left, and rings.*

BOIS-D'ENGHIEN. Oh no, another one? . . . Who is it this time?

BOUZIN. I beg your pardon, but . . .

BOIS-D'ENGHIEN. I know, the bill . . . Later, not now! . . . Look, do me a favor, will you? I can't go to the door like this. Would you see who that is?

BOUZIN. Well, I suppose . . .

> *He makes a move toward the door that opens onto the landing.*

BOIS-D'ENGHIEN, *pointing to the other door, upstage.* No no, this way. You go all the way down and turn right. Whoever it is, just say I'm sorry but I can't see anybody.

BOUZIN. If you insist . . .

> *He exits through the upstage door as* THE GENERAL *rings the bell again.*

BOIS-D'ENGHIEN. What the devil gets into people, ringing the bell at this hour of the morning?

THE GENERAL, *furious.* Caramba! Me van a hacer esperar toda la vida?

> *He rings again, long and impatiently.*

BOIS-D'ENGHIEN, *with a little laugh.* Not very patient, whoever it is!

BOUZIN'S VOICE, *far left.* Just a minute . . . I'm coming.

THE GENERAL, *backing up toward the middle of the landing.* Bueno! Ees about time, I theenk! (BOUZIN *opens the door.*) Monsieur Bodégué . . .

BOUZIN, *taking a step or two onto the landing, then suddenly recognizing* THE GENERAL. My God, it's that cannibal!

> *He does a rapid about-face, dashes back into the apartment, and slams the door in* THE GENERAL'S *face.*

THE GENERAL, *beside himself.* Poussin! Poussin! What you mean, cannonball? (*Ringing the bell and pounding on the door.*) Open the door, Poussin! Open heem! Open heem!

BOIS-D'ENGHIEN, *attracted by the noise, opening the other door and poking his head out.* Now really, who on earth . . . Oh, it's you, General!

THE GENERAL, *shoving* BOIS-D'ENGHIEN *aside and bursting into the apartment.* Ees you! Bueno! I take care of you later! First you tell me, Poussin he ees here, no?

BOIS-D'ENGHIEN. Well, as a matter of fact . . .

THE GENERAL. He call me "cannonball" thees Poussin. I keel heem!

> *He moves far right.*

BOUZIN, *appearing suddenly at the upstage door, panic-stricken.* Monsieur, it's that madman, that gen . . . (*Recognizing* THE GENERAL.) Aaaah! Again?

> *He slams the door and disappears.*

THE GENERAL. Ees heem! (*About to run after him.*) Now I catch heem, thees Poussin! Es un hombre muerto!

BOIS-D'ENGHIEN, *trying to hold him back.* Please, General . . . Really . . .

THE GENERAL. Out of the way, Bodégué! Ees your turn later!

> *He pushes* BOIS-D'ENGHIEN *aside and dashes out the up-*

> *stage door in pursuit of*
> BOUZIN.

BOIS-D'ENGHIEN. Of course, they had to pick my place to come tear each other apart.

> *He opens the door to the landing and puts his head out to watch the proceedings. A moment later* BOUZIN *appears through the door down left, slams it and makes a dash for the staircase.*

BOUZIN, *passing in front of* BOIS-D'ENGHIEN *without stopping.* For God's sake, don't tell him which way I went!

BOIS-D'ENGHIEN, *laughing.* No, no! Don't worry, I won't.

> BOUZIN *begins sprinting up the stairs, suddenly colliding with* THE FLORIST, *who is just on his way down.*

THE FLORIST, *indignantly.* You could watch where you're going!

> *With a look of scorn he continues down the stairs out of sight, as* BOUZIN, *oblivious, disappears.*

THE GENERAL, *bursting through the door, down left.* Where ees he? Where ees Poussin?

BOIS-D'ENGHIEN. He went that way . . . Downstairs!

THE GENERAL, *leaning over the railing.* Ah, bueno, I see heem! (*Rushing headlong for the staircase.*) Es muerto, Poussin! Nobody he call me "cannonball" and leeve!

> *He disappears out of sight, down the stairs. After a moment* BOUZIN *appears at the top of the staircase, slumped over the railing.*

BOIS-D'ENCHIEN. That's right, go chase him! You'll have a good run for your money!

BOUZIN, *disheveled, coming down the stairs cautiously.* Is he gone?

BOIS-D'ENCHIEN, *laughing.* I should say he is! He just went running after you.

BOUZIN, *entering the dressing room and collapsing onto the armchair with a sigh.* Oh my . . .

BOIS-D'ENCHIEN, *closing the door, jokingly.* Well, I hope you've had yourself a pleasant trip!

BOUZIN. Just imagine! That . . . That barbarian! Why doesn't he leave me alone? What did I ever do to him? Good God, do I have to spend the rest of my life with that lunatic on my heels? What in the world has he got against me? Do you know?

BOIS-D'ENCHIEN, *pretending to be deeply serious.* Yes, I know. He's heard about you and Lucette Gautier. That's what he's got against you. He knows that you're her lover.

BOUZIN, *standing up to protest.* Me? Lucette Gautier? But . . . but that's absolutely absurd! It's not true! Tell him it's not true! There's never been anything between me and Mademoiselle Gautier! Never! (*Taking* BOIS-D'ENCHIEN's *smile for disbelief.*) I give you my word of honor!

BOIS-D'ENCHIEN. Never?

BOUZIN. Of course not! I . . . I don't know how Mademoiselle Gautier feels toward me . . . Perhaps . . . I mean, she's never said anything . . . But as far as I'm concerned, well . . . I hate to say it, but if she's been making up stories, she's just flattering herself, that's all! (*Pleading.*) Look, please, you've got to help me. Things can't go on like this. You know the General, don't you? Talk to him . . . Make him listen to reason. Help me clear up this absurd misunderstanding before it finishes me!

BOIS-D'ENCHIEN. Certainly . . . Anything to oblige.

> *Meanwhile,* LUCETTE *has appeared coming up the stairs. She stops on the landing, catches her breath for a moment, and finally strides up to the door, far left.*

LUCETTE. Oh, this isn't going to be easy!

> *She rings the bell.*

BOIS-D'ENCHIEN. What? Another one? (*A look of horror comes over* BOUZIN's *face.*) Bouzin, old boy, do me a favor and see who that is, would you?

BOUZIN, *taking refuge in back of the armchair.* Oh no! Not me! I'm sorry!

BOIS-D'ENCHIEN. But Bouzin—

BOUZIN. Oh no! If it's the General again, that's all I need!

> LUCETTE *rings again.*

BOIS-D'ENCHIEN, *calling attention to his state of undress.* But look . . . I can't very well go myself, can I?

BOUZIN. I don't care! I'm not going to open that door!

LUCETTE. Hm! No answer . . . He must know it's me.

> *She rings again.*

BOIS-D'ENCHIEN. Please, Bouzin . . .

BOUZIN, *adamant.* No, no, no! Absolutely not!

LUCETTE, *after pacing back and forth a few times, suddenly remembering.* Ah! What's the matter with me? I have that key of his that I found down my back. I can let myself in through the other door.

> *She takes the key out of her pocket, crosses over to the other door, and turns the key in the lock.*

BOIS-D'ENCHIEN, *hearing the noise.* What? . . . What's that? (*The door opens.*) Who's there?

LUCETTE, *entering, with all the self-possession at her command.* It's me!

BOUZIN. Lucette Gautier!

BOIS-D'ENCHIEN, *moving far right*. Luc . . . (*Checking himself, coldly.*) You? Here?

LUCETTE. Yes, me!

BOIS-D'ENCHIEN. Well, very nice! You do have your nerve, I'll say that for you!

LUCETTE, *very distinctly*. I have to speak to you.

BOUZIN, *between them, a little upstage*. You have to speak to me?

LUCETTE, *with a sneer in* BOUZIN's *direction*. To you? What on earth for? (*To* BOIS-D'ENCHIEN.) You, Fernand! (*To* BOUZIN.) Please leave us alone, Monsieur Bouzin.

BOIS-D'ENCHIEN, *haughtily*. That's hardly necessary! Whatever you have to say can be said in public, I'm sure.

LUCETTE, *emphatically*. I said I have to speak to you, Fernand! (*To* BOUZIN.) Now Monsieur Bouzin, will you please leave us alone!

BOIS-D'ENCHIEN, *condescendingly*. All right, Bouzin, just for a moment. You can wait in the next room. I'll call you as soon as . . . Mademoiselle Gautier has finished.

BOUZIN, *moving toward the upstage door*. Of course. (*Stopping as he reaches the door, aside.*) Do you suppose she could have followed me here?

He leaves.

BOIS-D'ENCHIEN, *containing himself*. Now then, what's this all about? What do you want?

LUCETTE. I came . . . to . . . (*Intimidated by* BOIS-D'ENCHIEN's *harsh look.*) to bring you your key.

BOIS-D'ENCHIEN. Thank you . . . Just put it down somewhere. (LUCETTE *puts the key on the washstand, after which there is a moment of uneasy silence.*) Well, I'm sure you have nothing else to tell me.

LUCETTE, *suddenly swallowing her pride*. Yes, I do, Fernand . . . I do! (*Throwing her arms around his neck.*) Fernand, I love you! That's what I have to tell you!

BOIS-D'ENGHIEN, *breaking away*. Oh no! None of that, thank you! I've had enough of that little game!

LUCETTE. Oh!

BOIS-D'ENGHIEN. No . . . I let myself be taken in for a long time, but there's a limit to everything. You think it's that easy? You go and ruin my marriage and make me a laughingstock with your preposterous little show. And then all you have to do is come back and say, "I love you," and you think I'll forget the whole thing just like that and put my ball and chain back on?

LUCETTE, *bitterly*. Your ball and chain?

BOIS-D'ENGHIEN. That's what I said! . . . Well, you're wrong, understand? So, you love me, do you? Well that's too bad, I couldn't care less! I'm fed up with your love! Fed up! And if you don't believe me . . . (*He opens the door to the landing.*) There! The door's open . . .

LUCETTE, *indignantly*. You . . . You're throwing me out! Me!

BOIS-D'ENGHIEN. Come, come . . . No hysterics . . . Just get out! Once and for all! Out!

LUCETTE. So, that's the way it is, is it? All right! You won't have to tell me twice. (*She leaves, but comes rushing back in just as* BOIS-D'ENGHIEN *is about to close the door after her.*) But I'm warning you. Once you let me cross that threshold, you'll never see me again!

BOIS-D'ENGHIEN. It's a bargain!

LUCETTE. Never! (*Once again she leaves, but returns as before, just as* BOIS-D'ENGHIEN *tries to close the door.*) Now don't forget what I said!

BOIS-D'ENGHIEN, *aside*. What do I have to do to get rid of her?

LUCETTE. Once you let me cross that—

BOIS-D'ENGHIEN. Yes, yes, yes! I understand!

LUCETTE. Then this is good-bye. (*She leaves and returns*

once again, but this time BOIS-D'ENGHIEN *has succeeded in closing the door.*) But just remember . . . (*Finding the door closed.*) Fernand, open this door! . . . Fernand, do you hear me?

BOIS-D'ENGHIEN, *inside.* Go away!

LUCETTE. Fernand, think what you're doing. Remember, this is forever and ever!

BOIS-D'ENGHIEN. Right! Forever and ever . . . and ever! Not a day less!

LUCETTE, *collapsing onto the bench next to the stairwell.* Oh, you wretch! You . . . you heartless wretch!

> *In the meantime,* BOIS-D'ENGHIEN *has gone to the coat peg, removed the dressing gown hanging from it, and rolled it into a ball.*

BOIS-D'ENGHIEN, *opening the door a crack and throwing the bundle at* LUCETTE's *feet.* And here! Don't forget this!

> *He closes the door immediately and goes back for the slippers.*

LUCETTE, *horrified.* Oh!

BOIS-D'ENGHIEN, *opening the door.* And these!

> *He flings the slippers at her and shuts the door.*

LUCETTE. Oh! . . . You . . . All right, if that's the way you want it! But don't you forget, this will be on your conscience. (*Melodramatic.*) You're . . . you're forcing me to make a very desperate move!

BOIS-D'ENGHIEN, *inside.* Yes, I'm sure.

LUCETTE, *taking out of her pocket the revolver she used in act 2.* You'll see! I still have that gun, remember? And this time I'm going to use it. I'm going to kill myself!

BOIS-D'ENGHIEN, *dashing out, leaving the door wide open.* You're going to . . . Again? (*Lunging at her.*) I'll take that!

LUCETTE, *resisting.* Oh no!

BOIS-D'ENGHIEN, *struggling with her.* Now look, will you give that to me!

LUCETTE. Let me go!

BOIS-D'ENGHIEN. Give that to me, I said!

LUCETTE. No, no, no! I won't!

BOIS-D'ENGHIEN. Oh yes you will!

> *He seizes the revolver by the barrel, while* LUCETTE *tries to pull it away. As a result the fan is drawn out and left in* BOIS-D'ENGHIEN's *hand. There is a momentary look of consternation on his face.*

LUCETTE, *mortified.* Oh dear!

BOIS-D'ENGHIEN. A fan! . . . Well I'll be . . .

LUCETTE, *becoming angry.* Now look, Fernand . . .

BOIS-D'ENGHIEN, *with a sarcastic laugh.* Ha ha ha! Look what she's going to kill herself with! One of her silly props!

LUCETTE, *fuming.* Now look . . .

BOIS-D'ENGHIEN. Ha ha ha! That's what I call a really desperate move! (*To* LUCETTE.) Faker! . . . Always playing to the gallery, aren't you!

LUCETTE, *in an absolute rage.* You . . . Oh! You've seen me for the last time! You . . . This time I'm through!

> *She turns on her heels and disappears down the stairs.*

BOIS-D'ENGHIEN. Yes, yes! Of course you are. (*Putting the fan down on the bench, near the stairwell, and picking up the dressing gown and slippers.*) Here, you're forgetting a few little things!

> *He throws them over the*
> *railing and down the stairs,*
> *one after the other.*

LUCETTE'S VOICE. Oh!

BOIS-D'ENGHIEN, *picking up the fan.* Ha! So she's going to kill herself! And to think I was fool enough to fall for a trick like that. And with a fan, no less! (*He reassembles the revolver and places it on the other bench, outside the apartment door, far left.*) Well at least I'll have a little peace from now on. (*He turns and is about to go back into his dressing room. All of a sudden, the window, far right, opens, and a gust of wind closes the door in his face.*) Now that's nice! (*Trying the door and finding it locked.*) Damn! (*Knocking.*) Jean! . . . Jean! . . . (*Remembering.*) Oh, of course . . . He's out, damn it! And I went and left the key inside. (*Not knowing which way to turn.*) Well this is a fine mess! What do I do now? I can't stay out here like this! (*Calling downstairs.*) Janitor! . . . Janitor!

BOUZIN, *timidly opening the upstage door in the dressing room after knocking for a moment, and looking in.* Monsieur Bois-d'Enghien, you haven't forgotten me, I hope . . . (*Looking around.*) Monsieur Bois-d'Enghien . . . Hm! I wonder where he went.

> *He notices the open window*
> *and goes over to close it.*

BOIS-D'ENGHIEN, *collapsing onto the bench by the stairs.* Now what? (*A general murmur of merriment is heard from the celebration upstairs.*) My God! That wedding! All those people!

BOUZIN. Well, if he's not here there's no sense wasting my time. I'll come back later.

> *He is about to leave.*

BOIS-D'ENGHIEN, *as an idea hits him.* Wait a minute . . . Bouzin is still in there. He'll hear me if I ring the bell.

> *He goes to the door, far left,*
> *and rings persistently.*

BOUZIN, *whose hand is already on the doorknob, petrified.*
Oh, my God! The General! It's the General again . . .
And I'm all alone!

> *He dashes back through the*
> *upstage door and closes it*
> *frantically behind him.*

BOIS-D'ENGHIEN, *still ringing.* Bouzin! . . . Bouzin! . . .
Oh, what's the use? (*He stops ringing.*) He can hear
the bell but he won't dare come to the door. (*Pacing*
up and down, as the noise from upstairs grows louder.)
Oh, this is great! Just great! (*Leaning over the railing*
and calling downstairs.) Janitor! . . . Janitor! . . .
(*Suddenly.*) Good God, somebody's coming!

> *He makes a run for the*
> *stairway, leaping up several*
> *steps at a time and dis-*
> *appearing momentarily, only*
> *to come running down again,*
> *in panic, as the sounds of*
> *the celebration grow louder.*

All those people . . . They're coming down! I'm
trapped! . . . I'm surrounded!

> *He huddles in the doorway,*
> *far left, trying not to be*
> *seen. The wedding party*
> *appears coming down the*
> *stairs, everyone talking at*
> *the same time. Amid the*
> *general commotion the fol-*
> *lowing comments can be*
> *heard.*

THE BRIDE'S FATHER. Come on, come on! Let's not be late.
THE BRIDE. But we have plenty of time, Papa.
THE GROOM. We're not due at the city hall till eleven.

> *Suddenly everyone notices*
> BOIS-D'ENGHIEN *and emits an*
> *"oh" of dismay.*

262

THE BRIDE'S FATHER. Who on earth . . .

BOIS-D'ENGHIEN, *putting on a bold front, addressing* THE BRIDE *with all the gallantry he can muster.* Congratulations, Madame! May I be the first—

> *Everyone, arms upraised in horror, cuts him off with an appropriate exclamation: "Shocking!" "Scandalous!" etc.*

THE BRIDE'S MOTHER. He's naked!

THE GROOM. In broad daylight!

THE BRIDE'S FATHER, *indignant.* Well, we'll see about that!

THE BRIDE'S MOTHER. We'll complain!

THE GROOM. We'll get the janitor. He'll take care of him!

BOIS-D'ENGHIEN, *sheepishly bowing and scraping his way to the door of his dressing room.* Ladies . . . Gentlemen . . .

THE BRIDE'S FATHER, *to* BOIS-D'ENGHIEN. Really, Monsieur! At your age!

> *The members of the party continue down the stairs, still muttering expressions of their shock and disapproval. As they disappear, they pass* THE GENERAL, *who is on his way up.*

BOIS-D'ENGHIEN, *in despair.* How in heaven's name did I get into this?

THE GENERAL. Bueno, Bodégué . . .

BOIS-D'ENGHIEN, *aside, exasperated.* Him again!

THE GENERAL, *suddenly noticing* BOIS-D'ENGHIEN'S *attire.* Caramba! Bodégué, for why you dress like thees? For why you no wear pants? Porqué, Bodégué?

BOIS-D'ENGHIEN, *furious.* "Porqué? . . . Porqué? . . ." I've locked myself out, that's porqué! The door blew shut in my face!

THE GENERAL, *laughing.* Ha ha ha! Ees for to laugh.

BOIS-D'ENGHIEN. I'm glad you think so! (*Aside.*) Imbecile!

THE GENERAL, *regaining his composure, mopping his brow.*
Bueno! . . . Ah, thees Poussin . . . He make me run
long way, thees Poussin!

> *He sits down on the bench*
> *near the stairwell, fanning*
> *himself with his hand.*

BOIS-D'ENGHIEN. And you didn't catch him, did you! . . .
Well, ha ha ha! "Is for to laugh," old boy!

THE GENERAL, *standing up.* Sí! Sí, I catch heem! I keeck
heem een pants, thees Poussin! . . . Only, ees no Poussin. Ees fonny theeng, I no onderstand . . . When he
turn round, ees someone else.

BOIS-D'ENGHIEN. Ha!

THE GENERAL. Oh, but I no feeneesh weeth heem yet! Thees
Poussin . . . Es un—

BOIS-D'ENGHIEN, *interrupting.* Un hombre muerto! I know!
That's fine! . . . Now what do you want me to do
about it?

THE GENERAL. Bueno! Ees no for thees I come. I come for
talk weeth you, Bodégué.

BOIS-D'ENGHIEN. Yes . . . Well, later, all right? I have
other things on my mind at the moment than a friendly
chat.

THE GENERAL. Porqué?

BOIS-D'ENGHIEN. "Porqué? . . . Porqué? . . ." (*Aside.*)
He's getting on my nerves with his "porqué"! (*To* THE
GENERAL.) Don't you understand? I'm locked out of my
apartment!

THE GENERAL. Bueno . . . Ees mirboble! I no mind . . .
We talk right here, no?

BOIS-D'ENGHIEN. No, no, no! For goodness' sake, not now!
(*Looking over the railing.*) Oh God, someone else!

> *He dashes for the stairway*
> *and runs up the steps out*
> *of sight.*

THE GENERAL. Now for why he go run like thees? (*Going*
up a few steps and calling.) Bodégué! . . . Bodégué!

BOIS-D'ENGHIEN'S VOICE. Yes . . . Later, later!

THE GENERAL, *aside.* Es loco! (*An elderly gentleman appears on the landing, nods good-day to* THE GENERAL, *and continues up the stairs as* THE GENERAL *returns his greeting.*) Buenos días! (*Calling.*) Bodégué! For why you stay upstairs? You come down, Bodégué, no?

> BOIS-D'ENGHIEN *reappears at the top of the stairs, bowing his way backward down the first few steps, obviously in the direction of the unseen gentleman, finally turning and coming down to the landing.*

BOIS-D'ENGHIEN. No, really! This is too much! (*Pacing back and forth, with* THE GENERAL *at his heels.*) I can't stand out here like this, with people going up and down every minute! (*Shaking the dressing room door, to no avail.*) Oh! . . . Damned door! (*To* THE GENERAL, *behind him.*) I don't suppose you know how to pick a lock, by any chance?

THE GENERAL. Peeck lock? Me? . . . What you theenk, I be bugler maybe?

BOIS-D'ENGHIEN. Bugler? . . . No, I don't think . . . Oh, never mind!

> *He begins pacing again.*

THE GENERAL. Bueno, Bodégué . . . I come for talk weeth you, no?

BOIS-D'ENGHIEN, *standing still, near the railing, angrily.* All right, what is it? What do you want of me?

THE GENERAL. What I want? Ees what I tell you yesterday what I want. Remember? I come for to keel you.

BOIS-D'ENGHIEN, *out of patience.* You . . . Oh, go to hell!

THE GENERAL, *bowing with a flourish.* Your obediente sirviente, señor Bodégué!

BOIS-D'ENGHIEN. Really? Well look, obedient servant, go find me a pair of pants!

THE GENERAL, *springing up angrily*. Qué es eso? Me? Find you pair of . . . Ho, ho, ho, Bodégué! Eef you know what ees good for you, you be more antisepteec, mi amigo!

BOIS-D'ENGHIEN. What?

THE GENERAL. Sí, sí! You no be so such septeec when I tell you theengs!

BOIS-D'ENGHIEN, *suddenly understanding*. General, you mean sceptic! (*With a sarcastic laugh.*) "Septic!" That's a good one. "Septic!" At least you could learn how to speak the language! S, c, e . . . . "Sceptic," not "septic," understand? You pronounce the c.

THE GENERAL. Bueno! Ees make no deefference. Septeec, scepteec . . . Ees all the same.

BOIS-D'ENGHIEN. Fine, have it your way. Now let's get this nonsense over with. So, you want to kill me, do you?

THE GENERAL. No!

BOIS-D'ENGHIEN. What do you mean, "no"? You just said—

THE GENERAL. I mean, ees for why I come, sí . . . But now I no more want to keel you.

BOIS-D'ENGHIEN. Oh? Well, how nice.

THE GENERAL, *with a sigh of resignation*. No, for becose I have just see Lucette Gautier, downstairs. (BOIS-D'ENGHIEN *shrugs his shoulders.*) And she say to me sometheeng . . . sometheeng I no like, but ees notheeng I can do. She say to me: "Mi general, I no be yours, never, except eef Bodégué he come back to me." Thees are her words.

BOIS-D'ENGHIEN, *recoiling*. What?

THE GENERAL. Sí! Ees what she say. Oh, for me ees very deeffeecult . . . When I theenk of terreeble skene, yesterday . . .

BOIS-D'ENGHIEN. The terrible what?

THE GENERAL. Skene . . . skene . . . Terreeble skene you make weeth Lucette, een front of everybody, at home of Baronesa!

BOIS-D'ENGHIEN. General, you mean "scene," not "skene"! S, c, e . . . "Scene." You don't pronounce the c.

THE GENERAL, *losing patience.* Bodégué . . . I warn you, you no make fool of me! I tell you just now "septeec," you tell me "scepteec." Bueno! Now I tell you "skene," you tell me "scene" . . . (*Threatening.*) Bodégué!

BOIS-D'ENGHIEN, *imitating his menacing inflection.* General!

THE GENERAL. Be careful, Bodégué! I warn you!

BOIS-D'ENGHIEN, *with a gesture of unconcern.* Bah! (*Aside.*) He's all bluff.

THE GENERAL, *suddenly calming down.* Bueno! Ees what I have to tell you. You no more go be angry weeth Lucette. You weel take her back. (*Categorically.*) Bueno!

BOIS-D'ENGHIEN. Bueno my foot! What do you mean, I'll take her back?

THE GENERAL. Sí!

BOIS-D'ENGHIEN, *leaning over as if to whisper something into his ear, then bellowing.* Never in a million years!

THE GENERAL. No? Then I go re-keel you back again!

BOIS-D'ENGHIEN, *pacing downstage.* That's right! Re-kill me back again! (*Returning to* THE GENERAL.) For heaven's sake, I wish you would make up your mind! First you want to kill me because I am Lucette's lover, and now you want to because I'm not! Just what do you want, anyway?

THE GENERAL. What I want? . . . Bodégué, you are estúpido!

BOIS-D'ENGHIEN. I beg your—

THE GENERAL. Sí, estúpido! . . . What I want? Ees Lucette what I want, for me!

BOIS-D'ENGHIEN. For you, exactly! For you, not for me!

THE GENERAL. Sí!

BOIS-D'ENGHIEN. All right then, leave me out of it. Take her, she's yours!

THE GENERAL. But I tell you, she say to me . . .

BOIS-D'ENGHIEN. Yes! I know, I know . . . (*After a mo-*

ment of reflection.) All right, I have just the way to get rid of her.

THE GENERAL. Ees true? Ah, Bodégué, you my friend!

BOIS-D'ENGHIEN. You're going to go tell her that you've seen me and that I absolutely refuse to take her back.

THE GENERAL. Porqué?

BOIS-D'ENGHIEN, *to the audience.* "Porqué"! (*To* THE GENERAL.) Porqué, old boy, you can tell her I said she had certain . . . shall we say, certain physical imperfections . . .

THE GENERAL. Cómo?

BOIS-D'ENGHIEN, *whispering in* THE GENERAL's *ear.* . . . that only an intimate acquaintance like myself could appreciate . . .

THE GENERAL, *at the top of his voice.* Imperfecciones? Lucette she have imperfecciones?

BOIS-D'ENGHIEN. Lucette? Of course not! Don't be absurd!

THE GENERAL. Bueno, then for why you tell me—

BOIS-D'ENGHIEN. But she does have vanity, General. She's a woman, after all, and women love themselves much more than they love us. Now you just tell her what I said, and believe me, she'll never want to see me again. She'll be all yours.

THE GENERAL, *delighted.* Ah, sí! Sí! I onderstand! Ah, Bodégué! . . . Fernando! . . . Gracias, gracias! . . . Muchas gracias!

BOIS-D'ENGHIEN. Yes, yes . . . You're quite welcome.

THE GENERAL. I go run to her. Good-bye Fernando! (*Shaking* BOIS-D'ENGHIEN's *hands warmly.*) Adios, mi amigo! . . . Y buena suerte! (*He runs to the stairs, then stops a moment.*) And Bodégué . . . Now I no go keel you no more.

> *He runs down the stairs.*

BOIS-D'ENGHIEN. Fine . . . I'm glad to hear it. I no go keel you either. (*As* THE GENERAL *disappears.*) Him and his damned . . . assassinomania!

*He begins pacing again. In
the meantime, the upstage
door in the dressing room
has opened, and* BOUZIN
makes a timid entrance.

BOUZIN, *looking around and listening.* It must be safe. I
don't hear anything. Anyway, I can't spend the whole
day in there!

*He goes to the dressing
room door, listens for a
moment, then opens it
cautiously and steps out.
He is about to close the
door behind him.*

BOIS-D'ENGHIEN, *stage left, noticing* BOUZIN *and dashing
toward him.* My God, don't close that door!

BOUZIN, *unable to stop himself in time, as the door slams
shut.* Oh dear!

BOIS-D'ENGHIEN, *pounding the door in despair.* Bouzin!
You . . . you idiot! I told you not to close the door,
damn it!

BOUZIN. I'm sorry . . . It all happened so fast . . .

BOIS-D'ENGHIEN. Oh! Great! Now I'm still locked out!

BOUZIN, *laughing.* But . . . What on earth are you doing
out here . . . like this? I mean, really . . .

BOIS-D'ENGHIEN. What am I . . . Believe me, I'm not out
here for my health!

He paces back and forth.

BOUZIN, *still laughing.* It looks terribly funny, you know!

BOIS-D'ENGHIEN, *furious.* Oh, you think so, do you? Well,
damn it, I can understand why! You're dressed, you
are!

*He sits down on the bench,
far left, without noticing
the revolver, and jumps up
again with an "oh" of surprise. As he looks at the*

> *revolver, then at* BOUZIN,
> *an idea obviously dawns on*
> *him. Picking up the revolver*
> *and holding it behind his*
> *back, he crosses over to*
> BOUZIN.

BOIS-D'ENGHIEN, *very pleasantly.* Bouzin . . .

BOUZIN, *smiling.* Monsieur?

BOIS-D'ENGHIEN. Bouzin . . . You're going to do me a great favor!

BOUZIN, *still smiling.* I am, Monsieur?

BOIS-D'ENGHIEN, *still as pleasantly as possible.* Give me your pants, Bouzin.

BOUZIN, *laughing.* Give you my . . . Ha ha ha! You must be mad!

BOIS-D'ENGHIEN, *suddenly changing his tone and threatening him.* Yes, I'm mad! You're right! I'm stark, raving mad! Now give me your pants!

> *He aims the revolver right*
> *at* BOUZIN.

BOUZIN, *terrified, backed up against the wall.* My God in heaven! . . . Monsieur Bois-d'Enghien!

BOIS-D'ENGHIEN. Give me your pants!

BOUZIN. Please, Monsieur Bois-d'Enghien! Please . . .

BOIS-D'ENGHIEN. Come on, be quick about it! Your pants, or I shoot!

BOUZIN. Of course, Monsieur Bois-d'Enghien . . . Anything you say! (*Petrified, he begins to remove his pants.*) My God, this is terrible! Running around without my pants, and in a strange house!

BOIS-D'ENGHIEN. Come on, let's go!

BOUZIN. Here, Monsieur Bois-d'Enghien . . . Here . . .

> *He gives him his pants.*

BOIS-D'ENGHIEN. Thank you. Now the coat.

> *He aims the revolver again.*

BOUZIN. My coat too? But . . . Monsieur! I won't have anything left!

BOIS-D'ENGHIEN. You heard me! Your coat!

BOUZIN, *giving it to him.* Of course, Monsieur Bois-d'Enghien . . . Here . . .

BOIS-D'ENGHIEN. Thank you!

BOUZIN, *huddling against the dividing wall, holding his hat against his stomach with both hands, to hide his shame.* Oh! Why did I ever set foot in this place?

> *In the meantime,* BOIS-D'ENGHIEN *has gone over to the bench, near the stairs, laid the revolver by his side, and begun to put on the pants. Once they are on, he gets up, moves far left, turning his back to the audience while buttoning up.* BOUZIN's *face lights up suddenly as he notices the revolver. Placing his hat back on his head, he tiptoes over to the bench and picks it up. With a jaunty air of self-assurance, cocking his hat to one side, he approaches* BOIS-D'ENGHIEN, *holding the revolver behind his back.*

BOUZIN, *as pleasantly as possible.* Monsieur Bois-d'Enghien?

BOIS-D'ENGHIEN, *as he finishes buttoning the pants.* Yes?

BOUZIN. My pants, please.

BOIS-D'ENGHIEN. What?

> *He laughs.*

BOUZIN, *aiming the revolver, in his most menacing voice.* You're going to give me my pants, or I'll kill you, understand?

BOIS-D'ENGHIEN, *putting on the coat.* Of course, old boy, right away.

BOUZIN. This is no joke! Give me my pants, or I shoot!

BOIS-D'ENGHIEN. Certainly, go right ahead.

BOUZIN, *pulling the trigger several times, in vain.* What . . .

BOIS-D'ENGHIEN. Only, you'd better do it right. Here, let
me show you. (*He pulls the fan from the barrel leaving
it in the hands of a horrified* BOUZIN.) There! It's easy
when you know how!

BOUZIN. I've been tricked!

> *He puts the fan back on the
> bench in disgust.*

BOIS-D'ENGHIEN, *laughing.* Poor Bouzin!

> *He picks up the fan, reas-
> sembles the revolver, and
> puts it in his pocket.*

THE JANITOR'S VOICE, *coming up the stairs.* This way, gentlemen.

BOUZIN, *looking over the railing.* Who's that? . . . Oh no!
(*To* BOIS-D'ENGHIEN.) There's someone coming!

BOIS-D'ENGHIEN, *unconcerned.* Really? . . . Pity!

BOUZIN, *bolting up the stairs, four at a time, as* BOIS-
D'ENGHIEN *watches, chuckling.* Help!

> *He disappears.*

BOIS-D'ENGHIEN, *taking a few leisurely strides.* Ah, it feels
good to be wearing clothes again . . . even if they're
not my own!

THE JANITOR, *reaching the landing, followed by two
policemen.* This way . . . After you . . .

> THE POLICEMEN *pass in front
> of him.*

BOIS-D'ENGHIEN, *aside.* Now what's all this? (*To* THE JANI-
TOR.) Are you gentlemen looking for someone?

THE JANITOR. Yes . . . Some damned fool who's running
around the building in his underwear!

BOIS-D'ENGHIEN. In his underwear? (*Aside.*) Oh dear!
Poor Bouzin! (*Aloud.*) I haven't seen him. He's not up
here.

THE JANITOR, *at the stairs.* He must be. The people from

the Brugnot wedding made a complaint. I had to go
call the police. (*Following* THE POLICEMEN *up the
stairs.*) After you . . . He must be upstairs somewhere.
Anyway, he won't go far. There's only six floors.

> *They disappear.*

BOIS-D'ENGHIEN, *following them up a few steps, aside.* Poor
Bouzin! He just doesn't have much luck!

> *All of a sudden, from down-
> stairs, a female voice is
> heard vocalizing in arpeg-
> gios.* BOIS-D'ENGHIEN *looks
> up in surprise. A moment
> later* VIVIANE *appears,
> wearing a rose in her hair
> and carrying a roll of sheet
> music. She is followed by*
> MISS BETTING.

VIVIANE. Here we are!

BOIS-D'ENGHIEN, *joining them in two gigantic strides.*
Viviane! You? Here? But—

VIVIANE, *determined.* Yes, Fernand . . . Me! I've come to
tell you that I love you! There, I've said it!

BOIS-D'ENGHIEN. But . . . I thought . . . I mean, after
last night . . . After what happened . . .

VIVIANE. I don't care, Fernand . . . None of that matters.
I only know one thing. Last night I suddenly realized
you were exactly the kind of man I've always dreamed
of!

BOIS-D'ENGHIEN. I am? (*To the audience.*) See what happens when you show them your manly physique!

> MISS BETTING *makes an ap-
> propriately inquisitive ges-
> ture to* VIVIANE, *obviously
> anxious to know who the
> gentleman is.*

VIVIANE. Fernand, let me introduce you to Miss Betting,
my governess.

BOIS-D'ENGHIEN, *turning toward them.* Oh?

VIVIANE, *duplicating her spoken words with sign language,*
to MISS BETTING. This is Professor Capoul, my singing
teacher.

BOIS-D'ENGHIEN. What?

> MISS BETTING *nods in recog-*
> *nition, and directs a flurry*
> *of sign language to* VIVIANE.

VIVIANE, *replying in kind.* That's right . . . The famous
Professor Capoul.

BOIS-D'ENGHIEN, *aside to* VIVIANE *as* MISS BETTING, *smiling,*
looks on in admiration. What . . . What kind of nonsense is this?

VIVIANE. Well, I couldn't very well tell her where we were
going. She never would have taken me. I had to say I
was coming for a singing lesson.

BOIS-D'ENGHIEN. But she'll find out . . .

VIVIANE. Hardly! You can see for yourself she's deaf as a
post. She doesn't speak either.

BOIS-D'ENGHIEN. You mean . . . You have a deaf-mute for
a governess?

VIVIANE. Yes . . . Mamma says that way she can't go fill-
ing my head with a lot of nonsense.

BOIS-D'ENGHIEN, *shrugging his shoulders.* Oh . . .

VIVIANE, *suddenly waxing romantic.* Tell me, Fernand . . .
Is it true you've had simply dozens of women running
after you?

BOIS-D'ENGHIEN. What? (*Modestly.*) Well, I . . .

VIVIANE. Please say it's true! I'll love you all the more!

BOIS-D'ENGHIEN. Really? Why, in that case . . . I've had
swarms of them!

VIVIANE, *delighted.* You have? And have there been any
who wanted to kill themselves for you?

BOIS-D'ENGHIEN, *reflecting for a moment, categorically.*
Fifteen! As a matter of fact, there was one just a little
while ago. (*Reaching into his pocket for the revolver.*)
I had a devil of a time taking this away from her!

> *He puts it back in his*
> *pocket.*

VIVIANE, *ecstatic.* A revolver! Oh! . . . I would be out of
my mind not to love a man with a past like that!

BOIS-D'ENGHIEN, *about to take her in his arms.* Viviane!

VIVIANE. No, no! Not in front of Miss Betting!

BOIS-D'ENGHIEN. Oh!

> VIVIANE *and* BOIS-D'ENGHIEN,
> *to cover their embarrassment,*
> *throw a little offhand laugh*
> *at* MISS BETTING, *who, with-*
> *out understanding why,*
> *joins in. Suddenly she stops*
> *laughing and directs a*
> *sign language question to*
> VIVIANE.

VIVIANE, *laughing.* That's right.

BOIS-D'ENGHIEN, *laughing along with her.* What did she
say?

VIVIANE. She wants to know what we're doing out here on
the landing. Let's go in, shall we?

BOIS-D'ENGHIEN. Go in? I only wish we could! I've gone
and locked myself out.

VIVIANE. Oh my! What about my lesson? Miss Betting will
begin to wonder.

BOIS-D'ENGHIEN. Never mind . . . You can tell her that we
great artists always give our lessons out on the landing.
We can breathe better. There's so much more room.

VIVIANE, *with some trepidation.* Well . . .

> *She passes on the informa-*
> *tion to* MISS BETTING, *who*
> *looks at* BOIS-D'ENGHIEN
> *inquisitively, with a gesture*
> *of surprise.*

BOIS-D'ENGHIEN, *to* MISS BETTING, *mouthing his words*
slowly. That's right! Big . . . Lots of room . . . Better
for the diaphragm . . .

VIVIANE, *showing* MISS BETTING *to the bench, far left.* Now, you can sit right here while I take my lesson. (MISS BETTING *sits down.*) There! (*With a sigh of relief.*) Everything is ready for Mamma, whenever she gets here.

BOIS-D'ENGHIEN, *shocked.* Ready for . . . You mean your mother is coming here? You're going to let her find—

VIVIANE, *interrupting him with a good-natured remonstrance.* No, no, no . . . That's enough! You mustn't talk any more!

BOIS-D'ENGHIEN. What?

VIVIANE, *unrolling her music.* This is my singing lesson, remember? If you have anything to say, you'll have to sing it to me.

BOIS-D'ENGHIEN. Sing it to you? You want me to—

VIVIANE. Of course. Miss Betting thinks I'm taking my lesson, doesn't she? (*She gives him one sheet of music and keeps the other.*) Here!

BOIS-D'ENGHIEN. But . . . You just told me, she's deaf as a post. Can't we just make believe we're singing? She'll never know the difference.

VIVIANE. Oh no, Fernand! That would never do! She's such a sweet thing, I simply couldn't bear deceiving her!

BOIS-D'ENGHIEN, *with a meaningful look to the audience.* Oh . . .

VIVIANE. Now then, what were you saying?

BOIS-D'ENGHIEN. I was saying that if your mother ever finds you here—

VIVIANE, *reminding him.* No, no, no! Sing it to me, I said!

BOIS-D'ENGHIEN. Hm! Of course . . . (*He clears his throat and opens out the music.* VIVIANE *follows the notes in her copy. Singing to the melody of Escamillo's song in act 2 of* Carmen, *from "Votre toast, je peux vous le rendre . . ."*)

> If your mother ever finds you here,
> After that scene last night,
> There will be fireworks!

VIVIANE, *continuing the melody.*
> I left Mamma a note,
> And said I've run away,
> But that she could find me here with you,
> Here with you . . .
>> *On the last notes, she pulls
>> the rose from her hair and
>> flings it at* BOIS-D'ENGHIEN.
>> *He is about to continue, but*
>> MISS BETTING *interrupts with
>> vigorous applause, and di-
>> rects a question to* VIVIANE,
>> *who nods assent.*

BOIS-D'ENGHIEN, *speaking.* What did she say?

VIVIANE, *speaking.* She said we must be singing something
from *Carmen.*

BOIS-D'ENGHIEN, *to* MISS BETTING, *mouthing his words.*
Yes, that's right . . . *Carmen* . . . (*To the audience.*)
Of course, we've taken a liberty or two! (*To* VIVIANE.)
Now look, that's all very well and good, but—

VIVIANE. No, no! Please! . . . Sing it!

BOIS-D'ENGHIEN, *resigned.* Oh . . . (*Singing, continuing
the melody from "Le cirque est plein, c'est jour de
fête . . ."*)
> That's all very well and good, I'm sure,
> But when she finds you here,
> She's going to take a fit!

VIVIANE, *continuing.*
> Oh yes, she'll rant and rave,
> But since I've gone this far,
> I know that she'll let me have my way,
> Just wait and see!
>> *During the preceding action,
>> the entire domestic staff
>> of the building, attracted by
>> the singing, has assembled
>> on the stairs, from both*

> *directions, unseen by the*
> *principals.*

BOIS-D'ENGHIEN, *delighted, speaking.* She will?

VIVIANE, *speaking.* Certainly!

BOIS-D'ENGHIEN, *in a rapturous outburst, singing to the melody of "Toréador, en garde . . ."*

> Ah, Viviane, my da-a-a-arling . . .

> *All of a sudden, the domes-*
> *tics pick up the melody with*
> *lusty shouts of "Toréador!*
> *Toréador!" They all break*
> *into laughter and applause.*
> BOIS-D'ENGHIEN *and* VIVIANE
> *turn round, horrified.* MISS
> BETTING *appears nonplussed.*

VIVIANE, *speaking.* What?

BOIS-D'ENGHIEN, *speaking, to the group.* You . . . What in the name of . . . Who invited you? Get out! . . . Come on, get out of here!

> *The domestics leave gradu-*
> *ally, grumbling as they go.*

MADAME DUVERGER, *appearing on the landing like a whirl-wind.* Viviane!

BOIS-D'ENGHIEN, *mistaking her for one of the domestics.* You heard me! Out! (*Recognizing her.*) Aaah! Madame . . .

VIVIANE. Mamma!

> MISS BETTING *gets up and*
> *crosses over to* MADAME
> DUVERGER, *extending her*
> *hand to her.*

MADAME DUVERGER, *to* MISS BETTING, *indignantly.* You! Aren't you ashamed, bringing my little girl here, with this . . . this gentleman! (MISS BETTING, *puzzled, says something to her in sign language.*) Oh . . . Never mind! I should know better by now!

BOIS-D'ENGHIEN, *formally.* Madame Duverger, once again

I have the honor of asking for your daughter's hand in marriage . . .

MADAME DUVERGER. You have the . . . Never, Monsieur! Never! (*To* VIVIANE.) Oh, you poor, foolish child! After a scandal like this, nobody will have you! Nobody!

VIVIANE. Don't be silly, Mamma! He'll have me . . . (*To* BOIS-D'ENGHIEN.) Won't you?

BOIS-D'ENGHIEN. Of course, I just said . . .

MADAME DUVERGER. Never! Do you understand?

VIVIANE. But Mamma! He's exactly the kind of man I've always dreamed of. I love him, and I'll never marry anyone else!

MADAME DUVERGER, *taking* VIVIANE *in her arms, as if to protect her from* BOIS-D'ENGHIEN. Him? Do you know what you're saying? That . . . that heaven-only-knows-what of Lucette Gautier!

BOIS-D'ENGHIEN. But I'm not her heaven-only-knows-what any more!

MADAME DUVERGER. Really, Monsieur! Do you expect me to believe that after what I saw last night?

BOIS-D'ENGHIEN, *self-possessed*. Ah, but that's just the point, Madame. I'm afraid you may have jumped to a rather hasty conclusion . . .

MADAME DUVERGER. Rubbish! I know what I saw.

BOIS-D'ENGHIEN. Yes, but did you know that I was merely telling Mademoiselle Gautier that she and I were through? I was saying good-bye to her, forever!

MADAME DUVERGER, *with a sneer*. Monsieur, what do you take me for? You were hardly dressed for saying good-bye. On the contrary, need I remind you that you were hardly dressed at all!

BOIS-D'ENGHIEN, *unruffled*. Exactly! Just before you came in I said to her: "Look here, Lucette. I never want to see you again, understand? In fact, I never want to see anything that reminds me of you. Not even . . . not even these clothes of mine that you've touched!"

MADAME DUVERGER. Oh?

BOIS-D'ENGHIEN. And then, true to my word, I began taking them off. If you had come in a minute later, I wouldn't have had a stitch left.

MADAME DUVERGER, *shocked.* You what?

VIVIANE. You see, Mamma? Everything is all right now. You can let me marry Monsieur Bois-d'Enghien after all!

BOIS-D'ENGHIEN. Of course!

VIVIANE. Besides, no one else will have me. You said so yourself.

MADAME DUVERGER. Oh . . .

VIVIANE. Say yes, Mamma! Please say yes!

MADAME DUVERGER, *resigned but unenthusiastic.* Oh . . . You poor dear child . . . If you're sure this is what you want . . .

VIVIANE. Oh yes! It is! It is!

MADAME DUVERGER. If you're absolutely sure . . . (*Sighing.*) Oh . . . Very well.

VIVIANE. Ah! Mamma!

BOIS-D'ENGHIEN. Mother!

VIVIANE, *running up to* MISS BETTING, *who has been looking on in bewilderment, and accompanying her words with signs.* Miss Betting! Isn't it wonderful? (*Pointing to* BOIS-D'ENGHIEN.) We're going to be married!

> MISS BETTING *points alternately to* VIVIANE *and* BOIS-D'ENGHIEN, *with a look of utter confusion. In the meantime,* JEAN *has appeared at the upstage door in the dressing room.*

JEAN, *entering and looking around.* Hm! He must have gone out.

> *He opens the door to the landing.*

BOIS-D'ENGHIEN. Ah, Jean! Finally! What took you so long?

JEAN. I went to half a dozen locksmiths, Monsieur, but I couldn't find a single one who was free.

BOIS-D'ENGHIEN. That doesn't matter. I won't be needing one anyway.

JEAN, *aside.* A nice time to tell me!

> *He turns and leaves through the upstage door, muttering to himself.*

BOIS-D'ENGHIEN, *at the open door.* Shall we go in, ladies? Mother . . . Viviane . . .

> *Just as they are all about to enter the dressing room, there is a loud commotion from upstairs. They turn to one another in surprise.*

VIVIANE. Oh my!

BOIS-D'ENGHIEN. What do you suppose that can be?

THE JANITOR, *coming down first.* We've got him now! We had to chase him over half the rooftops in the neighborhood, but we've got him now.

> BOUZIN *appears, in a state of disarray, dragged along by* THE POLICEMEN *and followed by the group of jeering domestics.*

BOIS-D'ENGHIEN. Bouzin!

MADAME DUVERGER. Monsieur!

VIVIANE, *as* MISS BETTING *covers her eyes.* Shocking!

> *The three ladies rush into the dressing room.*

THE POLICEMEN. Come on you, let's go!

BOUZIN, *dragging his feet.* No, no! Wait! It's all a mistake! (*As he passes* BOIS-D'ENGHIEN, *at the door.*) Monsieur, for heaven's sake, tell them!

281

BOIS-D'ENGHIEN, *hypocritically*. For shame, Bouzin! At your age!

> *He enters the dressing room and closes the door in* BOUZIN's *face.*

BOUZIN. Oh!

THE POLICEMEN. Come on, come on! To the station with you!

BOIS-D'ENGHIEN, *aside, chuckling, as the ladies leave through the upstage door*. It's really an awfully dirty trick, I suppose . . . Oh well, I know the chief of police. A word from me and he'll be out in no time.

THE POLICEMEN. Come on, you! To the station!

BOUZIN. In the name of Posterity . . . I'm innocent! I'm innocent!

> *He disappears down the stairs, amid the hoots and shouts of the domestics.*

CURTAIN

Going to Pot

On purge Bébé

CHARACTERS

FOLLAVOINE
CHOUILLOUX
TRUCHET

JULIE
MADAME CHOUILLOUX
ROSE
BABY

Going to Pot *is a revised version of Norman R. Shapiro's transla-tion first published in the* Tulane Drama Review, *Autumn 1960.*
Illustration: Feydeau shortly before his death

FOLLAVOINE'S *study. Down right, a door leading to* FOLLA-
VOINE'S *bedroom. Up right, the door to his wife's room. Upstage center, a double door leading to the hall. On each side
of this door, a cabinet, the front of which is formed by two
glassed panels, covered on the inside by an opaque material
concealing the interior. Stage left, running almost the entire
length of the wall, a large window appropriately curtained
in the style of the period. Near this window, a large desk,
facing the audience and covered with various articles: a
dictionary, miscellaneous books, folders, loose papers scat-
tered here and there, a box of rubber bands, etc. Under the
desk, a wastepaper basket. Behind it, a chair. In front of it,
to the left, an armchair. Up right, not far from the doors, a
sofa placed slightly diagonally. To the right of this sofa, an
end table; to the left, a small chair.*

At rise, FOLLAVOINE *is seen bent over his desk, busily consulting
his dictionary.*

FOLLAVOINE. Let's see now, Aleutian Islands . . . Aleutian
   Islands . . . Aleutian—(*A knock is heard at the door.*
   FOLLAVOINE *answers angrily without looking up from
   his dictionary.*) Come in! Come in! (*To* ROSE, *entering.*)
   What is it?
ROSE. It's Madame, Monsieur. She wishes to see you.
FOLLAVOINE, *impatiently.* Good! Let her come and see me.
   She knows where I am.
ROSE. Madame is in the bathroom. She says she's too busy
   to be disturbed.
FOLLAVOINE. Oh really? Well, you can tell her I'm busy
   too. I'm sorry, but I'm working.
ROSE, *indifferently.* Yes, Monsieur.
FOLLAVOINE, *in the same tone of voice.* What does she
   want anyway?
ROSE. I couldn't say, Monsieur.
FOLLAVOINE. Well, go find out.
ROSE. Yes, Monsieur.
FOLLAVOINE, *under his breath.* Too busy . . . (*Calling to*

ROSE *as she reaches the door, up right.*) Wait a minute!
While you're here . . .

ROSE. Monsieur?

FOLLAVOINE. You wouldn't know, off hand . . . where the
Aleutians are? . . .

ROSE. Monsieur?

FOLLAVOINE. The Aleutians. You wouldn't happen to know
where they are, would you?

ROSE. Oh no! No, Monsieur. I don't put things away around
here. Madame is the one who—

FOLLAVOINE, *standing up straight.* What? "Put things
away . . ."! What are you talking about? The Aleutians! The Aleutians! They're islands, idiot! Islands.
Earth surrounded by water. You know what that is?

ROSE, *opening her eyes wide.* Earth surrounded by water?

FOLLAVOINE. Yes. Earth surrounded by water. What do
you call it?

ROSE. Mud?

FOLLAVOINE. Mud? No, no . . . not mud! It's mud when
there's just a little earth and a little water. When there's
a lot of earth and a lot of water it's called an island.

ROSE, *amazed.* Oh?

FOLLAVOINE. That's what the Aleutians are. Islands. You
understand? They aren't in the apartment.

ROSE, *trying her best to understand.* Oh yes, Monsieur.
They're outside the apartment.

FOLLAVOINE. Of course they're outside the apartment!

ROSE. Yes, Monsieur, I understand. But I haven't seen them,
Monsieur.

FOLLAVOINE. That's fine! Thank you.

ROSE, *trying to justify herself.* I haven't been in Paris very
long. You understand . . .

FOLLAVOINE. Yes, yes. That's fine.

ROSE. And I get out so little!

FOLLAVOINE. Yes. That's right, that's right. (*He pushes
her gently toward the door, and she leaves.*) Ha! It's

incredible! That girl doesn't know a thing. Absolutely
nothing. What did she learn in school, I wonder? (*He
crosses to his desk, leaning against it once again to con-
sult the dictionary.*) Now let's see. Eleutians . . . Eleutians . . . That's funny. "Elephant, Eleusis, elevate . . ."
But no Eleutians! It should be right here between
"Eleusis" and "elevate." Bah! This dictionary is worth-
less!

> JULIE *enters in a flurry of
> agitation. She is dressed in
> a dirty bathrobe, with
> curlers in her hair and her
> stockings down around her
> ankles. A covered wash-
> bucket, full of water, is hang-
> ing from her arm.*

JULIE. Well! Very nice! Too busy to speak to me!

FOLLAVOINE, *jumping at the sudden intrusion.* Julie! For
God's sake, don't burst in here like that!

JULIE, *sarcastically.* Oh, I beg your pardon! Are you really
too busy to speak to me . . . darling?

FOLLAVOINE, *angrily.* You're a fine one to talk! Why must
I always come running? Why—

JULIE, *with an acid smile.* Of course. You're absolutely
right. We're only married, after all!

FOLLAVOINE. So? What difference—

JULIE. Oh! If I were someone else's wife, I'm sure you
could find the time—

FOLLAVOINE. All right! . . . That's enough! I'm busy!

JULIE, *putting down her bucket where she stands, center stage, and moving right.* Busy! He's busy! Isn't that
fine!

FOLLAVOINE. Yes, that's what I said. Busy! (*Suddenly
noticing* JULIE's *bucket.*) What's that doing here?

JULIE. What?

FOLLAVOINE. Are you crazy, bringing your wash-bucket in
here?

JULIE. Where? What wash-bucket?

FOLLAVOINE, *pointing to it.* That!

JULIE. Oh, that's nothing. (*As ingenuously as possible.*) It's just my dirty water.

FOLLAVOINE. And what am I supposed to do with it?

JULIE. It's not for you, silly. I'm going to empty it out.

FOLLAVOINE. In here?

JULIE. Of course not! What kind of a question . . . Do I usually empty my dirty water in your study? Really, I do have a little sense, you know.

FOLLAVOINE. Then why bring it in here in the first place?

JULIE. Because I just happened to have the bucket in my hand when Rose brought me your answer . . . your charming answer. (*Sarcastically.*) I didn't dare keep you waiting!

FOLLAVOINE. And you couldn't leave it outside the door?

JULIE, *becoming annoyed at* FOLLAVOINE'*s criticism.* Oh, for heaven's sake! If it bothers you so much it's your own fault. You shouldn't have said you were too busy to talk to me. Busy! I can just imagine! With what?

FOLLAVOINE, *grumbling.* With certain things—

JULIE. What things?

FOLLAVOINE. Certain things, I said . . . I was looking up the Aleutian Islands in the dictionary. There! Now you know.

JULIE. The Aleutian Islands? The Aleutian . . . Are you insane? You're going there I suppose?

FOLLAVOINE. No, I'm not going there!

JULIE, *sitting down on the sofa.* Then what difference could it possibly make where they are? Why does a porcelain manufacturer have to know about the Aleutian Islands, of all things?

FOLLAVOINE, *still grumbling.* If you think I give a damn! Believe me, if it was just for myself . . . But it's for Baby. He comes up with such questions! Children think their parents know everything. (*Imitating his son.*)

"Daddy, where's the Aleutian Islands?" (*In his own voice.*) "Ha?" (*Baby's voice.*) "The Aleutians, Daddy, the Aleutians?" Believe me, I heard him the first time. The Aleutians . . . How should I know where they are? You, do you know?

JULIE. Yes, I think . . . they're . . . I've seen them somewhere, on a map . . . but I don't remember exactly—

FOLLAVOINE. Ah! Just like me. But I couldn't tell Baby that I didn't remember exactly! What would he think of his father? So I tried to use my ingenuity. "Shame on you," I told him. "You shouldn't ask such questions. The Aleutians! That's not for children!"

JULIE. Ha ha! That's your ingenuity? What a stupid answer!

FOLLAVOINE. Unfortunately, it happens to be one of the questions in his geography lesson.

JULIE. Naturally!

FOLLAVOINE. Why do they have to keep teaching children geography nowadays! With railroads and boats that take you anywhere you want to go . . . And with timetables that tell you everything—

JULIE. What? What has that got to do with it?

FOLLAVOINE. Just what I said. When you're looking for a city, who has to go running to a geography book? Just look at a timetable!

JULIE. And that's how you help your son? A lot of good that does him.

FOLLAVOINE. Well, damn it! What do you want from me? I did my best. I tried to look as if I really knew the answer but just didn't want to talk about it. So I said to him: "Look, if I tell you the answer, what good will it do you? It's better if you try to find it out for yourself. Later on, if you still want to know, I'll tell you." So I close the door and make a beeline for the dictionary to look it up. What do I find? Zero.

JULIE. Zero?

FOLLAVOINE. Nothing. Absolutely nothing.

JULIE, *skeptical*. In the dictionary? Let me have a look.

FOLLAVOINE. Sure, sure! Look to your heart's content! (JULIE *begins scanning the page*.) Really, you should have a talk with Baby's teacher. Tell her not to fill his head with things even grown-ups don't know . . . and that aren't in the dictionary.

JULIE, *suddenly looking up from the dictionary, with a sarcastic laugh*. Oh no! Ha ha ha! . . . Of all the stupid . . . Ha ha ha!

FOLLAVOINE. What's so funny?

JULIE. You've been looking under the E's!

FOLLAVOINE, *not quite understanding*. Well? Isn't it in the E's?

JULIE, *very condescending*. In the E's? The Aleutians? No wonder you couldn't find it!

FOLLAVOINE. All right then, if it's not in the E's, where is it?

JULIE, *turning to another page*. You'll see, you'll see . . . "Illegible, illegitimate, ill-fated, ill-favored . . ." Hm! (*Surprised*.) Now how did that happen?

FOLLAVOINE. What?

JULIE. It isn't there.

FOLLAVOINE, *triumphantly*. Aha! I told you, know-it-all!

JULIE, *embarrassed*. I don't understand. It should be between "illegitimate" and "ill-fated."

FOLLAVOINE. Maybe now you'll believe me when I tell you that dictionary is useless. You can look for a word under any letter you please, it's all the same. You'll never find the one you're looking for.

JULIE, *still staring at the open page*. I just don't understand—

FOLLAVOINE. That should teach you!

JULIE. Well at least I looked under the I's. That's a lot more logical than the E's.

FOLLAVOINE. Sure! "More logical than the E's." Ha ha! Why not the A's while you're at it?

JULIE. "The A's . . . the A's!" What are you talking about, "the A's!" (*She gradually changes her tone.*) The A's . . . As a matter of fact, maybe . . . Aleutians, Aleutians . . . It seems to me . . . A . . . A . . . A . . .

FOLLAVOINE, *imitating.* Ayayayayay!

JULIE, *scanning the columns quickly.* "Aleph, Aleppo, alert, Aleut . . ." (*Triumphant.*) Aha! I've found it! "Aleutian Islands!"

FOLLAVOINE, *rushing to her side.* You've found it? You've found . . . (*In his haste he accidentally kicks* JULIE's *bucket, which has been sitting on the floor since her entrance.*) Damn!

> FOLLAVOINE *picks up the bucket and, not knowing where to put it, places it on a corner of his desk.*

JULIE. There, large as life: "Aleutian Islands, a chain of islands extending southward from Alaska, belonging to the United States."

FOLLAVOINE, *with a pleased expression, as if he had found it himself.* Fine, fine!

JULIE. And it even gives the area and the population: "1,461 square miles, 1,300 inhabitants."

FOLLAVOINE. Isn't that always the way! A minute ago we didn't know the first thing about them, and now we know more than we need. That's life!

JULIE. And to think we were looking under the E's and the I's.

FOLLAVOINE. We could have looked till doomsday.

JULIE, *picking up her bucket.* And all the time it was right there, in the A's.

FOLLAVOINE, *proudly.* Just like I said.

JULIE, *appalled.* You? Oh, now, just a moment! You said it . . . Yes, you said it, but you didn't mean it.

FOLLAVOINE, *moving toward* JULIE. What are you talking about, I didn't mean it?

JULIE. Absolutely not! You were making fun of me. "Sure, why not the A's while you're at it?"

FOLLAVOINE. Now wait just a minute—

JULIE. It was at that very moment that I got a sudden vision of the word.

FOLLAVOINE. "Vision!" That's wonderful! She got a vision of the word! I tell her why not look in the A's, and suddenly she gets a vision! Just like a woman!

JULIE. Oh! That's too much! Really! Who took the dictionary and looked it up? Who, I ask you?

FOLLAVOINE, *sarcastically.* Sure, under the I's. Ha!

JULIE. Like you, looking in the E's! But who found it in the A's? Answer me that! Who?

FOLLAVOINE, *sitting down at his desk and raising his eyes to the ceiling in an offhand manner.* Very clever! After I tell you to look in the A's.

JULIE, *shaking the bucket furiously as she speaks.* Oh! You know perfectly well I found it! I found it! I—

FOLLAVOINE, *rushing to take the bucket from her.* All right! You found it! You found it! There, are you happy?

> *He looks on all sides for a*
> *place to put it.*

JULIE. What are you looking for?

FOLLAVOINE, *sharply.* Nothing! Just some place to put this . . . this damned . . .

JULIE. Well, put it on the floor!

FOLLAVOINE, *placing it on the floor, angrily.* There!

JULIE, *picking up the argument.* The nerve! To say that you found it when you know perfectly well that I—

FOLLAVOINE, *out of patience.* You're right! I admit it. You found it! You, you, you! All alone!

JULIE. Absolutely! And don't think you're doing me any favors either. Trying to tell me I didn't have a vision—

FOLLAVOINE. All right, all right! That's enough! Now, for God's sake, go get dressed. It's about time. Already eleven o'clock and you're still running around in that filthy bathrobe . . .

JULIE. Of course! Change the subject!

FOLLAVOINE. Just look at yourself! Charming! Curlers in your hair, stockings down around your ankles . . .

JULIE, *pulling up her stockings.* And whose ankles should they be around? Yours? . . . There, I've fixed them. Are you happy?

FOLLAVOINE. Ha! If you think they'll stay up for more than half a minute the way you fixed them! It wouldn't kill you to wear garters, you know.

JULIE. And how am I supposed to attach them? I'm not wearing a corset.

FOLLAVOINE. Then go put one on, for God's sake! Who's stopping you?

JULIE. Why not? Maybe you'd like me to put on a hoop-skirt just to clean the bathroom!

> *While speaking she has
> picked up the bucket and
> moved toward her room.*

FOLLAVOINE. Well who the devil tells you to clean the bathroom in the first place? You have a maid, don't you? What on earth is she for?

JULIE, *returning in a huff and depositing the bucket at* FOLLAVOINE's *feet.* I should let my maid clean the bathroom?

FOLLAVOINE, *moving off, stage right, to avoid another discussion.* Bah!

JULIE. Thank you just the same! Let her scratch and break everything! My mirrors, my bottles . . . Oh no! I'd rather do it myself.

*She sits in the armchair near
the desk, casually resting
one leg on the bucket, as if it
were a footstool.*

FOLLAVOINE. Then why, may I ask, do you have a maid if
you won't let her do anything?

JULIE. She . . . she helps me.

FOLLAVOINE. Sure, sure she does. You do her work, and
she helps you! How?

JULIE, *embarrassed.* She . . . well . . . she watches me.

FOLLAVOINE. Isn't that nice. She watches you. I pay the
girl a salary like that just to stand and watch you.
Lovely!

JULIE. Oh please! Don't talk about money all the time. It's
so . . . so middle class!

FOLLAVOINE. Middle class! Middle . . . Listen! I think
when I give her such a salary I'm entitled to—

JULIE, *getting up and approaching* FOLLAVOINE. And besides, what are you complaining about? Do *I* get a
salary? No. So, if it doesn't cost you any more, what's
the difference who does the housework?

FOLLAVOINE. The difference . . . the difference is that I'm
paying a maid to do the housework for my wife. I'm not
paying a wife to do the housework for my maid. If
that's how it is, we could do without the maid.

JULIE, *indignant.* Aha! I knew that's what you were getting
at! I knew it! You begrudge me a maid!

FOLLAVOINE. Wait a minute! What are you talking about
. . . "begrudge you a maid"?

JULIE. Just what I said.

FOLLAVOINE, *out of replies, in desperation.* For God's
sake, pull up your stockings!

JULIE, *angrily complying.* Oh! (*Picking up the argument.*) Such a fuss just because I like to clean the bathroom myself. (*She moves toward* FOLLAVOINE's *desk,*

talking as she goes.) I'm sure you're the first husband to criticize his wife for being a good housekeeper.

FOLLAVOINE. Now just a moment! There's a difference between being a good housekeeper and—

JULIE, *nervously arranging the papers spread over the desk.* I suppose you'd rather see me do like other women we know. Go out every day, spend all my time at the hairdresser's . . .

FOLLAVOINE, *seeing how* JULIE *is disturbing his papers.* What are you doing?

He rushes to the desk.

JULIE, *still on the same subject.* . . . at the dressmaker's . . .

FOLLAVOINE, *defending his papers as best he can.* Please!

JULIE. . . . at the races . . .

FOLLAVOINE. Please! For heaven's sake!

JULIE. . . . out in the morning, out at night, always running around, running around, spending your money . . . *your* money!

FOLLAVOINE. Will you please—

JULIE. A wonderful life you'd like me to lead.

FOLLAVOINE. . . . leave those papers alone! Leave them alone!

He pulls her away, stage left.

JULIE. Now what's the matter?

FOLLAVOINE, *trying to put his papers back in order.* My papers, damn it! That's what's the matter! Who asked you to touch them?

JULIE. I can't stand seeing such a mess.

FOLLAVOINE. Then look the other way. Just leave my papers alone!

JULIE. Your papers, your papers! If you think I care about your papers . . .

She moves to leave, picking up her bucket as she passes.

FOLLAVOINE. Fine! Then prove it. Go putter around in your own room! (*Grumbling under his breath.*) Always fussing with something, always—

> *While speaking he sits down at his desk.*

JULIE, *returning to the desk and picking up the argument again.* So that's how you'd like me to be, I suppose?

FOLLAVOINE, *exasperated, almost shouting.* How I'd like you to be? How I'd like you to be what? What on earth are you talking about?

JULIE. Like those other women. That's what I'm talking about.

FOLLAVOINE, *thoroughly exasperated.* I don't care! Just leave my papers alone! That's all I'm asking!

JULIE, *moving stage right with long, sultry movements, simulating the walk of a socialite, and still carrying the bucket, dangling precariously from her arm.* A highbrow? Maybe that's what you'd like me to be? (*Changing her tone.*) Sorry! I wasn't cut out for that sort of thing. My family—

FOLLAVOINE. All right! All right! That's fine!

JULIE, *moving to his desk and placing the bucket on some of his papers just as he is about to pick them up.* My family—

FOLLAVOINE, *watching incredulouly.* Oh! For God's sake!

JULIE, *louder than the preceding times.* My family didn't bring me up—

FOLLAVOINE. Oh!

JULIE. . . . to be a gadabout or a socialite. They taught me how to be a good housekeeper.

FOLLAVOINE. Look, that's lovely. Very interesting. But it's already after eleven and—

JULIE. That's how I was brought up . . . Just to be a good housekeeper, and never depend on someone else to do my work. Because in life, you can never tell when some day you're going to have to take care of yourself.

*She moves stage right with
a self-righteous air.*

FOLLAVOINE, *out of arguments.* Fix your stockings!

JULIE. Oh! (*Without troubling to sit down, she fixes first
one stocking then the other.*) That's how my family
brought me up, ever since I can remember. Now it's
second nature. (*She sits down in the armchair near the
desk.*) Whether it's right or wrong, that's how I am. I
take after my mother.

FOLLAVOINE, *busily looking through his papers, answering
half-unconsciously.* Ah yes! Mother-in-law.

JULIE, *turning to him with a sharp reply.* No! My mother!

FOLLAVOINE, *still half-unconsciously.* That's what I said,
didn't I?

JULIE. No, you didn't! When I say "my mother," it sounds
tender and affectionate. It's polite. When you say
"mother-in-law" it sounds sarcastic and mean.

FOLLAVOINE, *as before.* Sure, sure. You're absolutely right.

JULIE. If I say "my mother" I mean "my mother." You
don't have to remind me that she's your mother-in-law!

FOLLAVOINE. Look . . . I assure you, if I said "mother-in-
law" it's only because as far as *I'm* concerned your
mother—

JULIE, *jumping up as if on fire and holding on to the
edges of the desk while lunging toward* FOLLAVOINE.
What? What? My mother is what? Has she ever done
anything to you? Has she ever—

FOLLAVOINE, *recoiling.* No! No! No! I didn't say that. All
I said was that as far as I'm concerned your mother is
my—

JULIE. That's enough! That's enough! Leave my mother
alone!

FOLLAVOINE, *speechless.* What?

JULIE. I don't know why you're always picking on my poor
mother. Always making fun of her. It just isn't right!

FOLLAVOINE. Me? What did I—

JULIE. And why? Just because I committed the . . . the crime of bringing my wash-bucket into your study.

FOLLAVOINE. Now listen—

JULIE. All that fuss over a wash-bucket! (*She picks it up from the desk.*) See! I'm taking it out. Now you won't have anything to argue about.

> *She moves toward the door.*

FOLLAVOINE, *mumbling, trying to look absorbed in his papers.* Fine! . . . Fine!

JULIE. You'd think I was a criminal!

> *She arrives at the door of her room and stops. A thought goes through her mind. She turns around, returns to the desk, and places the bucket in the same spot as before.*

And don't you forget it, either. Next time you want to find fault with me—

FOLLAVOINE. Now just a minute! Not that damned bucket again?

JULIE, *ignoring his remark.* The next time you want to find fault with me, be man enough to come right out with it . . . without dragging my poor mother into it!

FOLLAVOINE. But for God Almighty's sake! What did I say? What did I say, damn it?

JULIE. Oh, nothing at all! Of course not! Now go and deny it, hypocrite!

FOLLAVOINE, *with no strength left to argue.* Oh!

> *He gets up and moves down stage right.*

JULIE, *going over to his desk and once again meddling with his papers.* I know perfectly well what you were going to say.

FOLLAVOINE, *turning toward* JULIE. But I wasn't going to . . . (*Suddenly he notices* JULIE *arranging his papers.*) Oh no! No! Not again? (*He rushes to stop her.*)

Once and for all, will you please leave those papers
alone! . . . What's this mania all of a sudden to play
with my papers?

JULIE, *with a self-important air.* I like to see things in their
place.

FOLLAVOINE, *giving up.* Ha! You like to see things in their
place. That's a good one! How about this? This . . .
this . . .

JULIE, *taking the bucket.* So? What about it?

FOLLAVOINE, *grumbling.* Like to see things in their place!
My foot! If you're so neat why don't you go get
dressed? A minute ago you were almost out the door
. . . You and that damnable bucket! Why didn't you
just keep going? Why—

JULIE. I have to speak to you.

FOLLAVOINE, *gently pushing her toward her room.* Later!
Later!

JULIE. This can't wait until later. It's important.

FOLLAVOINE. Look! Whatever it is, it'll have to wait. It's
already after eleven. Chouilloux and his wife are coming to lunch and you aren't even dressed yet. Look at
you!

JULIE. "Chouilloux and his wife"! I wouldn't give two
cents for either one of them!

FOLLAVOINE. Maybe not. Just don't forget that Chouilloux
is an important man to have on my side. He's the one
who—

JULIE. I don't care who he is. He'll wait. Who's more important, Chouilloux or Baby?

FOLLAVOINE, *realizing that another argument is imminent.*
Baby? Baby? What are you talking about?

JULIE, *passing in front of him, toward stage left.* Go
ahead! Tell me Chouilloux is more important!

> She sits down in the chair
> by the desk, holding the
> bucket on her lap.

FOLLAVOINE, *almost shrieking.* What are you talking about? What? . . . "Chouilloux . . . Baby . . . Baby . . . Chouilloux!" Of course Baby's more important! I don't see . . . Just because I'm going out of my way to be nice to Chouilloux . . . What on earth does that have to do with Baby? (*He tries to calm down.*) Now look, be reasonable. Chouilloux will be here any minute now. He's coming before lunch so we can talk about some very important business.

JULIE. Talk all you want. I'm not stopping you.

FOLLAVOINE. But I'm telling you, he'll be here any minute. You aren't going to let him see you like that, I hope! That filthy bathrobe, that . . . that bucket on your lap, and those damned stockings down around your ankles again!

JULIE, *putting down the bucket angrily in front of her.* Oh! That's all you can talk about! My stockings! (*She stands up, puts one foot on the bucket, and adjusts the stocking.*) I suppose Chouilloux never saw stockings fall down before. When his wife gets up in the morning I suppose she puts on an evening gown!

FOLLAVOINE, *while* JULIE *nervously adjusts the other stocking.* Believe me, I don't know what she wears when she gets up. All I know is that nobody . . . nobody wears what you're wearing when they invite people they don't know to lunch.

JULIE, *running through* FOLLAVOINE's *papers, apparently looking for something.* Never mind! You make up for me. You're overdressed!

FOLLAVOINE. I happen to be dressed just right. When people come to lunch . . . (*He notices what* JULIE *is doing.*) What are you looking for? Just what are you looking for?

JULIE, *taking some elastic bands from a box.* Your elastic bands.

FOLLAVOINE. My . . . What on earth for?

JULIE. Maybe then you'll stop hounding me about my
stockings.

> *She puts an elastic around*
> *each leg to hold up the*
> *stockings.*

FOLLAVOINE. Just a minute! I need those for my reports.
They aren't garters.

JULIE. They aren't garters, because no one uses them for
garters. But if I'm using them for garters, then they
are garters. See?

FOLLAVOINE. God! What a mess!

JULIE, *shrugging her shoulders.* You make me laugh.
You're dressed "just right"! "Just right"! I've never
seen anything more ridiculous. Eleven in the morning
and you look as if you're going to a wedding or something. And for Chouilloux! That fool! Letting his wife
two-time him the way she does!

FOLLAVOINE, *looking at her with an air of amazement.* His
wife? Two-time him? What do you know about all that?

JULIE, *happy to have a ready answer.* All I know is what
you told me. You yourself.

FOLLAVOINE. Me?

JULIE. I don't even know the man. I wouldn't make up a
story about someone I don't even know.

FOLLAVOINE. What a terrible thing to say! His wife . . .
two-timing him!

JULIE. It must be true. You told me.

FOLLAVOINE. All right, all right! I told you. But when I
told you I didn't know Chouilloux would turn out to be
so important to me. Now I realize—

JULIE, *giving him tit for tat.* So now his wife doesn't two-
time him any more?

FOLLAVOINE. No . . . Yes . . . I mean, what's the difference? It's none of our business! That's not why we're
inviting him to lunch!

JULIE. Fine!

FOLLAVOINE. The fact is, Chouilloux is an important man. He can do a lot for me.

JULIE. Like what?

FOLLAVOINE. Like a big business deal I'm working on. I don't have time to go into it.

JULIE. That's all you think about. Business deals.

FOLLAVOINE. Look. Does it bother you so much that his wife is two-timing him? What difference does it make—

JULIE. Bother me? Ha ha ha! Not at all! She could do the same thing with a dozen men and it wouldn't bother me. The only thing that bothers me is that you have to go and invite her here for lunch. That woman . . . Here, in my house!

FOLLAVOINE. What could I do? I couldn't very well invite him and not invite her.

JULIE. And her boyfriend, Horace Truchet? You had to invite him too?

FOLLAVOINE. Of course I did. The three of them go everywhere together. If I didn't invite Truchet it would have looked bad. Even Chouilloux would have wondered why.

JULIE, *crossing her arms indignantly.* Lovely! Just lovely! We get all three of them! The whole triangle! Just lovely! (*She picks up her bucket and moves stage right.*) Nice friends to bring home to your wife! And a fine example for Baby!

FOLLAVOINE. Baby? What does Baby know? He's only seven.

JULIE. He won't be seven forever.

FOLLAVOINE. No. But meanwhile that's all he is.

JULIE. Very nice! Your own child, and you don't care how he grows up. You don't care about anything . . . if he's healthy, if he's sick . . .

FOLLAVOINE. Now just what is that supposed to mean? What have I done now?

JULIE, *placing the bucket on the floor, center stage, then moving to join* FOLLAVOINE, *who has just sat down at the desk.* If you'd only listen! For an hour I've been trying to tell you that Baby isn't feeling well. But can I get a word in edgewise? Ha! Every time I open my mouth and say "Baby" you say "Chouilloux"! That's all you're interested in: "Chouilloux! Chouilloux!" All the time: "Chouilloux"!

FOLLAVOINE, *losing his patience.* What is it? What do you have to tell me? ·

JULIE. I have to speak to you.

FOLLAVOINE. Go ahead! Speak! I'm listening!

JULIE. Hm! It's about time!

> *She moves center stage and sits down on the bucket, as if it were a stool.*

FOLLAVOINE. Oh no! No!

JULIE, *taken aback.* What?

FOLLAVOINE. You can't find any other place to sit? You think that's what a wash-bucket is for?

JULIE. What difference does it make? I'm perfectly comfortable.

FOLLAVOINE. I'm not asking you if you're comfortable! A wash-bucket isn't something to sit on. Will you please sit on a chair like every other human being!

JULIE, *with sarcasm.* My, my! Aren't we proper! (*She looks at him scornfully for a moment, then gets up.*) Such affectation!

FOLLAVOINE. Affectation my foot! You could slip and knock that thing over. If you think I want your dirty water all over my rug—

JULIE. So what? It could stand a washing.

FOLLAVOINE. Thanks just the same! If you don't mind, I'd rather not! Now what's all this talk about Baby? What do you have to tell me?

JULIE, *sarcastically.* Oh, is it all right? You're sure I may?

FOLLAVOINE. Yes . . . you *may!*

JULIE, *bringing the small chair to the desk and sitting next to* FOLLAVOINE. Well, I'll tell you. I'm worried.

FOLLAVOINE. Oh?

JULIE. It's about Toto.

FOLLAVOINE. I know, you've said that! . . . Why? What's the matter?

JULIE. He hasn't gone this morning.

FOLLAVOINE, *repeating like an echo, without understanding.* He hasn't gone this morning.

JULIE. No.

FOLLAVOINE. Where?

JULIE. Where? Where? . . . Nowhere! "He hasn't gone" . . . period. That's all. Do I have to spell it out for you?

FOLLAVOINE, *suddenly understanding.* Ah! . . . Oh, oh! . . . He hasn't gone.

JULIE. That's right. We've tried all morning. Four different times. No luck. Absolutely nothing. Once I thought . . . maybe . . . almost . . . But no. No luck.

FOLLAVOINE, *offhand.* So? He's a little constipated. So what?

JULIE, *annoyed.* "A little constipated . . . so what?"

FOLLAVOINE. Yes. What do you want me to do about it?

JULIE, *horrified.* Oh! What do I want you . . . Oh!

FOLLAVOINE. For God's sake! I can't go *for* him, I don't suppose!

JULIE, *getting up.* Oh! Very clever! You're a comedian. Of course you can't go *for* him!

FOLLAVOINE. So?

JULIE. No one's asking you to go *for* him! Still, just because you can't go *for* someone, that's no reason to let them burst! Really, how can you be so heartless?

FOLLAVOINE, *getting up and moving toward* JULIE, *replying almost good-humoredly.* Heartless? Now look . . . really! You don't expect me to start crying just because Baby's a little constipated?

JULIE. I think you should take it seriously. Constipation is no joke.

FOLLAVOINE, *incredulous.* Oh?

JULIE, *with conviction.* I remember reading in a book . . .

a history book . . . that an illegitimate son of Louis the
Fifteenth almost died of a stubborn case of constipation.
And he was only seven.

FOLLAVOINE. All right. But it was a stubborn case, and he
was illegitimate. There's no connection.

JULIE. But Baby is seven, and he's constipated, just like
him.

FOLLAVOINE. So? Give him some medicine. That's all you
have to do.

JULIE. I know, I know.

FOLLAVOINE. Well then, what's the trouble? Go give it to
him.

JULIE. Thank you! Thank you very much! I didn't need
you to tell me that. The problem is what I should give
him. There are so many different kinds.

FOLLAVOINE. Give him a little castor oil. It's as good as
anything else.

JULIE, *grimacing at the thought.* Ugh! Castor oil? Oh no!
No, I can't stomach it. It makes me sick!

FOLLAVOINE. You? Who's talking about you? It's for your
son, not for you.

JULIE. That doesn't matter. Just looking at it . . . just
talking about it makes me . . . No, no! Definitely not!
And besides, I don't see why you're making such a fuss.
We have a full bottle of mineral oil. There's no reason
why I shouldn't use that just because you insist on
castor oil.

FOLLAVOINE. Me! Just because I—

JULIE, *categorically.* Mineral oil! That's what I'll give
him, mineral oil.

FOLLAVOINE. Fine, fine! Give him mineral oil. I don't
know why you bothered to ask me in the first place.

JULIE. To find out what I should do.

FOLLAVOINE. Sure, I believe you!

> *He sits at the desk and be-*
> *gins to busy himself.*

JULIE. If you think it's going to be fun trying to make him take it.

FOLLAVOINE, *engrossed in his papers.* What?

JULIE. His mineral oil.

FOLLAVOINE. Oh . . .

> *He becomes increasingly absorbed in his papers.*

JULIE. It's always the way. Every time I let his grandmother take him out.

FOLLAVOINE, *mechanically, still wrapped up in his work.* What grandmother?

JULIE, *sarcastic.* What? How many does he have? Your mother lives in Düsseldorf. Who do you suppose I'm talking about? My mother, of course!

FOLLAVOINE. Of course, your mother.

JULIE. Yes! (*Imitating him.*) "*Your* mother! *Your* mother!" I know she's my mother! That's all you can ever say: "Your mother." As if you were blaming me for it!

FOLLAVOINE. Me? . . . What?

JULIE, *taking up her original thought.* I don't understand. Every time she takes Baby out, it never fails. She fills him so full of junk—

FOLLAVOINE, *still absorbed in his work.* All grandmothers are like that.

JULIE. I don't care, she shouldn't do it. I told her especially—

FOLLAVOINE. Look. I'm sure she didn't think that—

JULIE, *becoming angry.* You're right! That's just the trouble. She didn't think.

FOLLAVOINE, *indulgent.* Well, after all . . .

JULIE, *furious.* Never mind! Don't tell me "Well, after all." I'll never understand it, the way you always stand up for my mother, always taking her side against me. I say she shouldn't do it. That's all there is to it! She shouldn't do it!

FOLLAVOINE, *to end the discussion.* Fine, fine! You're right!

JULIE. What happens? Baby doesn't go, and now we have to give him something for it. Lovely!

FOLLAVOINE. So? Why all the fuss? I admit it's a nuisance, but for heaven's sake, it isn't going to kill him.

JULIE. Oh! "It isn't going to kill him!" Well I should hope not! . . . What a thing to say about your own child! Your own child! . . . He *is* yours, you know!

FOLLAVOINE. I should hope so!

JULIE. I'm not like Madame Chouilloux, I assure you! I don't go around letting my "cousin" . . . my *"cousin"* . . . do my husband's work for him! I assure you—

FOLLAVOINE. All right, all right! That's enough! Enough!

JULIE. When I have a child, I have it with my own husband! I assure you—

FOLLAVOINE. Well whoever said you didn't? Who? . . . Who?

JULIE, *sitting in the chair near the desk.* A wonderful father you are! It would serve you right if he wasn't your child! Believe me—

FOLLAVOINE. Oh?

JULIE. It would serve you right if . . . if he was someone else's. If I had him with . . . with . . . (*Picking the first name that comes to her.*) . . . with Louis the Fifteenth.

FOLLAVOINE, *amused, despite his anger.* Louis the Fifteenth?

JULIE. Yes!

FOLLAVOINE. Ha ha! Good God! That would be something!

JULIE. That's right, laugh! Go ahead, laugh!

FOLLAVOINE, *exasperated.* Now listen. That's enough! Everything is settled. It's over, finished. We've decided Baby needs some medicine. All right, go give it to him.

JULIE. It's so easy to say. But if you think it won't be a struggle—

FOLLAVOINE. So it's going to be a struggle. Too bad! That's that! Now for God's sake go get dressed, and let me have a little quiet. Chouilloux will be here, and I don't even know what I'm going to say to him.

> *He gets up and moves over*
> *toward one of the cabinets.*

JULIE, *getting up, moving toward her room and mumbling to herself.* When I think of making him take that awful stuff! The poor little thing! It makes me sick just thinking about it.

FOLLAVOINE, *turning around from the cabinets and noticing the bucket, which* JULIE *has left in the middle of the floor.* Julie! Julie!

JULIE. What?

FOLLAVOINE, *pointing to it.* Will you please get that thing out of here! Believe me, I've seen enough of it!

JULIE, *furious, moving toward the bucket.* Oh! That's all I hear. "The bucket, the bucket!" If it isn't "Chouilloux" it's "the bucket"! Oh! . . .

FOLLAVOINE. Well, for God's sake! My study is hardly the place to flaunt a damned wash-bucket around!

> *While speaking he takes a*
> *chamber pot from the cabi-*
> *net, displaying it during*
> *his last few words.*

JULIE, *sarcastic.* That's a good one! That really is! I suppose your study is the place to "flaunt" a chamber pot!

FOLLAVOINE. A chamber pot?

JULIE. That's what I said. Unless that thing in your hands is a new idea for a hat!

FOLLAVOINE. How can you compare your wash-bucket to . . . to this? A wash-bucket . . . A wash-bucket is nothing but a . . . a wash-bucket. A common, ordinary,

everyday thing . . . A thing you try to keep out of sight.
But this . . . this is—

JULIE. A chamber pot! A common, ordinary, everyday
thing you try to keep out of sight!

FOLLAVOINE, *lyrically.* Maybe that's all it is for you, for
someone who doesn't know any better. But for me . . .
for me it's a thing of beauty, the fruit of my labors.
It's the result of my intellect. It's my product, my . . .
my bread and butter.

JULIE, *with a sarcastic little curtsy.* Then eat it, why don't
you.

FOLLAVOINE, *placing the chamber pot on the end table
by the sofa.* Ha ha! Very funny! But you won't joke
about it when it begins making a small fortune for us!

JULIE. A fortune? From chamber pots?

FOLLAVOINE. That's what I said. You might not think so,
but with the help of God . . . and Chouilloux . . . we
can be rich overnight.

JULIE. What? What kind of nonsense—

FOLLAVOINE. It's no nonsense. I didn't mention it before
because I wanted it to be a surprise, if everything
works out all right. It's all a part of the government's
plan to improve conditions in the army. They're trying
to make the soldiers as comfortable as they can, almost
treating them with kid gloves. Why, they've even given
them house slippers.

JULIE. House slippers? For soldiers?

FOLLAVOINE. That's right.

JULIE, *sarcastically.* My, how very military!

FOLLAVOINE. And that's not all. They've just come up with
a way to keep the men from catching cold.

JULIE. Oh?

FOLLAVOINE. Instead of making them go out at night, in
all kinds of weather, every time . . . Well, instead,
they're going to give each soldier his own chamber pot.

JULIE, *appalled.* No!

FOLLAVOINE. Personal, with his own number on it.

JULIE. That should be lovely!

FOLLAVOINE. Soon they'll be taking bids to see what this new equipment should be made of, and who's going to manufacture it. Naturally, I decided to make a bid for my porcelain. That's where Chouilloux comes in. He's the chairman of the committee that's examining all the different models before the government decides to award the contract. Now you can see why I have to play up to him, can't you? Since I have the patent for unbreakable porcelain, if I can only make an impression on him, it'll be in the bag.

JULIE. And then what?

FOLLAVOINE. "Then what?" What do you mean, "then what?" If everything goes right we'll make a fortune. I'll be the army's exclusive supplier.

JULIE. The army's exclusive supplier of chamber pots?

FOLLAVOINE, *proudly.* Of every single chamber pot in the army.

JULIE. And . . . and everyone will know?

FOLLAVOINE. Of course! Everyone will know!

JULIE. Oh no! No, no, no, no, no, no! I don't want to be known as the wife of the man who sells chamber pots! Oh no!

FOLLAVOINE, *taken aback.* What? What are you talking about? We'll make a fortune, I tell you.

JULIE. I don't care! It's revolting!

FOLLAVOINE. But for goodness' sake, how different is it from what I'm doing now? I sell chamber pots every day of the week. Not so many, maybe, but I sell them.

JULIE, *moving to the desk.* Oh! You sell them, you sell them! Of course you sell them. But you sell other things too. It's only natural for a porcelain manufacturer to sell things made of porcelain. All kinds of things. But to specialize! To become all of a sudden the man who sells nothing but chamber pots . . . No! No, not even for the government!

FOLLAVOINE. You don't know what you're saying! Just think—

JULIE. I have thought! Oh no! Thank you just the same! I refuse to go through life crowned with a chamber pot! I can just hear people now, wherever I go: "Who is that lady? . . . Oh, she's the wife of the man who makes the chamber pots." No, no! Thank you just the same!

FOLLAVOINE, *becoming more and more disconcerted by* JULIE's *objections*. Listen, for heaven's sake! Whatever you do, don't talk like that when Chouilloux is here. That's all I need!

JULIE, *disdainfully*. Oh! Don't worry! I have nothing to say to your Chouilloux!

FOLLAVOINE. Maybe there's a way we can work things out . . . with a middleman or something. But please, just one thing, don't ruin this for me. I'm begging you. When Chouilloux gets here, for God's sake, be nice to him, be polite—

JULIE. Well, really! I don't think I'm exactly in the habit of being impolite. I do know how to act in society.

FOLLAVOINE. Of course you do . . .

JULIE. My father once had the President to dinner, you know . . .

FOLLAVOINE. Sure, before you were born!

JULIE. Never mind! He still had him to dinner. And—

FOLLAVOINE. That's right, that's right. Now please . . . (*He pushes her gently toward her room.*) Go give Baby his medicine, and get dressed. And take your bucket while you're at it.

JULIE, *moving off toward her room, accompanied by* FOLLAVOINE. I've got my bucket, I've got it. Really, I don't need you to tell me what to do all the time.

The doorbell rings.

FOLLAVOINE. Ah! There's the bell. It must be Chouilloux. Now please, please hurry up and finish dressing. If he came in here now—

JULIE, *on the threshold.* So he'd see me. Who cares?

FOLLAVOINE, *gently pushing her out.* If it's all the same with you, I'd rather he didn't! (*He closes the door and comes down stage right.*) Oh! Women, women, women! Can they make life complicated! (*He picks up the chamber pot, walks back and forth a little while waiting to receive his guest.*) What on earth is that girl waiting for? Why doesn't she show him in? (*He goes to the door, upstage center, opening it slightly to peek out, then opens it all the way, surprised not to see anyone.*) Nobody? (*Calling backstage.*) Rose! Rose!

> *He returns to the desk, without closing the door.*

ROSE, *on the threshold.* Monsieur?

FOLLAVOINE, *standing at his desk, with the chamber pot in his left hand.* Who was that? Who just rang?

ROSE. It was a lady, Monsieur. She wanted you to pull one of her teeth.

FOLLAVOINE. What?

ROSE. I told her the dentist lives upstairs.

FOLLAVOINE. What a nuisance! Always the same mistake, day in, day out.

ROSE, *staring at the chamber pot.* Oh! Monsieur!

FOLLAVOINE. What?

ROSE. Excuse me, Monsieur, but . . . did you know . . . did you know . . .

FOLLAVOINE, *impatiently.* Did I know what?

ROSE. That . . . that you have your . . . your chamber pot in your hand?

FOLLAVOINE. Yes, yes. I know.

ROSE. Oh! I thought maybe it was a mistake. Excuse me, Monsieur.

FOLLAVOINE. And besides, it isn't just a chamber pot. It's a piece of military equipment.

> *He places the pot on a stack of papers on his desk.*

ROSE. Oh my! It's funny how much it looks like a chamber pot, Monsieur!

FOLLAVOINE. That's right, that's right! You can leave now. (*Rose goes out.* FOLLAVOINE *sits at his desk and begins to make various calculations.*) Now let me see. If we figure that in peacetime there are about . . . hm . . . three hundred thousand men in the army. That means three hundred thousand chamber pots. And if each pot costs—

JULIE, *still dressed as in the preceding scene, appearing suddenly in the doorway.* Maximilien, would you come here a minute.

FOLLAVOINE, *absorbed in his calculations.* Shhh! Can't you see I'm busy?

JULIE, *moving downstage, still carrying the bucket.* I'm asking you to come here a minute! Baby won't take his medicine.

FOLLAVOINE. Well then, make him take it! Show him who's boss! (*Suddenly noticing the bucket.*) Oh no!

JULIE. What?

FOLLAVOINE, *standing up.* Are you bringing that thing in here again?

JULIE. Well, I didn't have time to empty it yet. Now please, come and help me with—

FOLLAVOINE, *in a rage.* No, no, no! I've seen enough of that damned thing! Now get it out of here! Get it out of here!

JULIE. But I'm telling you that Baby—

FOLLAVOINE. I said get it out of here!

JULIE. But Baby—

FOLLAVOINE. I don't care! Get that thing out of here!

JULIE. But—

FOLLAVOINE. Out! Out! Out!

JULIE, *haughtily placing the bucket in the middle of the floor.* Now just you wait a minute! I'm sick and tired of hearing about my bucket!

FOLLAVOINE. What?

JULIE. That's all you can say: "Get it out of here! Get it out of here!" I'm not your maid, you know!

FOLLAVOINE, *unable to believe his ears.* I beg your pardon!

JULIE. You'd think I was supposed to do everything around here! If my bucket bothers you so much, you can get rid of it yourself!

FOLLAVOINE. Me?

JULIE. I brought it in, you can take it out.

FOLLAVOINE. But for God's sake! It's your dirty water, not mine!

JULIE. Well then, I give it to you. There! It's yours!

>*She moves off toward her*
>*room.*

FOLLAVOINE, *following her and trying to catch her by the hem of her robe.* Julie! Are you out of your mind? Julie!

JULIE. It's yours, I said! It's all yours!

>*She runs into her room.*

FOLLAVOINE. Julie! Get this thing out of here! Julie!

ROSE, *entering suddenly from the hall and presenting* MONSIEUR CHOUILLOUX, *a very well-dressed and distinguished gentleman.* Monsieur Chouilloux.

FOLLAVOINE. Get this thing—

CHOUILLOUX. Good afternoon, my friend.

FOLLAVOINE, *still at* JULIE's *door, without turning around.* Oh shut up! (*He turns around suddenly, as* ROSE *leaves, and recognizes* CHOUILLOUX.) Monsieur Chouilloux! Oh! Monsieur Chouilloux, I didn't realize . . . I . . . Oh! Please excuse me!

CHOUILLOUX. Am I a little early?

FOLLAVOINE. No, no . . . not at all. I . . . I was just speaking to my wife. I . . . I didn't hear you ring.

CHOUILLOUX. Oh, but I did ring. And the young lady let me in. (*Trying to be funny.*) I don't walk through the walls, you know!

FOLLAVOINE, *obsequiously.* Ha ha ha! Very good! Very good!

CHOUILLOUX, *modestly.* Well, really—

FOLLAVOINE, *hurrying to take his hat.* Here . . . I'll take that.

CHOUILLOUX. Much obliged. (*He moves downstage and stops short, amazed at the sight of* JULIE's *bucket.*) My word!

FOLLAVOINE, *putting the hat on one of the cabinets, then dashing downstage to place himself between* CHOUILLOUX *and the bucket.* Oh, I beg your pardon! I . . . this . . . my . . . my wife was here a moment ago and . . . and this . . . she must have forgotten this . . . this . . . Rose! Rose!

ROSE'S VOICE. Yes, Monsieur.

FOLLAVOINE. Come in here! (*To* CHOUILLOUX.) Really, I don't know what to say. Especially at a time when I have the honor . . . the great honor . . .

CHOUILLOUX, *bowing quickly several times.* Oh, please! Please—

FOLLAVOINE, *bowing in emulation of* CHOUILLOUX. Oh, but it is! It is an honor, Monsieur Chouilloux! A great honor!

CHOUILLOUX. Too kind! Much too kind!

ROSE, *appearing at the door.* You called, Monsieur?

FOLLAVOINE. Yes. Take Madame's bucket out of here, will you?

ROSE, *surprised.* Oh! Whatever is it doing in here?

FOLLAVOINE. She . . . she left it. By mistake.

ROSE. Oh my! She must be looking high and low for it.
She picks it up.

FOLLAVOINE. That's right! Now go take it to her. And while you're there, tell her Monsieur Chouilloux is here.

ROSE. Yes, Monsieur.
She leaves.

CHOUILLOUX. Please, don't trouble her on my account.

FOLLAVOINE. It's no trouble at all. If I don't hurry her a

little . . . You know how women are. Never ready!

CHOUILLOUX. Ah! Believe me, I can hardly say the same for Madame Chouilloux. Every morning she gets up at the crack of dawn, always the first one up. She does a lot of hiking, you know. It's splendid exercise for her. Of course, at my age . . . I'm afraid that sort of thing is a little strenuous. She does have her cousin, though. She takes her exercise with him.

FOLLAVOINE, *trying to be agreeable.* Yes, yes! So I've been told.

CHOUILLOUX. Of course, that suits me fine.

FOLLAVOINE. Yes . . . it keeps it all in the family.

CHOUILLOUX. That's right. All in the family. And then too, it doesn't tire me out. (*They laugh. Turning to move upstage,* CHOUILLOUX *catches sight of the chamber pot on the desk.*) Ah! I see you've been working on our little venture.

FOLLAVOINE, *following him.* Yes, yes . . .

CHOUILLOUX, *with conviction.* That's the chamber pot.

FOLLAVOINE. That's the . . . Yes, yes! You recognized it?

CHOUILLOUX, *modestly.* Well . . . (*Observing it carefully.*) You know, it doesn't look bad at all. Not bad at all. And you say it's made of unbreakable porcelain?

FOLLAVOINE. That's right. Absolutely unbreakable.

CHOUILLOUX. Fine! Of course, you understand this is the feature that especially attracts the undersecretary and myself.

FOLLAVOINE. Yes, yes . . .

CHOUILLOUX. Because if it were just ordinary porcelain, you know, we really wouldn't be interested.

FOLLAVOINE. Oh no! I agree with you!

CHOUILLOUX. You just look at it and it breaks.

FOLLAVOINE. In no time at all.

CHOUILLOUX. It would be a waste of the government's money.

FOLLAVOINE. Absolutely! Whereas this one . . . Just look!

It's solid, it will never wear out. Here, take it, feel it. You're an expert.

CHOUILLOUX. Oh, not really!

FOLLAVOINE. Yes, you are! Here, feel how light it is.

CHOUILLOUX, *taking the pot and weighing it in his hand.* Why yes, you're right. Strange, it scarcely seems to weigh anything at all.

FOLLAVOINE. And feel how nice it is to touch. See? You could almost say it would be a pleasure . . . Well, you understand . . . (*Changing his tone.*) Now of course, we can make it in white or in color. If you want, for the army . . . maybe with stripes. Blue, white and red.

CHOUILLOUX. Oh, I don't think so. That would be rather pretentious.

FOLLAVOINE. Yes, you're absolutely right. And it would be a needless expense.

CHOUILLOUX. At any rate, we have time to think about all that. (*Placing the pot on the table and approaching* FOLLAVOINE.) You know, we've had a look at some enamel samples too. They aren't bad either.

FOLLAVOINE. Oh! Monsieur Chouilloux! No, you don't mean that! You wouldn't consider enamel!

CHOUILLOUX. Why not?

FOLLAVOINE. Well really! It's not for my own personal interest. I leave that out of it entirely. But Monsieur Chouilloux . . . Enamel? . . . It has such an unpleasant smell. And besides, it isn't nearly as clean as porcelain. Really, there's no comparison.

CHOUILLOUX. Of course, there are two sides to the—

FOLLAVOINE. Not to mention the question of health. Certainly you must know that most cases of appendicitis come from using enamel utensils.

CHOUILLOUX, *half laughing, half serious.* Well, as far as that goes, I don't think . . . considering the use they're going to be put to . . .

FOLLAVOINE. Ah, but you never know! The youth today

317

are so thoughtless! Just picture a few soldiers. They want to try out their new equipment . . . They mix up a big punch, piping hot. The heat cracks the enamel, a few chips fall into the punch. They drink, they swallow . . . Well, you can imagine what I mean, can't you?

CHOUILLOUX, *still amused.* Not really! I assure you I never had the experience of drinking punch from a—

FOLLAVOINE. No! But you *were* in the army.

CHOUILLOUX. I'm afraid not. When I went for my physical examination they made me undress, and then someone said to me: "Your eyes are no good." That settled my military career then and there. I've been in the War Ministry ever since.

FOLLAVOINE. Oh? Well, anyway, Monsieur Chouilloux, take my word for it. No enamel! Take vulcanized rubber, if you must, or even celluloid. Of course, in the long run nothing is as good as porcelain. The only trouble is that it's generally too fragile. But once that's taken care of . . . Look, let me show you. (*He takes the pot from the table.*) You'll see how solid it is. (*He raises the pot in the air as if to throw it to the floor, then changes his mind.*) No! Here, with the rug, it wouldn't prove anything. But in there, in the hall, on the bare floor . . . Just watch! (*While talking he goes to open the door upstage center, then returns center stage beside* CHOUILLOUX, *still holding the pot.*) Over there, Monsieur Chouilloux, over there! (CHOUILLOUX *takes a few steps in that direction;* FOLLAVOINE *holds him back*). No, no. Stay right here but look over there! (FOLLAVOINE *prepares to hurl the pot.*) Watch closely now! (*He winds up to throw.*) One! Two! Three! (*He throws it through the doorway.*) There!

> At the very moment he says "There!" the pot hits the floor and breaks into a

> *thousand pieces. For a*
> *moment the two characters*
> *stand gazing in astonish-*
> *ment.**

CHOUILLOUX. It broke!

FOLLAVOINE. Hm!

CHOUILLOUX. It broke!

FOLLAVOINE. Yes . . . it . . . it broke.

CHOUILLOUX, *walking over to the door.* No, no doubt about it. It's not an optical illusion.

FOLLAVOINE, *joining him.* No . . . no . . . It broke all right. Funny, I don't understand it. That's the first time . . . Believe me, it's the first time that ever happened.

CHOUILLOUX, *moving downstage.* Perhaps it hit a flaw.

FOLLAVOINE, *joining him.* Perhaps. That must be it. Of course! Anyway, it really doesn't matter. It just proves that . . . that . . . Well, like they always say: "The exception proves the rule." Because I assure you, it never breaks. Never.

CHOUILLOUX. Never?

FOLLAVOINE. Never! . . . Well, all right, maybe one in a thousand.

CHOUILLOUX. Ah! One in a thousand.

FOLLAVOINE. Yes, and . . . and even then . . . Look, I'll prove it to you. (*He goes to the same cabinet and takes out another pot.*) Here's another one. You'll see. We'll be able to throw it all over the place. You'll see. Forget about the first one. It wasn't baked right.

CHOUILLOUX. I see. It was half-baked.

FOLLAVOINE, *placing himself in the center of the stage, next to* CHOUILLOUX. There. Now watch. One! Two!

---

* *Author's note: Should the pot fail to break as it hits the floor—as has occasionally happened—the actor playing the role of Follavoine may simply say: "You see! Unbreakable! And you know, you can throw it as many times as you like. Just to prove it to you, watch: One! Two! Three! . . . There!" etc.*

(*Suddenly changing his mind.*) No, wait. Here. You throw this one yourself.

> *He hands the pot to*
> CHOUILLOUX.

CHOUILLOUX. Me?

FOLLAVOINE. Certainly! That way you'll get a better idea.

CHOUILLOUX. Oh?

> FOLLAVOINE *moves off a little, stage left.* CHOUILLOUX *takes his place.*

FOLLAVOINE. Go ahead!

CHOUILLOUX. All right. (*Swinging the pot.*) One! Two!

> *He stops, obviously nervous.*

FOLLAVOINE. Go on, go on! What's the matter?

CHOUILLOUX. Nothing . . . It's just . . . It's the first time I've ever bowled with a . . . with a . . . I feel silly.

FOLLAVOINE. Go ahead! Don't be afraid. I assure you, one in a thousand.

CHOUILLOUX. One! Two! And three!

> *He flings the pot.*

FOLLAVOINE. There!

> *Once again the pot breaks as it hits the floor. The two characters stand motionless, thunderstruck.*

CHOUILLOUX, *walking to the door after a little while, to survey the damage.* It broke!

FOLLAVOINE, *joining him.* It broke! . . . It . . . It . . . I . . .

CHOUILLOUX. Two in a thousand!

FOLLAVOINE. All right! Two in a thousand! Look, I just don't understand it. There must be something . . . It must be the way we throw them. I know when my foreman throws them . . . Never, absolutely never!

CHOUILLOUX. Never?

FOLLAVOINE. Never!

CHOUILLOUX, *sitting down on the sofa while* FOLLAVOINE

shuts the door upstage center. That's very interesting.

FOLLAVOINE, *sensing* CHOUILLOUX's *doubt.* But . . . certainly you must be able to appreciate the difference between ordinary breakable porcelain and—

CHOUILLOUX. And unbreakable porcelain.

FOLLAVOINE. Yes! (*Sheepishly.*) Still, I can tell I haven't exactly convinced you.

CHOUILLOUX. Oh, but you have . . . You have! I understand perfectly. They're the very same pots. Only, instead of breaking, they don't break.

FOLLAVOINE. Exactly!

CHOUILLOUX. Very interesting.

JULIE, *entering suddenly from her room in the same state of undress, but this time without the bucket.* Maximilien, will you please come here a minute? This child will drive me insane! I can't do a thing with him!

FOLLAVOINE, *leaping toward* JULIE *and speaking to her in angry, muffled tones.* What? Are you crazy? Coming in here like that! Just look at yourself! (*Pointing to* CHOUILLOUX, *who has risen at* JULIE's *entrance.*) Monsieur Chouilloux is here!

JULIE. Monsieur Chouilloux can go hang!

CHOUILLOUX. What?

FOLLAVOINE, *in a near frenzy.* No! No! What are you saying? Please, for God's sake! (*Awkwardly making introductions.*) Monsieur Chouilloux . . . My wife . . .

CHOUILLOUX, *bowing respectfully.* Madame.

JULIE, *very quickly.* Yes, yes! How do you do. You'll excuse me for coming in like this, won't you?

CHOUILLOUX, *very gallant.* Please, Madame, think nothing of it. A beautiful woman looks good no matter what she wears!

JULIE, *hardly listening to the compliment.* Thank you. (*To* FOLLAVOINE.) Now look, Baby is being very difficult. I can't even mention the word "laxative."

FOLLAVOINE. Well that's just too bad! I'm sorry for you!

But I'm discussing serious business with Monsieur Chouilloux. I've got more important things on my mind than giving your son a laxative!

JULIE, *scandalized, to* CHOUILLOUX. Oh! That's a father for you, Monsieur Chouilloux! That's a father!

CHOUILLOUX, *not knowing what to answer.* Well . . .

FOLLAVOINE, *in a commanding voice.* Will you please go get dressed! I'm absolutely ashamed that you should let anyone see you like that! I should think you would have a little dignity, a little—

JULIE. Oh, please! If you think I care how I look at a time like this!

CHOUILLOUX, *trying to appear interested.* Is your child ill, Madame?

JULIE. Yes, he is.

FOLLAVOINE, *shrugging his shoulders.* But it's nothing, Monsieur Chouilloux. Nothing at all.

JULIE, *as if to prove her assertion.* He hasn't gone all morning!

CHOUILLOUX. Oh?

FOLLAVOINE. All right. So . . . so his bowels are taking a little rest.

JULIE. And he . . . *he* says it's nothing! Nothing! For him it's nothing! What does he care?

FOLLAVOINE. Well, why all the fuss? All he needs is a laxative.

JULIE. I know, I know! But just try giving it to him if you're so smart! That's why I asked you to come in. Ha! I should have known better! All the nice jobs are for me!

FOLLAVOINE. For heaven's sake, you'd think it was something serious.

CHOUILLOUX, *shaking his head, with conviction.* No, no . . . of course it isn't serious. But still, you should never take something like that too lightly.

JULIE. Aha! You hear that? And he knows what he's talking about!

FOLLAVOINE, *obsequiously*. Oh? Really, Monsieur Chouilloux?

CHOUILLOUX. Of course! (*To* JULIE.) Is the child usually subject to . . . if I may ask . . . to constipation?

JULIE. Well . . . yes, as a matter of fact. A little.

CHOUILLOUX. He is? Well, you should watch that. Some fine day, if it ever develops into enteritis, he'll have a job getting rid of it.

JULIE, *to* FOLLAVOINE. You see?

CHOUILLOUX. I know all about it. I had a case that lasted five years!

JULIE, *instinctively turning her head towards her son's room*. Oh! (*Turning her head back toward* CHOUILLOUX.) Poor dear!

CHOUILLOUX, *nodding*. Thank you.

JULIE. What?

CHOUILLOUX. Oh, I thought you were talking to me.

JULIE. No, no . . .

CHOUILLOUX, *continuing his story*. Yes indeed! Five long years! I caught it in the war.

JULIE. 1870?

CHOUILLOUX. No, 1888.

JULIE, *looking at him quizzically*. 1888? But . . . there was no war in 1888.

CHOUILLOUX. No, Madame. You misunderstand. When I say "in the war" I mean the War Ministry. I'm an official there.

JULIE. Oh, I see.

FOLLAVOINE. Yes, Monsieur Chouilloux is—

JULIE. Yes, I know!

CHOUILLOUX. I used to get terribly thirsty. I didn't care what water I drank. Any water at all. I thought I was smart. Why listen to all that talk about germs . . . mi-

crobes? Water from the faucet? Bah! Why not? Well!
I can tell you, I wasn't so smart! Before long I had a
good case of enteritis. For three years I almost lived
in the clinic at Plombières trying to get rid of it.

JULIE, *jumping to conclusions.* Oh! Then you think we
should take Baby to Plombières?

CHOUILLOUX. No, no! His case sounds more like the . . .
the constipated form of enteritis. For him the clinic at
Chatel-Guyon would be better. You see, my case was
different. I had rather a . . . (*Sensing an audience.*)
Shall we sit down?

FOLLAVOINE, *while* CHOUILLOUX *and* JULIE *sit down on
the sofa.* By all means, Monsieur Chouilloux. Please
go on!

CHOUILLOUX. I had rather a . . . if you don't mind . . .
a . . . a relaxed enteritis.

JULIE. Oh?

FOLLAVOINE, *affecting great interest.* You don't say!

CHOUILLOUX. Yes. So in my case Plombières was recommended. Oh! What a treatment!

JULIE, *thinking only of* BABY. And what's the treatment
at Chatel-Guyon?

CHOUILLOUX. At Chatel . . . Why, I wouldn't know. I was
never there. But at Plombières! Every morning, an in-
ternal rinse: a quart, maybe a quart and a half—

JULIE. Yes, that's fine, Monsieur Chouilloux. But at
Chatel-Guyon do they—

CHOUILLOUX. Really, I don't know. I was never there.
(*Continuing.*) Then, after the rinse, I would have a
bath. For a whole hour. Then a massage—

JULIE, *impatient.* Yes, but—

CHOUILLOUX. And then lunch. Nothing but bland foods:
broths, noodles, macaroni, rice puddings—

JULIE. But what about Chatel-Guyon?

FOLLAVOINE, *angrily.* Monsieur Chouilloux keeps telling
you he was never there!

CHOUILLOUX. I'm sorry, but I really don't know—

FOLLAVOINE. He can only tell you about his diet at Plombières.

JULIE, *ingenuously.* But I don't care about his diet at Plombières.

CHOUILLOUX, *taken aback.* Oh? Excuse me! I thought—

JULIE. Why should I care about his diet at Plombières when Baby needs the diet at Chatel-Guyon? (*Getting up.*) Monsieur Chouilloux, you're an intelligent person. You know what I mean.

CHOUILLOUX. Of course! Of course!

JULIE. He might as well be telling me how they go fishing off the Grand Banks of Newfoundland! It would be very interesting, but it wouldn't have anything to do with Baby's health!

CHOUILLOUX, *trying to be agreeable.* That's right.

JULIE. I'm not here to listen to stories. I have to give Baby his medicine.

FOLLAVOINE, *who has had all he can take.* Fine! Then go . . . go give Baby his medicine! Go—

JULIE, *to* CHOUILLOUX, *very politely.* You will excuse me, Monsieur Chouilloux?

CHOUILLOUX, *rising.* Please . . .

JULIE, *to* FOLLAVOINE, *dryly.* And you won't come with me?

FOLLAVOINE. No! No! No!

JULIE. Oh! What a father! What a father!

FOLLAVOINE. Sure, sure! You're right! . . . Now go get dressed!

JULIE. What a father!

She leaves, up right.

FOLLAVOINE, *watching her leave.* The idea, coming in here dressed like that! Really, Monsieur Chouilloux, I don't know . . .

CHOUILLOUX. Your wife is a most charming person, I must say.

FOLLAVOINE. Yes! Charming, absolutely charming! At times she's a little . . . But outside of that . . . charming! I'm sorry you haven't seen her at her best. Believe me, when she dresses up—

CHOUILLOUX. Yes, I can just imagine.

FOLLAVOINE. Without her curlers and all that . . . She really has such beautiful hair, you know . . . A nice natural curl . . .

CHOUILLOUX. Oh?

FOLLAVOINE. Of course, when you see her like this . . . And especially now, when she's worried about her Baby . . .

CHOUILLOUX, *sitting in the chair near the desk.* Oh, I'm sure there's no need to be concerned.

FOLLAVOINE, *following him.* None at all! But just try to tell her that! You saw what happened when you mentioned the clinic at Chatel-Guyon? Now that's all she'll be able to think about: Chatel-Guyon!

CHOUILLOUX. I do hope I haven't said anything to—

FOLLAVOINE. No, no! Not at all! I just couldn't help laughing to myself when you began talking about your diet at Plombières.

He laughs.

CHOUILLOUX, *joining in.* That didn't interest her in the slightest.

FOLLAVOINE, *still laughing.* Not a bit.

CHOUILLOUX. Ha ha! And all the time I thought . . . Ha ha!

While CHOUILLOUX *and* FOL- LAVOINE *are laughing heartily, the door to* JULIE's *room opens suddenly.* JULIE *appears, dragging* BABY *with one hand, and with the other holding a glass. Against her chest she is pressing a bottle of mineral oil.*

JULIE. All right! Now you just wait and see what your father has to say! He's absolutely furious with you! (*To* FOLLAVOINE.) Go ahead, tell him. (*Seeing that* FOLLAVOINE *and* CHOUILLOUX *are still laughing, she gives her husband a quick kick in the shins, addressing him in a low but frantic voice, so that* BABY *cannot hear.*) Will you please listen to me!

FOLLAVOINE, *jumping at the blow.* Owww! . . . What on earth—

JULIE. I'm telling Baby you're furious with him. If he sees you both splitting your sides—

FOLLAVOINE. What? What? Now what's the matter?

JULIE, *sending* BABY *to him.* The matter is that I'm asking you to make your son obey! Will you please give him his medicine!

FOLLAVOINE. Me?

JULIE. Yes, you! (*She places the bottle and the glass on the end table near the sofa.*) There! There's the bottle and the glass. I give up!

FOLLAVOINE. But why me all of a sudden?

JULIE. If you don't mind! You *are* his father, you know! If you don't show a little authority once in a while . . .

FOLLAVOINE, *looking at the ceiling, then at* CHOUILLOUX, *with a sigh of resignation.* Excuse me for a moment, Monsieur Chouilloux.

CHOUILLOUX. Please!

FOLLAVOINE, *severely, to* BABY. Now then, young man. What's the meaning of this? I'm very angry with you, do you understand?

BABY, *stamping his foot.* I don't care! I don't wanna waxative!

FOLLAVOINE. What?

JULIE, *on edge.* There! You see? That's what I've been putting up with for the last half hour.

CHOUILLOUX, *putting his hand on* BABY's *shoulder.* Come now! Is that any way for a big boy to talk?

> BABY *pulls himself away,*
> *petulantly.*

FOLLAVOINE, *who has seen his son's gesture.* Where are your manners? Now say hello to the gentleman.

BABY, *stamping his foot.* I don't care! I don't wanna waxative!

FOLLAVOINE, *shaking* BABY *by the shoulders.* Well just you listen to me! No one's asking you what you want! Little brat! What makes you think—

JULIE, *jumping to* BABY's *defense, pulling* FOLLAVOINE *away.* Oh! You brute! Leave him alone!

FOLLAVOINE. Oh!

> *He stifles a curse, angrily*
> *stalks over to his desk, but*
> *without sitting down.*

JULIE, *to* CHOUILLOUX. Really, we'll have to think of some way to make him take it. His tongue is all coated. (*To* BABY.) Show your tongue to the gentleman.

CHOUILLOUX, *trying to be agreeable.* Wait just a moment. (*He goes down on one knee to see* BABY *more easily, then takes a reading glass from his pocket to inspect his tongue.*) Now then, let's see!

JULIE. Go on, darling, show him your tongue.

> BABY *sticks out his tongue.*

CHOUILLOUX. It looks all right to me.

JULIE. Still, you can tell by his breath. (*To* BABY.) Go ahead, say "aaah" in the nice man's face.

CHOUILLOUX, *instinctively protecting himself.* Oh, thank you just the same.

JULIE. What? You don't mean to say you're afraid of a baby's breath?

CHOUILLOUX. Not at all! It's just—

JULIE. Well then? (*To* BABY, *pushing his head toward*

328

CHOUILLOUX's *face*.) Go on, darling, say "aaah" in his face.

CHOUILLOUX. No! Really, I assure you, it isn't necessary! I can tell perfectly well . . . (*He sits down and addresses* BABY *as agreeably as he can.*) Now then young man, what's the trouble? Is that any way for a big boy to act? (*No reply from* BABY.) What's your name?

> BABY *sulks but doesn't*
> *answer.*

FOLLAVOINE. Go ahead, tell the gentleman your name!

BABY. I don't wanna waxative.

FOLLAVOINE, *champing at the bit*. Oh! (*to* CHOUILLOUX.) His name is Toto.

CHOUILLOUX. Ah?

FOLLAVOINE. It's short for Alexander.

CHOUILLOUX. Oh? How unusual . . . (*To* BABY.) And how old are you? Six?

JULIE, *offended*. He's seven, if you please!

CHOUILLOUX. Well now! You're seven years old and your name is Toto. And when a young man's name is Toto, and he's seven years old, should he make such a fuss about taking a little medicine?

BABY. I don't care, I don't wanna waxative!

CHOUILLOUX. That's not very nice. What will you say when you grow up and you have to go to war?

JULIE, *drawing* BABY *to her, as if to protect him, and rapping the desk to ward off a curse*. What are you saying!

BABY, *hiding in his mother's skirts*. I don't care! I don't wanna go to war!

CHOUILLOUX. No, you don't want to. But if there's a war, you'll have to go.

BABY. I don't care! I'll wun away . . . to Switzerwand!

CHOUILLOUX. What?

JULIE, *covering him with kisses*. Ah! Mamma's little angel! Isn't he smart!

CHOUILLOUX, *to* FOLLAVOINE. Congratulations, Monsieur!
I suppose he has you to thank for such ideas!

FOLLAVOINE, *defending himself.* No! Of course not! (*To*
BABY.) You should never say things like that! You
understand . . . Alexander?

JULIE, *taking* BABY *to the sofa.* For goodness' sake, leave
the poor child alone! You don't have to make him
think about such things at his age. He's Mamma's little darling! Now he's going to be a big brave man and
take his medicine. There!

> *While speaking she has filled
> the glass on the end table.*

BABY. I don't wanna waxative!

JULIE. But I tell you, you have to—

FOLLAVOINE, *coming over to the sofa.* Now look, Toto. If
you took it right away it would all be over by now.
You'd be all finished.

BABY. I don't care! I don't wanna!

FOLLAVOINE. Listen here! You're going to obey, you understand?

BABY, *running stage left.* I don't wanna!

CHOUILLOUX, *standing up, to* BABY. When I was your age
. . . when I was very small . . . if my parents told me to
do something . . . Well, believe me—

BABY, *right in* CHOUILLOUX's *face.* Aw shuddup!

> JULIE *and* FOLLAVOINE *ex-
> change shocked glances.*

CHOUILLOUX. What did he say?

FOLLAVOINE, *grabbing* BABY *and quickly placing him behind his back.* Nothing! Nothing!

CHOUILLOUX, *letting it pass, sitting down in the armchair.*
Oh . . .

FOLLAVOINE, *furious, shaking* BABY. Now look, I've had
enough of this nonsense! You're going to do what
you're told, and be quick about it! You're not going
to get away with—

JULIE, *pulling* BABY *from his grasp*. Really! Are you insane? Do you have to beat the poor child?

FOLLAVOINE, *aside to* JULIE. You . . . you heard what he said! He said "shut up!" He—

JULIE. All right, so he said "shut up!" It's not a dirty word!

FOLLAVOINE, *trying not to swear*. Oh!

JULIE, *to* BABY, *caressing him*. Mamma's little baby!

> *She takes him to the sofa and sits down.*

FOLLAVOINE, *sitting down at the desk and finally giving vent to his rage*. Damn! . . . Oh! Goddamn!

JULIE, *to* BABY, *kissing him as she speaks*. Never you mind! Your father is just a nasty man. But don't you be afraid. Mamma's right here.

FOLLAVOINE, *furious*. That's lovely! Just lovely! Start putting ideas like that in his head!

JULIE, *taking the full glass of mineral oil from the end table*. And why not? When you begin bullying the poor little thing! And especially now, when he's not well!

FOLLAVOINE, *turning his chair, back to* JULIE, *as if to ignore her completely*. All right, then. From now on leave me out of it!

JULIE. With pleasure! (*To* BABY, *as sweetly as possible, and putting the glass to his lips*.) There! Now be a dear and take your medicine.

BABY, *pursing his lips and moving his head away*. No, I don't wanna!

JULIE, *casting a look of rage at* FOLLAVOINE; *then, controlling herself, in a cajoling voice, to* BABY. Please! Just for me?

BABY. No! I don't wanna!

JULIE, *repeating her glance to* FOLLAVOINE; *then, again to* BABY. Please angel, be a dear!

BABY. No!

JULIE, *gritting her teeth*. Oh! (*Casting a vicious look at*

FOLLAVOINE.) You see what happens when you inter-
fere!

FOLLAVOINE, *stupefied.* When I—

JULIE. Yes, you! (*To* BABY.) Now listen, Toto! If you
take your medicine like a good boy, Mamma's going
to give you a peppermint.

BABY. Gimmee a peppermint first!

JULIE. No, afterwards!

BABY. Now! Now!

JULIE. Well, I'll let you have it now, but only if you
promise to take your medicine.

BABY. Okay.

JULIE. You promise?

BABY. Okay.

JULIE. Your word of honor?

BABY, *in a long drawl.* Okay!

JULIE. All right, I believe you. (*To* FOLLAVOINE, *who is
still facing the other direction, his eyes toward the ceiling in an attitude of resignation.*) Father! (FOLLAVOINE,
absorbed in thought, doesn't answer.) Maximilien!

CHOUILLOUX, *mechanically.* Maximilien!

FOLLAVOINE, *as if walking from a dream.* Hm? . . . Ha?
. . . What?

JULIE, *curtly.* The box of peppermints!

CHOUILLOUX. The box of peppermints!

FOLLAVOINE, *opening his desk drawer with the sigh of a
martyr and taking out the box.* The box of peppermints! (*He gets up, at the same time addressing*
CHOUILLOUX.) Please forgive me, Monsieur Chouilloux.
I didn't mean to subject you to a family crisis.

CHOUILLOUX. Not at all! This is very interesting . . . for
someone who never had children . . .

FOLLAVOINE, *giving the box to* JULIE. Here!

JULIE, *taking out a peppermint.* Thank you. (*To* BABY.)
Now open wide, angel . . . There!

FOLLAVOINE, *to* CHOUILLOUX. Still, this is hardly why I invited you to lunch!

CHOUILLOUX, *casually*. Oh, well . . .

JULIE, *to* BABY. Good?

BABY. Yup!

JULIE, *holding the glass out to him*. That's fine! Now be an angel and take your medicine.

BABY, *running off*. No! I don't wanna waxative!

JULIE, *taken aback, placing the glass on the end table*. What?

FOLLAVOINE, *on edge*. There! Goddammit! There!

JULIE. But Toto, you promised! I gave you a peppermint!

BABY. I don't care! I don't wanna waxative!

FOLLAVOINE, *hardly able to contain himself*. Oh, that child! That child!

JULIE, *furious, addressing* FOLLAVOINE *while chasing* BABY *around the room*. Is that all you can say? "That child! That child!" Instead of helping me! You can see I have my hands full!

> *She lifts* BABY *bodily and carries him over to the sofa.*

FOLLAVOINE, *livid with rage*. What? For God's sake! Just a minute ago you told me—

JULIE. Oh! Forget it! I should have known—

> *While speaking she walks toward her room.*

FOLLAVOINE. All right . . . What do you want? What? What? What are you going to do?

JULIE. What do you think? I'm going to try something else. That's what I'm going to do! (*Once at the threshold she turns and looks directly at* CHOUILLOUX.) Oh! He has to pick a time like this to invite people to lunch!

> *She slams the door as she leaves.*

FOLLAVOINE, *jumping up, absolutely mortified*. Oh!

333

CHOUILLOUX, *rising, to* FOLLAVOINE. What did she say?

FOLLAVOINE, *innocently.* Who? . . . Who?

CHOUILLOUX. Your wife. What did she say?

FOLLAVOINE. My wife? . . . Nothing! . . . Nothing! She said: "I . . . I don't know what time . . . we can have a bite of lunch!"

CHOUILLOUX, *sitting down.* Oh well, it really doesn't matter.

FOLLAVOINE, *going over to* BABY, *who is still on the sofa, and taking his hand to make him get up.* Shame on you, Toto! Breaking your word like that! You should be ashamed of yourself! Shouldn't he, Monsieur Chouilloux?

CHOUILLOUX, *more circumspect.* Oh, really . . . I . . . I'd rather stay out of it. Really . . .

FOLLAVOINE, *bending over to* BABY's *height, and speaking to him as rationally as possible.* Now look, Toto! You're seven years old. That means you're a young man. You shouldn't be acting like a baby any more. Now if you behave and take your medicine, like a big boy, I have a surprise for you.

> *He straightens up.*

BABY, *curious.* What?

FOLLAVOINE. Well . . . I'll tell you where the Aleutian Islands are. How about that!

BABY. Oh! I don't care! I don't wanna know!

FOLLAVOINE. That's not very nice. Especially after all the trouble we had finding them! . . . I'll tell you. They're near Alaska.

BABY, *indifferent.* Oh.

FOLLAVOINE. And besides, they have an area of . . . of . . . They have a population of . . . Oh! Forget it!

> *He lets go of* BABY *and*
> *starts moving stage left.*

BABY, *catching him by his coat.* And Wake Michigan?

FOLLAVOINE. What?

BABY. Where's Wake Michigan, Daddy?

FOLLAVOINE, *mechanically repeating the question.* "Where's Lake Michigan?"

BABY. Yes! Wake Michigan!

FOLLAVOINE. All right! I heard you! (*Aside.*) Him and his damned questions! (*To* CHOUILLOUX.) Lake Michigan, Monsieur Chouilloux? . . . You wouldn't remember offhand where it is?

CHOUILLOUX. Lake Michigan? . . . Why certainly. It's in America . . . the United States . . .

FOLLAVOINE. Of course! What was I thinking of?

CHOUILLOUX. In the state of Michigan.

FOLLAVOINE. Of course! Michigan! I couldn't remember the name of the state, that's all.

CHOUILLOUX. Lake Michigan! . . . (*Reminiscing.*) Why, in '77 I went swimming in it.

FOLLAVOINE. No! You? (*To* BABY, *bending over and pointing to* CHOUILLOUX.) You see, Toto! You were looking for Lake Michigan. Well, what do you know! Here's a man . . . You wouldn't think anything just to look at him . . . But you know what? He's gone swimming in it! . . . Now I hope after that you'll be a good boy and take your medicine!

BABY, *returning to the sofa.* No! I don't wanna!

FOLLAVOINE, *raising his eyes to heaven, in despair.* Oh!

CHOUILLOUX. He has a mind of his own, your son!

FOLLAVOINE, *with conviction.* You can say that again!

JULIE, *arriving with a second glass just like the first and approaching the sofa.* All right! Here's another glass! (*She fills it with mineral oil.*) And just to show Baby how easy it is . . . You know what? Daddy's going to drink a big glass too!

FOLLAVOINE. What?

JULIE, *putting the glass under his nose.* Aren't you!

FOLLAVOINE, *taking refuge behind his desk.* Me? Not on your life! Thank you just the same!

335

JULIE, *curtly, in a low voice.* For heaven's sake! You're not going to say no!

FOLLAVOINE. Oh yes I am! Wild horses wouldn't get me to drink that stuff! You can drink it! You, not me!

JULIE. Oh! You won't even do a little thing like that for your own son!

FOLLAVOINE, *pushing away the glass that* JULIE *obstinately keeps putting to his lips.* My own son! My own son! . . . He's your son too, you know!

JULIE, *setting the glass on the desk.* I see! I should do all the dirty work, I suppose! Of course! All the dirty work! Maybe you don't think I've done enough for him since he was born? And even before! Maybe you think it was easy carrying him for nine months! (*Waxing poetic.*) Nine long months, in the depths of my womb!

FOLLAVOINE. Ha! In the depths of your womb! Where did you dig that one up? The depths of your womb!

BABY. Mamma!

JULIE. What is it, angel?

BABY. Why . . . why d'you cawwy me nine mumphs? Why didn't Daddy?

JULIE, *lifting* BABY *and placing him on the sofa, where she sits down.* Ha! Why? Because your father . . . If you had to wait for him to do it . . . He knew that was one job I had to do myself!

FOLLAVOINE, *to* CHOUILLOUX. Really, I ask you. Is that something to tell a baby?

BABY. You shoulda asked anuvver man.

FOLLAVOINE, *furious.* There! How do you like that! "You should have asked another man!" Very nice!

JULIE, *sarcastic, ostensibly to* BABY. Oh, you know! They're all alike!

BABY. Oh no! I won't be wike dat!

JULIE, *caressing him.* That's my little angel. At least you have a heart.

FOLLAVOINE, *to* CHOUILLOUX. Really, Monsieur Chouil-

loux, I don't know what to say. Subjecting you to . . .
It's incredible, absolutely incredible!

CHOUILLOUX, *getting up.* Not at all! It's charming! Children
say such clever things. Out of the mouths of babes, you
know!

JULIE, *to* BABY. You see the difference between a father
and a mother! Your father won't even take a laxative
for you!

BABY. I don't care! I don't want him to take a waxative!

FOLLAVOINE, *moving to the sofa.* Ha ha! You see! He's
more reasonable than you are!

CHOUILLOUX, *joining* FOLLAVOINE. He doesn't want his
Daddy to drink it.

BABY, *pointing to* CHOUILLOUX. I want *him* to dwink it!

FOLLAVOINE. Ayyyy!

CHOUILLOUX, *instinctively withdrawing.* What?

JULIE, *happy to be able to please her son.* You want him
to drink it? All right! He'll drink it!

> *She takes the glass from the
> end table and, with* BABY
> *clinging to her skirts, moves
> toward* CHOUILLOUX.

FOLLAVOINE, *stopping her.* For God's sake! You aren't
serious!

JULIE, *brushing him aside.* Shhh! Don't butt in! (*To*
CHOUILLOUX.) Here, Monsieur Chouilloux, be a dear.

CHOUILLOUX, *fuming.* Really! That child is impossible!
Oh—(JULIE *has placed the glass forceably to his lips
just as he says his last words, with the result that, while
sighing his "oh" he accidentally takes a mouthful.*)
Aaaaah! Pfaw! Pfuiii!

JULIE, *still accompanied by* BABY, *continuing to hold the
glass out to* CHOUILLOUX. Be an angel, Monsieur Chouilloux. Drink a little just to make him happy.

> *She presses the glass to his
> lips once again.*

CHOUILLOUX, *spitting.* Ah! Ptui! Ptui! No, no! My dear woman! No! No thank you!

FOLLAVOINE, *beside himself.* Julie!

JULIE, *to* CHOUILLOUX. Just a little. Just half a glass.

> *She approaches him again.*

CHOUILLOUX, *defending himself.* No, no! Really, I'd love to help, but—

FOLLAVOINE. Julie! You can't be serious! Monsieur Chouilloux isn't here to . . . to take that!

JULIE. My goodness! How can a grown man make so much fuss over a little mineral oil?

CHOUILLOUX, *backed up against the chair, stage left.* That's all well and good, but—

JULIE. A child I can understand. But a man of your age? (*Wheedling.*) Now be a dear, Monsieur Chouilloux.

> *She puts the glass under*
> *his nose.*

FOLLAVOINE. Julie! For heaven's sake!

CHOUILLOUX. No, no! I'm terribly sorry! Not a laxative! With my intestines . . . Absolutely not!

FOLLAVOINE. Of course not!

JULIE. Come now! What can half a glass of mineral oil do to your intestines?

FOLLAVOINE. Julie!

JULIE. And besides, if I have to choose between Baby's health and your intestines, there's no question—

FOLLAVOINE. Julie! Please!

CHOUILLOUX. Look here, my dear woman! I don't even know if your child needs a laxative!

JULIE, *drawing* BABY *aside in a flurry of agitation.* Oh! For goodness sake! Not in front of Baby! That's all I need!

FOLLAVOINE. Julie!

CHOUILLOUX, *to* JULIE. I beg your pardon if I've said something—

JULIE. After all my trouble! After all my begging and coaxing—

FOLLAVOINE. Julie! Julie!

JULIE, *insisting.* And now you go tell him he shouldn't take his medicine!

CHOUILLOUX. Not at all! Only, I thought—

JULIE, *ready to chew his head off.* You thought! You thought!

FOLLAVOINE. Julie!

JULIE. What do you know about it? Where did you find out? At Plombières? . . . You couldn't have! The diet is just the opposite at Plombières! You said so yourself! Just the opposite!

CHOUILLOUX. All right! I take it back! I take it back!

FOLLAVOINE. Julie! Please! That's enough!

JULIE, *moving stage right with* BABY, *her rage unabated.* And what business is it of his anyway? He should mind his own business! Do I butt in when I see his wife making him a laughingstock? Two-timing him with her *cousin!*

> *She places the glass on the end table.*

CHOUILLOUX, *electrified.* What did you say?

FOLLAVOINE, *not knowing where to turn or what to say.* God in heaven!

> *Without thinking any more of* CHOUILLOUX, JULIE *has lifted* BABY *onto the sofa and sits down next to him.*

CHOUILLOUX. My wife? . . . Her cousin? . . .

FOLLAVOINE. No, Monsieur Chouilloux! It isn't true!

CHOUILLOUX, *pushing* FOLLAVOINE *aside.* Leave me alone! Leave me alone! . . . I . . . I . . . Aaaah! (*He clutches his throat as if choking with rage.*) Water! Water!

> *He notices the other glass that* JULIE *had set on the desk and rushes over to it, forgetting what it contains, emptying it with a healthy swallow.*

FOLLAVOINE. Oh!

BABY, *delighted.* Mamma! Mamma! Wook!

> *He jumps up and down,*
> *pointing gleefully at* CHOUIL-
> LOUX *and finally climbs*
> *playfully onto his father's*
> *chair.*

JULIE, *to* CHOUILLOUX, *as he swallows the medicine.* There!
Now why couldn't you do that right away, instead of
making such a fuss?

FOLLAVOINE, *out of his mind.* Monsieur Chouilloux! For
heaven's sake!

> *Suddenly* CHOUILLOUX's *face*
> *becomes contorted, his eyes*
> *glazed; he begins to cast*
> *frantic glances all around*
> *the room. Then, apparently*
> *remembering where* FOLLA-
> VOINE *keeps his chamber*
> *pots, he rushes madly toward*
> *the cabinet.*

FOLLAVOINE, *realizing what he is looking for, running after*
him. No! No! Not that way! . . . There aren't any
more! (*He pushes him toward the door, down right.*)
That way! In there! (CHOUILLOUX *rushes precipitously*
from the room; FOLLAVOINE *closes the door behind*
him, then turns angrily to JULIE.) Congratulations!
Isn't that lovely! Just lovely! Now you've done it!

> *He paces nervously.*

JULIE. Well! He should have minded his own business!

FOLLAVOINE. Telling him he's a laughingstock! . . . That
his wife is two-timing him!

JULIE. Well? Isn't it true?

FOLLAVOINE. That's no reason to tell it to him, to his face!

BABY. Mamma!

JULIE. What is it, angel? Do you want your medicine?

BABY. No! . . . What's a waffingstock?

JULIE, *with a sarcastic smile.* Ha! (*Pointing to the door through which* CHOUILLOUX *has just made his hurried exit.*) You just saw one, darling. That man who just ran out. He's a laughingstock because his wife is two-timing him!

FOLLAVOINE, *suddenly stops pacing and turns around.* Is that something to tell a child? I ask you, is that—

JULIE. If he drank it right away, when I asked him—

FOLLAVOINE. Sure! A laxative! That's all, just a laxative! . . . You're incredible! Absolutely incredible!

> *He begins pacing again.*

JULIE. Well! When someone invites you to their house you take what they give you! He has no manners, that's his trouble! Of all things! He comes here for the first time and what does he talk about? . . . His intestines! Really! Where was he brought up?

FOLLAVOINE. Oh! You're a fine one to talk! You . . . You ask him to . . . to purge himself, for God's sake!

JULIE, *rising to join* FOLLAVOINE. What? Since when did I ask him to "purge" himself? What business is it of mine if he "purges" himself? I asked him to drink a little mineral oil, that's all! I didn't ask him to "purge" himself!

FOLLAVOINE. "I asked him to drink a little mineral oil, that's all!" Sure, that's all! It's not your fault if he just happens to purge himself, in the bargain!

JULIE, *sitting in the armchair, with* BABY *by her side.* Anyway, that's his business. What do I care!

> *The doorbell rings.*

FOLLAVOINE. And what about me? Now I'll never get the contract!

JULIE. Oh! That's all you care about!

FOLLAVOINE. It's all down the drain now!

ROSE, *entering.* Madame Chouilloux and Monsieur Truchet.

FOLLAVOINE. Oh no! No! (*To* JULIE.) You talk to them! After all this . . . No! I couldn't!

> *He walks toward the door,*
> *down right.*

JULIE, *getting up.* What? But Maximilien, I don't even know them!

FOLLAVOINE. Too bad! You'll think of something!
He goes out.

MADAME CHOUILLOUX, *entering in great haste, followed by* TRUCHET. Ah! Madame Follavoine, I presume?

JULIE, *bewildered.* What? . . . No! . . . I mean yes! Yes!
*She is backed up against
the desk, with* BABY *hiding
behind her skirts.*

MADAME CHOUILLOUX. I am so delighted, my dear! I was afraid we might be late. (*Noticing* JULIE's *attire.*) But I'm so happy to see I was mistaken.

JULIE, *embarrassed.* Yes . . . Well . . . You must excuse me! I . . . I haven't dressed yet. You see . . . I . . .

MADAME CHOUILLOUX. Please, my dear! You really mustn't stand on ceremony for us! (*Introducing.*) Monsieur Truchet, my cousin . . . It was so good of you, my dear, to insist—

TRUCHET. I do hope you haven't put yourself out . . .

JULIE. No, no! Not at all!

MADAME CHOUILLOUX, *catching sight of* BABY's *head as he peeks from behind* JULIE's *robe.* Oh, my dear! Is this your adorable little girl?

JULIE, *presenting* BABY. No! . . . Yes! . . . That is, he's a little boy!

MADAME CHOUILLOUX, *surprised.* Oh? Well, at that age, don't you know? It's so hard to tell the difference.

JULIE, *trying to be agreeable.* Of course!

TRUCHET. And your husband? He will be joining us, I hope?

JULIE, *pointing to the door down right.* Yes! . . . Yes! He's in there.

BABY, *ingenuously.* Wiv a waffingstock! And . . . and his wife is a two-timer!

JULIE, *to* BABY, *quickly pulling him behind her.* Shhh!

MADAME CHOUILLOUX, *wondering if she has heard correctly.* What was that?

JULIE. Nothing! Nothing! He's . . . he's one of my husband's employees . . . A German fellow, you know . . . Laffingstock . . . Helmut Laffingstock!

MADAME CHOUILLOUX. And his wife . . .

JULIE. . . . is a Tuteheimer! One of the Düsseldorf Tuteheimers!

MADAME CHOUILLOUX. Oh, my dear. What delightful names!

JULIE, *with a forced laugh.* Yes, aren't they!

MADAME CHOUILLOUX. Laffingstock! And his wife, a Tuteheimer! . . . Oh, that reminds me. My husband should be arriving any moment.

JULIE. He's here! He's here!

MADAME CHOUILLOUX. Oh? With them?

JULIE. "Them"? Who?

MADAME CHOUILLOUX. Why, with your husband, and . . . Herr Laffingstock.

JULIE. Oh! . . . Yes! . . . Yes, of course! (*At a loss for something to say.*) Please, won't you sit down?

> MADAME CHOUILLOUX *sits down on the sofa while* TRUCHET *moves upstage in search of another chair. Just at that moment, the door, down right, opens, and* CHOUILLOUX *comes storming through, followed by* FOLLAVOINE. *They are both talking at the same time.*

FOLLAVOINE. But Monsieur Chouilloux! I assure you—

CHOUILLOUX. Leave me alone!

MADAME CHOUILLOUX, *going to her husband.* Ah! Abélard!

CHOUILLOUX. You! . . . You wretch!

MADAME CHOUILLOUX *and* TRUCHET, *stupefied.* What?

FOLLAVOINE, *standing by the sofa.* God in heaven!

CHOUILLOUX, *pointing to his wife.* There she is! Look at her! The adulteress!

MADAME CHOUILLOUX. Me?

CHOUILLOUX, *going to* TRUCHET, *and pointing to him.* There he is! The faithless friend!

TRUCHET. But—

CHOUILLOUX, *pointing to himself.* And here he is! Look at him! Here he is, the trusting husband! . . . The blind fool! . . . The laughingstock!

FOLLAVOINE, *who has joined* CHOUILLOUX, *center stage.* God in heaven! (*To* CHOUILLOUX.) But Monsieur—

MADAME CHOUILLOUX. This is absurd, my dear! Utterly absurd!

TRUCHET. Whoever told you such things?

CHOUILLOUX. Who told me? Who? Who? (*Pointing to* FOLLAVOINE.) There! Ask him who told me! (*Pointing to* JULIE.) Ask her!

FOLLAVOINE. It isn't true, Monsieur Chouilloux! It isn't true!

MADAME CHOUILLOUX, *going to* CHOUILLOUX. My dear—

CHOUILLOUX, *waving her aside with a broad gesture.* Out of my sight, woman! I've seen the last of you! (*Moving towards* TRUCHET.) And as for you, Monsieur Truchet, I shall meet you on the field of honor!

> *He goes to pick up his hat.*

MADAME CHOUILLOUX, *running after him.* Abélard! For goodness' sake, listen to me! At least let me—

TRUCHET, *following him also.* Chouilloux, my friend—

CHOUILLOUX. Enough!

> *He leaves, followed by his wife.*

TRUCHET, *returning, and going directly to* FOLLAVOINE. Did you tell him all those things?

FOLLAVOINE. No! No! It's all a misunderstanding . . . a terrible misunderstanding!

TRUCHET. I see! Well, you'll pay for it, my friend!

> *He slaps him across the face.*

FOLLAVOINE, *seeing stars.* Aaaah!

TRUCHET. Monsieur, you may choose your weapon! Good day!

>   *He leaves in a huff.*

FOLLAVOINE, *rubbing his cheek.* Oh! That . . . That . . .
Damn!

JULIE, *after a while, hands on her hips, looking* FOLLAVOINE
up and down with a contemptuous little smile. Well! I
hope you're happy now! What a fine mess you've got us
into!

FOLLAVOINE, *unable to believe his ears.* What? . . . Me?
. . . Are you going to stand there and tell me it's all
my fault?

JULIE, *shrugging her shoulders.* Of course it is! Who told
you to go and invite all those people for lunch?

FOLLAVOINE. Me? . . . Me? . . .

JULIE. Oh! Leave me alone! You'll never change!

>   *She leaves, furious, up right.*

FOLLAVOINE. My fault! It's all my fault! I have a duel
on my hands on account of her, and it's my fault! (*He
collapses onto the sofa.*) Oh no! No! That woman! She's
going to drive me out of my mind! She . . . I . . .

>   *Choking with indignation,*
>   *he notices the other glass of*
>   *mineral oil on the end table,*
>   *and forgetting its contents*
>   *grabs it up and swallows it in*
>   *one gulp.*

BABY, *who has been watching the scene.* Oh!

FOLLAVOINE. Aaaah! Pfaw! Ptuiii!

>   *He makes a beeline for his*
>   *room, down right.*

BABY, *as soon as* FOLLAVOINE *is gone, clapping his hands
together in glee.* Goody! Goody! (*He goes to the table
near the sofa, takes the empty glass, turns it upside
down to make sure it is really quite empty, then once
again begins clapping.*) Goody! Goody! (*Running up
right to* JULIE's *room, glass in hand, he opens the door
and calls.*) Mamma! Mamma!

JULIE's VOICE. What? What is it?

BABY. Mamma! C'm here!

JULIE, *entering and joining* BABY. What is it, Mamma's little angel?

BABY, *without batting an eyelash.* Wook. I dwank it.

                        He holds out the empty glass.

JULIE. What?

BABY, *turning the glass upside down to prove it is empty.* I dwank my waxative.

JULIE, *kneeling beside him.* You drank it? Oh! You little angel! What a good boy! Now you see, it wasn't so terrible after all!

BABY, *with a malicious smile.* Oh no!

FOLLAVOINE, *bursting into the room wearing his hat and coat.* No! I won't stay here another minute! I've had enough!

                        He goes to his desk and
                        takes a few papers, which he
                        nervously arranges in his
                        briefcase before leaving.

JULIE, *without even noticing* FOLLAVOINE's *actions.* Maximilien! Baby took his medicine!

FOLLAVOINE. I don't give a good goddamn!

                        He storms out of the room.

JULIE, *shocked.* Oh! . . . Did you hear that? Did you hear . . . He doesn't give a . . . (*To* BABY.) See, that's your father for you! He doesn't give . . . Well! It's a lucky thing you have your mother, precious! And you'll always love her, angel, won't you!

                        She covers him with kisses.

CURTAIN